enVision® Geometry
Assessment Resources

SAVVAS
LEARNING COMPANY

Copyright © 2024 by Savvas Learning Company LLC. All Rights Reserved. Printed in the United States of America.

This publication is protected by copyright, and permission should be obtained from the publisher prior to any prohibited reproduction, storage in a retrieval system, or transmission in any form or by any means, electronic, mechanical, photocopying, recording, or otherwise. The publisher hereby grants permission to reproduce pages, in part or in whole, for classroom use only, the number not to exceed the number of students in each class. Notice of copyright must appear on all copies. For information regarding permissions, request forms, and the appropriate contacts within the Savvas Learning Company Rights Management group, please send your query to the address below.

Savvas Learning Company LLC, 15 East Midland Avenue, Paramus, NJ 07652

Savvas® and **Savvas Learning Company®** are the exclusive trademarks of Savvas Learning Company LLC in the U.S. and other countries.

Savvas Learning Company publishes through its famous imprints **Prentice Hall®** and **Scott Foresman®** which are exclusive registered trademarks owned by Savvas Learning Company LLC in the U.S. and/or other countries.

enVision® and **Savvas Realize®** are exclusive trademarks of Savvas Learning Company LLC in the U.S. and/or other countries.

Unless otherwise indicated herein, any third party trademarks that may appear in this work are the property of their respective owners, and any references to third party trademarks, logos, or other trade dress are for demonstrative or descriptive purposes only. Such references are not intended to imply any sponsorship, endorsement, authorization, or promotion of Savvas Learning Company products by the owners of such marks, or any relationship between the owner and Savvas Learning Company LLC or its authors, licensees, or distributors.

SAVVAS
LEARNING COMPANY

ISBN-13: 978-1-4184-0208-2
ISBN-10:   1-4184-0208-7

enVision® Geometry

Geometry Readiness Assessment

Progress Monitoring Assessments

Topic 1 Assessments and Lesson Quizzes

Topic 2 Assessments and Lesson Quizzes

Benchmark Assessment 1

Topic 3 Assessments and Lesson Quizzes

Topic 4 Assessments and Lesson Quizzes

Benchmark Assessment 2

Topic 5 Assessments and Lesson Quizzes

Topic 6 Assessments and Lesson Quizzes

Benchmark Assessment 3

Topic 7 Assessments and Lesson Quizzes

Topic 8 Assessments and Lesson Quizzes

Benchmark Assessment 4

Topic 9 Assessments and Lesson Quizzes

Topic 10 Assessments and Lesson Quizzes

Benchmark Assessment 5

Topic 11 Assessments and Lesson Quizzes

Topic 12 Assessments and Lesson Quizzes

Benchmark Assessment 6

ASSESSMENT GUIDE
CONTENTS

SavvasRealize.com

Activity

Clear and purposeful assessment is at the heart of effective instruction. This Assessment Guide offers general information about assessment as well as specific information about assessment resources in **enVision® Geometry** The Assessment Guide is divided into the following parts.

Page

vi **Why and When to Assess**

viii **What to Assess**

xi **How to Assess**

xii **Assessment Data**

ASSESSMENT GUIDE
WHY AND WHEN TO ASSESS

enVision® Geometry offers the most important key to success on standards-based assessments: daily core instruction that has the same rigor as the assessments. A hallmark of the program is the formative assessment integrated into core instruction through high-cognitive-level, question-driven classroom conversations.

> "enVision® Geometry offers the most important key to success on standards-based assessments: daily core instruction that has the same rigor as the assessments."

Type of Assessment	Why and When to Use This Assessment	Instructional Outcomes Informed by Assessment Results
Diagnostic Assessment	Why: **Diagnose students' readiness** for learning by assessing prerequisite content When: **Before** instruction	• Develop individual study plans. • Make grouping decisions. • Prescribe specific activities to fill gaps in understanding of prerequisite content.
Progress Monitoring Assessment	Why: **Measure students' growth across time** toward specific learning goals When: **Before** the start of instruction of grade level content and **anytime** during the year to measure growth	• Determine students' level of understanding and mastery of grade-level concepts and skills. • Inform instructional activities on the content. • Determine efficacy of curriculum.
Formative Assessment	Why: **Monitor students' progress** on learning content When: **During** daily lessons	• Prescribe specific remediation or enrichment activities on the content. • Provide alternative instruction (reteach). • Alter the pace of instruction. • Adjust the instructional plan for a topic.
Summative Assessment	Why: **Measure students' learning** of the content When: **After** a group of lessons	• Provide specific remediation activities on the content.

Assessment Guide

All of the assessments listed below are available as both print and digital resources. Most of the digital assessments are auto-scored.

		enVision® Geometry Mathematics Resources
Progress Monitoring Assessment	At the START of the YEAR, DURING the YEAR, and/or at the END of the YEAR	✓ **Progress Monitoring Assessment, Forms A, B, and C** Assess students' conceptual understanding and procedural skill and fluency with on-level content. Establish a baseline from which growth can be measured.
Diagnostic Assessment	At the start of the YEAR	✓ **Geometry Readiness Assessment** Diagnose students' areas of strength and weakness; results can be used to prescribe differentiated intervention.
	At the start of a TOPIC	✓ **Topic Readiness Assessment** Diagnose students' proficiency with topic prerequisite concepts and skills; results can be used to generate personalized study plans.
Formative Assessment	During a LESSON	✓ **Try It!** Assess students' understanding of concepts and skills presented in each example; results can be used to modify instruction as needed. ✓ **Do You Understand? and Do You Know How?** Assess students' conceptual understand and procedural fluency with lesson content; results can be used to review or revisit content.
	At the end of a LESSON	✓ **Lesson Quiz** Assess students' conceptual understanding and procedural fluency with lesson content; results can be used to prescribe differentiated instruction.
Summative Assessment	At the end of a TOPIC	✓ **Topic Assessment, Form A and Form B** Assess students' conceptual understanding and procedural fluency with topic content. Additional Topic Assessment with ExamView® ✓ **Topic Performance Assessment, Form A and Form B** Assess students' ability to apply concepts learned and proficiency with the Mathematical Thinking and Reasoning Standards.
	After a group of TOPICS and At the end of the YEAR	✓ **Benchmark Assessments** Assess students' understanding of and proficiency with concepts and skills taught throughout the school year; results can be used to prescribe intervention.

Assessment Guide

ASSESSMENT GUIDE
WHAT TO ASSESS

The assessment resources in **enVision® Geometry** assess all aspects of the program, from content and skill to practice and process expectations.

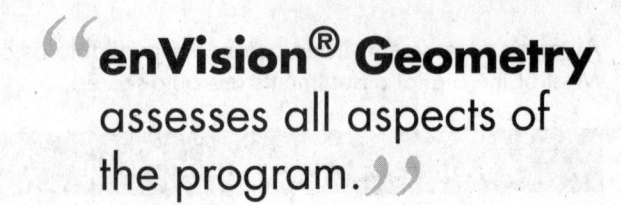

"**enVision® Geometry** assesses all aspects of the program."

What to Assess	enVision® Geometry Resources
Math Content • Conceptual understanding • Procedural skill and fluency • Applications	• **Lesson Quizzes** • **Topic Assessments** • **Topic Performance Assessments** • **Benchmark Assessments** • **Progress Monitoring Assessments**
Math Practices and Processes	• **Performance Assessments** • **Habits of Mind** in the Teacher's Edition and Student Companion
Cognitive Complexity • Depth of Knowledge (DOK)	• **Item Analysis Charts** include a "DOK" column that identifies the DOK level for each item.

Assessment Guide

Cognitive Rigor Matrix for Mathematics

Depth of Knowledge (DOK)

TYPE OF THINKING	DOK LEVEL 1: Recall and Reproduction	DOK LEVEL 2: Basic Skills and Concepts	DOK LEVEL 3: Strategic Thinking and Reasoning	DOK LEVEL 4: Extended Thinking
Remember	• Recall conversions, terms, facts.			
Understand	• Evaluate an expression. • Locate points on a grid or number on number line. • Solve a one-step problem. • Represent math relationships in words, pictures, or symbols.	• Specify, explain relationships. • Make basic inferences or logical predictions from data/observations. • Use models/diagrams to explain concepts. • Make and explain estimates.	• Use concepts to solve non-routine problems. • Use supporting evidence to justify conjectures, generalize, or connect ideas. • Explain reasoning when more than one response is possible. • Explain phenomena in terms of concepts.	• Relate mathematical concepts to other content areas, other domains. • Develop generalizations of the results obtained and the strategies used and apply them to new problem situations.
Apply	• Follow simple procedures. • Calculate, measure, apply a rule (e.g., rounding). • Apply algorithm or formula. • Solve linear equations. • Make conversions.	• Select a procedure and perform it. • Solve routine problem applying multiple concepts or decision points. • Retrieve information to solve a problem. • Translate between representations.	• Design investigation for a specific purpose or research question. • Use reasoning, planning, and supporting evidence. • Translate between problem and symbolic notation when not a direct translation.	• Initiate, design, and conduct a project that specifies a problem, identifies solution paths, solves the problem, and reports results.
Analyze	• Retrieve information from a table or graph to answer a question. • Identify a pattern/trend.	• Categorize data, figures. • Organize, order data. • Select appropriate graph and organize and display data. • Interpret data from a simple graph. • Extend a pattern.	• Compare information within or across data sets or texts. • Analyze and draw conclusions from data, citing evidence. • Generalize a pattern. • Interpret data from complex graph.	• Analyze multiple sources of evidence or data sets.
Evaluate			• Cite evidence and develop a logical argument. • Compare/contrast solution methods. • Verify reasonableness.	• Apply understanding in a novel way, provide argument or justification for the new application.
Create	• Brainstorm ideas, concepts, problems, or perspectives related to a topic or concept.	• Generate conjectures or hypotheses based on observations or prior knowledge and experience.	• Develop an alternative solution. • Synthesize information within one data set.	• Synthesize information across multiple sources or data sets. • Design a model to inform and solve a practical or abstract situation.

Developed by Hess, Carlock, Jones, & Walkup (2009) and adopted by the Smarter Balance Assessment Consortium. Integrates Webb's Depth-of-Knowledge Levels with a modified Bloom's Taxonomy of Educational Objectives shown in the first column.

Assessment Guide

ASSESSMENT GUIDE
HOW TO ASSESS

enVision® Geometry offers a variety of assessment tools that help teachers evaluate student understanding.

Observational assessment in math is especially important for English language learners or students who struggle with reading and writing.

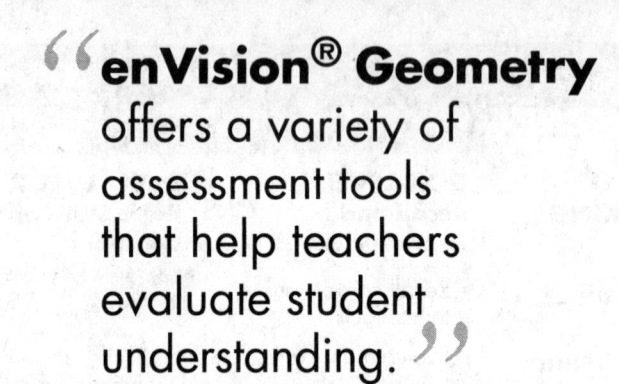

> "enVision® Geometry offers a variety of assessment tools that help teachers evaluate student understanding."

How to Assess		enVision® Geometry Resources
Observational Assessment	Walk around and observe as students do work in class. Listen as students reply to questions in class.	• **Try It!** is in-class assessment right after instruction to check whether students understand Example content. • **Do You Understand? Do You Know How?** is in-class assessment to see if students are ready for independent practice. • **Guiding questions** in the Teacher's Edition give students a chance to explain their thinking in whole-class, small-group, or individual settings.
Portfolio Assessment	Collect samples of student work.	• **Written assessments** that show representative samples of student work can be especially helpful during parent-teacher conferences.
Performance-Based Assessment	Assign tasks that assess complex thinking and ask for explanations.	• **Performance Assessments** are complex, multi-part tasks and ask for explanations. Topic Performance Assessments and Practice Performance Assessments are online and in print.
Program Assessments	Measure students' understanding of lesson, topic, and grade-level content using paper-based and online assessments.	• **Program assessments**, available in print and online, use items like those found on the state assessment to assess students' understanding of concepts and skills.

enVision® Geometry provides resources to facilitate data-driven decision making.

Online assessments at SavvasRealize.com generate a variety of helpful reports and provide ways to group students and prescribe differentiation.

> "enVision® Geometry provides resources to facilitate data-driven decision making."

Assessment Data Resources in enVision® Geometry

Collecting Assessment Data	• **Data from online assessments** include a variety of class and individual reports that show results for an item, an assessment, or a group of assessments. Also available are individual and class reports on standards mastery.
	• **Data from other assessments** can include more than students' scores. Examine and discuss students' work on assessments to gain and record valuable insights into what individual students understand and where they are still struggling.
Using Assessment Data	• **Form groups** based on assessment data for the purposes of making instructional decisions and assigning differentiated resources.
	• **Assign differentiation** based on assessment data. Differentiation is assigned automatically after students complete online Lesson Quizzes, Topic Assessments, and Benchmark Assessments.

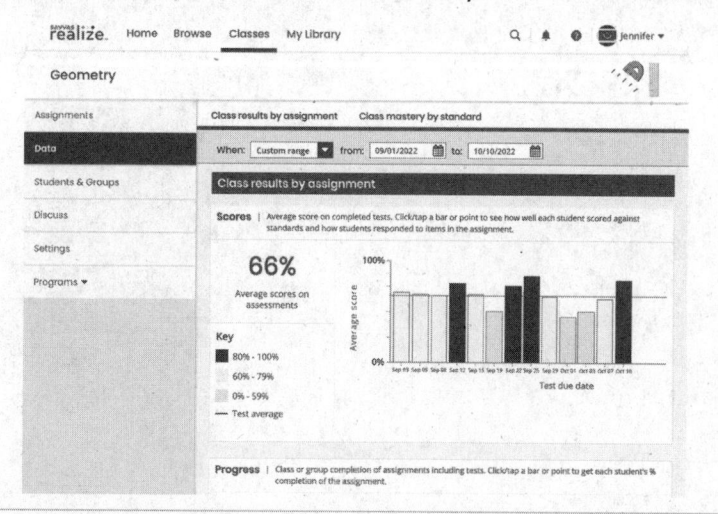

Geometry Readiness Assessment

1. What is the equation of the line?

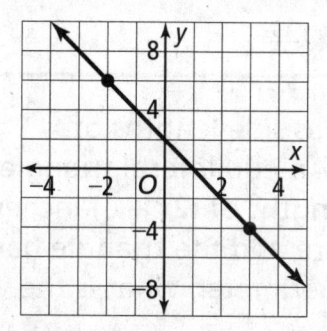

   Ⓐ $y = -2x + 2$
   Ⓑ $y = 2x + 2$
   Ⓒ $y = x + 1$
   Ⓓ $y = -x + 1$

2. Find the value of x.
   $\frac{5}{6}x - \frac{1}{3} = 4 + \frac{1}{2}x$

   Ⓐ $x = 11$
   Ⓑ $x = \frac{77}{16}$
   Ⓒ $x = 13$
   Ⓓ $x = \frac{13}{4}$

3. Greta draws one side of equilateral △PQR on the coordinate plane at points P(−2, 2) and Q(6, 2). Which ordered pair is a possible coordinate of vertex R?

   Ⓐ (−2, −6)
   Ⓑ (0, 8)
   Ⓒ (2, 8.9)
   Ⓓ (2, −8.9)

4. What is the approximate volume of the composite figure? Use 3.14 for π. Round to the nearest hundredth.

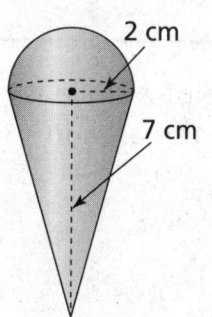

   Ⓐ 29.31 cm³
   Ⓑ 33.49 cm³
   Ⓒ 46.05 cm³
   Ⓓ 62.80 cm³

5. **Part A** Which figure is a translation of Figure A?

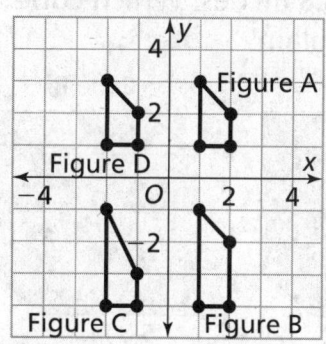

   Ⓐ Figure B
   Ⓑ Figure C
   Ⓒ Figure D
   Ⓓ None of the above

   Part B Describe the translation from Figure A to its congruent figure.

   Ⓐ 3 units left
   Ⓑ 3 units right
   Ⓒ Reflected across the y-axis
   Ⓓ 5 units down

6. The graph of a line passes through the points (3, 18) and (6, 33). What is the equation of the line?

Ⓐ $y = 2x + 12$

Ⓑ $y = 0.5x + 3$

Ⓒ $y = -5x + 33$

Ⓓ $y = 5x + 3$

7. The circumference of a circle is 6π inches. What is the area in terms of π?

Ⓐ 3π in.^{2}

Ⓑ 9π in.^{2}

Ⓒ 12π in.^{2}

Ⓓ 36π in.^{2}

8. Cube A has a volume of 216 cubic inches. The edge lengths of Cube B measure 5.8 inches. Which cube is larger? Explain.

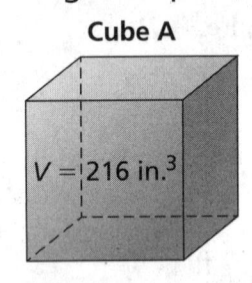

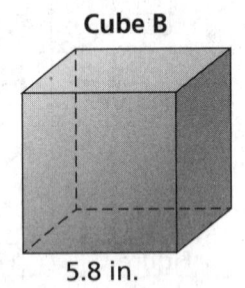

Cube A
$V = 216$ in.^{3}

Cube B
5.8 in.

Ⓐ Cube A, because its volume is greater than the volume of Cube B.

Ⓑ Cube A, because its surface area is greater than the volume of Cube B.

Ⓒ Cube B, because its volume is greater than the volume of Cube A.

Ⓓ Cube B, because its edge length is greater than the edge length of Cube A.

9. Which of the following could be the side lengths of a right triangle?

Ⓐ 3, 4, $\sqrt{5}$

Ⓑ 9, 12, 21

Ⓒ 24, 32, 40

Ⓓ $\sqrt{8}$, $\sqrt{14}$, 22

10. A square has side lengths of $2x$ inches. An equilateral triangle has side lengths of $(2x + \frac{1}{3})$ inches. If the square and the triangle have the same perimeter, what is the value of x?

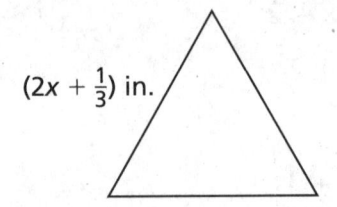

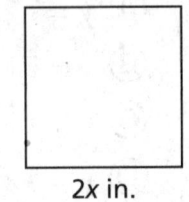

$(2x + \frac{1}{3})$ in.

$2x$ in.

Ⓐ 2

Ⓑ $\frac{1}{14}$

Ⓒ $\frac{1}{2}$

Ⓓ $\frac{3}{2}$

11. What is the equation of the line?

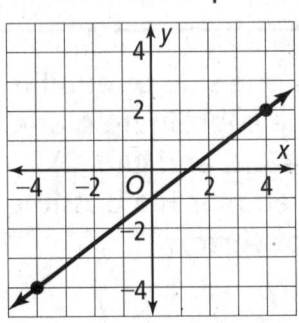

Ⓐ $y = x - 1$

Ⓑ $y = \frac{4}{3}x - 1$

Ⓒ $y = \frac{3}{4}x - 1$

Ⓓ $y = -\frac{4}{3}x + 1$

12. Richard takes a hang gliding lesson. He lifts off at the top of a hill and glides downward for the first 5 minutes. Then he soars at a consistent elevation for 10 minutes. The last 3 minutes he glides upward until he lands on a smaller hill. Use the information about when Richard's elevation is increasing, decreasing, or constant to choose the graph that best approximates Richard's gliding lesson over time.

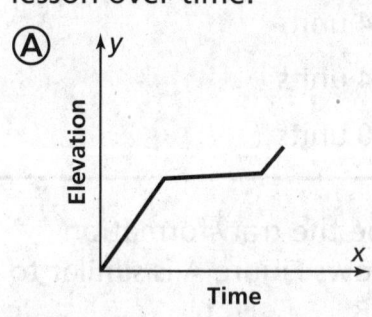

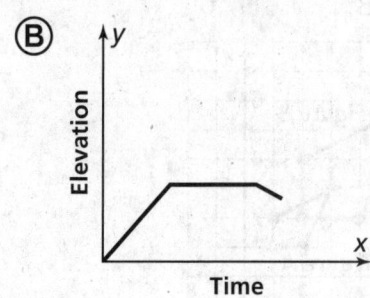

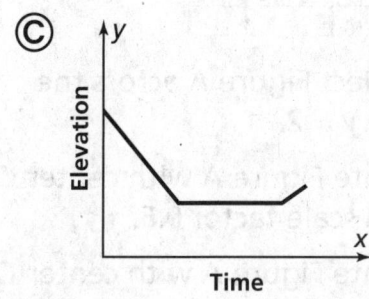

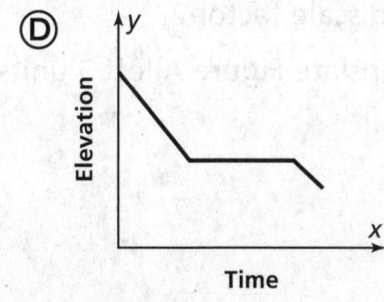

   Ⓐ
   Ⓑ
   Ⓒ
   Ⓓ

13. How many solutions does the system of equations have? Explain.

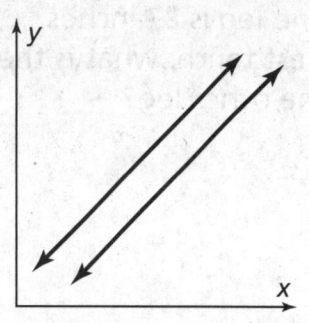

   Ⓐ One; the lines intersect at only one point.
   Ⓑ None; the lines are perpendicular.
   Ⓒ Infinitely many; the lines are parallel.
   Ⓓ None; the lines are parallel.

14. The coordinates of $\triangle PQR$ are $P(1, 1)$, $Q(2, 2)$, and $R(3, 1)$. If $\triangle PQR$ is rotated 90° counterclockwise about the origin, what are the vertices of $\triangle P'Q'R'$?

   Ⓐ $P'(-1, 1), Q'(-2, 2), R'(-1, 3)$
   Ⓑ $P'(-1, -1), Q'(-1, -3), R'(-2, -2)$
   Ⓒ $P'(1, -1), Q'(2, -2), R'(3, -1)$
   Ⓓ $P'(-1, -1), Q'(-2, -2), R'(-3, 1)$

15. If two triangles are similar, which of the following is NOT true about them?

   Ⓐ Corresponding angles are always equal.
   Ⓑ Corresponding sides are always equal.
   Ⓒ The lengths of corresponding sides have the same scale factor.
   Ⓓ A transformation from one triangle to the other must include a dilation.

16. The length of the hypotenuse of a right triangle is 30 inches. The length of one leg is 27 inches. To the nearest tenth, what is the length of the other leg?

   Ⓐ 7.5 in.
   Ⓑ 13.1 in.
   Ⓒ 29.5 in.
   Ⓓ 40.4 in.

17. What is the measure of ∠2?

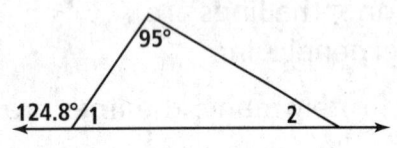

   Ⓐ 180°
   Ⓑ 75°
   Ⓒ 65.2°
   Ⓓ 29.8°

18. The drawing shown is a scale figure of Carlos's bedroom. Given that the dimensions of Carlos's bedroom are 12 ft × 10 ft, what is the scale of Carlos's drawing?

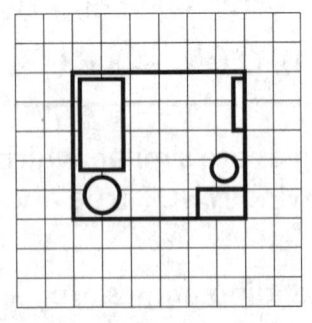

   Ⓐ 1 unit = 12 feet
   Ⓑ 1 unit = 2 feet
   Ⓒ 2 units = 1 foot
   Ⓓ 1 unit = 10 feet

19. What is the perimeter of △LMN? Round to the nearest tenth.

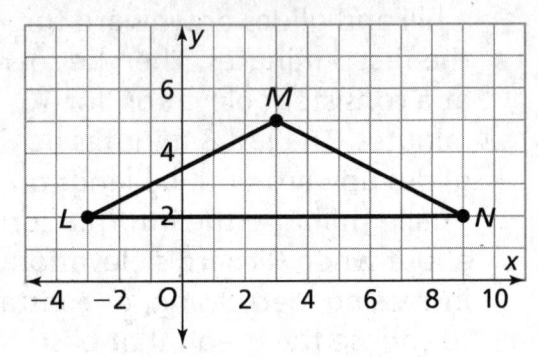

   Ⓐ 19.4 units
   Ⓑ 22.4 units
   Ⓒ 25.4 units
   Ⓓ 30.0 units

20. Describe the transformation that shows Figure A is similar to Figure B.

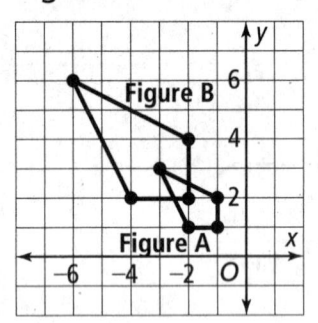

   Ⓐ Reflect Figure A across the line $y = 2$.
   Ⓑ Dilate Figure A with center O and scale factor 0.5.
   Ⓒ Dilate Figure A with center O and scale factor 2.
   Ⓓ Translate Figure A left 3 units.

21. Which angle(s) are congruent to ∠1?

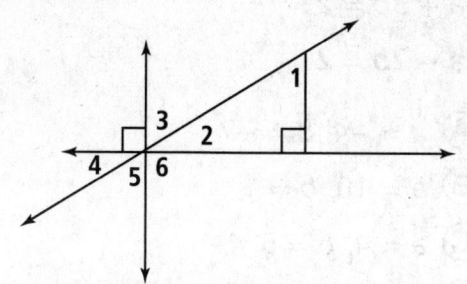

Ⓐ ∠2
Ⓑ ∠2, ∠4
Ⓒ ∠3, ∠5
Ⓓ ∠6

22. What is the sum of the interior angle measures of a regular hexagon?

Ⓐ 180°
Ⓑ 360°
Ⓒ 540°
Ⓓ 720°

23. What is the solution to the system?

$y = \frac{3}{2}x + 3$
$y = 1.5x + 3$

Ⓐ (−1.5, 0)
Ⓑ (1, −6)
Ⓒ No solution
Ⓓ Infinitely many solutions

24. Solve for x.

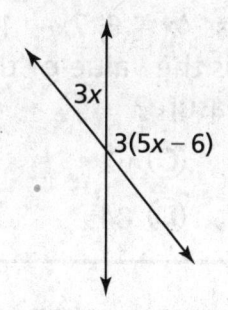

$3x$
$3(5x - 6)$

Ⓐ $x = 10$
Ⓑ $x = 11$
Ⓒ $x = 15$
Ⓓ No solution

25. The net of a rectangular prism with a square base is shown. Use the net to find the surface area of the prism.

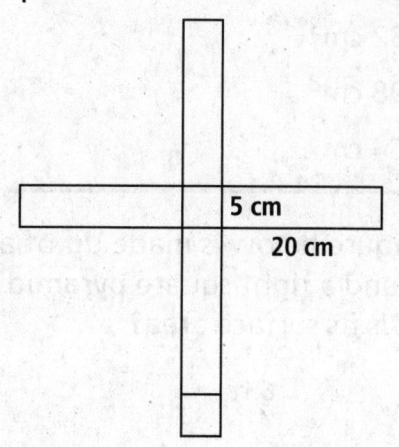

5 cm
20 cm

Ⓐ 100 cm²
Ⓑ 450 cm²
Ⓒ 500 cm²
Ⓓ 2500 cm²

26. If the angle measures of a triangle can be expressed as $4x + 6$, $7x - 14$, and $48 - x$, what is the value of the smallest angle measure?

    (A) 14
    (B) 34
    (C) 62
    (D) 84

27. What is the approximate volume of the cylinder? Use $\frac{22}{7}$ for π. Round to the nearest cubic centimeter.

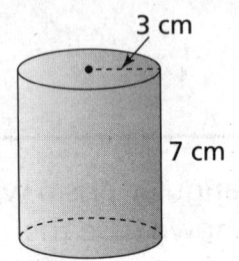

    3 cm
    7 cm

    (A) 66 cm³
    (B) 132 cm³
    (C) 198 cm³
    (D) 264 cm³

28. The figure below is made up of a cube and a right square pyramid. What is its surface area?

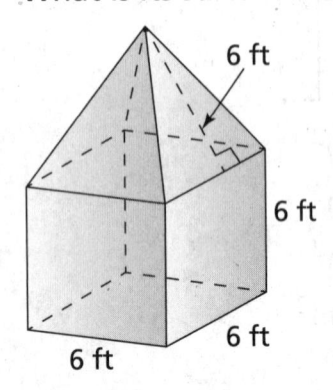

    6 ft
    6 ft
    6 ft
    6 ft

    (A) 216 ft²
    (B) 252 ft²
    (C) 288 ft²
    (D) 324 ft²

29. Solve the system of equations.

    $2a + 3b = 23$
    $3a - 2b = 2$

    (A) $a = -4$, $b = -7$
    (B) $a = 10$, $b = 1$
    (C) $a = 4$, $b = 5$
    (D) No solution

30. The perimeter of a garden is 88 feet. The length is 12 feet greater than the width.

    Part A

    Choose the equations you could use to find the dimensions of the garden.

    (A) $L + W = 12$
        $2L + 2W = 88$

    (B) $L = W + 12$
        $2L + 2W = 88$

    (C) $L + W = 44$
        $L + 12 = W$

    (D) $LW = 88$
        $L = W + 12$

    Part B

    Find the dimensions of the garden and its area.

    (A) Length = 26 ft, width = 18 ft, area = 468 ft²
    (B) Length = 40 ft, width = 28 ft, area = 1120 ft²
    (C) Length ≈ 17.2 ft, width ≈ 5.1 ft, area ≈ 87.72 ft²
    (D) Length = 28 ft, width = 16 ft, area = 448 ft²

Progress Monitoring Assessment Form A

1. Triangle A'B'C' is a dilation of △ABC. What is AB?

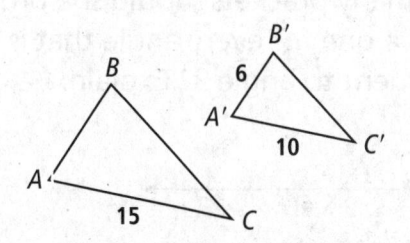

   AB = ☐

2. A ray of sunlight forms a 24°-angle with the ground. What is the length of the shadow cast by a person 1.82 m tall?

   Ⓐ 0.81 m
   Ⓑ 1.99 m
   Ⓒ 4.09 m
   Ⓓ 4.47 m

3. Triangle XYZ is rotated 90° counterclockwise about the origin to produce △X'Y'Z'. What are the coordinates of △X'Y'Z'?

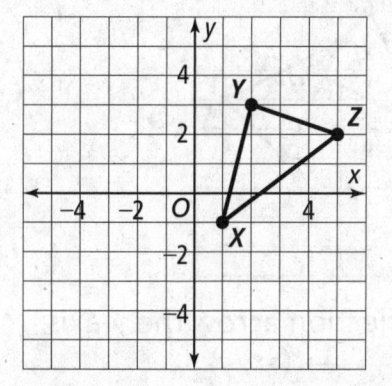

   Ⓐ X'(1, 1), Y'(−3, 2), Z'(−2, 5)
   Ⓑ X'(−1, −1), Y'(3, −2), Z'(2, −5)
   Ⓒ X'(−1, −1), Y'(−2, 3), Z'(−5, 2)
   Ⓓ X'(0, 0), Y'(1, 4), Z'(4, 3)

4. Which statement must be true?

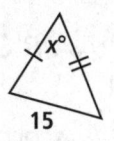

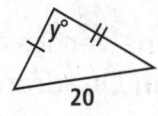

   Ⓐ x < y
   Ⓑ x = y
   Ⓒ x > y
   Ⓓ No relationship between x and y can be determined from the information given.

5. A square pyramid has a surface area of 20 cm². A dilation of the pyramid has a surface area of 80 cm². What is the scale factor of the dilation?

   Ⓐ $\frac{1}{2}$
   Ⓑ 2
   Ⓒ 4
   Ⓓ 16

6. A circle has center (5, −4) and radius 8. Which gives the equation for the circle?

   Ⓐ $(x + 5)^2 + (y - 4)^2 = 8$
   Ⓑ $(x - 5)^2 + (y + 4)^2 = 8$
   Ⓒ $(x + 5)^2 + (y - 4)^2 = 64$
   Ⓓ $(x - 5)^2 + (y + 4)^2 = 64$

7. Suppose △ABC has coordinates A(2, 3), B(5, 1), C(4, 4), and △ABC is mapped to △A'B'C' by a reflection across the line $y = -5$ followed by a translation 1 unit left. Select all the statements that are true about △A'B'C'.

   ☐ A. All the vertices of △A'B'C' are in Quadrant II.

   ☐ B. All the vertices of △A'B'C' are in Quadrant IV.

   ☐ C. The x-coordinates of A', B', and C' are all negative.

   ☐ D. The y-coordinates of A', B', and C' are all positive.

   ☐ E. The y-coordinates of A', B', and C' are all negative.

8. Point Q'(9, −5) is the image of Q after a translation down 2 units and right 4 units. What are the coordinates of Q?

   Ⓐ (5, −3)
   Ⓑ (1, 1)
   Ⓒ (3, −5)
   Ⓓ (1, −1)

9. Camille is making a wall-mounted bookshelf. It has 2 shelves, with a third piece of wood intersecting them. To support the shelves, Camille orders some L-brackets to put between the shelves and the crosspiece. She measures angle 3. How many brackets should she order to have one for every angle that is congruent to angle 3? Explain.

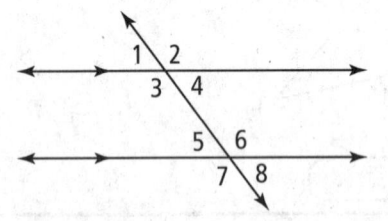

   Ⓐ 2; ∠2 is congruent to ∠3.
   Ⓑ 3; ∠2, ∠6 are both congruent to ∠3.
   Ⓒ 2; ∠6 is congruent to ∠3.
   Ⓓ 4; ∠2, ∠6, ∠7 are all congruent to ∠3.

10. Describe the transformation that maps △EFG to △UVW and represent it algebraically using coordinates.

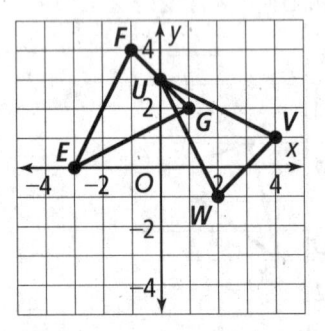

    Ⓐ reflection across the y-axis; $(x, y) \longrightarrow (-x, y)$
    Ⓑ translation 5 units right and 1 down; $(x, y) \longrightarrow (x + 5, y - 1)$
    Ⓒ rotation 90° clockwise about the origin; $(x, y) \longrightarrow (y, -x)$
    Ⓓ rotation 90° counterclockwise about the origin; $(x, y) \longrightarrow (-y, x)$

11. A farmer is putting up fences. He wants to keep his horse in the section marked △WZT. Each side must be at least 20 ft long in order for the horse to have enough room. Find the length of $\overline{ZT}$ and use that to decide if the section is big enough.

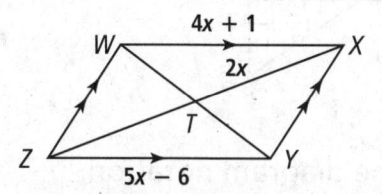

Ⓐ 7; no, there is not enough space.

Ⓑ 14; no, there is not enough space.

Ⓒ 28; yes, there is enough space.

Ⓓ 29; yes, there is enough space.

12. A chord is 15 cm long. It is 9 cm from the center of the circle. What is the approximate radius of the circle?

Ⓐ 7.5 cm   Ⓒ 11.7 cm
Ⓑ 9 cm   Ⓓ 12 cm

13. In the figure shown, what additional information is needed to show that △ABC ≅ △DEF by AAS?

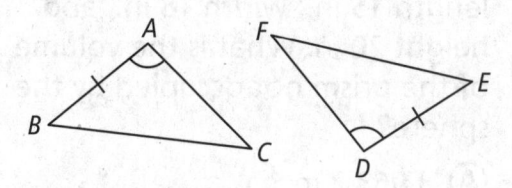

Ⓐ $m\angle C \cong m\angle E$
Ⓑ $\angle B \cong \angle E$
Ⓒ $\angle C \cong \angle F$
Ⓓ There is not enough information given.

14. Jamal is partway through constructing a figure relating to a triangle. So far he has constructed the perpendicular bisectors of two of the sides of the triangle. Which of the following could Jamal be constructing?

Ⓐ centroid
Ⓑ circumcenter
Ⓒ incenter
Ⓓ altitude

15. Which term best describes the quadrilateral formed by A(2, 3), B(4, 6), C(8, 9), and D(5, 5)?

Ⓐ quadrilateral
Ⓑ parallelogram
Ⓒ rhombus
Ⓓ kite

16. When constructing the perpendicular bisector of a segment, which of the following steps should be done first?

Ⓐ Draw an arc with the compass.
Ⓑ Draw a line with the straightedge.
Ⓒ Set the length of the compass to longer than half the length of the segment.
Ⓓ Set the point of the compass on an endpoint.

17. Find *BD*.

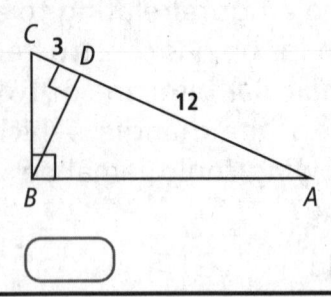

18. A pizza restaurant is located in a town with a population density of 1000 people per square mile. What delivery radius will allow the pizza restaurant to deliver to approximately 20,000 people?

Ⓐ 2.2 miles
Ⓑ 2.5 miles
Ⓒ 4.5 miles
Ⓓ 6.4 miles

19. A cross section of a square pyramid is formed by an intersection with a plane that is perpendicular to the base. Which best describes the shape of a possible cross section?

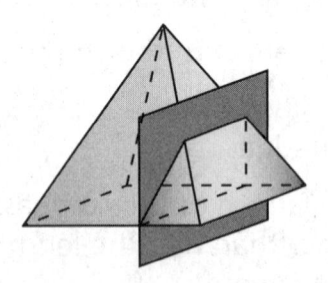

Ⓐ parallelogram
Ⓑ rectangle
Ⓒ square
Ⓓ trapezoid

20. Sort the following steps into ones that are required, and ones that are not required to show that △*ABC* ≅ △*DEC*.

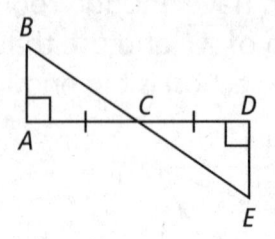

1. By the diagram notation, $m\angle BAC = m\angle CDE$, and $AC = CD$.

2. By the properties of congruent triangles, ∠*ABC* ≅ ∠*DEC*.

3. By the Angle-Side-Angle theorem, △*ABC* ≅ △*DEC*.

4. By the Vertical Angles Theorem, ∠*BCA* ≅ *DCE*.

	required	not required
Step 1	☐	☐
Step 2	☐	☐
Step 3	☐	☐
Step 4	☐	☐

21. A sphere of radius 7 in. is placed inside a rectangular prism with length 15 in., width 18 in., and height 20 in. What is the volume of the prism not occupied by the sphere?

Ⓐ 3,963.2 in.^{3}
Ⓑ 4,028.0 in.^{3}
Ⓒ 4,787.2 in.^{3}
Ⓓ 5,224.1 in.^{3}

22. Part A The sum of the measures of the interior angles in a convex polygon is 1,260. How many sides does the polygon have?

Ⓐ 5
Ⓑ 7
Ⓒ 9
Ⓓ 14

Part B What assumption would you need to make to find the measure of each interior angle?

Ⓐ The polygon is irregular.
Ⓑ Each side is at least 1 cm long.
Ⓒ The measure of each angle is no more than 90.
Ⓓ The polygon is regular.

23. What is cos C?

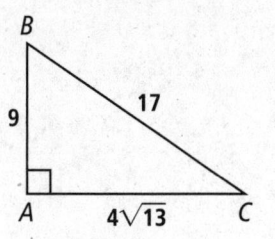

Ⓐ $\dfrac{4\sqrt{13}}{17}$
Ⓑ $\dfrac{9\sqrt{13}}{52}$
Ⓒ $\dfrac{9}{17}$
Ⓓ $\dfrac{4\sqrt{13}}{9}$

24. Segment AB is tangent to ⊙T at B. What is the radius of ⊙T?

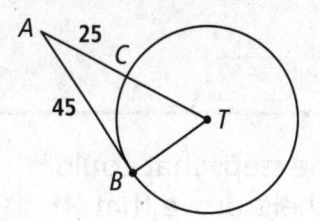

Ⓐ 20
Ⓑ 25
Ⓒ 28
Ⓓ $10\sqrt{14}$

25. The coordinates of points A and B are A(4, −2) and B(12, 10). What are the coordinates of the point that is $\frac{1}{4}$ of the way from A to B?

Ⓐ (1, −0.5)
Ⓑ (6, 1)
Ⓒ (10, 7)
Ⓓ (3, 2.5)

26. Where applicable, match the solid to the letter of the figure that forms it when rotated about the given axis of rotation.

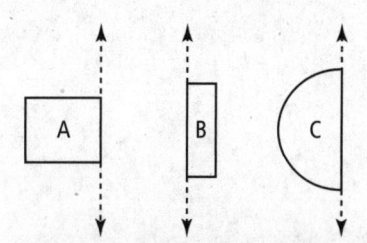

Solid	A	B	C
Cone	❏	❏	❏
Cylinder	❏	❏	❏
Sphere	❏	❏	❏

27. If a circle has equation $(x-3)^2 + (y+1)^2 = 49$, what is its domain?

    ☐ ≤ x ≤ ☐

28. Select all the steps that could be used to help prove that parallelogram ABCD is a rhombus.

    ☐ A. Check that each vertex is a right angle.

    ☐ B. Check that all side lengths are equal.

    ☐ C. Check that the diagonals are perpendicular.

    ☐ D. Check that the diagonals are the same length.

    ☐ E. Check that the adjacent sides are different lengths.

29. Which maps △ABC to a triangle that is similar, but not congruent, to △ABC?

    Ⓐ reflection over the x-axis

    Ⓑ rotation 270° counterclockwise about the origin

    Ⓒ translation right 2 units and up 3 units

    Ⓓ dilation with scale factor 2 about the origin

30. Select all the scale factors of dilations with center A that map △ABC to △AEF.

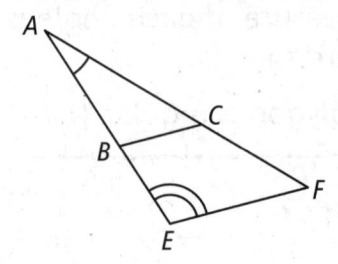

    ☐ A. $\frac{AE}{AB}$

    ☐ B. $\frac{AF}{AC}$

    ☐ C. $\frac{AC}{AF}$

    ☐ D. $\frac{BC}{EF}$

    ☐ E. $\frac{EF}{BC}$

31. Choose a reason for each statement in the proof table for the following:

$\overline{BD}$ divides sides $\overline{AC}$ and $\overline{CE}$ into proportional segments.

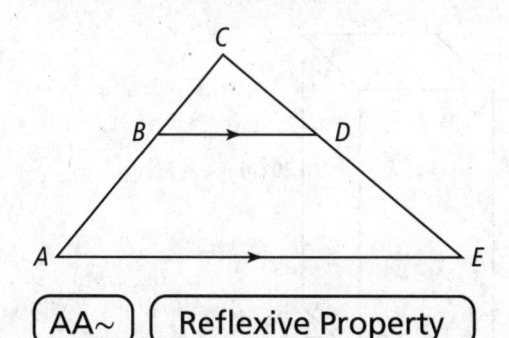

[AA~] [Reflexive Property]

[Corresponding side lengths of similar triangles are proportional.]

[If parallel lines are cut by a transversal, the corresponding angles are congruent.]

Statements	Reasons
1. $\angle C \cong \angle C$	1.
2. $\angle CBD \cong \angle CAE$	2.
3. $\triangle CBD \sim \triangle CAE$	3.
4. $\dfrac{CB}{CA} = \dfrac{CD}{CE}$	4.

32. Part A

What is EF?

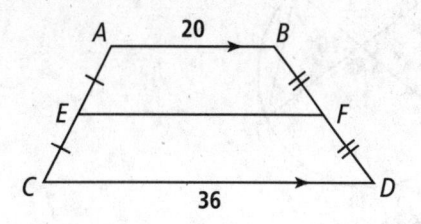

Ⓐ 26
Ⓑ 28
Ⓒ 30
Ⓓ cannot be determined

Part B

Select all the reasoning statements that support your solution.

☐ A. ABCD is a dilation of EFCD.
☐ B. E is the midpoint of $\overline{AC}$ and F is the midpoint of $\overline{BD}$.
☐ C. EF is the geometric mean of AB and CD.
☐ D. $\overline{EF}$ is halfway between $\overline{AB}$ and $\overline{CD}$.
☐ E. The lengths of $\overline{AC}$ and $\overline{BD}$ are needed to solve the problem.

33. In $\triangle ABC$, angle C is a right angle and $BC > AC$. Select all the statements that are true.

☐ A. $m\angle B > m\angle A$
☐ B. $\sin A > \sin B$
☐ C. $\sin A < \sin B$
☐ D. $\cos A > \cos B$
☐ E. $\cos A < \cos B$

34. Find the measure of ∠T.

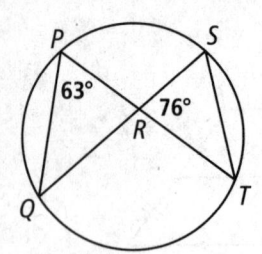

Ⓐ 28°
Ⓑ 41°
Ⓒ 63°
Ⓓ 82°

---

35. What is the area of △JKL, in square units?

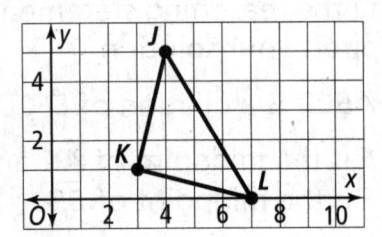

Ⓐ $\sqrt{17}$
Ⓑ $2\sqrt{17}$
Ⓒ 8.5
Ⓓ 34

---

36. A chef adds minced garlic to the container of butter shown. How many ounces of garlic will he need for the final product to have 0.002 ounces of garlic per cubic centimeter of butter?

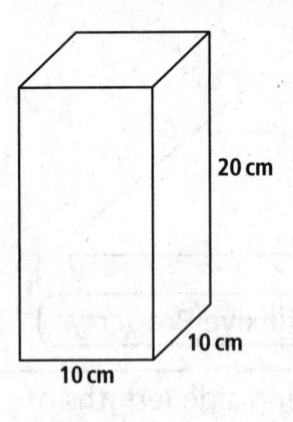

20 cm
10 cm
10 cm

---

37. If the arc shown has length 8 units, what is the area of the sector to the nearest tenth of a square unit?

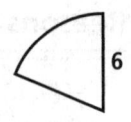

6

Ⓐ 76.3
Ⓑ 24.0
Ⓒ 7.6
Ⓓ 4.0

Name _____

Progress Monitoring Assessment Form B

1. Triangle $A'B'C'$ is a dilation of $\triangle ABC$. What is BC?

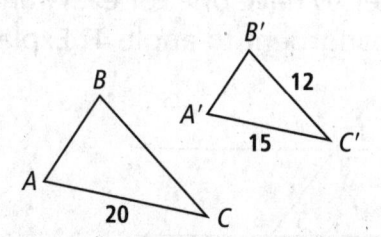

   $BC = \boxed{}$

2. A ray of sunlight forms a 31°-angle with the ground. What is the length of the shadow cast by a person 1.65 m tall?

   Ⓐ 0.99 m Ⓒ 2.75 m
   Ⓑ 1.92 m Ⓓ 3.20 m

3. Triangle XYZ is rotated 180° counterclockwise about the origin to produce $\triangle X'Y'Z'$. What are the coordinates of $\triangle X'Y'Z'$?

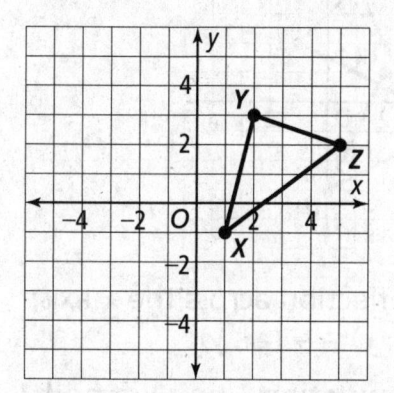

   Ⓐ $X'(1, -1)$, $Y'(3, 2)$, $Z'(2, 5)$
   Ⓑ $X'(-1, 1)$, $Y'(-3, -2)$, $Z'(-2, -5)$
   Ⓒ $X'(-1, 1)$, $Y'(-2, -3)$, $Z'(-5, -2)$
   Ⓓ $X'(0, 0)$, $Y'(1, 4)$, $Z'(4, 3)$

4. Which statement must be true?

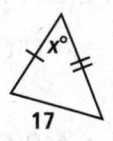

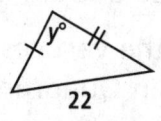

   Ⓐ $y < x$
   Ⓑ $x = y$
   Ⓒ $y > x$
   Ⓓ No relationship between x and y can be determined from the information given.

5. A square pyramid has a surface area of 10 cm². A dilation of the pyramid has a surface area of 90 cm². What is the scale factor of the dilation?

   Ⓐ $\frac{1}{3}$
   Ⓑ 3
   Ⓒ 9
   Ⓓ 81

6. A circle has center $(-7, -6)$ and radius 9. Which gives the equation for the circle?

   Ⓐ $(x + 7)^2 + (y + 6)^2 = 81$
   Ⓑ $(x - 7)^2 + (y - 6)^2 = 81$
   Ⓒ $(x + 7)^2 + (y + 6)^2 = 3$
   Ⓓ $(x - 7)^2 + (y - 6)^2 = 3$

7. Suppose △ABC has coordinates A(3, 3), B(6, 1), C(5, 4), and △ABC is mapped to △A'B'C' by a reflection across the line x = 1 followed by a translation 4 units down. Select all the statements that are true about △A'B'C'.

- [ ] A. All the vertices of △A'B'C' are in Quadrant II.
- [ ] B. All the vertices of △A'B'C' are in Quadrant III.
- [ ] C. The x-coordinates of A', B', and C' are all negative.
- [ ] D. The y-coordinates of A', B', and C' are all negative.
- [ ] E. None of the y-coordinates of A', B', and C' are positive.

8. Point Q'(2, −8) is the image of Q after a translation up 2 units and right 3 units. What are the coordinates of Q?

   Ⓐ (−1, −6)
   Ⓑ (0, −11)
   Ⓒ (−1, −10)
   Ⓓ (5, −6)

9. Ann is making a wall-mounted display shelf. It has 2 shelves, with a third piece of wood intersecting them. To support the shelves, Ann orders some L-brackets to put between the shelves and the crosspiece. She measures angle 4. How many brackets should she order to have one for every angle that is congruent to angle 4? Explain.

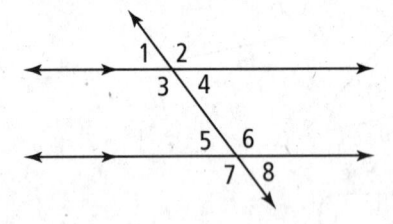

   Ⓐ 2; ∠1 is congruent to ∠4.
   Ⓑ 3; ∠1, ∠5 are both congruent to ∠4.
   Ⓒ 2; ∠5 is congruent to ∠4.
   Ⓓ 4; ∠1, ∠5, ∠8 are all congruent to ∠4.

10. Describe the transformation that maps △EFG to △UVW and represent it algebraically using coordinates.

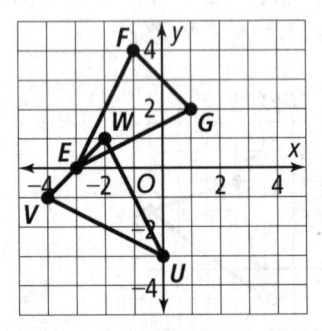

    Ⓐ reflection across the x-axis; (x, y) ⟶ (−x, y)
    Ⓑ translation 1 unit left and 3 units down; (x, y) ⟶ (x − 1, y − 3)
    Ⓒ rotation 90° clockwise about the origin; (x, y) ⟶ (y, −x)
    Ⓓ rotation 90° counterclockwise about the origin; (x, y) ⟶ (−y, x)

11. A gardener is putting up dividers in his vegetable gardens. He wants to keep zucchini in the section marked △WZT. Each side must be at least 20 ft long in order for the zucchini to have enough room. Find the length of $\overline{ZT}$ and use that to decide if the section is big enough.

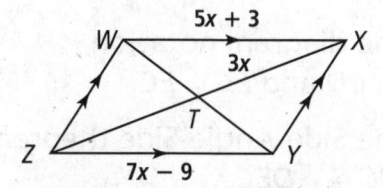

Ⓐ 6; no, there is not enough space.

Ⓑ 18; no, there is not enough space.

Ⓒ 33; yes, there is enough space.

Ⓓ 36; yes, there is enough space.

12. A chord is 8 cm long. It is 12 cm from the center of the circle. What is the approximate radius of the circle?

Ⓐ 4 cm   Ⓒ 12 cm
Ⓑ 10 cm   Ⓓ 12.6 cm

13. In the figure shown, what additional information is needed to show that △ABC ≅ △DEF by ASA?

Ⓐ m∠B = m∠F
Ⓑ ∠B ≅ ∠E
Ⓒ ∠C ≅ ∠F
Ⓓ There is not enough information given.

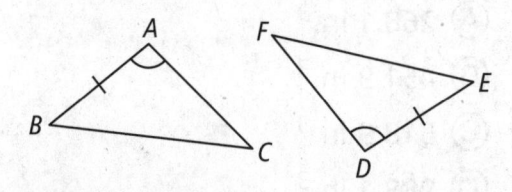

14. Will is partway through constructing a figure relating to a triangle. So far he has constructed the angle bisectors of two of the angles of the triangle. Which of the following could Will be constructing?

Ⓐ centroid
Ⓑ circumcenter
Ⓒ incenter
Ⓓ altitude

15. Which term best describes the quadrilateral formed by A(2, 8), B(4, 4), C(10, 2), and D(8, 6)?

Ⓐ quadrilateral
Ⓑ parallelogram
Ⓒ rhombus
Ⓓ kite

16. When constructing the bisector of an angle, which of the following steps should be done second?

Ⓐ Draw an arc with the compass.
Ⓑ Draw a line with the straightedge.
Ⓒ Set the length of the compass to any length.
Ⓓ Set the point of the compass on the vertex of the angle.

17. Find BD.

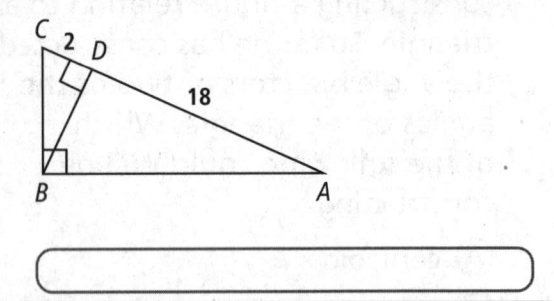

18. A pizza restaurant is located in a town with a population density of 1200 people per square mile. What delivery radius will allow the pizza restaurant to deliver to approximately 25,000 people?

Ⓐ 1.5 miles
Ⓑ 2.6 miles
Ⓒ 4.6 miles
Ⓓ 6.6 miles

19. A cross section of a square pyramid is formed by an intersection with a plane that is perpendicular to the base and passes through the vertex at the top of the pyramid. Which best describes the shape of a possible cross section?

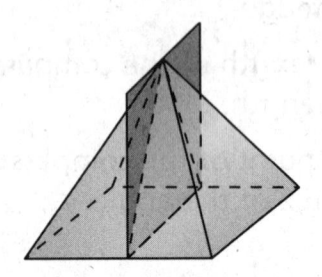

Ⓐ triangle
Ⓑ rectangle
Ⓒ square
Ⓓ trapezoid

20. Sort the following steps into ones that are required, and ones that are not required, to show that $\triangle ABC \cong \triangle DEC$.

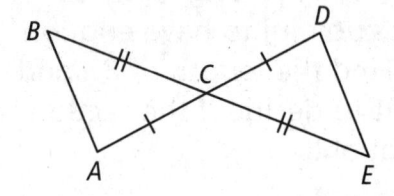

1. By the diagram notation, $AC = CD$ and $BC = EC$.
2. By the Side-Angle-Side theorem, $\triangle ABC \cong \triangle DEC$.
3. By the properties of congruent triangles, $\angle ABC \cong \angle DEC$.
4. By the Vertical Angles Theorem, $\angle BCA \cong \angle ECD$.

	required	not required
Step 1	☐	☐
Step 2	☐	☐
Step 3	☐	☐
Step 4	☐	☐

21. A sphere of radius 4 in. is placed inside a rectangular prism with length 9 in., width 8 in., and height 10 in. What is the approximate volume of the prism not occupied by the sphere?

Ⓐ 268.1 in.³
Ⓑ 451.9 in.³
Ⓒ 518.9 in.³
Ⓓ 988.1 in.³

22. **Part A** The sum of the measures of the interior angles in a convex polygon is 1,440. How many sides does the polygon have?

   Ⓐ 8
   Ⓑ 10
   Ⓒ 12
   Ⓓ 14

   Part B What assumption would you need to make to find the measure of each interior angle?

   Ⓐ The polygon is regular.
   Ⓑ The polygon is irregular.
   Ⓒ Each side is no more than 10 cm long.
   Ⓓ Each angle is no more than 90°

23. What is cos B?

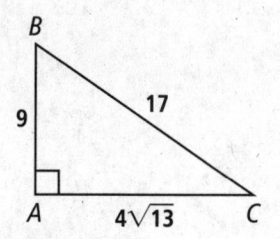

   Ⓐ $\frac{4\sqrt{13}}{17}$
   Ⓑ $\frac{9\sqrt{13}}{52}$
   Ⓒ $\frac{9}{17}$
   Ⓓ $\frac{4\sqrt{13}}{9}$

24. Segment AB is tangent to ⊙T at B. What is the radius of ⊙T?

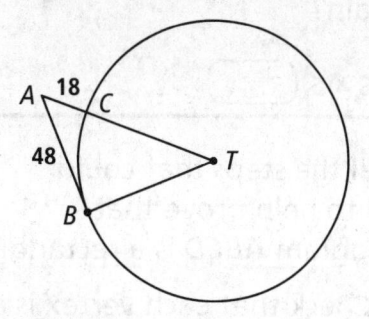

   Ⓐ 18
   Ⓑ 30
   Ⓒ $3\sqrt{210}$
   Ⓓ 55

25. The coordinates of points A and B are A(6, −3) and B(18, 3). What are the coordinates of the point that is $\frac{1}{3}$ of the way from A to B?

   Ⓐ (2, −1)
   Ⓑ (6, 1)
   Ⓒ (10, −1)
   Ⓓ (14, 1)

26. Match each solid to the letter of the figure that forms it when rotated about the given axis of rotation.

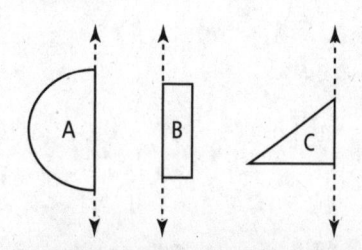

Solid	A	B	C
Cone	☐	☐	☐
Cylinder	☐	☐	☐
Sphere	☐	☐	☐

27. If a circle has equation $(x + .3)^2 + (y - 1)^2 = 49$, what is its domain?

   $\boxed{} \leq x \leq \boxed{}$

28. Select all the steps that could be used to help prove that parallelogram ABCD is a rectangle.

   ☐ A. Check that each vertex is a right angle.
   ☐ B. Check that all side lengths are equal.
   ☐ C. Check that the diagonals are perpendicular.
   ☐ D. Check that the diagonals are the same length.
   ☐ E. Check that the adjacent sides are different lengths.

29. Which maps △ABC to a triangle that is similar, but not congruent, to △ABC?

   Ⓐ reflection across the y-axis
   Ⓑ dilation with scale factor 3 about the origin
   Ⓒ rotation 90° counterclockwise about the origin
   Ⓓ translation left 4 units and up 5 units

30. Select all the scale factors of dilations with center A that map △ABC to △AEF.

   ☐ A. $\frac{EF}{BC}$
   ☐ B. $\frac{BC}{EF}$
   ☐ C. $\frac{AC}{AF}$
   ☐ D. $\frac{AF}{AC}$
   ☐ E. $\frac{AE}{AB}$

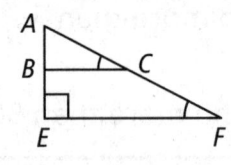

31. Choose a reason for each statement in the proof table for the following:

Given $\frac{CB}{CA} = \frac{CD}{CE}$, prove $\overline{BD} \parallel \overline{AE}$.

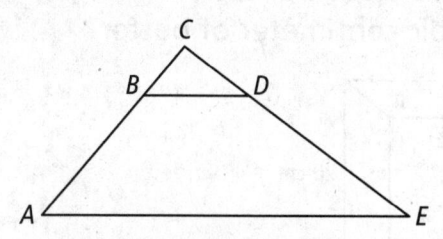

Reflexive Property

Given   SAS~

Corresponding angles of similar triangles are congruent.

If corresponding angles are congruent, the lines are parallel.

Statements		Reasons
1. $\frac{CB}{CA} = \frac{CD}{CE}$	1.	
2. $\angle C \cong \angle C$	2.	
3. $\triangle CBD \sim \triangle CAE$	3.	
4. $\angle CBD \cong \angle CAE$	4.	
5. $\overline{BD} \parallel \overline{AE}$	5.	

32. Part A

What is EF?

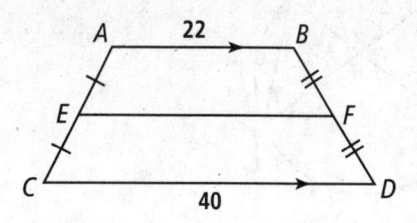

Ⓐ 31
Ⓑ 32
Ⓒ 34
Ⓓ cannot be determined

Part B

Select all the reasoning statements that support your solution.

☐ A. ABCD is a dilation of EFCD.
☐ B. E is the midpoint of $\overline{AC}$ and F is the midpoint of $\overline{BD}$.
☐ C. EF is the geometric mean of AB and CD.
☐ D. $\overline{EF}$ is halfway between $\overline{AB}$ and $\overline{CD}$.
☐ E. The lengths of $\overline{AC}$ and $\overline{BD}$ are needed to solve the problem.

33. In $\triangle ABC$, angle C is a right angle and BC > AC. Select all the statements that are true.

☐ A. sin A > sin B
☐ B. sin A < sin B
☐ C. tan A < tan B
☐ D. m∠A > m∠B
☐ E. m∠B > m∠A

34. Find the measure of ∠T.

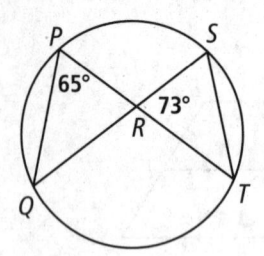

Ⓐ 34°
Ⓑ 42°
Ⓒ 65°
Ⓓ 84°

35. What is the area of △JKL, in square units?

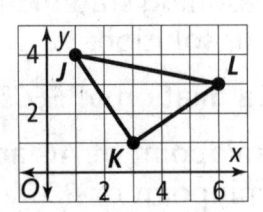

Ⓐ $\sqrt{13}$
Ⓑ $\frac{\sqrt{13}}{2}$
Ⓒ 6.5
Ⓓ 26

36. A chef adds dried herbs to the container of butter shown. How many ounces of dried herbs will she need for the final product to have 0.005 ounces of herbs per cubic centimeter of butter?

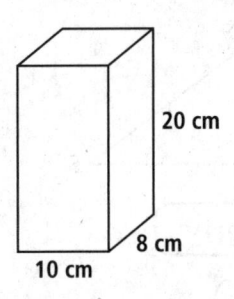

37. If the arc shown has length 12 units, what is the area of the sector to the nearest tenth of a square unit?

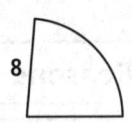

Ⓐ 15.3
Ⓑ 48.0
Ⓒ 85.9
Ⓓ 98.0

Name _____

Progress Monitoring Assessment Form C

1. Triangle A'B'C' is a dilation of △ABC. What is AC?

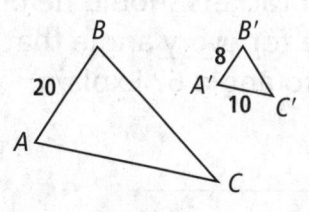

   AC = ☐

2. A ray of sunlight forms a 56°-angle with the ground. What is the length of the shadow cast by a person 2.03 m tall?

   Ⓐ 1.37 m   Ⓒ 3.01 m
   Ⓑ 2.45 m   Ⓓ 3.63 m

3. Triangle XYZ is rotated 90° clockwise about the origin to produce △X'Y'Z'. What are the coordinates of △X'Y'Z'?

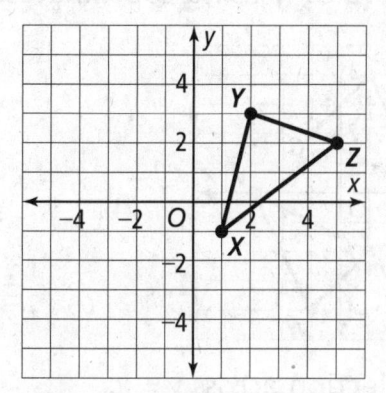

   Ⓐ X'(1, 1), Y'(−3, 2), Z'(−2, 5)
   Ⓑ X'(−1, 1), Y'(−2, −3), Z'(−5, −2)
   Ⓒ X'(−1, −1), Y'(3, −2), Z'(2, −5)
   Ⓓ X'(0, 0), Y'(1, 4), Z'(4, 3)

4. Which statement must be true?

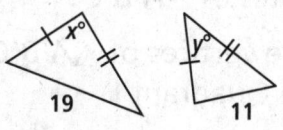

   Ⓐ x < y
   Ⓑ x = y
   Ⓒ x > y
   Ⓓ No relationship between x and y can be determined from the information given.

5. A square pyramid has a surface area of 40 cm². A dilation of the pyramid has a surface area of 10 cm². What is the scale factor of the dilation?

   Ⓐ $\frac{1}{16}$
   Ⓑ $\frac{1}{4}$
   Ⓒ $\frac{1}{2}$
   Ⓓ 2

6. A circle has center (−2, 1) and radius 7. Which gives the equation for the circle?

   Ⓐ $(x + 2)^2 + (y - 1)^2 = 7$
   Ⓑ $(x - 2)^2 + (y + 1)^2 = 7$
   Ⓒ $(x + 2)^2 + (y - 1)^2 = 49$
   Ⓓ $(x - 2)^2 + (y + 1)^2 = 49$

7. Suppose △ABC has coordinates A(2, 3), B(5, 1), C(4, 4), and △ABC is mapped to △A'B'C' by a reflection across the line y = 5 followed by a translation 1 unit down. Select all the statements that are true about the coordinates of △A'B'C'.

☐ A. All the vertices of △A'B'C' are in Quadrant I.

☐ B. All the vertices of △A'B'C' are in Quadrant IV.

☐ C. The x-coordinates of A', B', and C' are all positive.

☐ D. The x-coordinates of A', B', and C' are all nonnegative.

☐ E. The y-coordinates of A', B', and C' are all positive.

8. Point Q'(−1, −3) is the image of Q after a translation down 7 units and left 5 units. What are the coordinates of Q?

Ⓐ (6, 2)
Ⓑ (−8, 4)
Ⓒ (−8, −8)
Ⓓ (4, 4)

9. Corey is making a wall-mounted bookshelf. It has 2 shelves, with a third piece of wood intersecting them. To support the shelves, Corey orders some L-brackets to put between the shelves and the crosspiece. He measures angle 6. How many brackets should he order to have one for every angle that is congruent to angle 6? Explain.

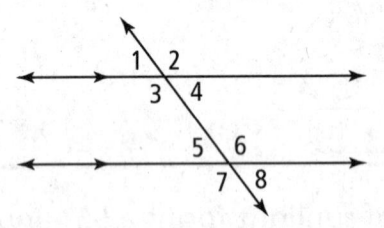

Ⓐ 2; ∠7 is congruent to ∠6.
Ⓑ 2; ∠3 is congruent to ∠6.
Ⓒ 3; ∠7, ∠3 are both congruent to ∠6.
Ⓓ 4; ∠7, ∠2, ∠3 are all congruent to ∠6.

10. Describe the transformation that maps △EFG to △VWU and represent it algebraically using coordinates.

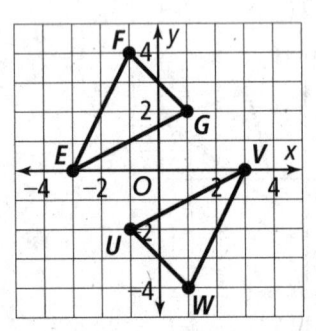

Ⓐ reflection across y = x; (x, y) ⟶ (y, x)

Ⓑ translation 4 units right and 4 units down; (x, y) ⟶ (x + 4, y − 4)

Ⓒ rotation 90° clockwise about the origin; (x, y) ⟶ (y, −x)

Ⓓ rotation 180° about the origin; (x, y) ⟶ (−x, −y)

11. A farmer is putting up fences. She wants to keep her sheep in the section marked $\triangle WZT$. Each side must be at least 20 ft long in order for the sheep to have enough room. Find the length of $\overline{ZT}$ and use that to decide if the section is big enough.

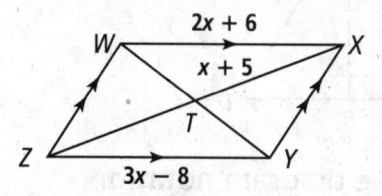

Ⓐ 14; no, there is not enough space.

Ⓑ 19; no, there is not enough space.

Ⓒ 34; yes, there is enough space.

Ⓓ 38; yes, there is enough space.

12. A chord is 17 cm long. It is 5 cm from the center of the circle. What is the approximate radius of the circle?

Ⓐ 5 cm

Ⓑ 8.5 cm

Ⓒ 9.9 cm

Ⓓ 11 cm

13. In the figure shown, what additional information is needed to show that $\triangle ABC \cong \triangle DEF$ by SAS?

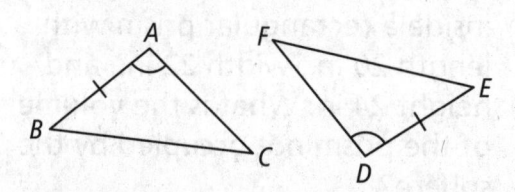

Ⓐ $AC = EF$

Ⓑ $\overline{AC} \cong \overline{DE}$

Ⓒ $\overline{AC} \cong \overline{DF}$

Ⓓ There is not enough information given.

14. Patricia is constructing a circle containing the three vertices of a triangle. Patricia says that she needs to construct the perpendicular bisectors of two sides of a triangle to find the center of the circle. Is she right? Explain.

Ⓐ Yes; she needs to construct two perpendicular bisectors to find the incenter.

Ⓑ No; she needs to construct two medians to find the centroid.

Ⓒ No; she needs to construct two altitudes to find the orthocenter.

Ⓓ Yes; she needs to construct two perpendicular bisectors to find the circumcenter.

15. Which term best describes the quadrilateral formed by $A(2, 8)$, $B(4, 4)$, $C(8, 2)$, and $D(6, 6)$?

Ⓐ quadrilateral

Ⓑ parallelogram

Ⓒ rhombus

Ⓓ kite

16. When constructing an angle bisector, the compass must be used to make three arcs. Do all three arcs need to have the same radius? Explain.

Ⓐ Yes, because you need the points of intersection of the angle and arcs to form a parallelogram.

Ⓑ Yes, because then the marks are equidistant from each other.

Ⓒ No; any three radii will work.

Ⓓ No; the second two arcs must have the same radius but it can be different from the first.

17. Find *BD*.

18. A pizza restaurant is located in a town with a population density of 1200 people per square mile. What delivery radius will allow the pizza restaurant to deliver to approximately 30,000 people?

Ⓐ 2.8 miles
Ⓑ 5.0 miles
Ⓒ 1.6 miles
Ⓓ 8.0 miles

19. A cross section of a square pyramid is formed by an intersection with a plane that is perpendicular to the base. Which shape cannot be a possible cross section?

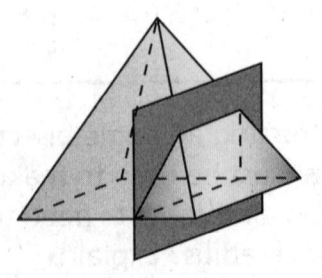

Ⓐ parallelogram
Ⓑ quadrilateral
Ⓒ trapezoid
Ⓓ triangle

20. Sort the following steps into ones that are required, and ones that are not required, to show that $\triangle ABC \cong \triangle DBC$.

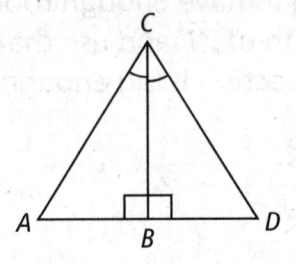

1. By the diagram notation, $m\angle ACB = m\angle DCB$.
2. Because all right angles are congruent, $m\angle ABC = m\angle DBC$.
3. By the Reflexive Property, $\overline{BC} \cong \overline{BC}$.
4. By the Angle-Side-Angle theorem, $\triangle ABC \cong \triangle DBC$.
5. By the properties of congruent triangles, $\angle CAB \cong \angle CDB$.

	required	not required
Step 1	☐	☐
Step 2	☐	☐
Step 3	☐	☐
Step 4	☐	☐
Step 5	☐	☐

21. A sphere of radius 9 in. is placed inside a rectangular prism with length 20 in., width 22 in., and height 24 in. What is the volume of the prism not occupied by the sphere?

Ⓐ 3,053.6 in.³
Ⓑ 7,506.4 in.³
Ⓒ 9,542.1 in.³
Ⓓ 13,613.6 in.³

22. **Part A** The sum of the measures of the interior angles in a convex polygon is 1,080. How many sides does the polygon have?

Ⓐ 6
Ⓑ 7
Ⓒ 8
Ⓓ 10

Part B What assumption would you need to make to find the measure of each interior angle?

Ⓐ The measure of each angle is at least 90.
Ⓑ Each side is at least 1 cm long.
Ⓒ The polygon is regular.
Ⓓ The polygon is irregular.

23. What is tan B?

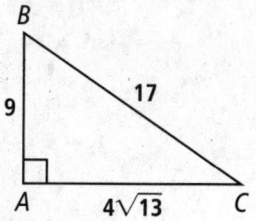

Ⓐ $\frac{4\sqrt{13}}{17}$
Ⓑ $\frac{9\sqrt{13}}{52}$
Ⓒ $\frac{9}{17}$
Ⓓ $\frac{4\sqrt{13}}{9}$

24. Segment AB is tangent to ⊙T at B. What is the radius of ⊙T?

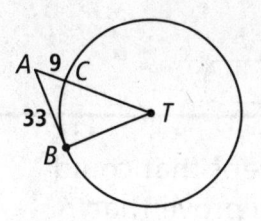

Ⓐ 9
Ⓑ 24
Ⓒ 56
Ⓓ $12\sqrt{7}$

25. The coordinates of points A and B are A(2, 16) and B(22, 4). What are the coordinates of the point that is $\frac{3}{4}$ of the way from A to B?

Ⓐ (17, 7)
Ⓑ (7, 13)
Ⓒ (16.5, 3)
Ⓓ (1.5, 12)

26. Where applicable, match the solid to the letter of the figure that forms it when rotated about the given axis of rotation.

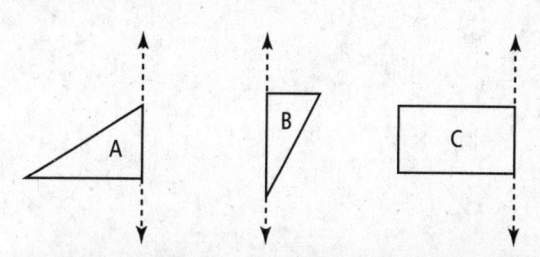

Solid	A	B	C
Cone	☐	☐	☐
Cylinder	☐	☐	☐
Sphere	☐	☐	☐

27. If a circle has equation $(x-8)^2 + (y-4)^2 = 49$, what is its domain?

$\boxed{} \leq x \leq \boxed{}$

28. Select all the steps that could be used to help prove that parallelogram ABCD is a square.
    - ☐ A. Check that each vertex is a right angle.
    - ☐ B. Check that all side lengths are equal.
    - ☐ C. Check that the diagonals are perpendicular.
    - ☐ D. Check that the diagonals are the same length.
    - ☐ E. Check that the adjacent sides are different lengths.

29. Which maps △ABC to a triangle that is similar, but not congruent, to △ABC?
    - Ⓐ reflection over the x-axis
    - Ⓑ rotation 180° about the origin
    - Ⓒ dilation with scale factor 1.5 about the origin
    - Ⓓ translation right 9 units and up 7 units

30. Select all the scale factors of dilations with center F that map △ABF to △DEF.

    - ☐ A. $\dfrac{FD}{FA}$
    - ☐ B. $\dfrac{AB}{DE}$
    - ☐ C. $\dfrac{DE}{AB}$
    - ☐ D. $\dfrac{FE}{FB}$
    - ☐ E. $\dfrac{FD}{FB}$

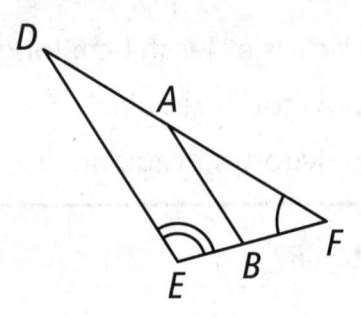

31. Choose a reason for each statement in the proof table for the following:

Given that $\triangle XYZ$ is a right triangle, and $\overline{WX}$ is an altitude of $\triangle XYZ$, $a^2 + b^2 = c^2$.

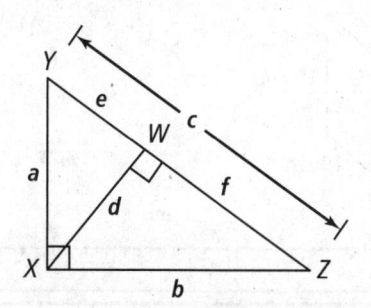

[Diagram of right triangle XYZ with altitude WX, labeled sides: a (XY), b (XZ), c (YZ), e (YW), f (WZ), d (WX)]

- Corresponding side lengths of similar triangles are proportional.
- Definition of perpendicular
- Reflexive Property
- AA~
- All right angles are congruent.

Statements	Reasons
1. $\triangle XYZ$ has right angle $\angle YXZ$; $\overline{WX}$ is an altitude of $\triangle XYZ$ with $\overline{WX} \perp \overline{YZ}$; $c = e + f$	1. Given
2. $\angle Y \cong \angle Y$; $\angle Z \cong \angle Z$	2.
3. $\angle YWX$ and $\angle ZWX$ are right angles.	3.
4. $\angle YXZ \cong \angle YWX$; $\angle YXZ \cong \angle ZWX$	4.
5. $\triangle XYZ \sim \triangle WYX$; $\triangle XYZ \sim \triangle WXZ$	5.

6. $\dfrac{c}{a} = \dfrac{a}{e}$; $\dfrac{c}{b} = \dfrac{b}{f}$	6.	
7. $a^2 = ce$; $b^2 = cf$	7. Multiplication Prop. of Equality
8. $a^2 + b^2 = ce + cf$	8. Addition Prop. of Equality
9. $a^2 + b^2 = c(e + f)$	9. Distributive Property
10. $a^2 + b^2 = c^2$	10. Substitution

32. Part A

What is AB?

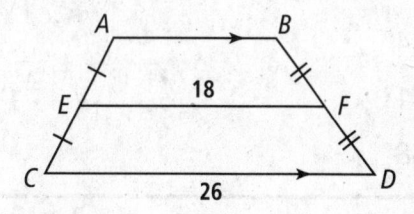

[Trapezoid with A, B on top, C, D on bottom, E on AC, F on BD; EF = 18, CD = 26]

Ⓐ 6
Ⓑ 8
Ⓒ 10
Ⓓ cannot be determined

Part B

Select all the reasoning statements that support your solution.

☐ A. ABCD is a dilation of EFCD.
☐ B. E is the midpoint of $\overline{AC}$ and F is the midpoint of $\overline{BD}$.
☐ C. EF is the geometric mean of AB and CD.
☐ D. $\overline{EF}$ is halfway between $\overline{AB}$ and $\overline{CD}$.
☐ E. The lengths of $\overline{AC}$ and $\overline{BD}$ are needed to solve the problem.

33. In △ABC, angle C is a right angle and AC > BC. Select all the statements that are true.

☐ A. m∠B > m∠A
☐ B. m∠A > m∠B
☐ C. sin A > sin B
☐ D. cos A < cos B
☐ E. tan A < tan B

34. Find the measure of ∠T.

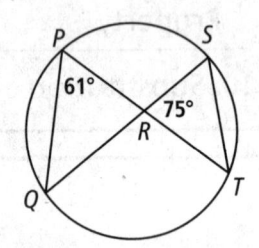

Ⓐ 30°
Ⓑ 44°
Ⓒ 61°
Ⓓ 88°

35. What is the area of △JKL, in square units

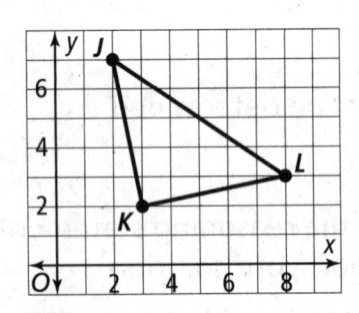

Ⓐ $\sqrt{13}$
Ⓑ 13
Ⓒ $\sqrt{26}$
Ⓓ 26

36. A chef adds grated basil to the container of olive oil shown. How many ounces of basil will she need for the final product to have 0.0025 ounces of basil per cubic centimeter of olive oil?

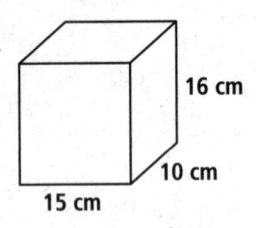

37. If the arc shown has length 12 units, what is the area of the sector to the nearest tenth of a square unit?

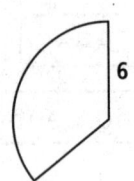

Ⓐ 36.0
Ⓑ 36.5
Ⓒ 72.0
Ⓓ 114.6

1 Readiness Assessment

1. What are the angles in a 30°–60°–90° triangle after it is rotated clockwise 45°?

   Ⓐ 45°–45°–90°
   Ⓑ 75°–105°–135°
   Ⓒ 30°–60°–90°
   Ⓓ None of the above

2. A line segment from (0, 0) to (4, 6) is reflected across the y-axis. What are the coordinates of the reflected line segment?

   Ⓐ (0, 0), (−4, 6)
   Ⓑ (4, 6), (0, 0)
   Ⓒ (0, 0), (4, −6)
   Ⓓ (−4, 6), (4, −6)

3. What is the measure of ∠XYZ?

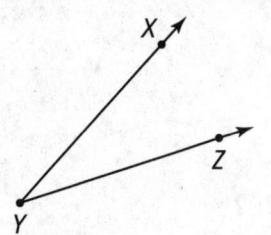

   Ⓐ 120°   Ⓒ 180°
   Ⓑ 90°   Ⓓ 30°

4. What is the name of the angle formed by ray BA and ray BC?

   Ⓐ ∠BAC
   Ⓑ ∠ABC
   Ⓒ ∠ACB
   Ⓓ ∠CAB

5. In △ABC, the measure of side c is 3.9 cm. If △DEF is a dilation of △ABC with a scale factor of 2.5, what is the measure of side f?

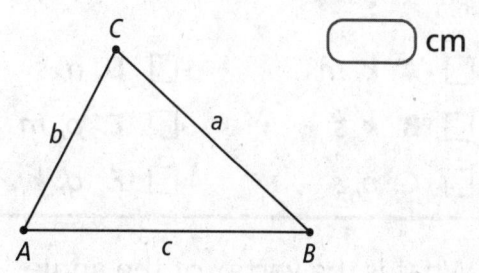

   ◯ cm

6. What is the distance between (−5, 0) and (0, 3)? Round your answer to 2 decimal places, if needed.

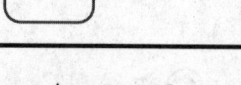

   ◯

7. In △ABC, if m∠CAD = 29, what is m∠DAB? ◯°

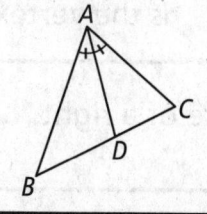

8. In the figure, which two lines appear to be parallel?

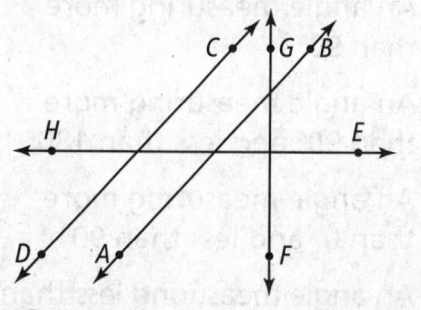

   Ⓐ lines AB and GF
   Ⓑ lines HE and GF
   Ⓒ lines AB and CD
   Ⓓ lines HE and CD

9. Select all the pairs of lines that appear to be perpendicular.

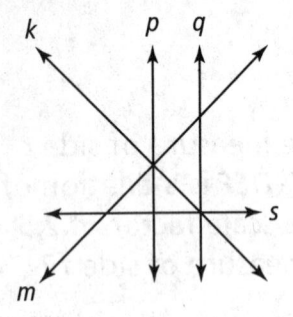

☐ A. k, m
☐ B. k, s
☐ C. p, s
☐ D. q, s
☐ E. p, m
☐ F. q, k

10. What is the vertex of the angle below?

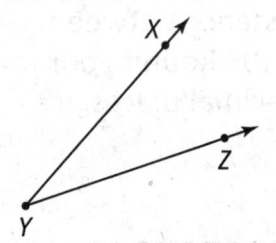

Ⓐ X
Ⓑ Y
Ⓒ Z
Ⓓ None of these is the vertex.

11. What is the measure of a right angle? ◯°

12. What is the best description of an acute angle?

Ⓐ An angle measuring more than 90°
Ⓑ An angle measuring more than 90° and less than 180°
Ⓒ An angle measuring more than 0° and less than 90°
Ⓓ An angle measuring less than 0°

13. In △ABC, what is the length of $\overline{BC}$?

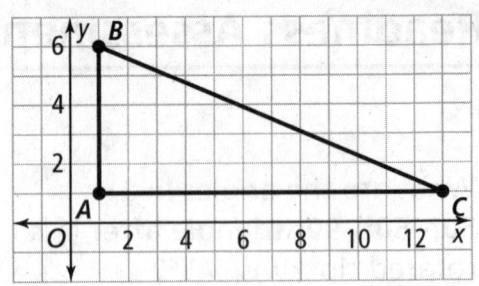

Ⓐ 13 units
Ⓑ 15 units
Ⓒ 17 units
Ⓓ 169 units

14. Is $2^2 + 3^2 = 4^2$ a true statement? Explain.

Ⓐ Yes; 7 + 9 = 16
Ⓑ No; 4 + 9 ≠ 16
Ⓒ Yes; 4 + 9 = 13
Ⓓ No; 7 + 9 ≠ 16

For Items 15–16, refer to the following figure.

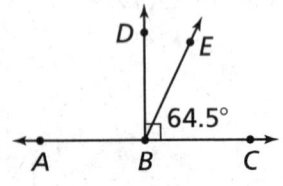

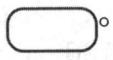

15. What is m∠DBE? ◯°

16. What is the sum of m∠ABD, m∠DBE, and m∠EBC?

Ⓐ 90°
Ⓑ 115.5°
Ⓒ 154.5°
Ⓓ 180°

1-1 Lesson Quiz

Measuring Segments and Angles

1. Select all the true statements. 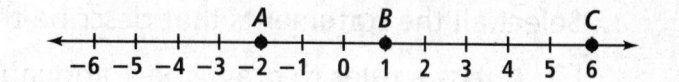
   - ☐ A. The length of $\overline{AB}$ is −3.
   - ☐ B. $BC = |6 - 1|$
   - ☐ C. $AB + AC = BC$
   - ☐ D. $AB + BC = AC$
   - ☐ E. The length of $\overline{BC}$ is 6.

2. The measure of ∠JML is 85°. Select all the true statements. 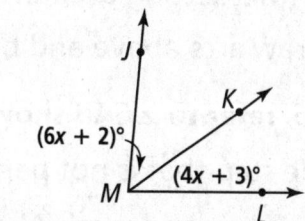
   - ☐ A. $m\angle JMK = 10°$
   - ☐ B. $m\angle KML = 11°$
   - ☐ C. $m\angle JMK = 50°$
   - ☐ D. $m\angle KML = 35°$
   - ☐ E. $m\angle JMK - m\angle KML = m\angle JML$

3. Points A, B, and C are collinear, and B lies between A and C. If $AC = 48$, $AB = 2x + 2$, and $BC = 3x + 6$, what is BC?

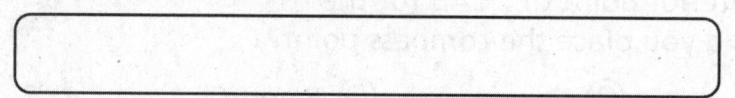

4. Point P is in the interior of ∠OZQ. If $m\angle OZQ = 125°$ and $m\angle OZP = 62°$. What is $m\angle PZQ$?

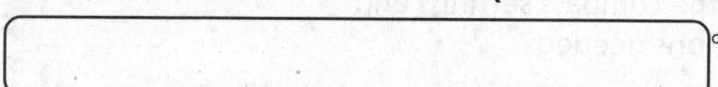

5. In the diagram shown, $m\angle XWZ = 90°$. What is x?

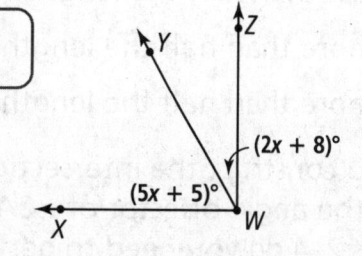

Name _____

1-2 Lesson Quiz
Basic Constructions

1. Select all the statements that describe the steps to copy $\overline{XY}$.

   ☐ A. Use a ruler to draw line ℓ and label point M.

   ☐ B. Use a straightedge to draw line ℓ and label point M.

   ☐ C. Place a compass point at X and open the compass to length XY.

   ☐ D. Using the same setting, place the compass at point M, draw an arc through line ℓ, and mark point N as the intersection.

   ☐ E. With a setting greater than $\frac{1}{2}XY$, place the compass point at X. Draw arcs above and below $\overline{XY}$.

For Items 2–5, refer to ∠CAB shown.

2. Select the step that is not part of the process for copying ∠CAB

   Ⓐ Draw a line and mark A' on it.

   Ⓑ Set the compass to length AB.

   Ⓒ Place the compass point at A' and mark an arc crossing the new line.

   Ⓓ Label the intersection of the arc and the new line C'.

3. In order to construct the interior point of ∠CAB for the angle bisector, where should you place the compass point?

   Ⓐ A Ⓑ B Ⓒ C Ⓓ B and C

4. In order to construct the perpendicular bisector of $\overline{AB}$, which statement describes the compass settings and the number of arc intersections needed?

   Ⓐ less than half the length of $\overline{AB}$; 1

   Ⓑ less than half the length of $\overline{AB}$; 2

   Ⓒ more than half the length of $\overline{AB}$; 1

   Ⓓ more than half the length of $\overline{AB}$; 2

5. If you construct the intersection of the perpendicular bisector of $\overline{AB}$ and the angle bisector of ∠CAB, then which of the constructions in Items 2–4 do you need to perform?

   Ⓐ 2 and 3   Ⓒ 3 and 4

   Ⓑ 2 and 4   Ⓓ 2, 3, and 4

enVision® Geometry • Assessment Sourcebook

1-3 Lesson Quiz

Midpoint and Distance

Items 1–3 refer to the graph shown.

1. What is the midpoint of $\overline{AB}$?

   (⬚ , ⬚)

2. What is the length of $\overline{AB}$? Round your answer to the nearest hundredth.

   ⬚

3. What are the coordinates of the point $\frac{3}{4}$ of the way from A to B?

   (⬚ , ⬚)

4. Select all the equations that represent the distance formula.
   - ☐ A. $d = \sqrt{(x_1 - x_2)^2 + (y_1 - y_2)^2}$
   - ☐ B. $d = \sqrt{(x_2 - x_1)^2 + (y_2 - y_1)^2}$
   - ☐ C. $d = \sqrt{(x_2 + x_1)^2 + (y_2 + y_1)^2}$
   - ☐ D. $d = \sqrt{|x_2 - x_1|^2 + |y_2 - y_1|^2}$
   - ☐ E. $d = \sqrt{(x_2 + x_1) - (y_2 + y_1)}$

5. What is an expression for the distance between the origin and a point $P(x, y)$?
   - Ⓐ $d = 0$
   - Ⓑ $d = \sqrt{x^2 + y^2}$
   - Ⓒ $d = \sqrt{x^2 - y^2}$
   - Ⓓ $d = \sqrt{y^2 - x^2}$

Name _____

enVision Geometry
SavvasRealize.com

1-4 Lesson Quiz
Inductive Reasoning

For Items 1–2, refer to diagram shown.

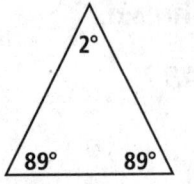

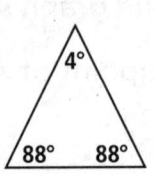

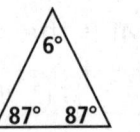

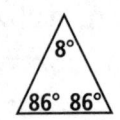

1. What is the measure of the vertex angle in the next triangle in the pattern?
   ⬚

   (Triangles shown with vertex angles 2°, 4°, 6°, 8° and base angles 89°/89°, 88°/88°, 87°/87°, 86°/86°. Not to scale.)

2. What conjecture can you make about the measure of the base angles in the *n*th triangle in the pattern?

   Ⓐ $180 - 2n$

   Ⓑ $\dfrac{180 - 2n}{2}$

   Ⓒ $\dfrac{180(n - 1)}{2}$

   Ⓓ $\dfrac{180 - n}{2}$

3. Which shape is a counterexample to the following statement? *All quadrilaterals with four congruent sides are squares.*

   Ⓐ rectangle

   Ⓑ trapezoid

   Ⓒ parallelogram

   Ⓓ rhombus

Use the table for Items 4 and 5.

4. Based on the data in the table, what is the sum of the interior angles of an 8-sided polygon?

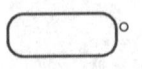

   ⬚°

Number of Sides	Sum of All Interior Angles
3	180°
4	360°
5	540°
6	720°

5. Select all of the conjectures you could make based on the table.

   ☐ A. The sum of the interior angles of a trapezoid equals 360°.

   ☐ B. The sum of all the interior angles of a regular hexagon is 540°.

   ☐ C. The sum of the interior angles of a rhombus is equal to the sum of the interior angles of a square.

   ☐ D. The sum of the interior angles of polygon increases by 180° with each additional side.

   ☐ E. Doubling the number of sides of a polygon doubles the sum of the interior angles.

Name _____

1-5 Lesson Quiz

Conditional Statements

1. Choose the words to identify the hypothesis and conclusion of the following statement: *A rectangle must have four congruent angles.*

    [hypothesis]   [conclusion]

    A polygon is a rectangle. [_____]

    The polygon has four congruent angles. [_____]

2. Choose a letter to identify the truth value of the following statement:

    [T]   [F]

    If a parallelogram has four right angles, then it is a rectangle. [_____]

3. Which statement is the converse of the following conditional?
    If a polygon has three sides, then it is a triangle.

    Ⓐ If a polygon does not have three sides, then it is not a triangle.

    Ⓑ If a polygon is not a triangle, then it does not have three sides.

    Ⓒ If a polygon is a triangle, then it does not have three sides.

    Ⓓ If a polygon is a triangle, then it has three sides.

4. Identify the biconditional for the following statement.

    If M is the midpoint of $\overline{AB}$, then $\overline{AM} \cong \overline{MB}$.

    Ⓐ M is the midpoint of $\overline{AB}$ only if $\overline{AM} \cong \overline{MB}$.

    Ⓑ $\overline{AM} \cong \overline{MB}$ only if M is the midpoint of $\overline{AB}$.

    Ⓒ M is the midpoint of $\overline{AB}$ if and only if $\overline{AM} \cong \overline{MB}$.

    Ⓓ If $\overline{AM} \cong \overline{MB}$, then M is the midpoint of $\overline{AB}$.

5. Select all the conditionals and truth values implied by the following biconditional.

    Two lines are parallel if and only if they do not intersect.

    ☐ A. If two lines are parallel, then they do not intersect; T.

    ☐ B. If two lines are not parallel, then they intersect; F.

    ☐ C. If two lines do not intersect, then they are parallel; T.

    ☐ D. If two lines intersect, then they are parallel; F.

    ☐ E. If two lines intersect, then they are not parallel; T.

enVision® Geometry • Assessment Sourcebook

Name _____

1-6 Lesson Quiz

Deductive Reasoning

Assume all given information to be true.

1. If $m\angle A$ is less than 90°, then $\angle A$ is an acute angle. The measure of $\angle A = 75°$. What can you logically conclude?

   Ⓐ $\angle A$ is acute.

   Ⓑ $\angle A$ is right.

   Ⓒ $\angle A$ is obtuse.

   Ⓓ Not enough information

2. What conclusion can you draw from the following statements?
   - If a figure is a square, then it has four sides.
   - If a figure has four sides, then it is not a triangle.

   Ⓐ If a figure is not a triangle, then it is a square.

   Ⓑ If a figure has four sides, then it is a square.

   Ⓒ If a figure is a square, then it is not a triangle.

   Ⓓ If a figure is not a triangle, then it has four sides.

3. Determine whether the hypothesis of each given conditional is true from the given information.

	Yes	No
If A, B, C, and D are collinear, then they lie in the same plane. A, B, C, and D lie in the same plane.	❑	❑
If $\overrightarrow{BD}$ bisects $\angle ABC$, then D lies in the interior of $\angle ABC$. D lies in the interior of ABC.	❑	❑

4. In the Law of Syllogism, suppose $p \rightarrow q$ and $q \rightarrow r$ are true, where p is "a polygon has three sides", q is "a polygon is a triangle", and r is "the interior angles of a polygon sum to 180°". Complete the statement.

   If p is true, then r is ❑ true.
   ❑ false.

5. If C lies between A and B on $\overline{AB}$, then $AC + CB = AB$. Choose the option you can logically conclude about $\overline{AB}$.

   5.5   5.2
   A ——— C ——— B

   Ⓐ $AB = 2(AC)$

   Ⓒ $AB = 10.7$

   Ⓑ $AB = 11$

   Ⓓ none of the above

Name _____

1-7 Lesson Quiz
Writing Proofs

For Items 1–2, refer to the figure shown.

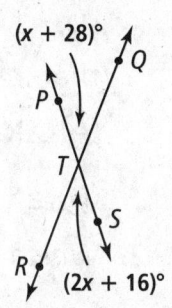

1. What is m∠PTR?
   Ⓐ 12°   Ⓑ 40°   Ⓒ 50°   Ⓓ 140°

2. What is m∠RTS?
   Ⓐ 12°   Ⓑ 40°   Ⓒ 50°   Ⓓ 140°

For Items 3–5, refer to the figure shown.

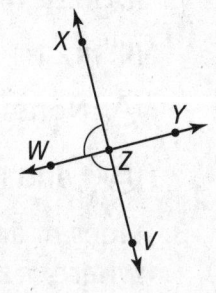

3. Select the correct options to supply the missing reasons in the proof.

| If two angles are supplementary to the same angle, then the two angles are congruent. | The sum of the measures of a linear pair is 180°. |

| Definition of perpendiular lines | Definition of linear pair |

| Supplementary congruent angles are right angles. | Transitive Property of Equality | Angle Addition Postulate |

Statement	Reason
1 ∠WZX ≅ ∠WZV	Given
2 ∠WZX and ∠WZV are a linear pair.	
3 m∠WZX + m∠WZV = 180°	
4 m∠WZX = m∠WZV = 90°	
5 $\overline{WY} \perp \overline{VX}$	

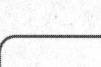

4. What is the measure of ∠XZW?
   m∠XZY = ( ) °

5. What is the measure of ∠YZW?
   m∠YZW = ( ) °

enVision® Geometry • Assessment Sourcebook

Name _____

1-8 Lesson Quiz
Indirect Proof

1. For an indirect proof, what must first be assumed to prove that ∠X is a right angle?

    Ⓐ ∠X is an acute angle.   Ⓒ ∠X is not a right angle.

    Ⓑ ∠X is an obtuse angle.   Ⓓ ∠X is a right angle.

2. Which two statements contradict each other?

    I. ∠1 and ∠2 are complementary angles.

    II. $m\angle 2 = 65°$

    III. $m\angle 1 + m\angle 2 + m\angle 3 = 90°$; $m\angle 3 \neq 0°$

    Ⓐ None   Ⓒ I and III

    Ⓑ I and II   Ⓓ II and III

3. Lines m and n cross to form ∠1, ∠2, ∠3, and ∠4 in some order, where $m\angle 1 = 30°$.

    • ∠1 and ∠4 are supplementary.

    • ∠1 and ∠2 are vertical angles.

    • $m\angle 3 = m\angle 4$

    Which angle has the same measure as ∠1? ∠ ▢

For Items 4–5, use the figure and the statements shown.

Given: $m\angle 1 + m\angle 2 = 180°$

Prove: $\ell \parallel m$

4. Which statement would complete an indirect proof by contrapositive?

    Ⓐ $m\angle 1 + m\angle 2 \neq 180°$

    Ⓑ $\ell \nparallel m$

    Ⓒ If $m\angle 1 + m\angle 2 \neq 180°$ then $\ell \nparallel m$.

    Ⓓ If $\ell \nparallel m$ then $m\angle 1 + m\angle 2 \neq 180°$.

5. What would be your first assumption in an indirect proof by contradiction?

    Ⓐ $m\angle 1 + m\angle 2 \neq 180°$

    Ⓑ $\ell \nparallel m$

    Ⓒ If $m\angle 1 + m\angle 2 \neq 180°$ then $\ell \nparallel m$.

    Ⓓ If $\ell \nparallel m$ then $m\angle 1 + m\angle 2 \neq 180°$.

Name _____

1 Topic Assessment Form A

1. If $DM = 25$, what is the value of r?

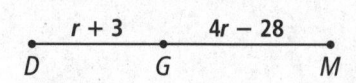

   D •——r + 3——• G •——4r − 28——• M

   Ⓐ 10
   Ⓑ 12
   Ⓒ 14
   Ⓓ 15

For Items 2–3, points P, Q, and S are collinear.

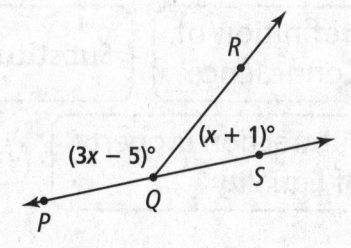

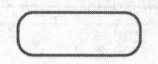

(diagram showing rays from Q to P, R, S with angles $(3x - 5)°$ for ∠PQR side and $(x + 1)°$ for ∠RQS... with R above, S to the right)

2. What is $m\angle PQR$?

   ☐

3. If a ray QT bisects $\angle RQS$, what is $m\angle TQS$?

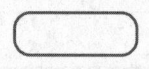

   ☐

4. Points L, M, and N are collinear. You are given $LM = 13$ and $LN = 20$. What is a possible value of MN?

   Ⓐ 6 Ⓒ 8
   Ⓑ 7 Ⓓ 9

5. Ray BD bisects $\angle ABC$ so that $m\angle DBC = x + 6$ and $m\angle ABD = 2x - 12$. What is x?

   Ⓐ 12 Ⓒ 16
   Ⓑ 14 Ⓓ 18

6. What are the coordinates of the point $\frac{1}{4}$ of the way from $A(-6, -3)$ to $B(10, 9)$?

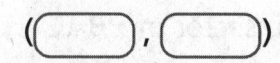

   (☐ , ☐)

For Items 7–8, suppose $\overline{XY}$ has one endpoint at $X(0, 0)$.

7. If $(3, 4)$ is the midpoint of $\overline{XY}$, what are the coordinates of point Y?

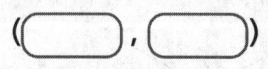

   (☐ , ☐)

8. What are the coordinates of Y if $(3, 4)$ is $\frac{1}{3}$ of the way from X to Y?

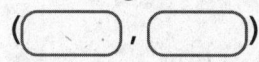

   (☐ , ☐)

For Items 9–10, use the choices to complete the sentences.

[AB] [A] [B] [C] [D]
[length AB] [length BC] [any length]

9. To construct a copy of $\angle ABC$ with $\overrightarrow{DE}$ as one ray, you can first use the compass to measure ☐, then place the point of the compass on ☐.

10. To construct the angle bisector of $\angle ABC$, you can first set the point of the compass on ☐, then draw an arc with the compass with ☐.

11. Which best describes what is formed by the construction of $\overline{CD}$?

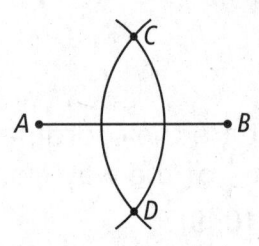

Ⓐ the angle bisector of ∠BAC
Ⓑ a 60° angle including $\overline{AB}$
Ⓒ the midpoint of $\overline{AB}$
Ⓓ the perpendicular bisector of $\overline{AB}$

For Items 12–13, use the diagram shown.

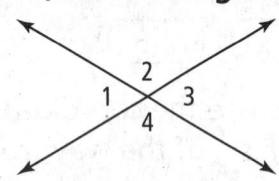

12. If $m\angle 1 = (4x + 2)$ and $m\angle 3 = (5x - 15)$, what is the value of x?

Ⓐ 14
Ⓑ 15
Ⓒ 16
Ⓓ 17

13. Select all statements that could be the first step of an indirect proof of the conditional below.

If $m\angle 2 = 110$, then $m\angle 1 = 70$.

☐ A. If $m\angle 2 = 110$, then $m\angle 1 = 70$.
☐ B. If $m\angle 1 \neq 70$, then $m\angle 2 \neq 110$.
☐ C. Assume if $m\angle 1 \neq 70$, then $m\angle 2 \neq 110$.
☐ D. Assume if $m\angle 2 \neq 110$, then $m\angle 1 \neq 70$.
☐ E. Assume if $m\angle 2 = 70$, then $m\angle 1 = 110$.

14. If $DM = 26$ and point G bisects $\overline{DM}$, what is the value of r?

Ⓐ 10
Ⓑ 13
Ⓒ 30
Ⓓ 52

15. Given: ∠1 and ∠2 are supplementary and ∠3 and ∠2 are supplementary.
Prove: $\angle 1 \cong \angle 3$

Use the reasons listed to complete the proof.

| Definition of Congruence | Substitution |
| Subtraction Property of Equality | Given |

Statements	Reasons
$m\angle 1 + m\angle 2 = 180$	
$m\angle 3 + m\angle 2 = 180$	
$m\angle 1 + m\angle 2 = m\angle 3 + m\angle 2$	
$m\angle 1 = m\angle 3$	
$\angle 1 \cong \angle 3$	

1 Topic Assessment Form B

1. If $DM = 35$, what is the value of r?

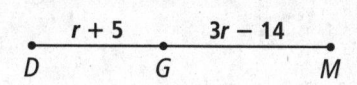

   D —— $r+5$ —— G —— $3r-14$ —— M

   Ⓐ 11
   Ⓑ 12
   Ⓒ 13
   Ⓓ 14

Items 2–3. Points P, Q, and S are collinear.

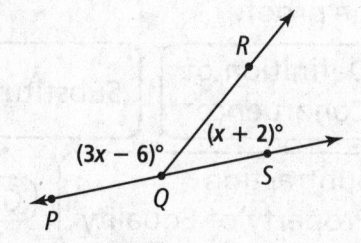

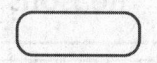

(diagram: rays from Q to P, R, and S; angle PQR = $(3x-6)°$, angle RQS labeled with $(x+2)°$)

2. What is $m\angle PQR$?

   [ ]

3. If a ray QT bisects $\angle RQS$, what is $m\angle TQS$?

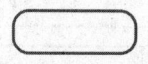

   [ ]

4. Points L, M, and N are collinear. You are given $LM = 18$ and $LN = 27$. What is a possible value of MN?

   Ⓐ 6   Ⓒ 8
   Ⓑ 7   Ⓓ 9

5. Ray BD bisects $\angle ABC$ so that $m\angle DBC = x + 8$ and $m\angle ABD = 2x - 15$. What is x?

   Ⓐ 16   Ⓒ 23
   Ⓑ 21   Ⓓ 28

6. What are the coordinates of the point $\frac{3}{4}$ of the way from $A(-6, -3)$ to $B(10, 9)$?

   ([ ] , [ ])

For Items 7–8, suppose $\overline{AB}$ has one endpoint at $A(0, 0)$.

7. If $(5, 3)$ is the midpoint of $\overline{AB}$, what are the coordinates of point B?

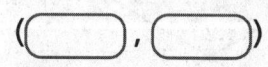

   ([ ] , [ ])

8. What are the coordinates of B if $(5, 3)$ is $\frac{1}{3}$ of the way from A to B?

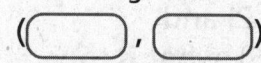

   ([ ] , [ ])

For Items 9–10, use the choices to complete the sentences.

[A] [C] [AB] [$\frac{1}{2}$ AB]

9. To construct a copy of $\overline{AB}$ on $\overleftrightarrow{CD}$, you can first use the compass to measure [ ], then place the point of the compass on [ ].

10. To construct the perpendicular bisector of $\overline{AB}$, you can first set the compass to measure [ ], next place the point of the compass on [ ], then draw an arc with the compass.

11. Which best describes what is formed by the construction of $\overline{AD}$?

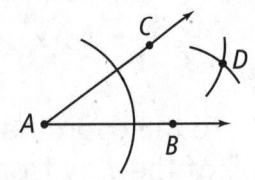

Ⓐ the angle bisector of ∠BAC
Ⓑ a 60° angle including $\overline{AB}$
Ⓒ the midpoint of $\overline{AB}$
Ⓓ the perpendicular bisector of $\overline{AB}$

For Items 12–13, use the diagram shown.

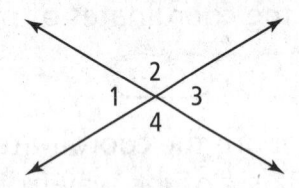

12. If $m\angle 1 = (4x + 2)$ and $m\angle 3 = (5x - 25)$, what is the value of x?

Ⓐ 27
Ⓑ 28
Ⓒ 30
Ⓓ 32

13. Select all statements that could be the first step of an indirect proof of the conditional below.

If $m\angle 2 = 95$, then $m\angle 3 = 95$.

☐ A. If $m\angle 3 \neq 95$, then $m\angle 2 \neq 95$.
☐ B. If $m\angle 2 = 95$, then $m\angle 3 = 95$.
☐ C. Assume if $m\angle 3 \neq 95$, then $m\angle 2 \neq 95$.
☐ D. Assume if $m\angle 2 \neq 95$, then $m\angle 3 \neq 95$.
☐ E. Assume if $m\angle 3 = 95$, then $m\angle 2 = 95$.

14. If $DM = 32$ and point G bisects $\overline{DM}$, what is the value of r?

Ⓐ 11
Ⓑ 16
Ⓒ 22
Ⓓ 72

---

15. Given: ∠1 and ∠2 are complementary and ∠3 and ∠2 are complementary.

Prove: $\angle 1 \cong \angle 3$

Use the reasons listed to complete the proof.

| Definition of Congruence | Substitution |
| Subtraction Property of Equality | Given |

Statements	Reasons
$m\angle 1 + m\angle 2 = 90$	
$m\angle 3 + m\angle 2 = 90$	
$m\angle 1 + m\angle 2 = m\angle 3 + m\angle 2$	
$m\angle 1 = m\angle 3$	
$\angle 1 \cong \angle 3$	

Name _____

1 Performance Assessment Form A

Alice and Raheem are each making a miniature replica of the De Young Museum. From a brochure, they have a drawing of the garden and first floor.

1. Measure the angles and side lengths of the Entry Court. Describe the shape of the Entry Court. What sides and angles are equivalent?

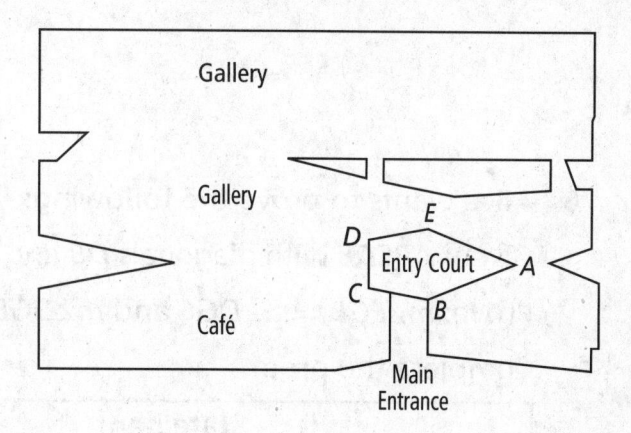

2. Alice plotted the entry court on graph paper. Find the midpoint of $\overline{CD}$. Construct the angle bisector of $\angle A$. Does the angle bisector pass through the midpoint?

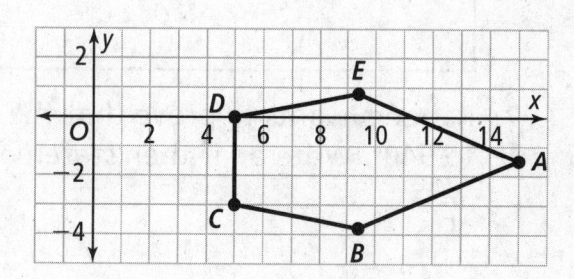

3. Construct a line perpendicular to the angle bisector through point E. Does the perpendicular line pass through point B? Is the midpoint of $\overline{BE}$ on the angle bisector? Explain.

4. Raheem said, "In pentagon $ABCDE$, if the angle bisector of $\angle A$ passes through the midpoint of $\overline{CD}$, then $AB = AE$, $BC = ED$, $m\angle B = m\angle E$, and $m\angle C = m\angle D$." Is that true? Explain.

5. Alice writes, "In a pentagon ABCDE, if AB = AE, BC = ED, m∠B = m∠E, and m∠C = m∠D, the angle bisector of ∠A passes through the midpoint of $\overline{CD}$." What is the converse of the statement Alice wrote? How does Alice's statement relate to Raheem's statement in Item 4?

6. Alice wants to prove the following:

    Given: ABCDE with diagonals $\overline{DB}$ and $\overline{EC}$ and intersection point G

    Prove: m∠EGB = m∠DGC and m∠DGE = m∠BGC

    Complete the proof.

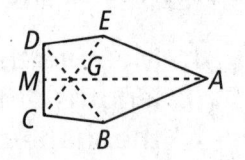

Statement	Reason

7. Raheem wants to prove that the sum of the angle measures of ABCDE is equal to 540°. Write an if-then statement Raheem can use to prove his conjecture.

8. Using the fact that the sum of the angle measures in a quadrilateral is equal to 360°, complete Raheem's proof.

Name _____

1 Performance Assessment Form B

enVision Geometry
SavvasRealize.com

G'ahan goes to Long Beach for the Grand Prix race every year. He has a map of the race track from last year.

1. Measure the angles and side lengths of ABCDE to estimate the measures on the track. Describe the shape of the polygon ABCDE. Which sides and angles are congruent?

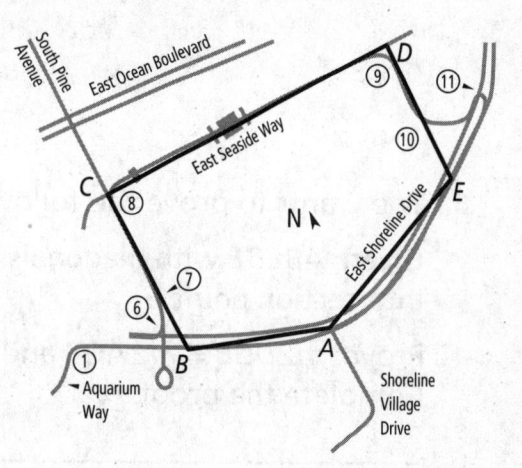

2. Louis plotted the track on graph paper. Find the midpoint of $\overline{CD}$. Construct the angle bisector of angle A. Does the angle bisector pass through the midpoint?

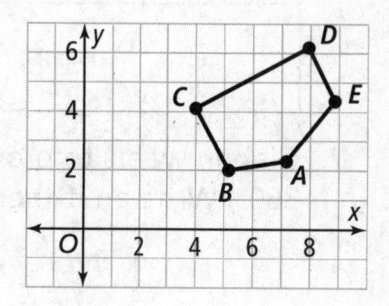

3. Construct a line perpendicular to the angle bisector through point E. Does the perpendicular line pass through point B? Is the midpoint of $\overline{BE}$ on the angle bisector? Explain.

4. G'ahan said, "In pentagon ABCDE, since the angle bisector of angle A does not pass through the midpoint of $\overline{CD}$, no sides or angles have equal measures." Is that true? Explain.

5. Zoe writes, "In a pentagon ABCDE, if $AB = DE$, $BC \neq ED$, $m\angle B \neq m\angle E$, and $m\angle C = m\angle D$, the angle bisector of angle A does not pass through the midpoint of $\overline{CD}$." What is the converse of the statement Zoe wrote? How does Zoe's statement relate to G'ahan's statement in Item 4?

6. Zoe wants to prove the following:

    Given: ABCDE with diagonals $\overline{DA}$ and $\overline{EB}$ and intersection point G

    Prove: $m\angle DGE = m\angle AGB$ and $m\angle BGD = m\angle EGA$
    Complete the proof.

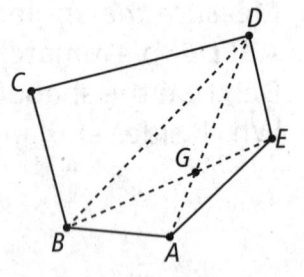

Statement	Reason

7. G'ahan wants to prove that the sum of the angle measures of ABDE is equal to 360°. Write an if-then statement G'ahan can use to prove his conjecture.

8. Using the fact that the sum of the angle measures in a triangle is equal to 180°, prove that the sum of the angle measures in ABDE is 360°.

2 Readiness Assessment

1. If $DG = 10$, what is the value of x?

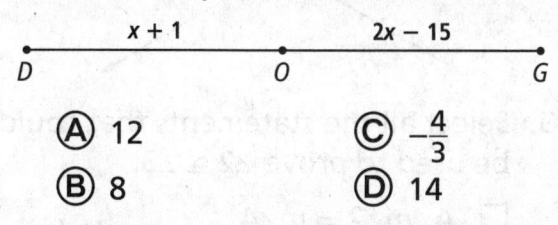

   D •———$x+1$———• O ———$2x-15$——• G

   Ⓐ 12
   Ⓑ 8
   Ⓒ $-\frac{4}{3}$
   Ⓓ 14

Use the figure for Items 2 and 3. Points P, Q, and S are collinear.

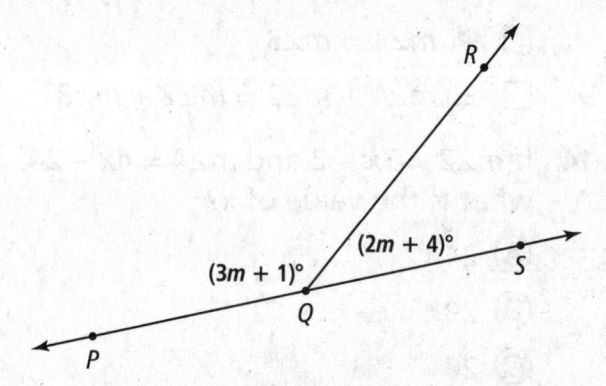

2. What is $m\angle SQR$? ☐

3. If $\overrightarrow{QT}$ bisects $\angle PQR$, what is the measure of $\angle PQT$? ☐

   (angles shown: $(3m+1)°$ and $(2m+4)°$ at Q with ray to R and ray to S; P on opposite side)

4. Points C, D, and E are collinear. If $CD = 18$ and $CE = 27$, what is a possible measure of DE?

   Ⓐ 6
   Ⓑ 7
   Ⓒ 8
   Ⓓ 9

5. $\overrightarrow{BD}$ bisects $\angle ABC$ so that $m\angle DBC = x + 2$ and $m\angle ABD = 2x - 5$. What is x?

   Ⓐ 2
   Ⓑ 7
   Ⓒ 6
   Ⓓ 8

6. What are the coordinates of the point $\frac{3}{4}$ of the way from $X(1, -6)$ to $Y(9, 10)$? (☐, ☐)

7. Point $(2, 6)$ is $\frac{2}{3}$ of the way from A to B. If A has coordinates $(-8, 6)$, what are the coordinates of B? (☐, ☐)

For Items 8–10, use the following conditional: If two angles are vertical angles, then they are congruent.

8. Which is the hypothesis of the conditional?

   Ⓐ Two angles are not vertical angles.
   Ⓑ The angles are congruent.
   Ⓒ The angles are not congruent.
   Ⓓ Two angles are vertical angles.

9. Which is the conclusion of the conditional?

   Ⓐ Two angles are not vertical angles.
   Ⓑ The angles are congruent.
   Ⓒ The angles are not congruent.
   Ⓓ Two angles are vertical angles.

10. Is the converse of the conditional true? Explain.

    Ⓐ No; if the angles are not vertical angles, they could still be congruent.
    Ⓑ Yes; if two angles are not congruent, then they cannot be vertical angles.
    Ⓒ No; if angles are congruent, they aren't necessarily vertical angles.
    Ⓓ Yes; if angles are vertical angles, then they are congruent.

For Items 11–12, use the Law of Detachment and the Law of Syllogism to make a conclusion.

11. If a triangle has congruent base angles, then the triangle is isosceles. In triangle ABC, $m\angle B = m\angle C$.

    Ⓐ $\angle B$ and $\angle C$ are base angles of the triangle.

    Ⓑ Triangle ABC is isosceles.

    Ⓒ $\angle A$ is the vertex of the triangle.

    Ⓓ Triangle ABC is not isosceles.

12. If the diagonals of a quadrilateral bisect each other, then it is a parallelogram. If a quadrilateral is a parallelogram, then opposite sides are congruent.

    Ⓐ If opposite sides of a quadrilateral are congruent, then it is a parallelogram.

    Ⓑ If opposite sides of a quadrilateral are congruent, then the diagonals bisect each other.

    Ⓒ Opposite sides of a parallelogram are congruent.

    Ⓓ If the diagonals of a quadrilateral bisect each other, then opposite sides are congruent.

For Items 13–14, use the diagram shown.

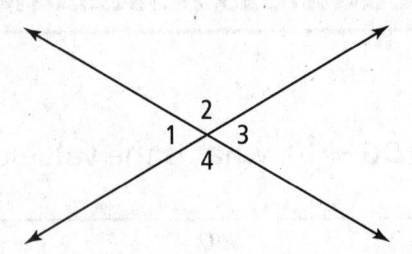

13. Select all the statements that could be used to prove $\angle 2 \cong \angle 3$.

    ☐ A. $m\angle 2 = m\angle 4$

    ☐ B. $m\angle 3 = m\angle 4$

    ☐ C. $m\angle 2 + m\angle 3 = m\angle 3 + m\angle 4$

    ☐ D. $m\angle 1 = m\angle 3$

    ☐ E. $m\angle 1 + m\angle 2 = m\angle 2 + m\angle 3$

14. If $m\angle 2 = 3x + 2$ and $m\angle 4 = 4x - 24$, what is the value of x?

    Ⓐ 24

    Ⓑ 29

    Ⓒ 26

    Ⓓ 27.3

2-1 Lesson Quiz

Properties of Parallel Lines

1. Select all the true statements.

   ☐ A. ∠3 ≅ ∠2 because they are alternate interior angles.

   ☐ B. m∠1 + m∠3 = 180 because they form a straight angle.

   ☐ C. ∠3 ≅ ∠6 because they are alternate interior angles.

   ☐ D. ∠1 and ∠6 are supplementary because ∠3 ≅ ∠6 and m∠1 + m∠3 = 180.

   ☐ E. ∠1 ≅ ∠3 because they are vertical angles.

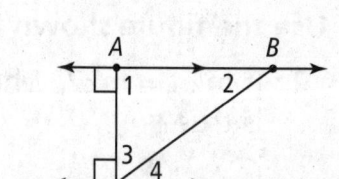

Use the figure shown for Items 2–4.

2. What is m∠2 + m∠3? Explain.

   Ⓐ 180; m∠1 + 90 = 180, so m∠2 + m∠3 = 180.

   Ⓑ 180; m∠1 + 90 = m∠2 + m∠3, so m∠2 + m∠3 = 180.

   Ⓒ 90; m∠1 + m∠2 + m∠3 = 180. m∠1 = 90, so m∠2 + m∠3 = 90.

   Ⓓ 90; ∠2 and ∠3 are corresponding angles, so m∠2 + m∠3 = 90.

3. If m∠4 = 35, find m∠2. Explain.

   Ⓐ 55; ∠2 and ∠4 are complementary angles, so m∠2 = 90 − m∠4.

   Ⓑ 35; ∠2 and ∠4 are corresponding angles, so m∠2 = m∠4.

   Ⓒ 145; ∠2 and ∠4 are supplementary angles, so m∠2 = 180 − m∠4.

   Ⓓ 35; ∠2 and ∠4 are alternate interior angles, so m∠2 = m∠4.

4. If m∠4 = 35, find m∠3. Explain.

   Ⓐ 55; ∠3 and ∠4 are complementary angles, so m∠3 = 90 − m∠4.

   Ⓑ 35; ∠3 and ∠4 are corresponding angles, so m∠3 = m∠4.

   Ⓒ 145; ∠3 and ∠4 are supplementary angles, so m∠3 = 180 − m∠4.

   Ⓓ 35; ∠3 and ∠4 are alternate interior angles, so m∠3 = m∠4.

5. In the figure shown, t ∥ x and k ∥ w. If m∠3 = 20, choose the list which includes all of the other angles that measure 20°.

   Ⓐ 1

   Ⓑ 7, 9, 14

   Ⓒ 1, 14, 16

   Ⓓ 1, 5, 7, 9, 11, 14, 16

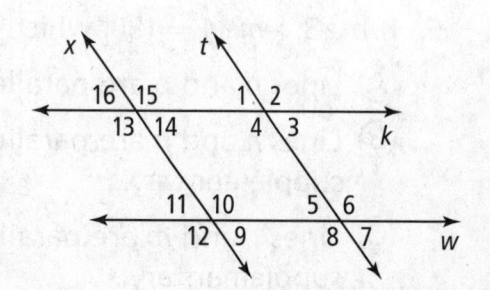

Name _____

2-2 Lesson Quiz

Proving Lines Parallel

1. Select all the true statements. 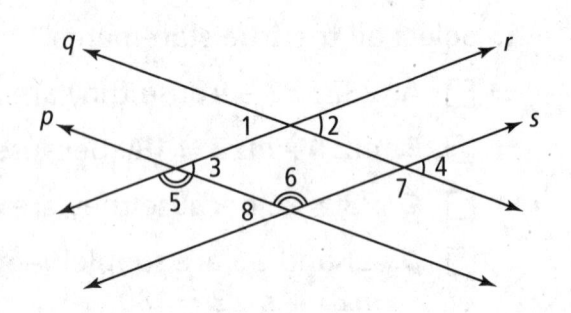
   - ☐ A. $p \parallel q$ because $\angle 2 \cong \angle 3$.
   - ☐ B. $p \parallel q$ because $\angle 5 \cong \angle 7$.
   - ☐ C. $r \parallel s$ because $\angle 2 \cong \angle 4$.
   - ☐ D. $r \parallel s$ because $\angle 5 \cong \angle 6$.
   - ☐ E. $r \parallel s$ because $\angle 5 \cong \angle 7$.

Use the figure shown for Items 2 and 3.

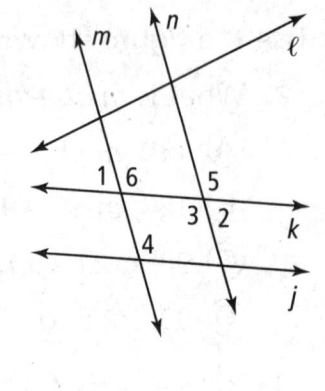

2. If $m\angle 1 = m\angle 2$, which of the following statements is true?
   - Ⓐ $k \parallel j$
   - Ⓑ $n \parallel m$
   - Ⓒ $\ell \parallel k$
   - Ⓓ $\ell \parallel m$

3. Which statement must be true to prove $j \parallel k$?
   - Ⓐ $\angle 2 \cong \angle 3$
   - Ⓑ $\angle 1 \cong \angle 4$
   - Ⓒ $m\angle 2 + m\angle 5 = 180$
   - Ⓓ $\angle 6 \cong \angle 4$

Use the figure shown for Items 4 and 5.

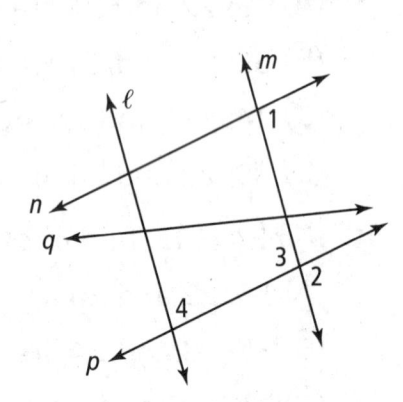

4. If $\angle 1 \cong \angle 2$, can you conclude that any of the lines are parallel? Explain.
   - Ⓐ Yes; lines n and p are parallel because corresponding angles are congruent.
   - Ⓑ No; $\angle 1$ and $\angle 2$ show no relationship.
   - Ⓒ Yes; lines ℓ and m are parallel because corresponding angles are congruent.
   - Ⓓ No; neither angle is formed by the transversal, line q.

5. If $m\angle 3 + m\angle 4 = 180$, which lines can you conclude are parallel? Explain.
   - Ⓐ Lines n and p are parallel because alternate interior angles are congruent.
   - Ⓑ Lines n and p are parallel because same-side interior angles are supplementary.
   - Ⓒ Lines ℓ and m are parallel because same-side interior angles are supplementary.
   - Ⓓ Lines ℓ and m are parallel because alternate interior angles are congruent.

Name _____

2-3 Lesson Quiz

Parallel Lines and Triangles

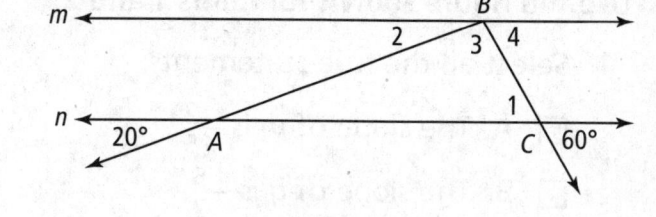

1. Select all true statements if n ∥ m.
   - ☐ A. m∠2 = 60
   - ☐ B. m∠3 = 100
   - ☐ C. m∠2 + m∠4 = 80
   - ☐ D. m∠2 + m∠3 = 80
   - ☐ E. m∠2 = 20

2. Select all the true statements.
   - ☐ A. 4x + 16 = 180
   - ☐ B. x = 49
   - ☐ C. m∠A = 99
   - ☐ D. From smallest to largest: ∠B, ∠C, ∠A
   - ☐ E. m∠C = 56

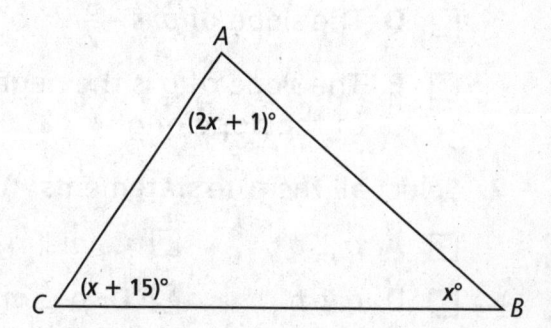

3. Line m is constructed as the first step to prove the Triangle Angle-Sum Theorem. Which of the following must be true in order to complete the proof?
   - Ⓐ m ∥ n
   - Ⓑ BC = AC
   - Ⓒ m∠1 + m∠2 = 90
   - Ⓓ m∠1 = m∠2

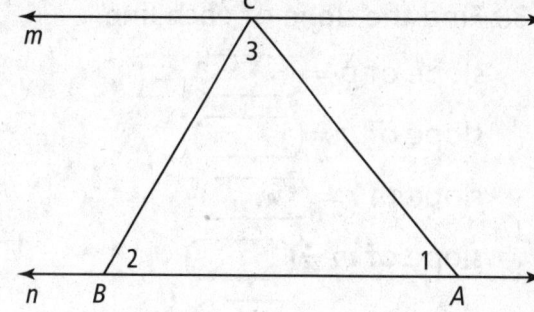

Use the figure shown for Items 4 and 5.

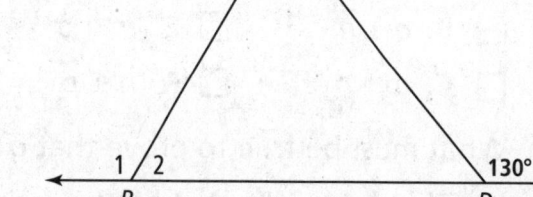

4. What is m∠1?
   - Ⓐ 130
   - Ⓑ 70
   - Ⓒ 60
   - Ⓓ 120

5. What kind of triangle is BCD? Explain.
   - Ⓐ Right triangle; m∠2 = 90
   - Ⓑ Acute triangle; m∠CDB = 180 − 130 = 50 and m∠2 = 180 − 70 − 50 = 60
   - Ⓒ Obtuse triangle; m∠CDB = 180 − 70 = 110
   - Ⓓ Isosceles triangle; m∠CDB = m∠2

enVision® Geometry • Assessment Sourcebook

Name _____

2-4 Lesson Quiz
Slopes of Parallel and Perpendicular Lines

enVision Geometry
SavvasRealize.com

Use the figure shown for Items 1 and 2.

1. Select all the true statements.

   ☐ A. The slope of m is $-\frac{2}{5}$.

   ☐ B. The slope of q is $-\frac{5}{2}$.

   ☐ C. The slope of n is $\frac{2}{5}$.

   ☐ D. The slope of p is $-\frac{5}{2}$.

   ☐ E. The slope of p is the negative reciprocal of the slope of q.

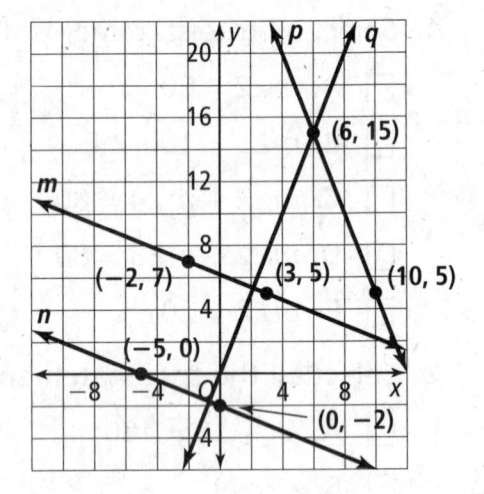

2. Select all the true statements.

   ☐ A. $p \perp q$ ☐ C. $m \parallel n$ ☐ E. $m \parallel q$
   ☐ B. $q \perp n$ ☐ D. $p \perp m$ ☐ F. $n \parallel q$

Use the figure shown for Items 3–5.

3. Find the slope of each line.

   slope of p = ⬚
   slope of q = ⬚
   slope of r = ⬚
   slope of m = ⬚
   slope of n = ⬚

4. Select all the true statements.

   ☐ A. $p \parallel q$ ☐ D. $p \perp m$
   ☐ B. $q \perp n$ ☐ E. $m \parallel p$
   ☐ C. $m \parallel n$ ☐ F. $n \perp p$

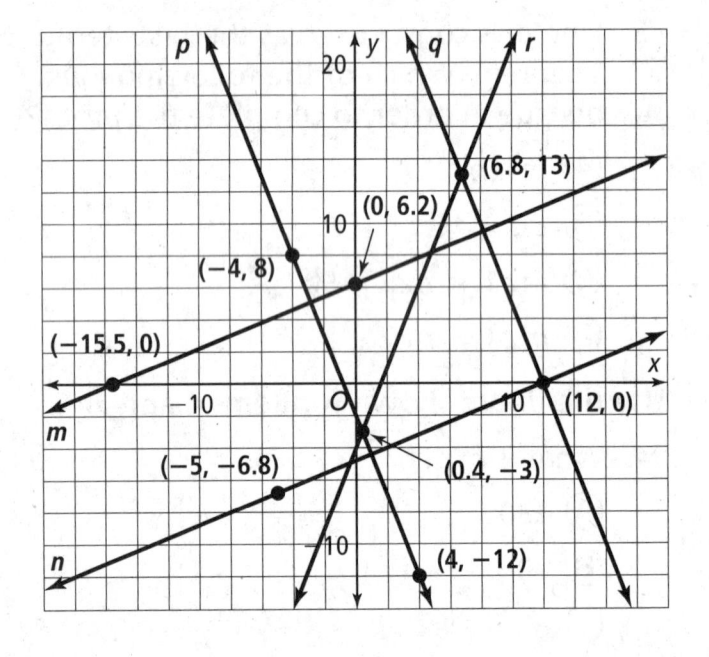

5. What must be true to prove that $q \perp n$?

   Ⓐ The slope of q must be the reciprocal of the slope of n.

   Ⓑ The slope of q must be the negative reciprocal of the slope of n.

   Ⓒ The slope of q must be the slope of n multiplied by -1.

   Ⓓ The slope of q must be -1 divided by the slope of n.

enVision® Geometry • Assessment Sourcebook

Name _____

2 Topic Assessment Form A

1. What type of lines are coplanar and do not intersect?
   - Ⓐ parallel
   - Ⓑ perpendicular
   - Ⓒ segments
   - Ⓓ transversal

For Items 2–5, lines ℓ and m are intersected by transversal t. $\ell \parallel m$

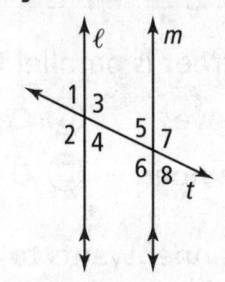

2. Select all the angles that are supplementary to $\angle 1$.
   - ☐ A. $\angle 3$ ☐ C. $\angle 5$ ☐ E. $\angle 7$
   - ☐ B. $\angle 4$ ☐ D. $\angle 6$ ☐ F. $\angle 8$

3. Select all the angles that are congruent to $\angle 5$.
   - ☐ A. $\angle 1$ ☐ C. $\angle 3$ ☐ E. $\angle 7$
   - ☐ B. $\angle 2$ ☐ D. $\angle 4$ ☐ F. $\angle 8$

4. Complete the following plan to prove that $\angle 3 \cong \angle 6$.

   Use the Same-Side Interior Angles Postulate to show that $\angle 3$ is supplementary to ☐.

   Show $\angle 6$ and ☐ are ☐ because they form a ☐.

   Since $\angle 3$ and $\angle 6$ are ☐ to the same angle, they are congruent to each other.

5. If $m\angle 2 = 112$, what is $m\angle 7$?

   $m\angle 7 =$ ☐

6. Select all the true statements given the figure.

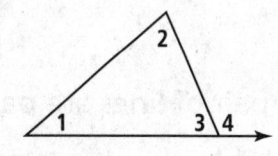

   - ☐ A. $m\angle 4 = m\angle 2$
   - ☐ B. $m\angle 4 = m\angle 1 + m\angle 2$
   - ☐ C. $m\angle 4 = 180 - m\angle 3$
   - ☐ D. $m\angle 4 = m\angle 1 + m\angle 2 + m\angle 3$
   - ☐ E. $m\angle 4 = m\angle 3 + m\angle 1$

For Items 7–9, use the figure shown.

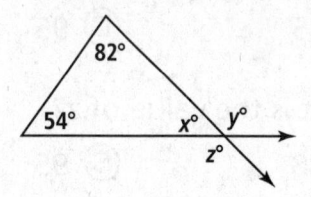

7. What is x?
   - Ⓐ 28
   - Ⓑ 44
   - Ⓒ 136
   - Ⓓ 224

8. What is y?

   $y =$ ☐

9. Select all the true statements.
   - ☐ A. $x = y$
   - ☐ B. $x + y = 180$
   - ☐ C. $y = z$
   - ☐ D. $x + z = 180$
   - ☐ E. $y + z = 180$

For Items 10–13, lines a, b, c, and d intersect as shown.

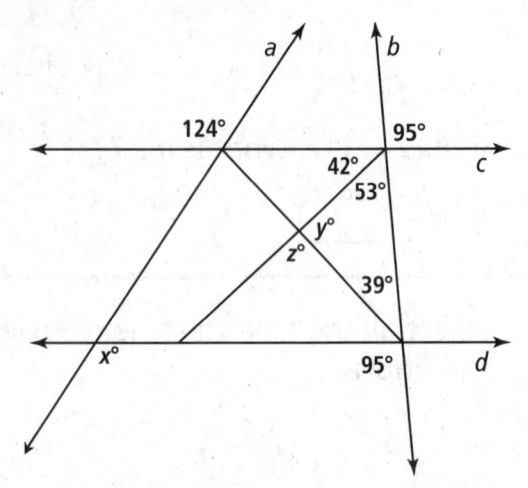

10. Which pair of lines are parallel?
    Ⓐ a and b
    Ⓑ a and c
    Ⓒ c and d
    Ⓓ b and d

11. What is the value of x?

    x = ◯

12. What is the value of y?
    Ⓐ 42
    Ⓑ 85
    Ⓒ 88
    Ⓓ 95

13. What is the value of z?
    Ⓐ 88
    Ⓑ 92
    Ⓒ 95
    Ⓓ 124

14. Two lines intersect to form ∠ABC. One step in constructing a line parallel to $\overleftrightarrow{BC}$ through point A is to construct an angle with vertex A. How should this angle be related to ∠ABC?

    Ⓐ The angles should be congruent.
    Ⓑ The angles should be complementary.
    Ⓒ The angles should be supplementary.
    Ⓓ The angles should have different measures.

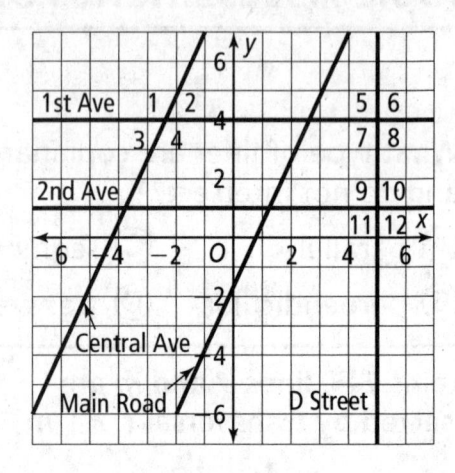

For Items 15–16, use the part of a city map shown.

15. Which street is parallel to 1st Ave?
    Ⓐ 2nd Ave
    Ⓑ Main Road
    Ⓒ Central Ave
    Ⓓ D Street

16. A city planner wants to build a road perpendicular to D Street. What is the slope of the new road?

    slope = ◯

17. What is the equation of a line that is parallel to the line $y = 2x + 7$ and passes through the point (–2, 4)?
    Ⓐ $y = -\frac{1}{2}x + 3$
    Ⓑ $y = 2x + 4$
    Ⓒ $y = -\frac{1}{2}x - 2$
    Ⓓ $y = 2x + 8$

18. What is the equation of a line that is perpendicular to the line $y = -\frac{1}{4}x - 1$ and passes through the point (3, 7)?
    Ⓐ $y = -4x + 19$
    Ⓑ $y = 4x - 5$
    Ⓒ $y = \frac{1}{4}x + \frac{25}{4}$
    Ⓓ $y = -4x + 31$

Name _____

2 Topic Assessment Form B

1. Which statement is true about parallel lines?
   - Ⓐ They are coplanar and intersect.
   - Ⓑ They are not coplanar and intersect.
   - Ⓒ They are coplanar and do not intersect.
   - Ⓓ They are not coplanar and do not intersect.

For Items 2–5, lines ℓ and m are intersected by transversal t. $\ell \parallel m$

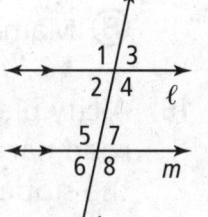

2. Select all the angles that are supplementary to $\angle 2$.
   - ☐ A. $\angle 3$
   - ☐ B. $\angle 4$
   - ☐ C. $\angle 5$
   - ☐ D. $\angle 6$
   - ☐ E. $\angle 7$
   - ☐ F. $\angle 8$

3. Select all the angles that are congruent to $\angle 6$.
   - ☐ A. $\angle 1$
   - ☐ B. $\angle 2$
   - ☐ C. $\angle 3$
   - ☐ D. $\angle 4$
   - ☐ E. $\angle 7$
   - ☐ F. $\angle 8$

4. Complete the following plan to prove that $\angle 4 \cong \angle 8$.

   Use the Same-Side Interior Angles Postulate to show that $\angle 4$ is supplementary to ◯.

   Show $\angle 8$ and ◯ are ◯ because they form a ◯.

   Since $\angle 4$ and $\angle 8$ are ◯ to the same angle, they are congruent to each other.

5. If $m\angle 4 = 105$, what is $m\angle 5$?

   $m\angle 5 =$ ◯

6. Select all the true statements given the figure.
   - ☐ A. $m\angle 4 = m\angle 1 + m\angle 2 + m\angle 3$
   - ☐ B. $m\angle 4 = m\angle 2 + m\angle 3$
   - ☐ C. $m\angle 4 = m\angle 3$
   - ☐ D. $m\angle 4 = 180 - m\angle 1$
   - ☐ E. $m\angle 4 = m\angle 1 + m\angle 2$

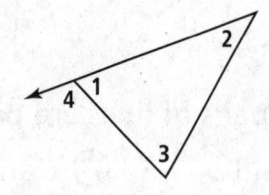

For Items 7–9, use the figure shown.

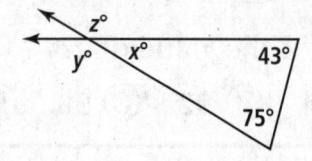

7. What is x?
   - Ⓐ 32
   - Ⓑ 62
   - Ⓒ 118
   - Ⓓ 242

8. What is y?

   $y =$ ◯

9. Select all the true statements.
   - ☐ A. $x = y$
   - ☐ B. $x + y = 180$
   - ☐ C. $y = z$
   - ☐ D. $x + z = 180$
   - ☐ E. $y + x = 180$

For Items 10–13, lines a, b, c, and d intersect as shown.

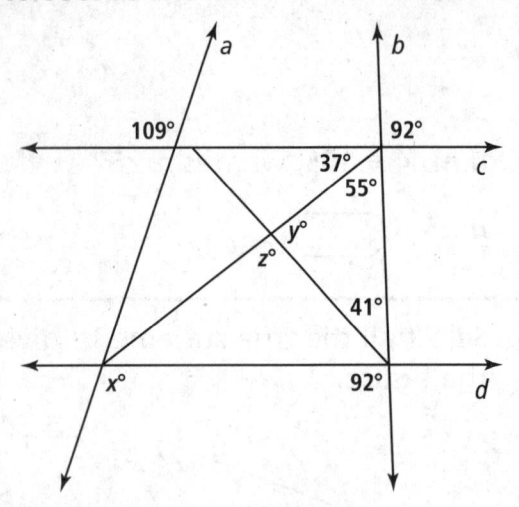

10. Which pairs of lines are parallel?
    Ⓐ a and b Ⓒ c and d
    Ⓑ a and c Ⓓ b and d

11. What is the value of x?
    x = ☐

12. What is the value of y?
    Ⓐ 37 Ⓑ 84 Ⓒ 88 Ⓓ 92

13. What is the value of z?
    Ⓐ 84 Ⓑ 92 Ⓒ 96 Ⓓ 109

14. Two lines intersect to form ∠ABC. One step in constructing a line parallel to $\overleftrightarrow{BC}$ through point A is to construct an angle congruent to ∠ABC with vertex A. Which theorem can you use to prove that the line you constructed is parallel to the given line?

    Ⓐ Same-Side Interior Angles Theorem
    Ⓑ Converse of the Same-Side Interior Angles Theorem
    Ⓒ Corresponding Angles Theorem
    Ⓓ Converse of the Corresponding Angles Theorem

For Items 15–16, use the part of a city map shown.

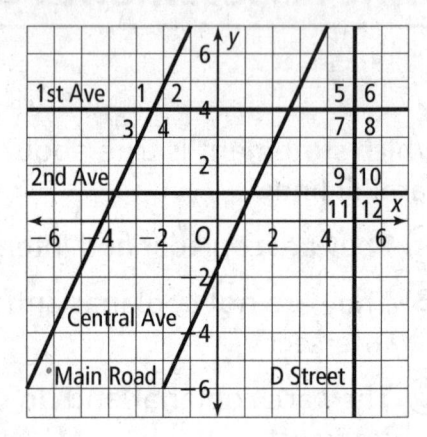

15. Which street is perpendicular to 1st Ave?
    Ⓐ 2nd Ave Ⓒ Central Ave
    Ⓑ Main Road Ⓓ D Street

16. A city planner wants to build a road parallel to 2nd Ave. What is the slope of the new road?

    slope = ☐

17. What is the equation of a line that is perpendicular to the line $y = 2x + 1$ and passes through the point (4, 6)?
    Ⓐ $y = -\frac{1}{2}x + 6$
    Ⓑ $y = 2x + 6$
    Ⓒ $y = -\frac{1}{2}x + 8$
    Ⓓ $y = 2x + 8$

18. What is the equation of the line parallel to the line $y = 3x - 4$ such that the distance between the y-intercepts is 10?
    Ⓐ $y = -3x + 6$
    Ⓑ $y = 3x + 6$
    Ⓒ $y = \frac{1}{3}x + 10$
    Ⓓ $y = -\frac{1}{3}x + 6$

enVision® Geometry Assessment Sourcebook

Name _____

2 Performance Assessment Form A

Luis is making a simple camera. The diagram shows how an object is projected onto the film.

1. Show that if the center axis bisects ∠APB, then it bisects ∠A'PB'.

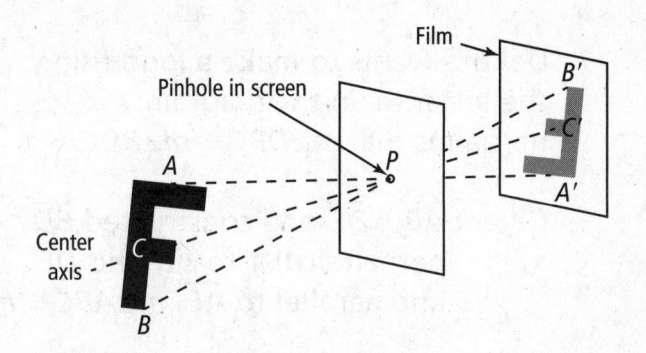

2. Luis uses a shoe box that is 14 inches long. He places the pinhole P in the center of the front, which is $7\frac{1}{2}$ in. × $5\frac{1}{8}$ in. If he needs to leave a half-inch border on the film, what is the largest image he can make?

3. In order to rotate an image 45°, Luis tries to rotate the shoe box 45°. His photo shown does not appear to be a rotation of 45°. Estimate the slopes of the parallel line segments.

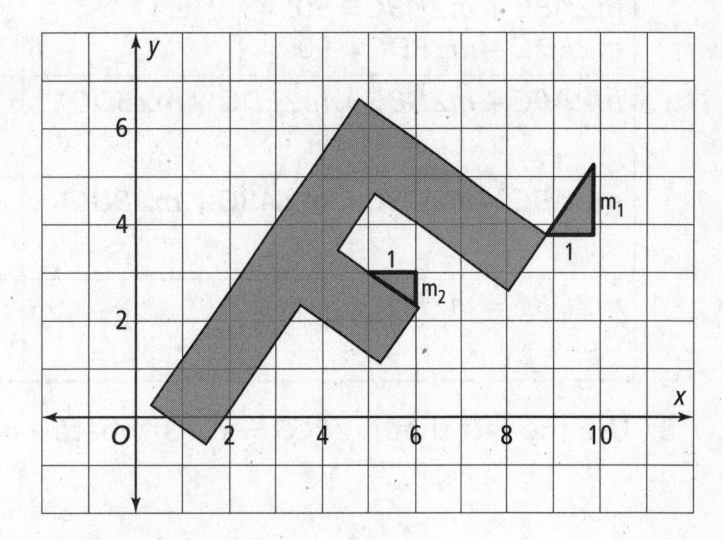

4. Show that there are perpendicular line segments in his photo.

5. Malia drew the slope triangles on the image. She explained, "If Luis had rotated the box 45°, then the legs of the slope triangles would be congruent." What should the slopes be according to Malia?

6. Malia claims that the closer the camera is to the object, the bigger the image. What relationship has she noticed that supports her claim?

7. Dakota wants to make a logo using the letter M. In the diagram, he claims that $m\angle DBC = m\angle BDC$.

   Given: $\overline{AB} \parallel \overline{DE}$ and constructed $\overline{BD}$ perpendicular to $\overline{AB}$ and $\overline{DE}$ and parallel to $\overline{AE}$, $m\angle ABC = m\angle EDC$

   Prove: $m\angle DBC = m\angle BDC$

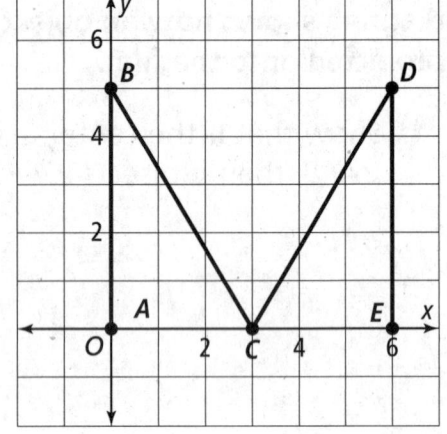

   Complete the proof.

$\overline{AB} \parallel \overline{DE}$, $\overline{BD} \parallel \overline{AE}$, $\overline{BD} \perp \overline{AB}$, $\overline{BD} \perp \overline{DE}$ $m\angle ABC = m\angle EDC$	
$\angle ABD$, $\angle BDE$ are right angles.	
$m\angle ABC + m\angle DBC = 90$, $m\angle EDC + m\angle BDC = 90$	
$m\angle ABC + m\angle DBC = m\angle EDC + m\angle BDC$	
$m\angle ABC + m\angle DBC = m\angle ABC + m\angle BDC$	
$m\angle DBC = m\angle BDC$	

8. Use the fact that $m\angle BCD = x + 3$, where x is $m\angle DBC$. Find x.

9. Find $m\angle BCD$ using the fact that $m\angle BCD = x + 3$.

2 Performance Assessment Form B

LaTanya is using a microscope to study the anatomy of an amoeba. The diagram shows how the image is enlarged by the microscope.

1. Show that if the center axis bisects ∠APB, then it bisects ∠A'PB'.

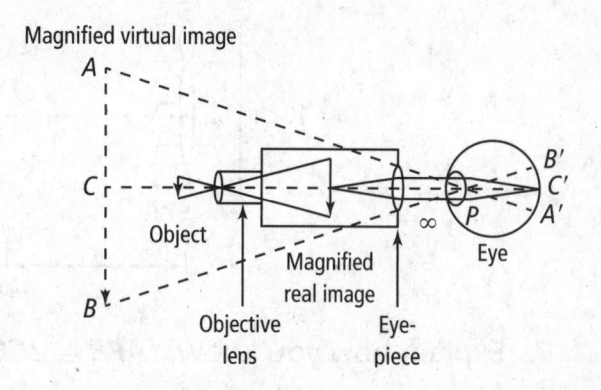

2. LaTanya enlarges the image 100 times to make a detailed sketch in her notebook. If the diameter of the amoeba on the slide is 1.04 mm, what is the size of the image she sees?

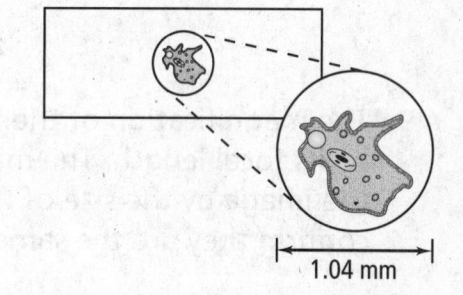

3. To change the orientation of the amoeba, LaTanya tries to rotate the slide 45°. Did she rotate the slide 45°? How can you tell?

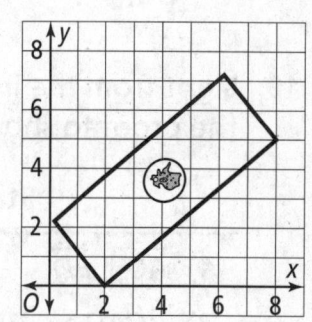

4. Estimate the slopes of the parallel line segments of the slide. Show that the edges of the slide are perpendicular.

5. Avery draws the slope triangles on the image. She says, "If LaTanya had rotated the slide 45°, then the legs of the slope triangles would be congruent." What should the slopes be according to Avery?

6. LaTanya claims that the closer the objective lens is to the slide, the bigger the image is. How is her claim supported by the diagram of the microscope lenses in Item 1?

Zachary uses a hand lens with a focal length of 5 cm to examine an insect 2 cm long. He holds the lens so the insect and his eye are both at the focal length from the insect. He sees an image 25 cm beyond the lens, the distance at which his eye focuses when using relaxed vision.

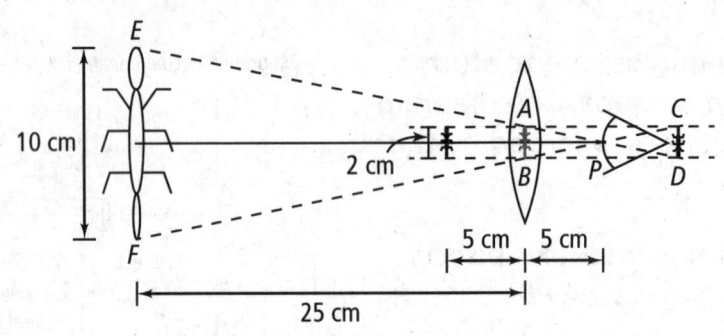

7. Explain how you know $\angle APB \cong \angle CPD$.

8. Point A and point B lie on $\overline{EP}$ and $\overline{FP}$, respectively. Is $\angle APB \cong \angle EPF$? Explain.

9. The magnification of the lens is the distance from the lens to the image divided by its focal length. The magnification can also be found by dividing the size of the image by the size of the subject. Calculate the magnification both ways and confirm they are the same value.

10. Light from the insect travels in parallel rays to the lens, so $\overleftrightarrow{AC} \parallel \overleftrightarrow{BD}$. Complete the proof to show $\angle APB \cong \angle CPD$.

Statements	Reasons
1) $\overleftrightarrow{AC} \parallel \overleftrightarrow{BD}$	1)
2) $\angle CAD \cong \angle BDA$ and $\angle ACB \cong \angle DBC$	2)
3) $m\angle CAD = m\angle BDA$ and $m\angle ACB = m\angle DBC$	3)
4) $m\angle CAD + m\angle ACB + m\angle APC = 180$ and $m\angle ACB + m\angle DBC + m\angle BPD = 180$	4)
5) $m\angle APC = m\angle BPD$	5)
6) $\angle APB \cong \angle BPD$	6)

Name _____

Benchmark Assessment 1

1. Order the steps from 1–5 for constructing a copy of ∠A.

   [ ] Place the compass point at A. Draw an arc that intersects both rays of ∠A. Label the points of intersection B and C.

   [ ] Place the compass point at C. Open the compass to the distance between B and C.

   [ ] Place the compass point at Y and draw an arc. Label the point Z where the two arcs intersect. Use a straightedge to draw $\vec{XZ}$.

   [ ] Use a straightedge to draw a ray with endpoint X.

   [ ] Place the compass point at X and draw an arc intersecting the ray. Mark the point Y at the intersection.

2. If point (p, q) is $\frac{1}{3}$ of the way from A to B, what are the values of p and q?

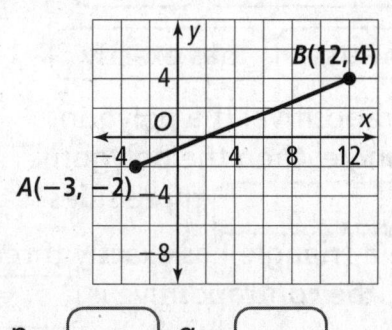

   [graph showing A(−3, −2) and B(12, 4)]

   $p = $ [ ], $q = $ [ ]

3. Point A has coordinates (−5, 3). If point (1, 6) is $\frac{3}{4}$ of the way from A to B, what are the coordinates of point B?

   ([ ] , [ ])

4. Select all the counterexamples for the conjecture, "If an angle is not acute, then it is obtuse."

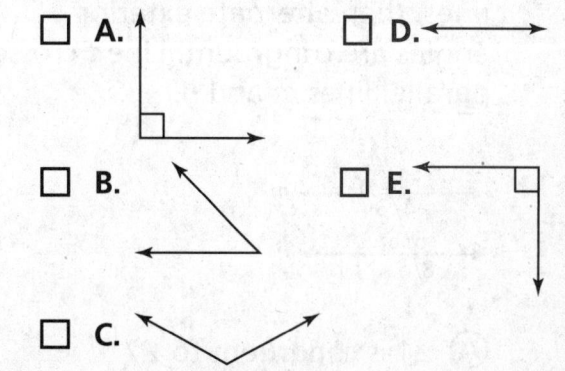

   ☐ A.   ☐ D.
   ☐ B.   ☐ E.
   ☐ C.

5. Complete the proof.

   Given: $m\angle 1 + m\angle 2 = 90$

   Prove: $m\angle 3 = 90$

   [∠1 ≅ ∠3] [$m\angle 1 + m\angle 2 = m\angle 3$]

   [the sum of ∠1 and ∠2]

   [$m\angle 3 = 90$] [∠1]

   ∠3 forms a vertical angle pair with [_____].

   So [_____] because vertical angles are congruent. Since $m\angle 1 + m\angle 2 = 90$ is given,

   [_____] by the transitive property of equality.

6. Identify two statements that contradict each other.

   I. ∠M is an obtuse angle.
   II. m∠M + m∠P = 90
   III. 180 − m∠M = 25
   IV. m∠P = 120

   Ⓐ I and II
   Ⓑ I and III
   Ⓒ I and IV
   Ⓓ III and IV

7. Which conclusion can you make from the given statements?

   If a transversal crosses parallel lines, then alternate exterior angles are congruent. Line t crosses parallel lines m and n.

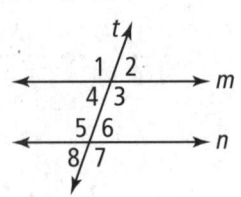

   Ⓐ ∠1 is congruent to ∠7
   Ⓑ ∠1 is congruent to ∠5
   Ⓒ ∠4 is congruent to ∠8
   Ⓓ ∠4 is congruent to ∠6

8. What is the value of x?

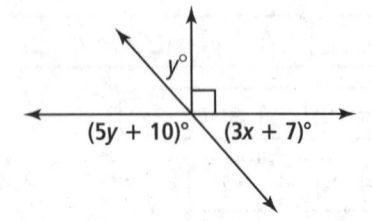

   Ⓐ 16
   Ⓑ 20
   Ⓒ 21
   Ⓓ 28

9. Complete the proof using the statements and reasons below.

   Given: ∠1 and ∠2 are vertical angles

   m∠2 + m∠3 = 90

   Prove: m∠1 + m∠3 = 90

Statements	Reasons
1) ∠1 and ∠2 are vertical angles m∠2 + m∠3 = 90	1) Given
2)	2) Vertical angles are congruent
3)	3)

   Substitution
   m∠1 = m∠3
   Vertical angles are congruent
   m∠1 = m∠2
   m∠1 + m∠3 = 90

10. Fill in the blanks to write the contrapositive of the following statement and complete its proof.

    If a polygon has more than three sides, then it is not a triangle.

    [true] [false] [is not]

    [conditional statement]

    [has more than] [is]

    [converse] [has exactly]

    Contrapositive: If a polygon [   ] a triangle, then the polygon [   ] three sides.

    Since a triangle has exactly three sides, the contrapositive is [   ].

    Since the contrapositive is [   ], the [   ] must be true.

11. When a transversal crosses a pair of parallel lines, which types of angle pairs are supplementary?

    Ⓐ alternate interior
    Ⓑ same-side interior
    Ⓒ alternate exterior
    Ⓓ vertical

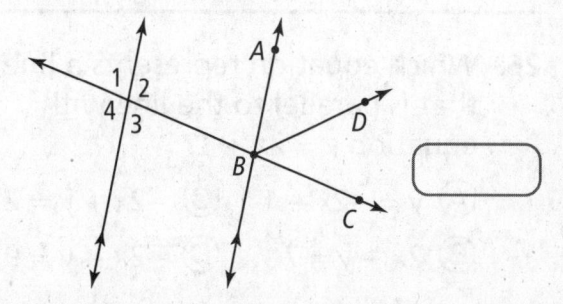

For Items 12–14, use the figure shown.

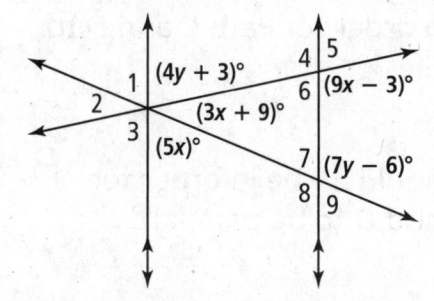

12. Select all the pairs of congruent corresponding angles.

    ☐ A. ∠1 and ∠4
    ☐ B. ∠2 and ∠4
    ☐ C. ∠4 and ∠7
    ☐ D. ∠3 and ∠6
    ☐ E. ∠1 and ∠7

13. What is $m\angle 2$?

    Ⓐ 12   Ⓑ 18   Ⓒ 45   Ⓓ 120

14. What is $m\angle 8$?

    Ⓐ 12   Ⓑ 18   Ⓒ 45   Ⓓ 120

15. If $DM = 60$, what is the value of r?

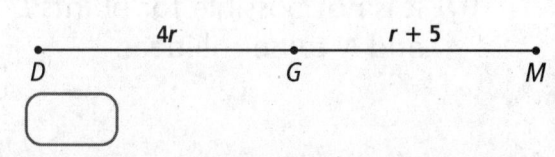

16. If $m\angle NOP = 37$ and $m\angle NOQ = 123$, what is $m\angle POQ$?

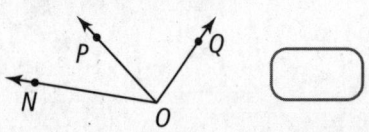

17. Given $a \perp c$ and $b \perp c$, what can you say about a and b? Explain.

    Ⓐ $a \perp b$; if two lines are perpendicular to the same line, then they are perpendicular to each other.
    Ⓑ a and b form a straight line; if two lines are perpendicular to the same line, then they form a straight line.
    Ⓒ a and b are intersecting lines; if two lines are perpendicular to the same line, then they are intersecting lines.
    Ⓓ $a \parallel b$; if two lines are perpendicular to the same line, then they are parallel to each other.

For Items 18 and 19, use the diagram shown.

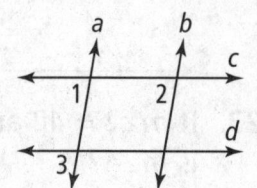

18. If $\angle 1 \cong \angle 3$, which conclusion can be made?

    Ⓐ $a \parallel b$ Ⓒ $c \perp a$
    Ⓑ $c \parallel d$ Ⓓ $b \perp d$

19. If $\angle 1 \cong \angle 2$, which conclusion can be made?

    Ⓐ $a \parallel b$ Ⓒ $c \perp a$
    Ⓑ $c \parallel d$ Ⓓ $b \perp d$

20. If $\vec{BD}$ bisects $\angle ABC$ and $m\angle 3 = 80$, what is $m\angle ABD$?

For Items 21 and 22, use the figure.

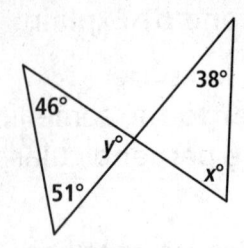

21. What is the value of y?

Ⓐ 83 Ⓒ 96
Ⓑ 89 Ⓓ 97

22. What is the value of x?

Ⓐ 38 Ⓒ 83
Ⓑ 59 Ⓓ 96

For Items 23 and 24, use the figure.

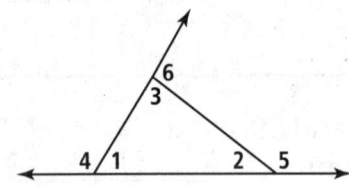

23. If $m\angle 2 = 42$ and $m\angle 6 = 126$, what is $m\angle 4$?

Ⓐ 12 Ⓑ 54 Ⓒ 96 Ⓓ 138

24. If $m\angle 4 = 96$ and $m\angle 5 = 138$, what is $m\angle 3$?

Ⓐ 42 Ⓑ 54 Ⓒ 84 Ⓓ 96

---

25. What is an equation of the line that is perpendicular to the line $y = -\frac{2}{3}x - 1$ and passes through the point $(-4, 2)$?

$y = \dfrac{\square}{\square}x + \square$

---

26. Which equation represents a line that is parallel to the line with equation $y = 2x + 1$?

Ⓐ $y = -2x + 1$ Ⓒ $-2x + y = 2$
Ⓑ $2x + y = 7$ Ⓓ $-2x - y = 9$

For items 27 and 28, use the figure.

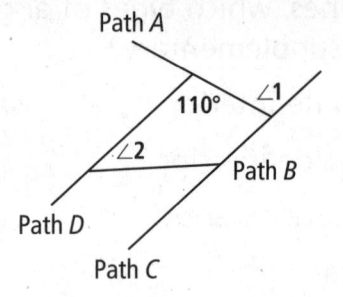

27. A city park has multiple paths around a green space. What should $\angle 2$ be in order for Path C and D to be parallel?

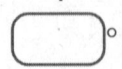

☐°

28. What should $\angle 1$ be in order for Path C and D to be parallel?

☐°

---

29. If $m \parallel n$ and the slope of line m is 3, what is the slope of line n?

Ⓐ $\frac{1}{3}$ Ⓒ -3
Ⓑ $-\frac{1}{3}$ Ⓓ 3

---

30. If $LM = 7$ and $LN = 12$, which of the following statements must be true?

Ⓐ If points L, M, and N are collinear, then $MN = 5$.

Ⓑ If $MN = 19$, then points L, M, and N cannot be collinear.

Ⓒ If points L, M, and N are collinear, then MN must be either 5 or 19.

Ⓓ It is not possible for points L, M, and N to be collinear.

3 Readiness Assessment

For Items 1–4, use the figure shown. Lines ℓ and m are intersected by transversal t and $\ell \parallel m$.

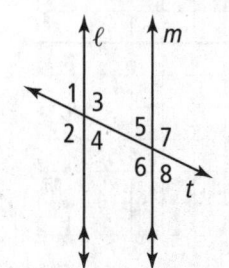

1. Select all the angles that are supplementary to ∠7.
   - A. ∠5
   - B. ∠2
   - C. ∠6
   - D. ∠8
   - E. ∠1
   - F. ∠3

2. Select all the angles that are congruent to ∠6.
   - A. ∠1
   - B. ∠3
   - C. ∠2
   - D. ∠4
   - E. ∠5
   - F. ∠8

3. Why is ∠4 ≅ ∠8?
   - Ⓐ ∠4 and ∠8 are alternate exterior angles.
   - Ⓑ ∠4 and ∠8 are alternate interior angles.
   - Ⓒ ∠4 and ∠8 are corresponding angles.
   - Ⓓ ∠4 and ∠8 are same-side interior angles.

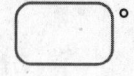

4. If $m\angle 3 = 126°$, what is $m\angle 5$?
   ___°

5. Given triangle XYZ, what is a?

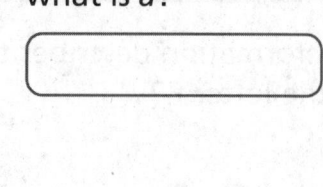

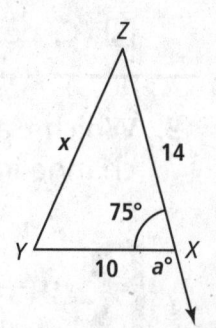

For Items 6–7, use the triangles shown.

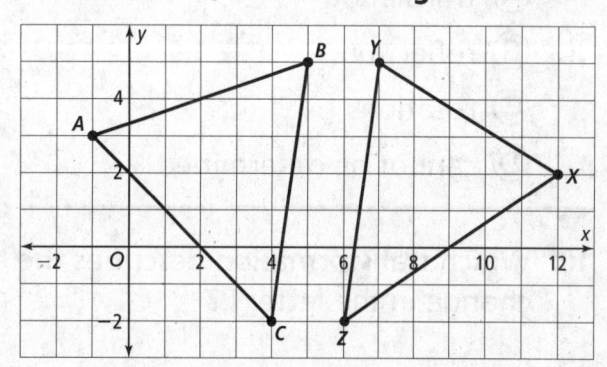

6. What is the exact value of BC?
   - Ⓐ 3.16
   - Ⓑ $5\sqrt{2}$
   - Ⓒ 7.07
   - Ⓓ 25

7. Is $\overline{AC}$ perpendicular to $\overline{XZ}$? Explain.
   - Ⓐ Yes; the slope of $\overline{AC}$ is 1, and the slope of $\overline{XZ}$ is −1.
   - Ⓑ Yes; the slope of $\overline{AC}$ is −1, and the slope of $\overline{XZ}$ is 1.
   - Ⓒ No; the slope of $\overline{AC}$ is 1, and the slope of $\overline{XZ}$ is not −1, it is $\frac{2}{3}$.
   - Ⓓ No; the slope of $\overline{AC}$ is −1, and the slope of $\overline{XZ}$ is not 1, it is $\frac{2}{3}$.

8. Select all types of lines that intersect and are coplanar.
   - ☐ A. parallel
   - ☐ B. transversal
   - ☐ C. perpendicular
   - ☐ D. segments
   - ☐ E. rays

9. Which transformation describes the change in the letter R?

   R → ᴚ

   - Ⓐ translation
   - Ⓑ reflection
   - Ⓒ rotation
   - Ⓓ cannot be determined

10. Which transformation describes the change in the letter L?

    L → ⌐

    - Ⓐ translation
    - Ⓑ reflection
    - Ⓒ rotation
    - Ⓓ cannot be determined

11. Which transformation describes the change in the letter F?

    F → F

    - Ⓐ translation
    - Ⓑ reflection
    - Ⓒ rotation
    - Ⓓ cannot be determined

For Items 12–14, use the coordinates plotted below.

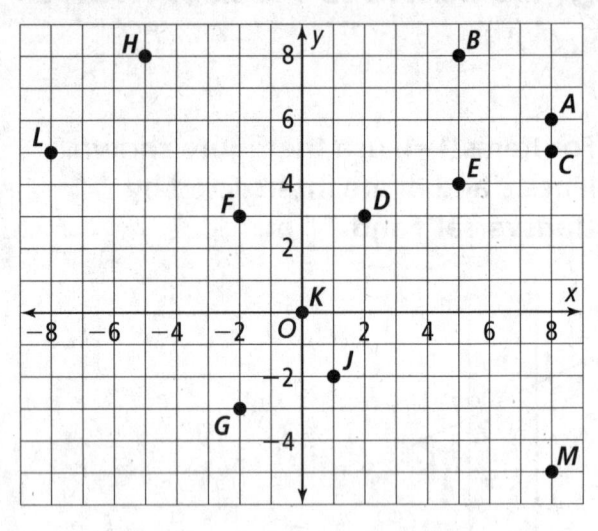

12. Which point is a reflection of C across the x-axis? ⬚

13. Which point is a 90° counterclockwise rotation of B around K? ⬚

14. Select all the true statements.
    - ☐ A. Point G is a translation of point F 6 units up.
    - ☐ B. Point F is a reflection of point D across the y-axis.
    - ☐ C. Point G is a rotation of point D 180° clockwise around K.
    - ☐ D. Point G is a rotation of point D 180° counterclockwise around K.
    - ☐ E. cannot be determined

enVision® Geometry · Assessment Sourcebook

Name _____

3-1 Lesson Quiz

Reflections

enVision Geometry
SavvasRealize.com

1. Triangle ABC has vertices A(−2, 5), B(1, 0), and C(6, −2). What are the coordinates of the vertices of △A'B'C' for $r_{y\text{-axis}}$?

   Ⓐ A'(5, −2), B'(0, 1) C'(−2, 6)
   Ⓑ A'(2, −5), B'(−1, 0), C'(−6, 2)
   Ⓒ A'(2, 5), B'(−1, 0), C'(−6, −2)
   Ⓓ A'(−2, −5), B'(1, 0), C'(6, 2)

2. What is the rule used to transform △ABC to its image?

   A(−3, 5), B(2, 8), C(−4, −5) and A'(−3, −5), B'(2, −8), C'(−4, 5)

   Ⓐ $r_m(x, y) = (−y, −x)$, where the equation of line m is y = −x
   Ⓑ $r_n(x, y) = (y, x)$, where the equation of line n is y = −x
   Ⓒ $r_{y\text{-axis}}(x, y) = (−x, y)$
   Ⓓ $r_{x\text{-axis}}(x, y) = (x, −y)$

For Items 3–5, use △ABC.

3. Suppose the equation of line s is y = 2. What are the coordinates of C' of △A'B'C' for r_s?

   (⬭ , ⬭)

4. Suppose the equation of line t is y = x. Which shows the graph of △A'B'C' for r_t?

   Ⓐ Ⓒ
   Ⓑ Ⓓ

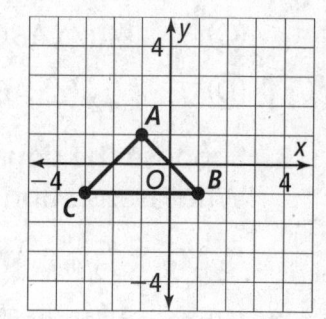

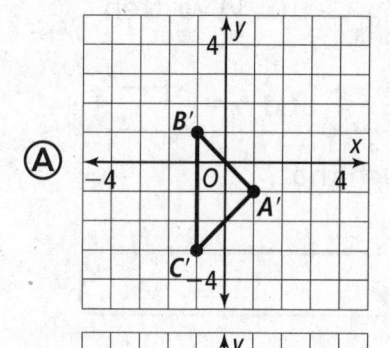

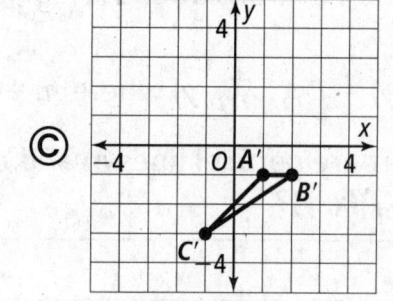

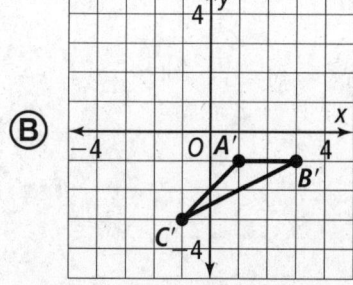

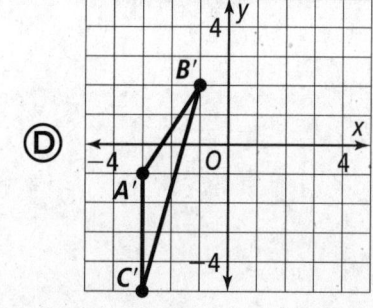

5. After a reflection of the figure, the image's vertices are A'(5, 1), B'(3, −1), and C'(7, −1). What is the line of reflection?

   Ⓐ y = 2   Ⓑ x = 2   Ⓒ y = −x   Ⓓ y = 2x

enVision® Geometry • Assessment Sourcebook

3-2 Lesson Quiz

Translations

For Items 1 and 2, use △ABC.

1. What are the vertices of △A'B'C' produced by $T_{\langle -3, 6 \rangle}(\triangle ABC) = \triangle A'B'C'$?

   Ⓐ A'(0, 6), B'(0, 4), C'(−3, 3)
   Ⓑ A'(6, 6), B'(6, 4), C'(3, 3)
   Ⓒ A'(0, −6), B'(0, −8), C'(−3, 9)
   Ⓓ A'(6, −6), B'(6, −8), C'(3, 9)

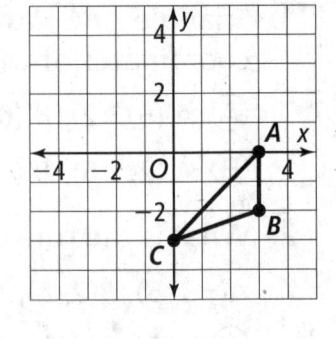

2. Suppose △DEF is the image of a translation of △ABC. If D is at (−6, −2), what translation rule maps △ABC to △DEF?

   Ⓐ $T_{\langle 9, 2 \rangle}(\triangle ABC) = \triangle DEF$
   Ⓑ $T_{\langle 9, -2 \rangle}(\triangle ABC) = \triangle DEF$
   Ⓒ $T_{\langle -9, 2 \rangle}(\triangle ABC) = \triangle DEF$
   Ⓓ $T_{\langle -9, -2 \rangle}(\triangle ABC) = \triangle DEF$

3. Suppose the equation of line p is x = 2 and the equation of line q is x = −1. What translation is equivalent to $r_p \circ r_q$?

   $r_p \circ r_q = T_{\langle m, n \rangle}$ where m = ☐ and n = ☐.

4. What is the composition of translations $(T_{\langle -3, 4 \rangle} \circ T_{\langle 8, -7 \rangle})(x, y)$ written as one translation?

   $(T_{\langle -3, 4 \rangle} \circ T_{\langle 8, -7 \rangle})(x, y) = T_{\langle m, n \rangle}(x, y)$ where m = ☐ and n = ☐.

5. How many units apart are parallel lines m and n such that $T_{\langle 0, -12 \rangle}(x, y) = (r_n \circ r_m)(x, y)$?

Name _____

3-3 Lesson Quiz
Rotations

For Items 1–2, use △BCD in the figure shown.

1. What are the vertices of the image $R_{(90°, O)}(\triangle BCD)$?

    Ⓐ B′(−3, −3), C′(−1, 4), D′(2, 0)

    Ⓑ B′(3, 3), C′(1, −4), D′(−2, 0)

    Ⓒ B′(3, −3), C′(1, 4), D′(0, 2)

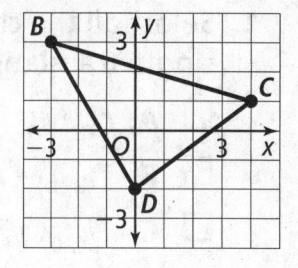

    Ⓓ B′(−3, −3), C′(−1, −4), D′(0, −2)

2. Select all the sequences of reflections that produce an image equivalent to the image $R_{(180°, O)}(\triangle BCD)$.

    ☐ A. $(r_{x\text{-axis}} \circ r_{y\text{-axis}})(\triangle BCD)$

    ☐ B. $(r_{y\text{-axis}} \circ r_{x\text{-axis}})(\triangle BCD)$

    ☐ C. $(r_{x\text{-axis}} \circ r_{x\text{-axis}})(\triangle BCD)$

    ☐ D. $(r_{y\text{-axis}} \circ r_{y\text{-axis}})(\triangle BCD)$

    ☐ E. $(r_{y=x} \circ r_{x\text{-axis}})(\triangle BCD)$

3. $\overline{AB}$ is rotated 120° clockwise about B. Then $\overline{AB}$ is rotated 45° counterclockwise about A. What is the image of A as a composition of transformations?

    Ⓐ $(R_{(120°, B)} \circ R_{(-45°, A)})(A)$

    Ⓑ $(R_{(-45°, A)} \circ R_{(120°, B)})(A)$

    Ⓒ $(R_{(-120°, B)} \circ R_{(45°, A)})(A)$

    Ⓓ $(R_{(45°, A)} \circ R_{(-120°, B)})(A)$

4. Suppose $R_{(140°, P)}(A) = B$ and $(r_{\overleftrightarrow{PD}} \circ r_{\overleftrightarrow{PC}})(A) = B$. What is $m\angle CPD$?

    ☐

5. How many times does the rotation $R_{(120°, P)}$ need to be applied to a figure to map the figure onto itself?

    ☐

Name _____

3-4 Lesson Quiz

Classification of Rigid Motion

1. Select all the compositions of rigid transformations that can be described as a single translation, rotation, or reflection.

   ☐ A. $r_m \circ r_n$

   ☐ B. $T_{\langle a, b \rangle} \circ r_m$

   ☐ C. $T_{\langle c, d \rangle} \circ T_{\langle a, b \rangle}$

   ☐ D. $r_m \circ T_{\langle a, b \rangle}$

   ☐ E. $r_m \circ r_n \circ r_p$

For Items 2–3, use triangles ABC and A'B'C'.

2. Which composition of two rigid transformations maps $\triangle ABC$ to $\triangle A'B'C'$?

   Ⓐ $r_{x\text{-axis}} \circ r_{y\text{-axis}}$

   Ⓑ $r_{y\text{-axis}} \circ r_{x\text{-axis}}$

   Ⓒ $T_{\langle -7, 0 \rangle} \circ r_{x\text{-axis}}$

   Ⓓ $T_{\langle -7, 0 \rangle} \circ r_{y\text{-axis}}$

3. Suppose m is the line with equation $y = -4$ and $\triangle A'B'C'$ is mapped to $\triangle A''B''C''$ by applying the glide reflection $T_{\langle 3, 0 \rangle} \circ r_m$. What are the coordinates of $\triangle A''B''C''$?

   Ⓐ $A''(-1, -3), B''(-3, -6), C''(1, -7)$

   Ⓑ $A''(-7, -3), B''(-8, -6), C''(-5, -7)$

   Ⓒ $A''(-2, -5), B''(0, -2), C''(-3, -1)$

   Ⓓ $A''(-8, -3), B''(-6, 4), C''(-9, 0)$

For Items 4–5, use triangles DEF and D'E'F'.

4. Complete the sentence.

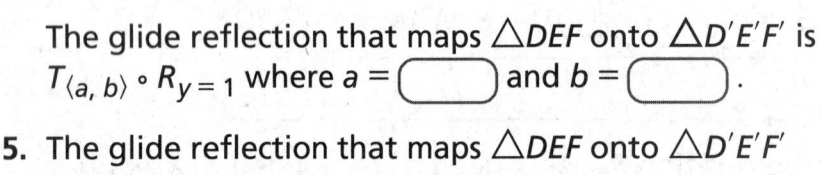

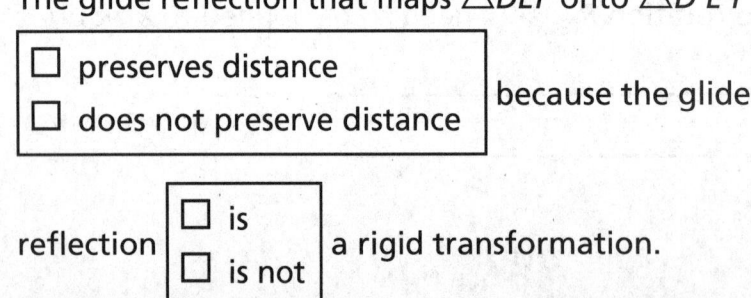

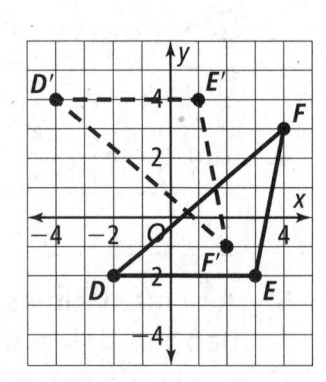

   The glide reflection that maps $\triangle DEF$ onto $\triangle D'E'F'$ is $T_{\langle a, b \rangle} \circ R_{y=1}$ where $a = \boxed{}$ and $b = \boxed{}$.

5. The glide reflection that maps $\triangle DEF$ onto $\triangle D'E'F'$

   ☐ preserves distance
   ☐ does not preserve distance

   because the glide

   reflection ☐ is
              ☐ is not a rigid transformation.

3-5 Lesson Quiz

Symmetry

For Items 1–3, use the regular pentagon shown.

1. How many lines of symmetry does the pentagon have?
   - Ⓐ 0
   - Ⓑ 1
   - Ⓒ 3
   - Ⓓ 5

2. What is the least angle of rotation in degrees that maps the pentagon onto itself?

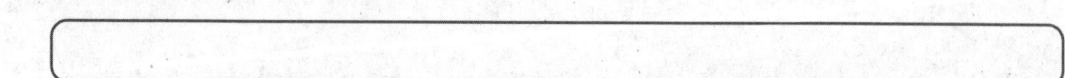

3. Does the pentagon have the following types of symmetry?

	Yes	No
Reflectional	❏	❏
Point	❏	❏

For Items 4–5, use the figure shown.

4. What reflection(s) map the figure onto itself?
   - Ⓐ r_m only
   - Ⓑ r_n only
   - Ⓒ r_m and r_n
   - Ⓓ none

5. Which rotation maps the figure onto itself?
   - Ⓐ $R_{(45°,P)}$
   - Ⓑ $R_{(90°,P)}$
   - Ⓒ $R_{(180°,P)}$
   - Ⓓ $R_{(270°,P)}$

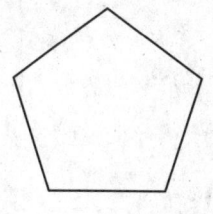

3 Topic Assessment Form A

1. Suppose △RST is translated and then reflected to form △R'S'T'. Select all of the statements that are true.

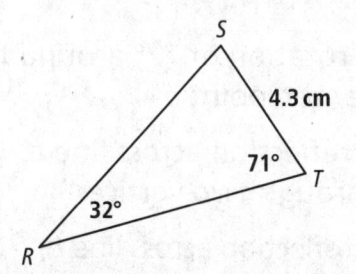

   ☐ A. length $\overline{R'S'}$ = 4.3 cm
   ☐ B. ∠R ≅ ∠R'
   ☐ C. m∠T' = 71
   ☐ D. $\overline{ST}$ ≅ $\overline{T'S'}$
   ☐ E. length $\overline{RT}$ > length $\overline{R'T'}$

2. Point T is at (−2, 5). What are the coordinates of point T' after a reflection across x = 0 and then y = 0? (☐ , ☐)

3. $\overline{PQ}$ is reflected across the line x = −1. Select all that apply.

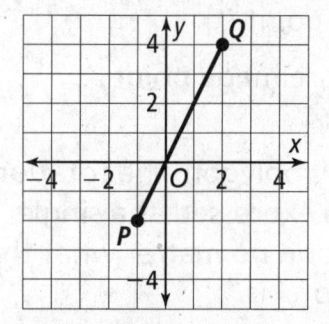

   ☐ A. $\overline{PQ}$ ≅ $\overline{P'Q'}$
   ☐ B. Q' is plotted at (−4, 4).
   ☐ C. Q' is plotted at (−4, −4).
   ☐ D. Q and Q' are in the same quadrant.
   ☐ E. P' and P are in the same quadrant.

4. Which transformation or sequence of transformations maps △ABC to △A'B'C'?

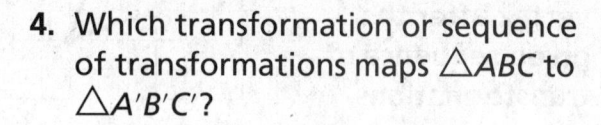

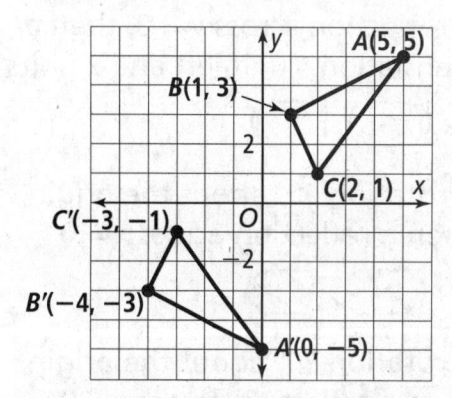

   Ⓐ a translation 5 units left
   Ⓑ a reflection across x = 0, then a translation 5 units left
   Ⓒ a reflection across y = 0, then a translation 5 units left
   Ⓓ a rotation 90° about the origin

5. Point P'(5, −4) is the image of point P(2, 3) under a translation. Select the image of (6, −2) under the same translation.

   Ⓐ (7, −1)   Ⓒ (9, −9)
   Ⓑ (13, −3)   Ⓓ (3, 5)

6. Given point A is not on line m, suppose A is reflected across line m. Which of the following is true?

   Ⓐ $\overline{AA'}$ is the bisector of line m.
   Ⓑ Line m is the perpendicular bisector of $\overline{AA'}$.
   Ⓒ Line m is parallel to $\overline{AA'}$.
   Ⓓ A = A'

For Items 7–10, use the figure shown. Find the coordinates of the specified vertex after the given sequence of transformations.

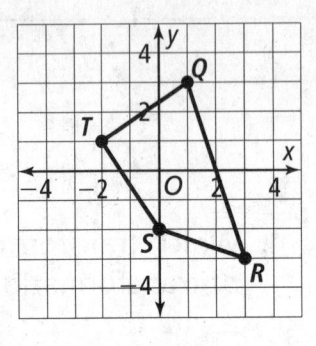

7. a reflection across y = 0, then a translation 1 unit left and 2 units up

    S': (☐, ☐)

8. a rotation 90° about the origin, then a reflection across x = 0

    R': (☐, ☐)

9. a rotation 90° about the origin, then a reflection across x = 0

    T': (☐, ☐)

10. a translation 2 units right, then a reflection across x = 0

    Q': (☐, ☐)

11. What type of symmetry does a rectangle have?

    Ⓐ Reflectional but not rotational symmetry.
    Ⓑ Rotational but not reflectional symmetry.
    Ⓒ Both reflectional and rotational symmetry.
    Ⓓ A rectangle is not symmetric.

12. If a figure is translated 3 units left and 3 units up which translation moves the image back to the original position?

    Ⓐ 3 units right and 3 units down
    Ⓑ 3 units left and 3 units up
    Ⓒ 3 units up
    Ⓓ 3 units left

13. Given the regular polygon, select all of the rotations and reflections that carry the figure onto itself.

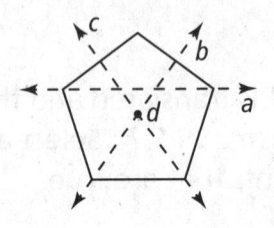

    ☐ A. a rotation of 72° around the center, point d
    ☐ B. a reflection across line a, through two vertices
    ☐ C. a reflection across line b, through one vertex, the center d
    ☐ D. a rotation of 60° around the center, point d
    ☐ E. a reflection across line c, and the midpoint of the opposite side

14. For a rotation x° about point P, which of the following is not true?

    Ⓐ For a preimage point A, $m\angle APA' = x$.
    Ⓑ The transformation rotates every point in the preimage x° about point P.
    Ⓒ For a preimage point A, $PA = PA'$.
    Ⓓ For any polygon, the rotation can be expressed as a single reflection no matter what the value of x is.

15. Point P'(−6, −4) is the image of point P(−2, 3) under a translation. What is the image of (5, −1) under the same translation?

    Ⓐ (9, 6)   Ⓒ (−1, −5)
    Ⓑ (1, −8)   Ⓓ (3, 2)

enVision® Geometry   Assessment Sourcebook

Name _____

3 Topic Assessment Form B

1. Suppose △NOP is rotated and then translated to form △N'O'P'. Select all of the statements that are true.

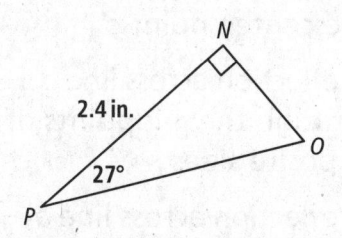

   [triangle NOP with right angle at N, 2.4 in from P to N, angle 27° at P]

   ☐ A. ∠N' is an acute angle.
   ☐ B. m∠O' = 27
   ☐ C. $\overline{NO}$ = 2.4 in
   ☐ D. ∠N ≅ ∠N'
   ☐ E. $\overline{PO}$ ≅ $\overline{O'P'}$

2. Point T is at (−6, 4). What are the coordinates of point T' after a reflection across x = 0 and then y = 0? (☐ , ☐)

3. $\overline{PQ}$ is reflected across the line y = 2. Select all that apply.

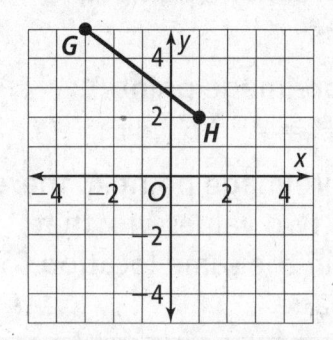

   [coordinate plane showing G at (-3, 5) and H at (1, 2)]

   ☐ A. G' is plotted at (3, 1).
   ☐ B. G' is plotted at (−3, −1).
   ☐ C. H and H' are in the same quadrant.
   ☐ D. $\overline{GH}$ ≅ $\overline{G'H'}$
   ☐ E. G and G' are in the same quadrant.

4. Which transformation or sequence of transformations maps △ABC to △A'B'C'?

   [coordinate plane showing A(5,5), B(1,3), C(2,1), and A'(0,-5), B'(-4,-3), C'(-3,-1)]

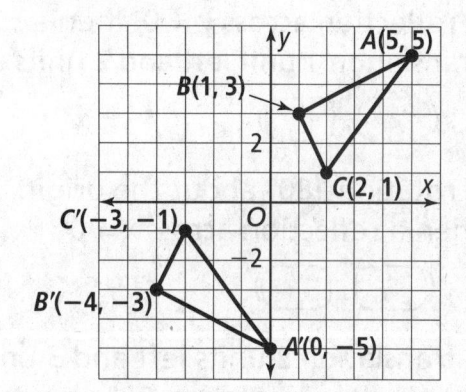

   Ⓐ a translation 5 units left, then a reflection across y = 0
   Ⓑ a translation 5 units left, then a rotation 90° about the origin
   Ⓒ a reflection across y = 0
   Ⓓ a rotation 90° about the origin

5. Point P'(−3, 2) is the image of point P(3, 8) under a translation. Select the image of (0, −6) under the same translation.

   Ⓐ (−3, −4)   Ⓒ (0, 10)
   Ⓑ (0, 6)   Ⓓ (−6, −12)

6. Given point A is on line m, suppose A is reflected across line m. Which of the following is true?

   Ⓐ $\overline{AA'}$ is the bisector of line m.
   Ⓑ Line m is the perpendicular bisector of $\overline{AA'}$.
   Ⓒ Line m is parallel to $\overline{AA'}$.
   Ⓓ A = A'

For Items 7–10, use the figure shown. Find the coordinates of the vertices of each image.

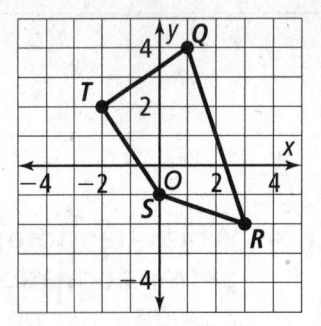

7. a reflection across y = 0, then a translation 1 unit left and 2 units up

   S': (,)

8. a rotation 180° about the origin, then a reflection across x = 0

   R': (,)

9. a translation 2 units left and 3 units down, then a rotation 90° about the origin

   T': (,)

10. a translation 3 units right, then a reflection across x = 0

    Q': (,)

11. What type of symmetry does a square have?

    Ⓐ Reflectional by not rotational symmetry.

    Ⓑ Rotational but not reflectional symmetry.

    Ⓒ Both reflectional and rotational symmetry.

    Ⓓ A rectangle is not symmetric.

12. If a figure is translated 5 units left and 3 units up, which translation moves the image back to the original position?

    Ⓐ 5 units right and 3 units down

    Ⓑ 5 units left and 3 units up

    Ⓒ 5 units up

    Ⓓ 5 units left

13. Given the regular polygon shown, select all of the rotations and reflections that carry the figure onto itself.

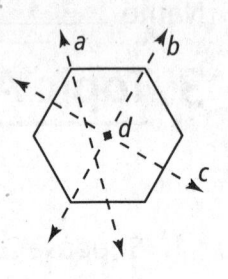

    ☐ A. a rotation of 120° around the center, point d

    ☐ B. a reflection across line c, through the midpoints of opposite sides

    ☐ C. a reflection across line a, through a vertex and a midpoint of an opposite side

    ☐ D. a reflection across line b, through one vertex, the center d

    ☐ E. a rotation of 60° around the center, point d

14. For a rotation $R_{(x°, P)}$, which of the following is not true?

    Ⓐ The transformation rotates every point in the preimage x° about a point P.

    Ⓑ For a preimage point A, PA = PA'.

    Ⓒ For a preimage point P, m∠PAP' = x.

    Ⓓ For a preimage point A, there are no two values of x that result in the same location for the image.

15. Point P'(−3, −2) is the image of point P(−1, 5) under a translation. What is the image of (2, −5) under the same translation?

    Ⓐ (9, −3)   Ⓒ (−2, −12)

    Ⓑ (0, −12) Ⓓ (−2, 2)

Name _____

3 Performance Assessment Form A

Rick is designing a series of icons for a new app. He has hired you to check some icons and to create some new ones. The icons will incorporate reflection, translation, and rotation.

Use what you know about transformations to answer Items 1 and 2.

1. Classify each transformation of △ABC as a translation, rotation, or reflection. If a reflection, identify the line of reflection. If a rotation, describe the point and degree of rotation.

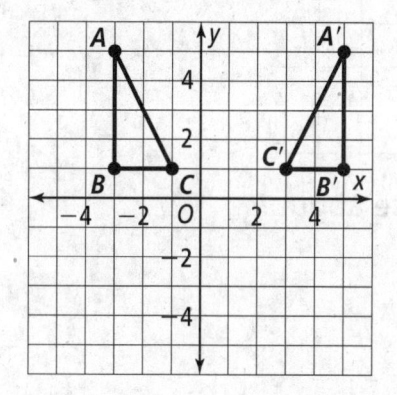

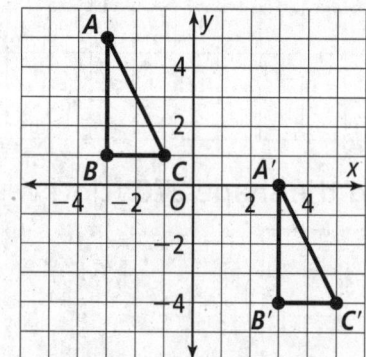

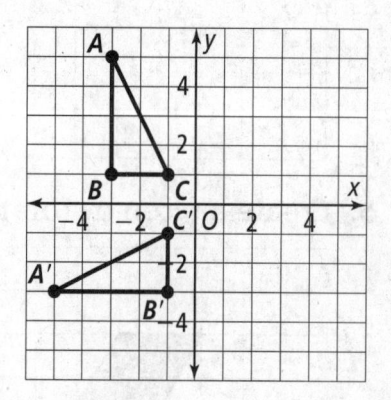

2. The keypad will have the following symbols. Which symbols have symmetry? Classify each symbol by listing the letter above it next to appropriate type of symmetry.

A B C D E F G H I J K L

Reflectional ☐

Translational ☐

Rotational ☐

3. The app will display a line segment on the keypad from 1 to 7, as shown. Describe a rigid transformation or series of rigid transformations that will allow the segment to be moved to run between 2 and 9. If that is not possible, describe why not.

4. Create an icon by translating the shape 5 units down and 3 units to the right. Each line in the grid represents one unit.

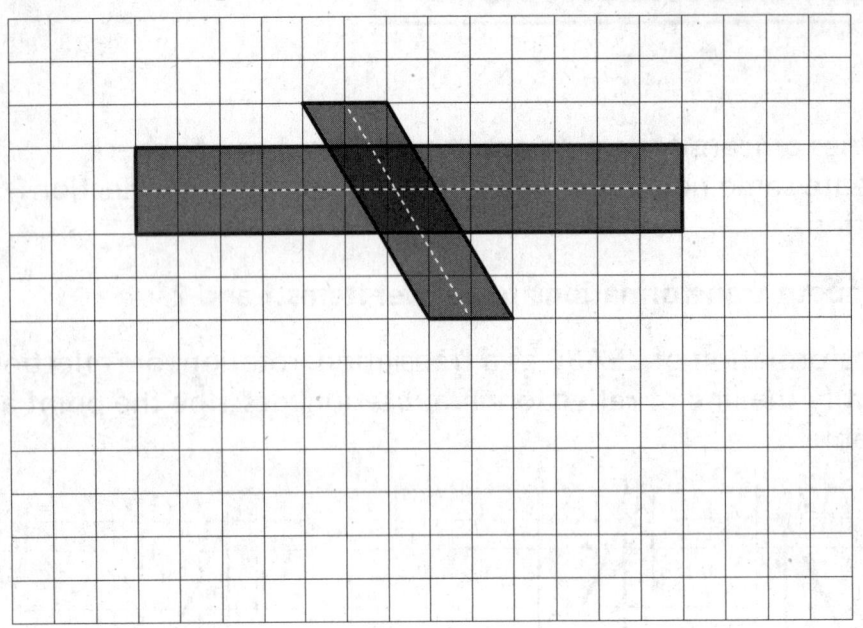

5. Create an icon by rotating the shape 270° clockwise about P.

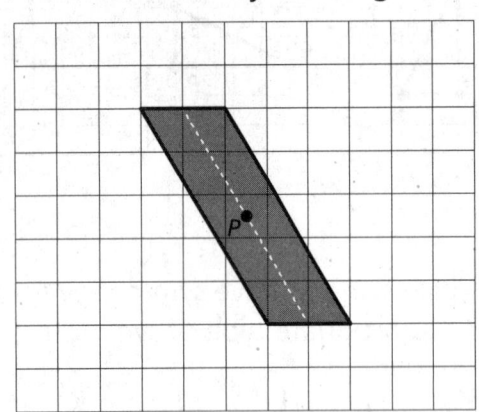

6. Rick draws the letter R in Quadrant I of this graph. What sequence of transformations can he use to map that R onto the other R shown on the graph? Each line in the grid represents one unit.

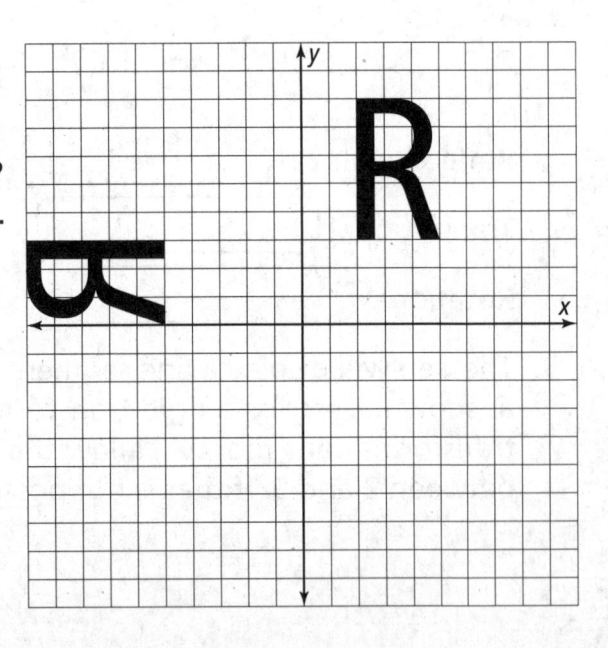

Name _____

3 Performance Assessment Form B

Jamie is studying Washington, D.C., and wants to make a presentation about the city using transformed images.

Use what you know about transformations to answer Items 1 and 2.

1. Classify each transformation of the symbol as a translation, rotation, or reflection. If a reflection, identify the line of reflection. If a rotation, describe the point and degree of rotation. Each line on the grid represents one unit.

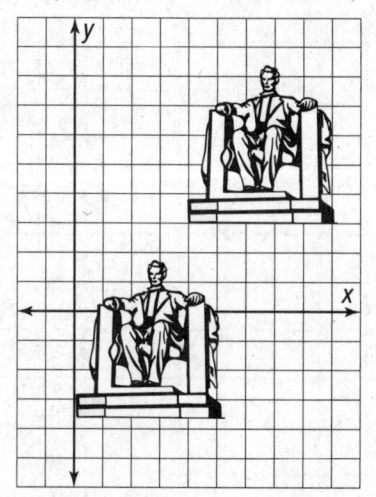

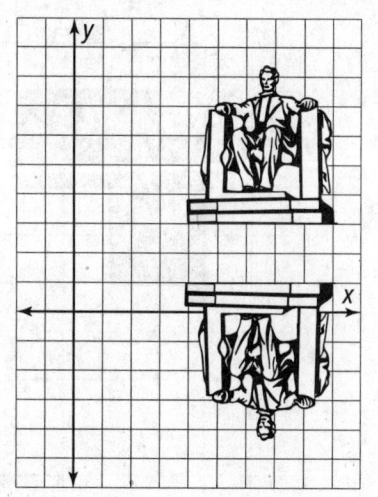

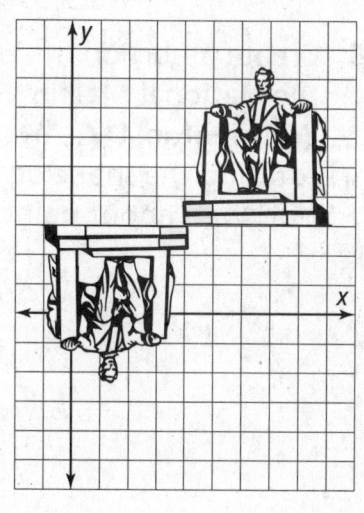

2. Two streets in Washington are shown on the map. Describe a rigid transformation or series of rigid transformations that will allow one street to be mapped onto the other. If that is not possible, describe why not. Each line on the grid represents one unit.

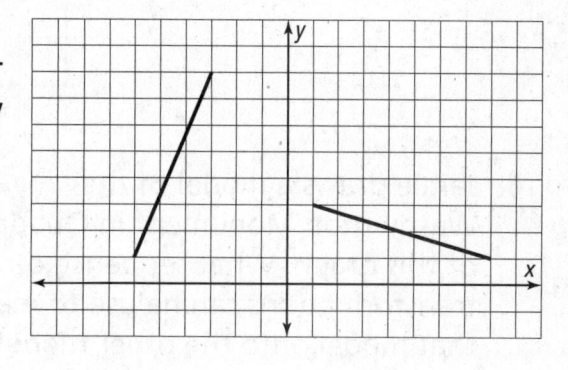

Dyani is studying city planning. She recognizes that transformations are a big part of laying out a city. She asks you to do some of the drawings.

Use your mathematical expertise to answer Items 3–6.

3. Create a portion of the National Mall in Washington, D.C., by reflecting the shape in line ℓ.

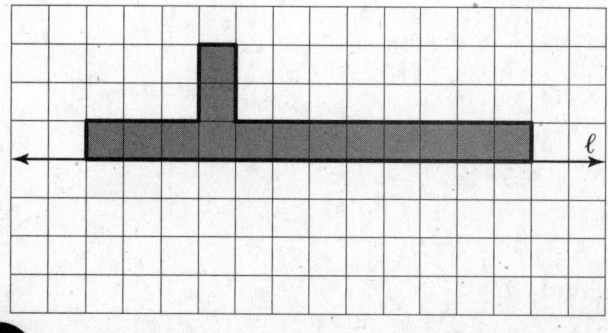

4. Create a portion of the National Mall in Washington, D.C., by translating the shape 5 units to the right. Each line on the grid represents one unit.

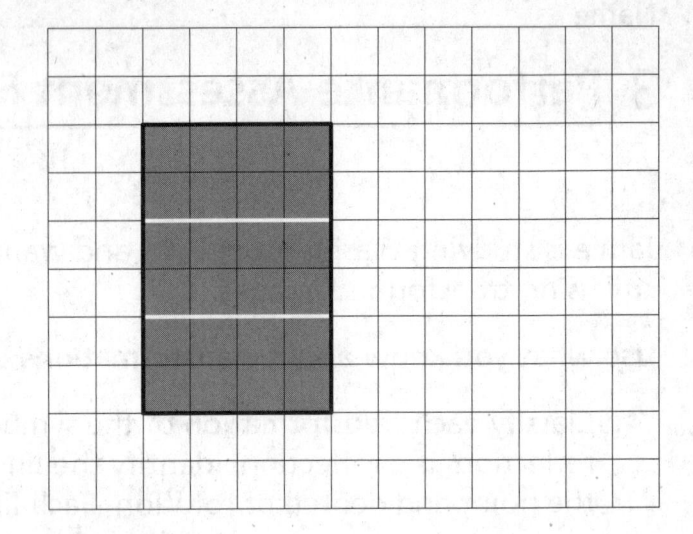

5. Create a portion of the National Mall in Washington, D.C., by rotating the shape 90° clockwise about point P.

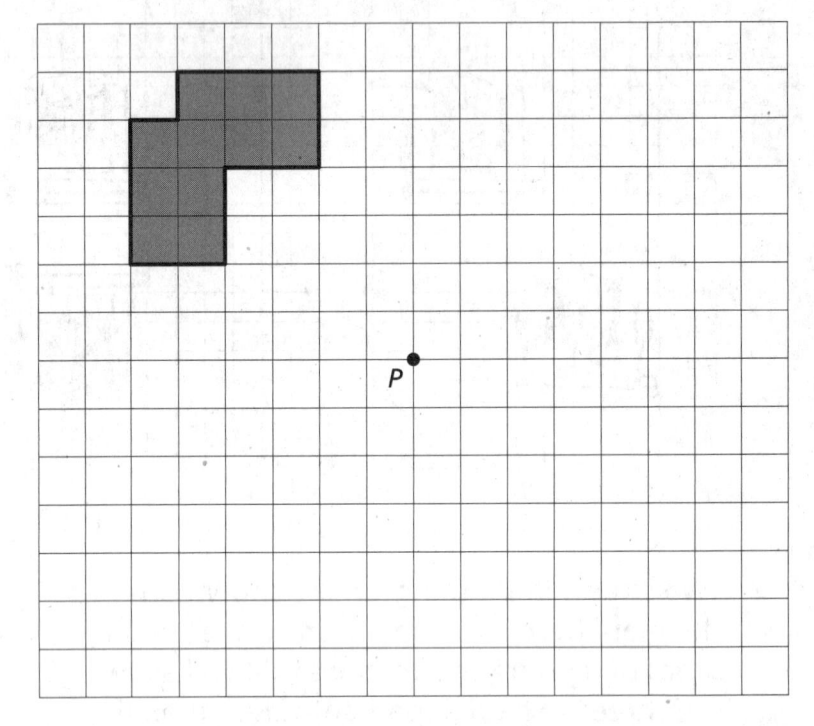

6. Jamie draws a model of the Washington Monument in Quadrant I of this graph. What sequence of transformations can he use to map that model onto the other model shown on the graph? Each line on the grid represents one unit.

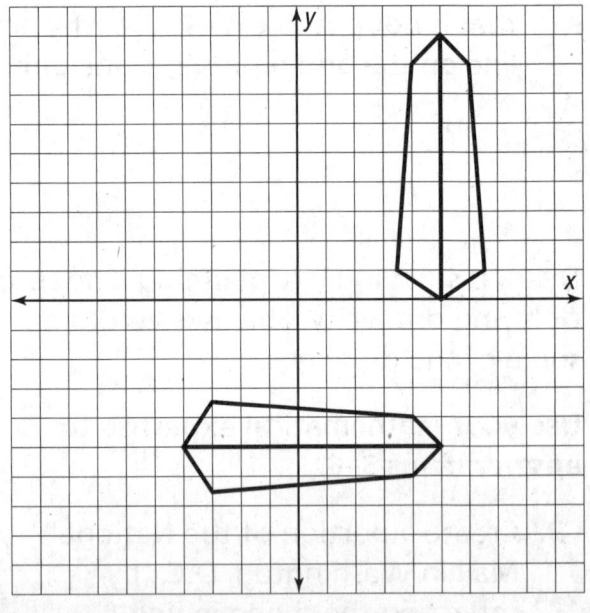

4 Readiness Assessment

Items 1–3. In the figure shown, the measures of all angles are equal, and AB = EF.

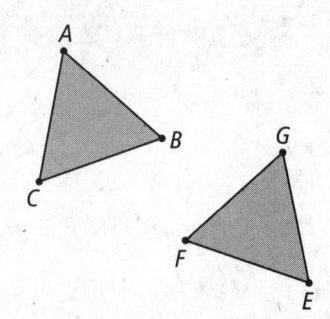

1. What sequence of transformations appears to map △ABC onto △EFG?
   - Ⓐ reflection and rotation
   - Ⓑ two translations
   - Ⓒ rotation and translation
   - Ⓓ none of the above

2. What are the measures of the angles in △ABC?
   - Ⓐ 60; 60; 60
   - Ⓑ 90; 60; 30
   - Ⓒ 90; 45; 45
   - Ⓓ 70; 60; 50

3. Is △EFG the same size and shape as △ABC? Explain.
   - Ⓐ No; △ABC and △EFG have different orientations, so they are not the same shape.
   - Ⓑ Yes; △ABC can be mapped to △EFG by a series of translations. Translations preserve size and shape.
   - Ⓒ No; △ABC and △EFG have different orientations, so they are not the same size.
   - Ⓓ Yes; △ABC can be mapped to △EFG by a rotation and a translation. Rotations and translations both preserve size and shape.

Items 4 and 5. Use the figure shown.

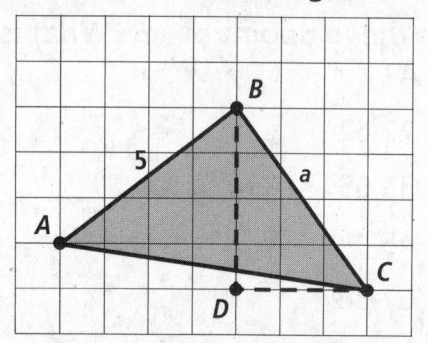

4. What is the measure of side a?
   ☐

5. What is the exact length of $\overline{AC}$?
   ☐ $\sqrt{\boxed{}}$

6. Does △ABC appear to be the same size and shape as △XYZ? Explain. 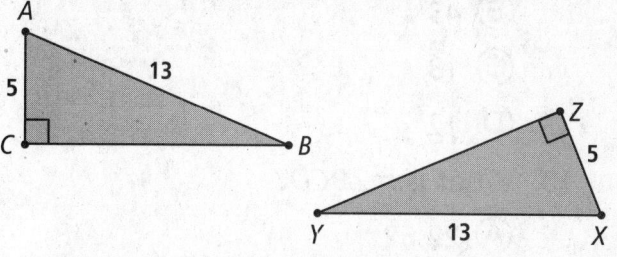
   - Ⓐ Yes; △ABC maps onto △XYZ with a translation and a rotation.
   - Ⓑ Yes; △ABC maps onto △XYZ with a translation and a reflection.
   - Ⓒ Yes; △ABC maps onto △XYZ with a rotation and a reflection.
   - Ⓓ No; the triangles are different sizes.

For Items 7–10, use the figure shown.

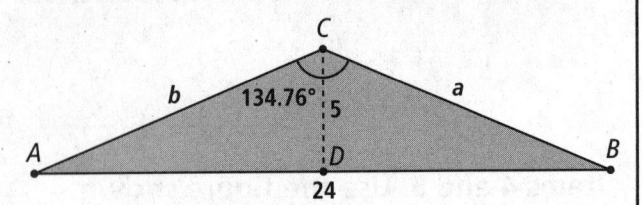

7. D is the midpoint of $\overline{AB}$. What is m∠A?
   - Ⓐ 22.62
   - Ⓑ 33.69
   - Ⓒ 45
   - Ⓓ 67.38

8. What is the length of side *a*?
   - Ⓐ 169
   - Ⓑ 43
   - Ⓒ 13
   - Ⓓ 12

9. What is the length of side *b*?
   - Ⓐ 169
   - Ⓑ 43
   - Ⓒ 13
   - Ⓓ 12

10. What is m∠BCD?
    - Ⓐ 22.62
    - Ⓑ 67.38
    - Ⓒ 90
    - Ⓓ 134.76

For Items 11–14, use the figure shown.

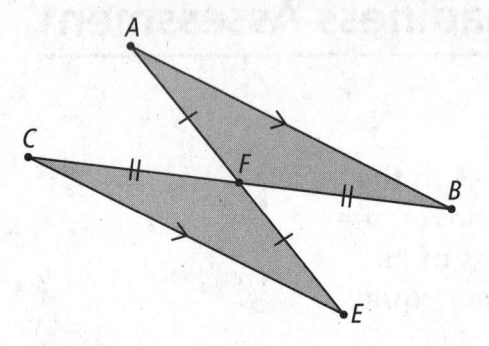

11. Does m∠BAF = m∠CEF? Explain.
    - Ⓐ Yes; they are vertical angles.
    - Ⓑ Yes; they are alternate interior angles.
    - Ⓒ Yes; they are alternate exterior angles.
    - Ⓓ No; the angles have no relationship.

12. Does m∠FBA = m∠CFE? Explain.
    - Ⓐ Yes; they are vertical angles.
    - Ⓑ Yes; they are alternate interior angles.
    - Ⓒ Yes; they are alternate exterior angles.
    - Ⓓ No; the angles have no relationship.

13. Which statement is true?
    - Ⓐ CF = AF
    - Ⓑ CF = EF
    - Ⓒ EF = BF
    - Ⓓ AF = EF

14. Is △FBA the same size and shape as △FCE? Explain.
    - Ⓐ Yes; △FBA is a reflection of △FCE.
    - Ⓑ No; the triangles have the same angle measures, but there is no information about the sides.
    - Ⓒ Yes; △FBA is a rotation of △FCE.
    - Ⓓ No; the triangles have different angle measures and side lengths.

4-1 Lesson Quiz
Congruence

Use the graph of two triangles for Items 1 and 2.

1. Select all the true statements given that △PQR ≅ △STU.

   ☐ A. PQ = ST   ☐ D. m∠P = m∠U
   ☐ B. PQ = TU   ☐ E. QR = SU
   ☐ C. m∠R = m∠U   ☐ F. m∠Q = m∠T

2. In the graph, △PQR ≅ △STU. Complete the statement below to describe a composition of rigid transformations that maps △PQR to △STU.

   Reflect △PQR across the line y = ◯.
   Then translate the resulting image ◯ units to the right.

Use the graph of four triangles for Items 3 and 4.

3. Which of the following statements is true?

   Ⓐ △JKL ≅ △MNO   Ⓒ △STU ≅ △MNO
   Ⓑ △JKL ≅ △PQR   Ⓓ △STU ≅ △JKL

4. Complete the statement below to prove that △MNO is not congruent to △PQR.

   The segment $\overline{QR}$ cannot be mapped to

   ☐ $\overline{JK}$ ☐ $\overline{NO}$ ☐ $\overline{MN}$ ☐ $\overline{MO}$ ☐ $\overline{SU}$

   by any composition of rigid transformations.

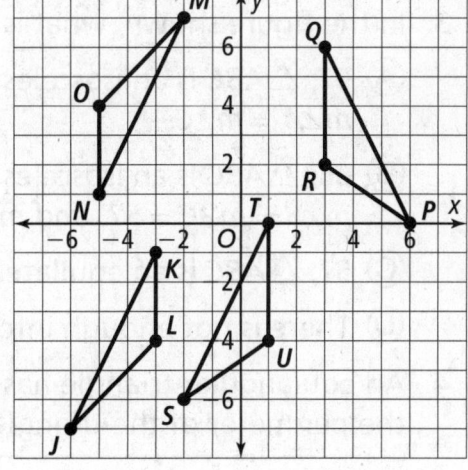

5. Which sequence of transformations could be used to show that PQRS is congruent to TUVW?

   Ⓐ translate PQRS 3 units left, then rotate it 90° about the origin

   Ⓑ translate PQRS 3 units down, then rotate it 90° about the origin

   Ⓒ translate PQRS 3 units left, then rotate it 180° about the origin

   Ⓓ translate PQRS 3 units down, then rotate it 180° about the origin

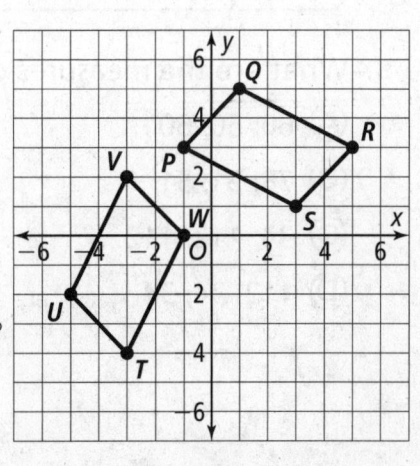

enVision® Geometry • Assessment Sourcebook

Name _____

4-2 Lesson Quiz

Isosceles and Equilateral Triangles

1. Which of the following statements is incorrect? 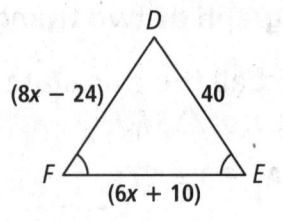
   - Ⓐ FE = 58
   - Ⓑ FE = 40
   - Ⓒ x = 8
   - Ⓓ DF = 40

2. Which of the following statements is incorrect?
   - Ⓐ A triangle with three congruent sides is equiangular.
   - Ⓑ The Isosceles Triangle Theorem can be applied to equilateral triangles.
   - Ⓒ The measure of each angle of an equilateral triangle is 120.
   - Ⓓ A triangle with three congruent angles is equilateral.

3. In the figure shown, what is m∠A? Explain. 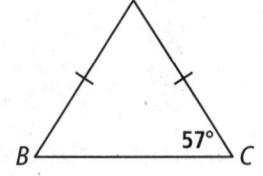
   - Ⓐ 57; △ABC is an isosceles triangle with base angles A and C. m∠A = m∠C.
   - Ⓑ 66; △ABC is an isosceles triangle with base angles B and C. m∠B = m∠C = 57, and m∠A + m∠B + m∠C = 180.
   - Ⓒ 57; △ABC is an equilateral triangle.
   - Ⓓ There is not enough information to find m∠A.

4. An equiangular triangle has one side of length six inches. What is the perimeter of the triangle, in inches?

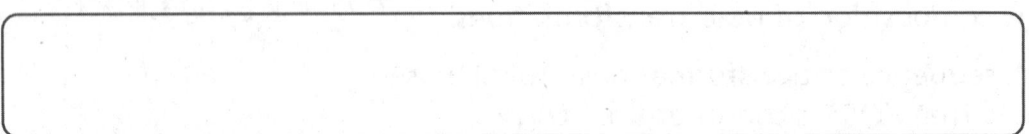

5. What are the measures of the angles in the triangle? 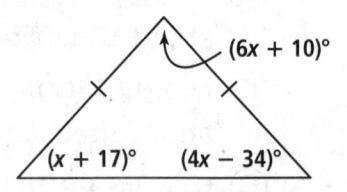
   - Ⓐ 60; 60; 60
   - Ⓑ 78; 51; 51
   - Ⓒ 34; 112; 112
   - Ⓓ 112; 34; 34

Name _____

4-3 Lesson Quiz

Proving and Applying the SAS and SSS Congruence Criteria

1. In the figure shown, which composition of rigid transformations will map one triangle onto the other?

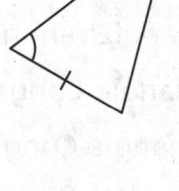

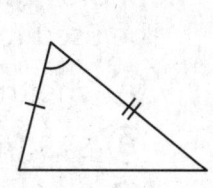

   Ⓐ a glide reflection

   Ⓑ a reflection followed by a translation

   Ⓒ two translations

   Ⓓ a rotation followed by a translation

2. Which theorem shows that △ABC ≅ △DEF?

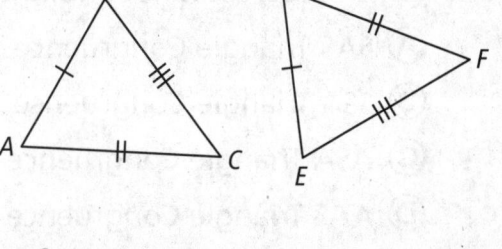

   Ⓐ The triangles are not congruent.

   Ⓑ SAS Triangle Congruence Theorem

   Ⓒ Isosceles Triangle Theorem

   Ⓓ SSS Triangle Congruence Theorem

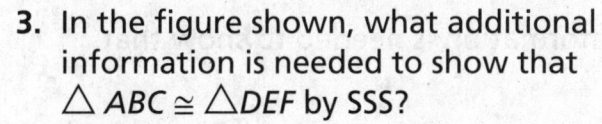

3. In the figure shown, what additional information is needed to show that △ABC ≅ △DEF by SSS?

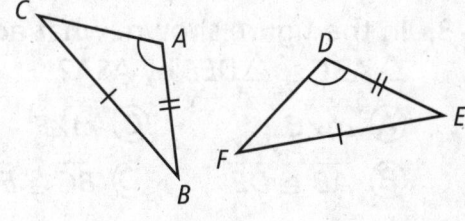

   Ⓐ m∠C

   Ⓑ $\overline{AC} \cong \overline{DF}$

   Ⓒ $\overline{AB} \cong \overline{DE}$

   Ⓓ m∠E

4. What are the necessary conditions to apply the SAS Triangle Congruence Theorem?

   Ⓐ One angle and two sides of one triangle are congruent to the corresponding parts of another triangle.

   Ⓑ Two angles and the included side of one triangle are congruent to the corresponding parts of another triangle.

   Ⓒ An angle and the two sides collinear with the angle's rays are congruent to the corresponding parts of another triangle.

   Ⓓ Two sides and any angle of one triangle are congruent to the corresponding parts of another triangle.

5. What value of x will make the triangles congruent by SSS?

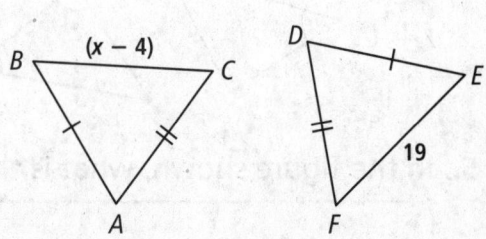

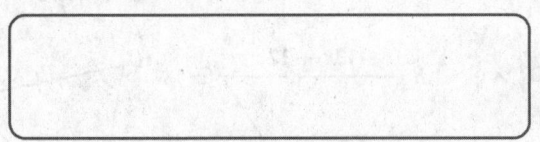

Name _____

4-4 Lesson Quiz

Proving and Applying the ASA and AAS Congruence Criteria

1. In the figure shown, which theorem can be used to show that △ABC ≅ △DEF?

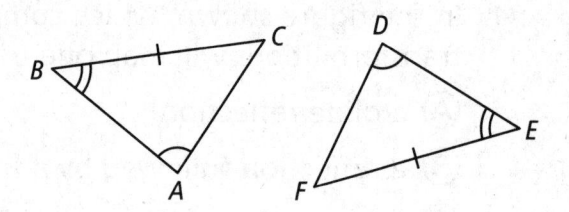

   (A) The triangles are not congruent.
   (B) SAS Triangle Congruence Theorem
   (C) AAS Triangle Congruence Theorem
   (D) ASA Triangle Congruence Theorem

2. Which theorem is not a valid theorem to show that two triangles are congruent?

   (A) SAS Triangle Congruence Theorem
   (B) SSA Triangle Congruence Theorem
   (C) ASA Triangle Congruence Theorem
   (D) AAS Triangle Congruence Theorem

3. In the figure shown, what additional information is needed to show that △ABC ≅ △DEF by ASA?

   (A) $m\angle C$
   (B) $\overline{AB} \cong \overline{DE}$
   (C) $m\angle F$
   (D) $\overline{BC} \cong \overline{EF}$

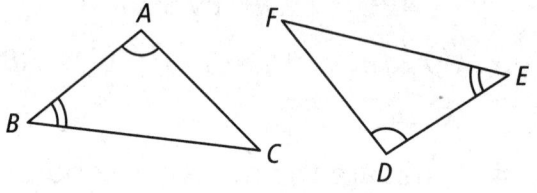

4. Select all the pairs of triangles that are congruent by ASA.

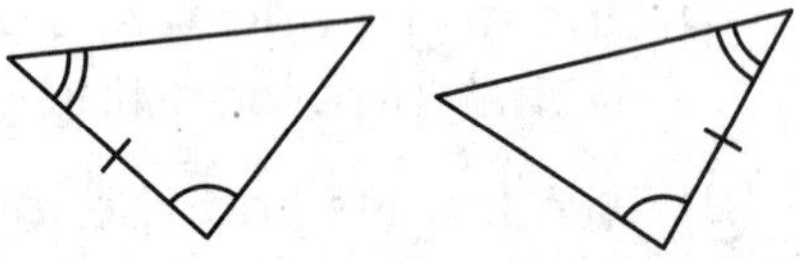

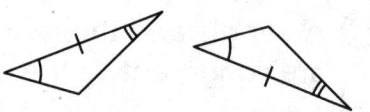

   ☐ A. 
   ☐ B. 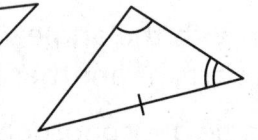 
   ☐ C. 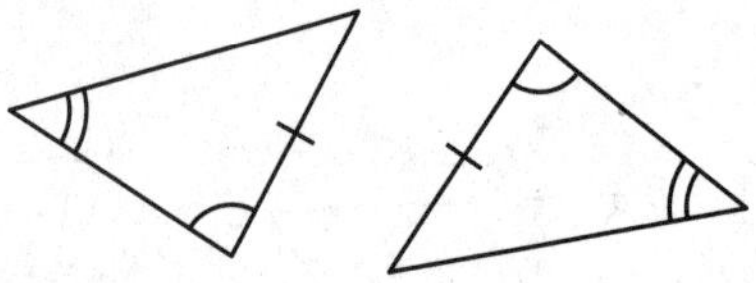
   ☐ D.
   ☐ E.
   ☐ F.

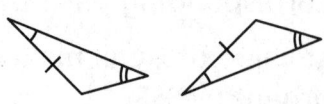

5. In the figure shown, what is the value of x?

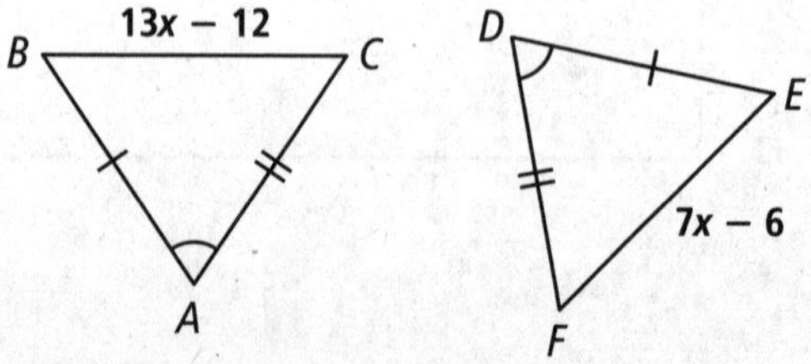

   (BC = 13x − 12, EF = 7x − 6)

enVision® Geometry • Assessment Sourcebook

4-5 Lesson Quiz
Congruence in Right Triangles

1. Which pair of triangles can be proven congruent using the Hypotenuse-Leg Theorem?

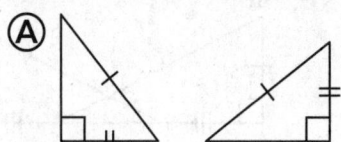

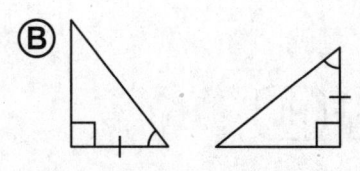

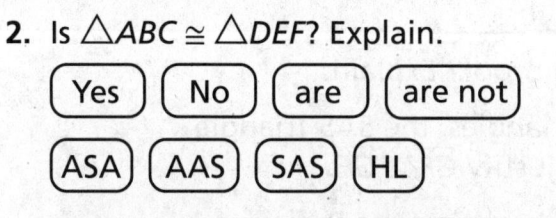

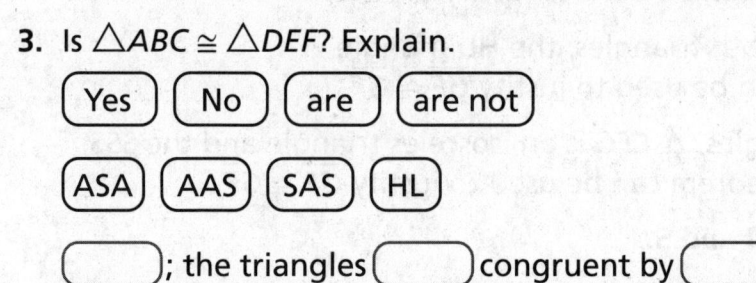

    Ⓐ   Ⓒ

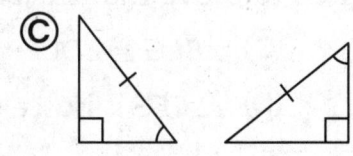

    Ⓑ   Ⓓ

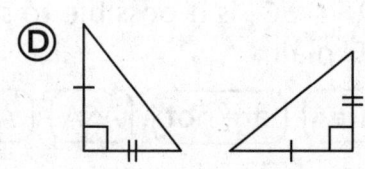

2. Is △ABC ≅ △DEF? Explain.

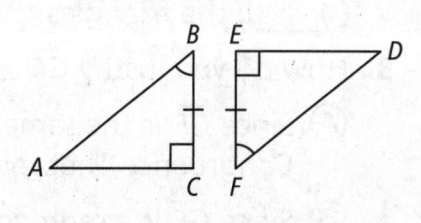

    [Yes] [No] [are] [are not]

    [ASA] [AAS] [SAS] [HL]

    ( ); the triangles ( ) congruent by ( ).

3. Is △ABC ≅ △DEF? Explain.

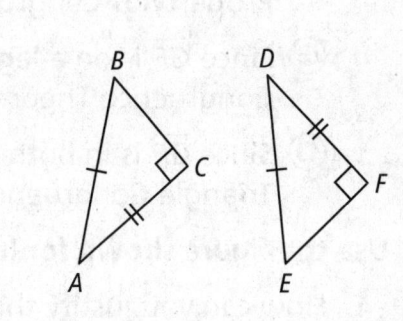

    [Yes] [No] [are] [are not]

    [ASA] [AAS] [SAS] [HL]

    ( ); the triangles ( ) congruent by ( ).

4. Select all the true statements for the figures shown.

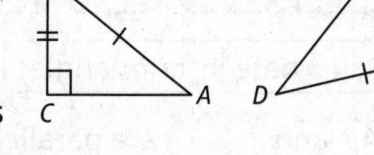

    ☐ A. If $m\angle D + m\angle E = 90$, then $m\angle F = 90$. The triangles are congruent by HL.

    ☐ B. If $m\angle D = 37$, then $m\angle A = 37$. The triangles are congruent by AAS.

    ☐ C. If $\angle E \cong \angle B$, then the triangles are congruent by SAS.

    ☐ D. If $\angle F$ is a right angle, then the triangles are congruent by HL.

    ☐ E. If $m\angle D + m\angle E = 90$, then $m\angle F = 90$. The triangles are congruent by SSA.

5. Are the two right triangles congruent? Explain.

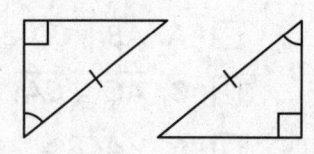

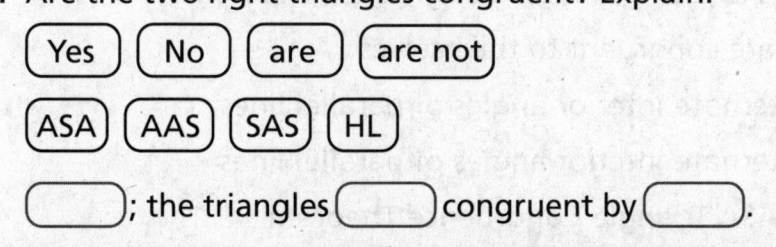

    [Yes] [No] [are] [are not]

    [ASA] [AAS] [SAS] [HL]

    ( ); the triangles ( ) congruent by ( ).

enVision® Geometry • Assessment Sourcebook

Name _____

4-6 Lesson Quiz

Congruence in Overlapping Triangles

Use the diagram shown for Items 1 and 2.

1. Which is a needed step to prove that △ABF ≅ △EDG?

   Ⓐ ∠BCD ≅ ∠BCD   Ⓒ ∠BCG ≅ ∠DCF
   Ⓑ $\overline{GF} \cong \overline{GF}$ Ⓓ △CFG is isosceles.

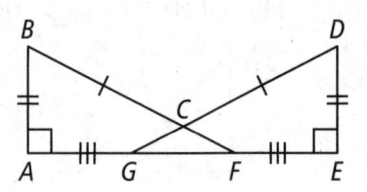

2. If a proof shows $\overline{AF} \cong \overline{EG}$, is it possible to show that △ABF ≅ △EDG? Explain.

   (Yes) (No) (are) (are not) (ASA) (AAS) (SAS) (HL)

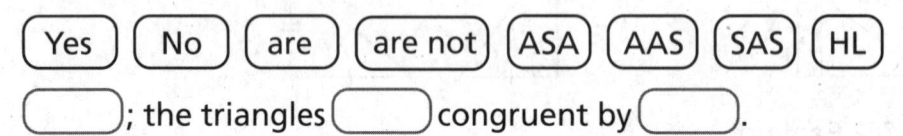

   (_____); the triangles (_____) congruent by (_____).

3. How do you justify $\overline{GF} \cong \overline{GF}$ as a step in a proof? Explain.

   Ⓐ Since $\overline{GF}$ is the same length in both triangles, the SAS Triangle Congruence Theorem can be used to justify $\overline{GF} \cong \overline{GF}$.

   Ⓑ Since $\overline{GF}$ is a segment shared by both triangles, the Reflexive Property of Congruence can be used to justify $\overline{GF} \cong \overline{GF}$.

   Ⓒ Since $\overline{GF}$ is on a leg of both triangles, the HL Triangle Congruence Theorem can be used to justify $\overline{GF} \cong \overline{GF}$.

   Ⓓ Since $\overline{GF}$ is in both triangles, △CFG is an isosceles triangle and the SSS Triangle Congruence Theorem can be used to justify $\overline{GF} \cong \overline{GF}$.

Use the figure shown for Items 4 and 5.

4. How can you justify that ∠ABE ≅ ∠CDE? Explain.

   ($\overline{AD}$) ($\overline{BC}$) ($\overline{CD}$) (vertical angles)

   (alternate interior angles) (alternate exterior angles)

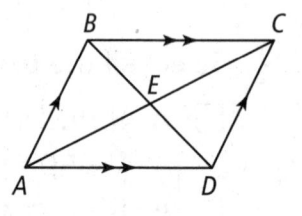

   $\overline{AB}$ and (_____) are parallel, so ∠ABE and ∠CDE form congruent

   (_____).

5. Select all the lines in the proof of △ABC ≅ △CDA that have the correct justification.

   ☐ A. $\overline{AB} \parallel \overline{CD}$ and $\overline{BC} \parallel \overline{AD}$, ASA Triangle Congruence Theorem

   ☐ B. $\overline{AC} \cong \overline{CA}$, figures are congruent to themselves

   ☐ C. ∠ACB ≅ ∠CAD, alternate interior angles of parallel lines

   ☐ D. ∠BAC ≅ ∠DCA, alternate interior angles of parallel lines

   ☐ E. △ABC ≅ △CDA, ASA Triangle Congruence Theorem

Name _____

4 Topic Assessment Form A

1. Is △PQR congruent to △XZY? Explain.

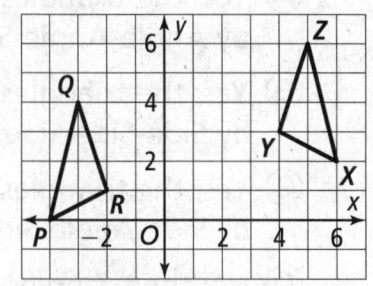

△PQR is ☐ congruent ☐ not congruent to △XZY because

☐ not enough information is given.
☐ △PQR maps to △XZY by a rotation 270° about the origin, then a translation 1 unit right and 3 units up.
☐ △PQR maps to △XZY by a translation 2 units up, then a reflection across x = 0.
☐ △PQR maps to △XZY by a reflection across x = −2, then a translation 6 units right and 2 units up

2. What theorem shows that △ACE ≅ △BCD? 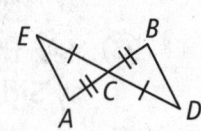
   Ⓐ Hypotenuse-Leg
   Ⓑ Angle-Angle-Side
   Ⓒ Angle-Side-Angle
   Ⓓ Side-Angle-Side

For Items 3–4, use △JKL and △LMN shown.

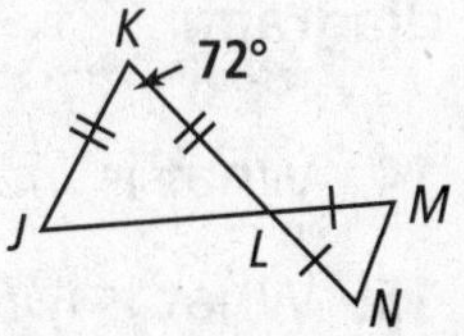

3. What is m∠KJL? ◯°

4. What is m∠LNM? ◯°

5. What composition of rigid transformations maps △PQR to △XZY?

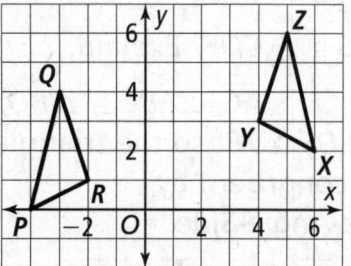

   Ⓐ a translation 1 unit right and 3 units up, then a rotation 270° about the origin
   Ⓑ a translation 2 units up, then a reflection across x = 0
   Ⓒ a reflection across x = −2, then a translation 6 units right and 2 units up
   Ⓓ a translation 6 units right, then a reflection across y = −2

6. Which triangle is congruent to △KLM?

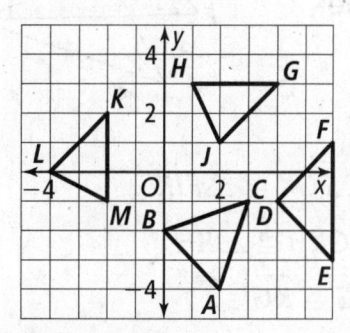

   Ⓐ △GJH
   Ⓑ △CBA
   Ⓒ △FDE
   Ⓓ none

enVision® Geometry   Assessment Sourcebook

For Items 7–9, refer to the diagram.

7. If m∠BHG = 100, what is m∠CED? ⬚°

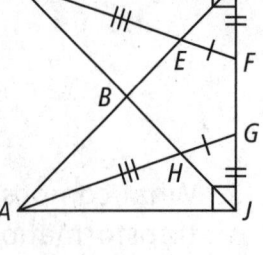

8. If m∠BEF = 100 and m∠CBE = 75, what is m∠DAG? ⬚°

9. Is △AJG ≅ △CDF? Explain.

   Ⓐ Yes; $\overline{CF} \cong \overline{AG}$, ∠ABC ≅ ∠JBD, and $\overline{DF} \cong \overline{JG}$, so the triangles are congruent by Side-Angle-Side.

   Ⓑ Yes; $\overline{CF} \cong \overline{AG}$, $\overline{DF} \cong \overline{JG}$, and ∠AJG ≅ ∠CDF, so the triangles are congruent by Side-Side-Angle.

   Ⓒ Yes; both triangles are right triangles, $\overline{CF} \cong \overline{AG}$, and $\overline{DF} \cong \overline{JG}$, so the triangles are congruent by Hypotenuse-Leg.

   Ⓓ No; the triangles are not congruent.

10. Select all the true statements about the figure.

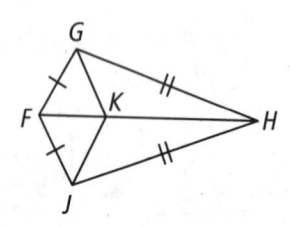

    ☐ A. △FGK ≅ △FJK
    ☐ B. ∠GKH ≅ ∠JKH
    ☐ C. $\overline{FG} \cong \overline{KG}$
    ☐ D. ∠GFH ≅ ∠JFH
    ☐ E. △GKH ≅ △JKH
    ☐ F. $\overline{FG} \cong \overline{JK}$

For Items 11–13, refer to the diagram.

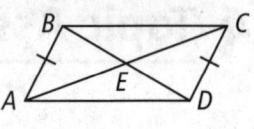

11. If ∠BAC ≅ ∠DCA, is △ABE ≅ △CDE? Explain.

    Ⓐ Yes; the triangles are congruent by Angle-Angle-Side.
    Ⓑ Yes; the triangles are congruent by Side-Side-Side.
    Ⓒ Yes; the triangles are congruent by Side-Angle-Side.
    Ⓓ No; the triangles are not congruent.

12. If $\overline{BD}$ bisects $\overline{AC}$ and $\overline{AC}$ bisects $\overline{BD}$, is △ABE ≅ △CDE? Explain.

    Ⓐ Yes; the triangles are congruent by Side-Angle-Side.
    Ⓑ Yes; the triangles are congruent by Side-Side-Side.
    Ⓒ Yes; the triangles are congruent by Angle-Angle-Side.
    Ⓓ No; the triangles are not congruent.

13. If $\overline{AB} \parallel \overline{CD}$, is △ACD ≅ △CAB? Explain.

    Ⓐ Yes; the triangles are congruent by Angle-Angle-Side.
    Ⓑ Yes; the triangles are congruent by Angle-Side-Angle.
    Ⓒ Yes; the triangles are congruent by Side-Angle-Side.
    Ⓓ No; the triangles are not congruent.

For Items 14–15, refer to the diagram.

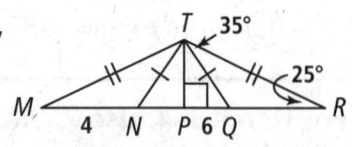

14. What is m∠MNT? ⬚°

15. What is MR? ⬚°

Name _____

4 Topic Assessment Form B

1. Is △STR congruent to △MNP? Explain.

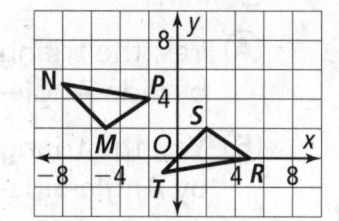

   △STR is ☐ congruent / ☐ not congruent to △MNP because

   ☐ not enough information is given.
   ☐ △STR maps to △MNP by a reflection across y = 2, then a translation 7 units left.
   ☐ △STR maps to △MNP by a rotation 90° about point T, then a translation 3 units right and 4 units up.
   ☐ △STR maps to △MNP by a translation 7 units left and 3 units up, then a reflection across x = −5.

2. What theorem shows that △TNP ≅ △TMQ? 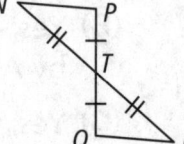
   Ⓐ Angle-Angle-Side
   Ⓑ Angle-Side-Angle
   Ⓒ Side-Angle-Side
   Ⓓ Hypotenuse-Leg

For Items 3–4, use △ABC and △CDE shown.

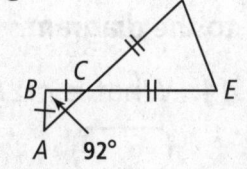

3. What is m∠BAC? ☐°

4. What is m∠CDE? ☐°

5. What composition of rigid transformations maps △ABC to △TUV?

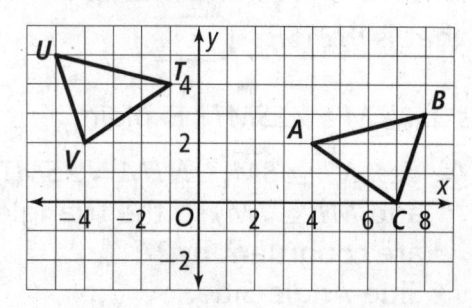

   Ⓐ a translation 3 units left and 2 units up, then a reflection across x = 0
   Ⓑ a rotation 90° about the origin, then a translation 1 unit right
   Ⓒ a reflection across y = 3, then a reflection across x = 1
   Ⓓ a reflection across x = 1, then a translation 1 unit left and 2 units up

6. Which triangle is congruent to △XYZ?

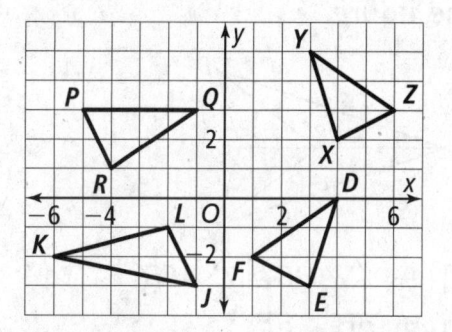

   Ⓐ △RQP
   Ⓑ △LKJ
   Ⓒ △EDF
   Ⓓ none

For Items 7–9, refer to the diagram shown.

7. If m∠NPM = 100, what is m∠TRM? ◯°

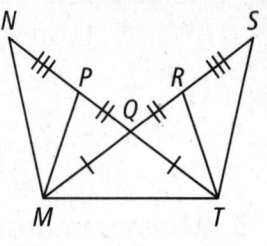

8. If m∠NMQ = 75 and m∠MQT = 95, what is m∠TSR? ◯°

9. Is △NTM ≅ △SMT? Explain.

   Ⓐ Yes; $\overline{NT} \cong \overline{SM}$, ∠NTM = ∠SMT, and $\overline{MT} \cong \overline{TM}$, so the triangles are congruent by Side-Angle-Side.

   Ⓑ Yes; $\overline{NT} \cong \overline{SM}$, $\overline{MT} \cong \overline{TM}$, and ∠NTM = ∠SMT, so the triangles are congruent by Side-Side-Angle.

   Ⓒ Yes; the triangles are right triangles, $\overline{NT} \cong \overline{SM}$, and $\overline{MT} \cong \overline{TM}$, so the triangles are congruent by Hypotenuse-Leg.

   Ⓓ No; the triangles are not congruent.

10. Select all the true statements about the figure.

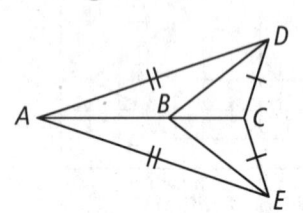

    ☐ A. △ADB ≅ △AEB
    ☐ B. $\overline{BD} \cong \overline{BE}$
    ☐ C. ∠BDC ≅ ∠BEC
    ☐ D. $\overline{AB} \cong \overline{BE}$
    ☐ E. △CDB ≅ △CAE
    ☐ F. ∠ABD ≅ ∠ABE

For Items 11–13, refer to the diagram.

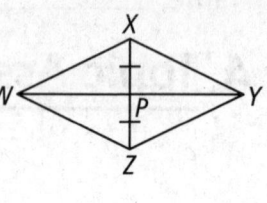

11. If $\overline{WX} \cong \overline{WZ}$, is △PXW ≅ △PZW? Explain.

    Ⓐ Yes; the triangles are congruent by Side-Angle-Side.
    Ⓑ Yes; the triangles are congruent by Angle-Side-Angle.
    Ⓒ Yes; the triangles are congruent by Side-Side-Side.
    Ⓓ No; the triangles are not congruent.

12. If $\overline{XZ} \perp \overline{WY}$ and $\overline{XY} \cong \overline{ZY}$, is △XYP ≅ △ZYP? Explain.

    Ⓐ Yes; the triangles are congruent by Hypotenuse-Leg.
    Ⓑ Yes; the triangles are congruent by Angle-Side-Angle.
    Ⓒ Yes; the triangles are congruent by Angle-Angle-Side.
    Ⓓ No; the triangles are not congruent.

13. If $\overline{XW} \parallel \overline{YZ}$ and ∠XWZ ≅ ∠ZYX, is △XWZ ≅ △ZYX? Explain.

    Ⓐ Yes; the triangles are congruent by Angle-Angle-Side.
    Ⓑ Yes; the triangles are congruent by Angle-Side-Angle.
    Ⓒ Yes; the triangles are congruent by Side-Angle-Side.
    Ⓓ No; the triangles are not congruent.

For Items 14–15, refer to the diagram.

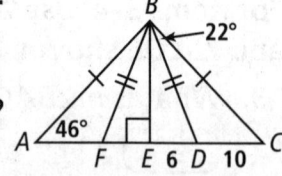

14. What is m∠BFD? ◯°

15. What is AC? ◯°

Name _____

4 Performance Assessment Form A

Darren is designing a leather collar for his rescued dog, Galgo. He has leather stamps in the shapes shown.

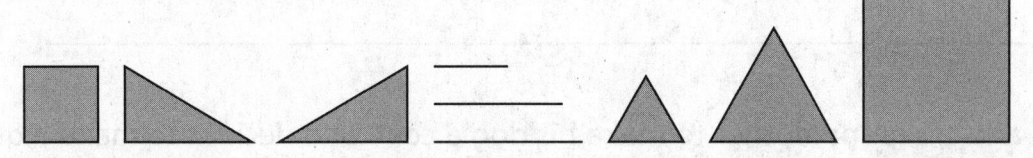

The lengths of the sides of the triangular stamps on the left are 1 cm, $\sqrt{3}$ cm, and 2 cm. The two rectangles are squares, and the two triangles on the right are equilateral triangles. The collar is 2 cm wide. Darren wants the design to use overlapping triangles, triangles that share a side, or both. He also wants the pattern to repeat several times around the collar.

1. Continue the design shown that Darren started.

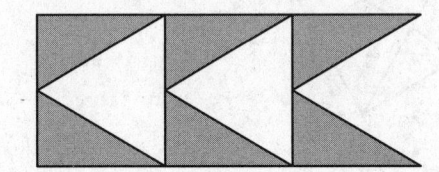

2. Add labels to the figures on the collar and write a proof that shows two of the small triangles are congruent.

3. Are two of the stamps congruent right triangles? Explain.

4. Make your own repeating design between the two horizontal lines for Galgo's collar and show that two of the triangles in your design, other than the shapes of the stamps, are congruent.

___

___

Darren asks his grandmother to make his dog a coat. She decides to make a quilted coat from scraps of fabric. She draws a design that looks like Galgo's head with nose at A and tips of the ears at C and D. She uses the design to draw a quilt pattern without overlaps or gaps along the sides.

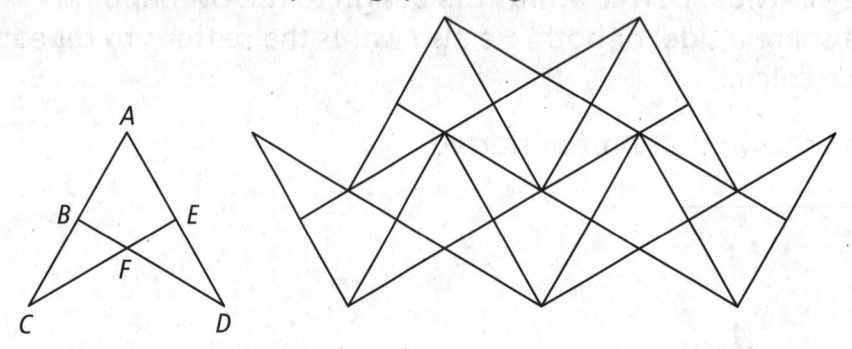

5. Darren knows that $m\angle A = 60$ and $m\angle ABD = 90$. What are the angle measures in the design? Explain.

Name _____

4 Performance Assessment Form B

Yama is designing a company logo. The company president requested for the logo to be made of triangles. Yama is proposing the design shown.

1. Identify two triangles in the diagram that are congruent. Draw separate diagrams of the two triangles, including any information that is shown in Yama's diagram.

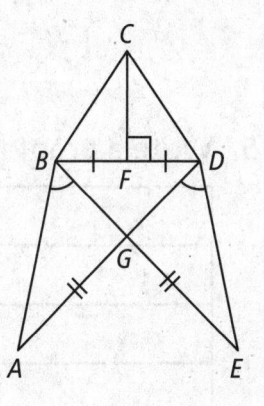

2. Write a proof to show the two triangles are congruent.

3. Identify an isosceles triangle in the diagram. Explain how you know.

4. Design your own logo that includes at least four triangles. At least two of the triangles must be congruent. Mark congruent angles and segments and right angles in your diagram.

5. Write a proof to show that two of the triangles in your design are congruent.

6. Suppose $m\angle HKM = 70$ and $m\angle LMH = 81$. The simplest way to find $m\angle JKH$ is to note that $\angle JKH$ and $\angle HKM$ are supplementary angles. Therefore:

   $m\angle JKH + m\angle HKM = 180$

   $m\angle JKH + 70 = 180$

   $m\angle JKH = 110$

   What is another way to find $m\angle JKH$?

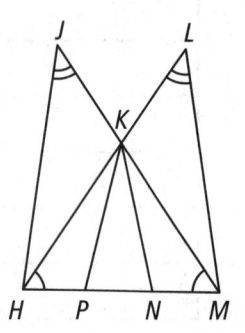

Benchmark Assessment 2

1. Select all of the following transformations that preserve distance.
   - ☐ A. Reflection over the y-axis
   - ☐ B. $(x, y) \rightarrow (6x, 6y)$
   - ☐ C. Rotation 90° clockwise about the origin
   - ☐ D. $(x, y) \rightarrow (x, -y)$
   - ☐ E. Dilation with scale factor 0.5 centered at the origin
   - ☐ F. $(x, y) \rightarrow (x - 8, y + 3)$

2. Use the Law of Detachment to make a conclusion.

   If a point is on the perpendicular bisector of a line segment, then the point is equidistant from the segment's endpoints.

   The midpoint of $\overline{AB}$ is X. $\overrightarrow{XY}$ is perpendicular to $\overline{AB}$. Point L is on $\overrightarrow{XY}$.

   Ⓐ Point L is not on the perpendicular bisector of $\overline{AB}$.
   Ⓑ Point L is equidistant to points X and Y.
   Ⓒ Point L is equidistant from points A and B.
   Ⓓ Point L is not equidistant from points A and B.

3. In △ABC, point D is the midpoint of $\overline{AC}$. Fill in the blanks to prove the Isosceles Triangle Theorem.

   [proven] [given] [SAS] [SSS]
   [BD] [BC] [AD] [CPCTC]

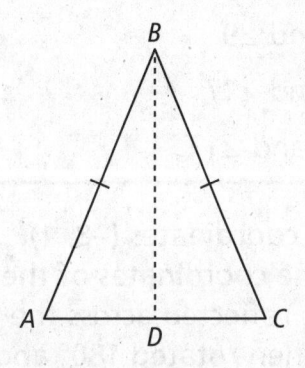

   Given: $\overline{AB} \cong \overline{BC}$
   Prove: $\angle A \cong \angle C$

   It is [   ] that $\overline{AB} \cong \overline{BC}$.
   By the Reflexive Property $\overline{BD} \cong$ [   ]. Since D is the midpoint of $\overline{AC}$, [   ] $\cong \overline{AC}$.
   So △ABD $\cong$ △CBD by [   ].
   Therefore $\angle A \cong \angle C$ by [   ].

4. The angle bisector of $\angle ABC$ is $\overrightarrow{BP}$. If $m\angle ABP = 6n$, what is $m\angle ABC$?
   Ⓐ 12
   Ⓑ 3n
   Ⓒ 12n
   Ⓓ $36n^2$

5. Select all the pairs of angles that are alternate interior angles.

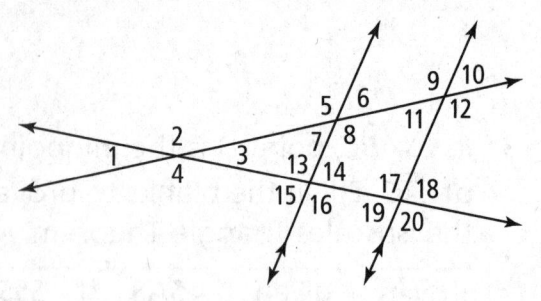

- [ ] A. ∠1 and ∠3
- [ ] B. ∠5 and ∠6
- [ ] C. ∠8 and ∠9
- [ ] D. ∠8 and ∠17
- [ ] E. ∠16 and ∠17

6. Point B has coordinates (−8, 1). What are the coordinates of the point when reflected across the y-axis and then rotated 180° about the origin?

Ⓐ (8, 1)
Ⓑ (−8, −1)
Ⓒ (−8, 1)
Ⓓ (8, −1)

7. Select all the equations that represent a line that is perpendicular to the line with equation $y = 2x - 8$.

- [ ] A. $y = \frac{1}{2}x + 1$
- [ ] B. $y = -\frac{1}{2}x + 1$
- [ ] C. $x + 2y = 5$
- [ ] D. $-x + 2y = -3$
- [ ] E. $-x - 2y = 9$

8. Quadrilateral ABCD has coordinates A(−2, 0), B(0, 4), C(4, 6), and D(2, 2).

What are the coordinates of the image of ABCD after applying the transformation $(x, y) \longrightarrow (-x, y)$ and then applying $(x, y) \longrightarrow (x, -y)$?

A'(☐ , ☐),
B'(☐ , ☐),
C'(☐ , ☐),
D'(☐ , ☐)

9. What rule maps ABCD to A'B'C'D'?

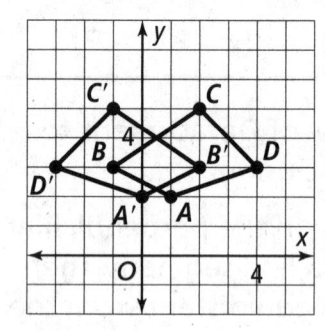

Ⓐ $r_{y\text{-axis}} \circ T_{\langle -1, 0 \rangle}$
Ⓑ $r_{x\text{-axis}} \circ T_{\langle 1, 0 \rangle}$
Ⓒ $T_{\langle 0, -1 \rangle} \circ r_{y\text{-axis}}$
Ⓓ $T_{\langle 0, 1 \rangle} \circ r_{x\text{-axis}}$

10. △ABC has vertices A(1, 3), B(2, 5), and C(5, 3). What are the coordinates of B' after the transformation $(x, y) \longrightarrow (-y, x)$, then translation 1 unit right and 4 units up?

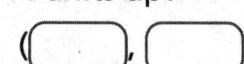

(☐ , ☐)

11. Use pentagon ABCD.

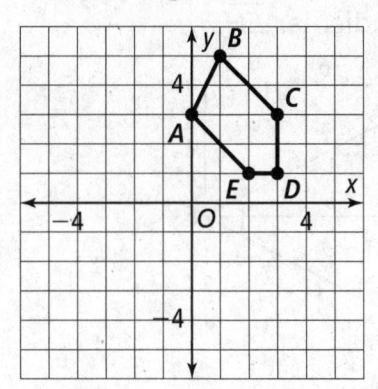

Part A

What are the coordinates of B' after the pentagon is reflected across the x-axis and then rotated 90° about the origin?

Ⓐ (1, 5)
Ⓑ (−1, 5)
Ⓒ (−5, 1)
Ⓓ (5, 1)

Part B

What are the coordinates of E' after the pentagon is rotated 270° about the origin and then reflected across the y-axis?

Ⓐ (−1, −2)
Ⓑ (1, 2)
Ⓒ (2, −1)
Ⓓ (2, 1)

---

12. Given △ABC with coordinates A(1, 3), B(4, 5), C(5, 2), what are the coordinates of △A'B'C' after reflecting across the y-axis, then translating left 1 unit and up 1 unit?

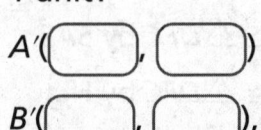

A'(☐ , ☐)

B'(☐ , ☐),

C'(☐ , ☐)

---

13. Write a rule for the glide reflection that maps △ABC with vertices A(−4, −2), B(−2, 6), and C(4, 4) to △A'B'C' with vertices A'(4, 2), B'(6, −6), and C'(12, −4).

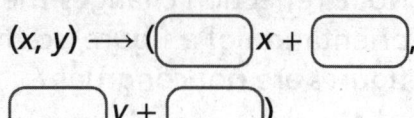

(x, y) ⟶ (☐ x + ☐ , ☐ y + ☐)

---

14. For the polygons below, select all the reflections that carry the figures onto themselves.

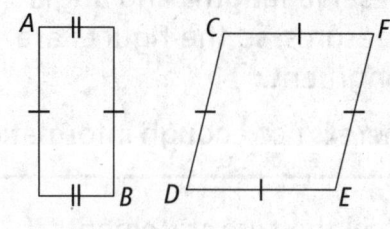

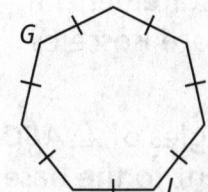

☐ **A.** Reflect the rectangle across a line through A and B.

☐ **B.** Reflect the parallelogram across a line through C and E.

☐ **C.** Reflect the parallelogram across a line through D and F.

☐ **D.** Reflect the regular heptagon across a line through G and J.

☐ **E.** Reflect the regular heptagon across a line through J and the midpoint of the side opposite J.

15. Triangle JKL is reflected across x = 0 and then translated 5 units up to create △J'K'L'. Are the two figures congruent? Explain.

Ⓐ No; a reflection changes the orientation of a figure, so the figures are not congruent.

Ⓑ No; a translation changes the position of a figure, so the figures are not congruent.

Ⓒ Yes; reflections and translations preserve lengths and angle measures, so the figures are congruent.

Ⓓ There is not enough information.

16. Select all the true statements if △ABC and △DEF are isosceles triangles.

☐ A. The base angles of △ABC are congruent to the base angles of △DEF.

☐ B. Two sides of △ABC are congruent.

☐ C. Two angles of △DEF are congruent.

☐ D. Two sides of △ABC are congruent to two sides of △DEF.

☐ E. △ABC is congruent to △DEF.

17. What are the coordinates of the point $\frac{4}{5}$ of the way from A to B?

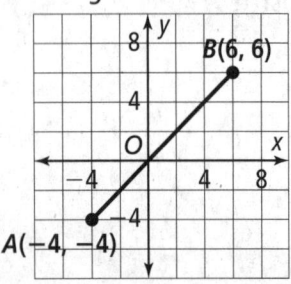

Ⓐ (−2, −2)
Ⓑ (0, 0)
Ⓒ (2, 2)
Ⓓ (4, 4)

18. $\overline{DF}$ is perpendicular to $\overline{GE}$ and $\overline{GE}$ is perpendicular $\overline{EH}$.

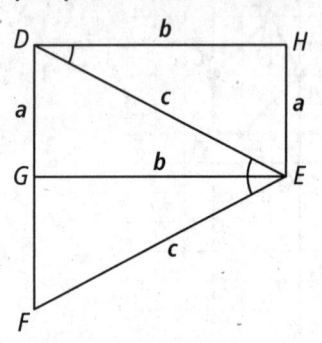

Part A

What is m∠DFE if m∠EDH = 18?

Ⓐ 9
Ⓑ 18
Ⓒ 36
Ⓓ 72

Part B

What is m∠DEH if m∠GDE = 63?

Ⓐ 27
Ⓑ 54
Ⓒ 63
Ⓓ 90

19. Select all the true statements about the figure shown.

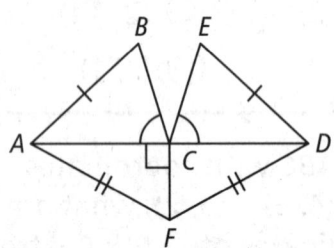

☐ A. △ABC ≅ △DEC by SAS.

☐ B. △ABC ≅ △DEC by SSS.

☐ C. △AFC ≅ △DFC by SAS.

☐ D. △AFC ≅ △DFC by HL.

☐ E. ∠C is a right angle

☐ F. There is not enough information to conclude that any of the triangles are congruent.

20. To prove that the Side-Angle-Side congruence criterion is true using transformations, start with the given information $\angle A \cong \angle D$ and

☐ $\overline{AB} \cong \overline{DE}$, $\overline{AC} \cong \overline{DF}$
☐ $\overline{AB} \cong \overline{DE}$, $\overline{BC} \cong \overline{EF}$
☐ $\overline{AB} \cong \overline{DE}$, $\angle B \cong \angle E$

and prove $\triangle ABC \cong \triangle DEF$.

Next, apply a translation to $\triangle ABC$ so that the image of A is

☐ D ☐ E ☐ F

21. Select all that apply about the reflection in the figure below.

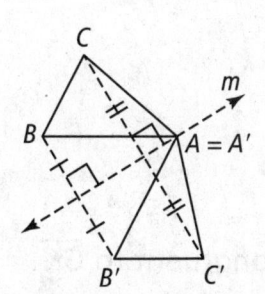

☐ A. $A' = A$
☐ B. $\overline{AC} > \overline{A'C'}$
☐ C. Line m is the perpendicular bisector of $\overline{BB'}$
☐ D. $\angle ABC \cong \angle A'B'C'$
☐ E. $\overline{BB'} \cong \overline{CC'}$

22. If $m\angle NOP = 24$ and $m\angle NOQ = 110$, what is $m\angle POQ$?

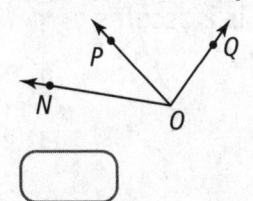

23. Which theorem can you use to prove that $\triangle GHJ$ and $\triangle GKJ$ are congruent?

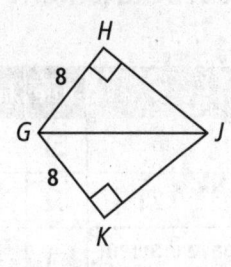

Ⓐ ASA
Ⓑ SAS
Ⓒ SSS
Ⓓ HL

24. Points A, B, and C are collinear. If $BC = 8.5$ and $AC = 13.2$, select all possible values of AB.

☐ A. 4.7
☐ B. 3.8
☐ C. 21.7
☐ D. 8.5
☐ E. 13.2

25. Match each figure with the types of symmetries it has.

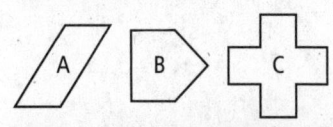

	A	B	C
Reflectional	☐	☐	☐
Rotational	☐	☐	☐

26. $T_{<x, y>}(\triangle ABC) = \triangle A'B'C'$

Use the properties of translations to determine if each statement is true or false.

	True	False
$\overline{AA'}$ is parallel to $\overline{BB'}$	☐	☐
$\overline{BB'} \cong \overline{CC'}$	☐	☐
$\triangle ABC$ and $\triangle A'B'C'$ have different orientations	☐	☐
The area of $\triangle ABC$ is smaller than the area of $\triangle A'B'C'$	☐	☐

27. If $a \perp c$, $c \parallel b$, $XS = 10$, and $XY = 24$ what is RY?

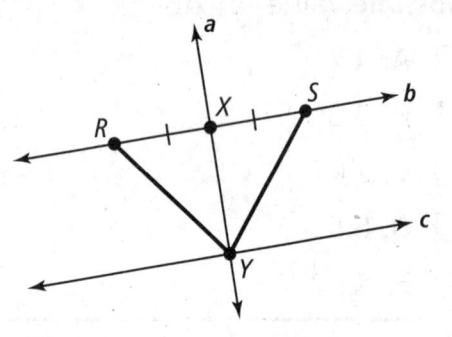

Ⓐ 10
Ⓑ 26
Ⓒ 24
Ⓓ 28

28. Select all of the statements that must be true if $m\angle 4 = m\angle 6$.

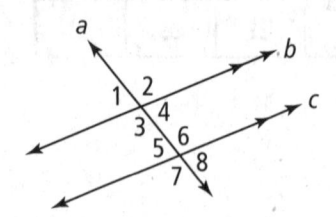

☐ A. $a \perp b$
☐ B. $m\angle 4 = 90$
☐ C. $m\angle 2 \neq m\angle 8$
☐ D. $m\angle 3 \neq m\angle 4$
☐ E. $m\angle 3 = m\angle 7$

29. $r_{(x°, p)}(\triangle ABC) = \triangle A'B'C'$

Use the properties of rotations to determine if each statement is true or false.

	True	False
$\triangle ABC$ and $\triangle A'B'C'$ have different orientations	☐	☐
$m\angle APB' = x°$	☐	☐
$PA = PA'$	☐	☐
The area of $\triangle ABC$ is equal to the $\triangle A'B'C'$	☐	☐

30. Use the diagram.

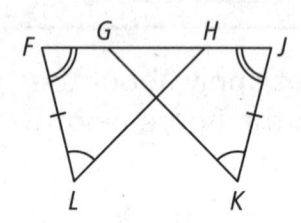

Part A

☐ $\overline{FH}$
☐ $\overline{FL}$ is congruent to $\overline{GK}$.
☐ $\overline{GJ}$
☐ $\overline{HL}$

Part B

The intersection of $\overline{GK}$ and $\overline{HL}$ is point P. Which triangle must be an isosceles triangle?

Ⓐ $\triangle FHL$
Ⓑ $\triangle GPH$
Ⓒ $\triangle JGK$
Ⓓ No triangle is isosceles.

Name _____

5 Readiness Assessment

1. Select all the true statements.
   - ☐ A. A triangle with side lengths 3.5, 3.5, and 9 is an isosceles triangle.
   - ☐ B. A triangle with side lengths 3, 4 and 5 is a right triangle.
   - ☐ C. A triangle with side lengths 3, 3 and 4 is an isosceles triangle.
   - ☐ D. A triangle with angles 60°, 60°, and 60° is an equilateral triangle.
   - ☐ E. A triangle with angles 80°, 80°, and 80° is an equilateral triangle.

2. A triangle has angle measures 24 and 85. What is the measure of the remaining angle?
   - Ⓐ 31
   - Ⓒ 71
   - Ⓑ 51
   - Ⓓ 91

3. In △ABC, m∠DEC = 110 and m∠EDC = 45. What is the measure of ∠ABC?

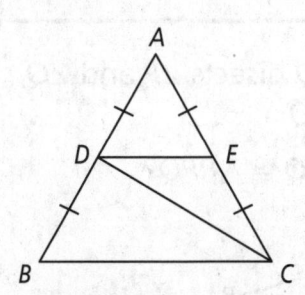

   - Ⓐ 50
   - Ⓒ 25
   - Ⓑ 65
   - Ⓓ 70

4. What is the midpoint between points (4, 7) and (1, 1)?
   (☐ , ☐)

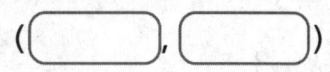

5. What is the endpoint of a segment with endpoint (−3, 5) and midpoint (2, 5)?
   (☐ , ☐)

6. In △ABC, m∠CBD = 80. What is the measure of ∠CAD?

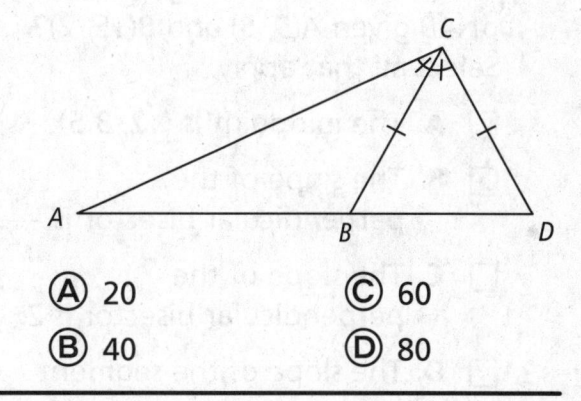

   - Ⓐ 20
   - Ⓒ 60
   - Ⓑ 40
   - Ⓓ 80

7. In △ABC, $\overrightarrow{AD}$ is an angle bisector and D lies on $\overline{BC}$. Select all statements that are true.
   - ☐ A. $\overrightarrow{AD}$ is a perpendicular bisector of $\overline{BC}$.
   - ☐ B. m∠CAD = m∠BAD
   - ☐ C. The intersection of $\overrightarrow{AD}$ and $\overline{BC}$ is the midpoint of $\overline{BC}$.
   - ☐ D. m∠BAC = 90
   - ☐ E. m∠ADC + m∠ADB = 180

8. What is the equation of the line that passes through (0, 3) and is perpendicular to $y = \frac{3}{4}x + 5$?

   Ⓐ $y = -\frac{3}{4}x + 3$
   Ⓑ $y = \frac{3}{4}x + 3$
   Ⓒ $y = \frac{4}{3}x + 3$
   Ⓓ $y = -\frac{4}{3}x + 3$

9. What is the equation of a line perpendicular to $y = \frac{1}{2}x + 3$ that has an x-intercept 8 units greater than the x-intercept of $y = \frac{1}{2}x + 3$?

   $y = \boxed{} x + \boxed{}$

10. Which of the following are true of $\overline{AB}$ given A(9, 5) and B(15, 2)? Select all that apply.

    ☐ A. The midpoint is (12, 3.5).
    ☐ B. The slope of the perpendicular bisector is $-\frac{1}{2}$.
    ☐ C. The slope of the perpendicular bisector is 2.
    ☐ D. The slope of the segment is $-\frac{1}{2}$.
    ☐ E. The distances from the endpoints of the segment to any point on the perpendicular bisector are equal.

11. What is the equation of a line perpendicular to the line through points (−3, 7) and (2, 5)?

    Ⓐ $y = -\frac{5}{2}x + 5\frac{4}{5}$
    Ⓑ $y = -\frac{2}{5}x + 5\frac{4}{5}$
    Ⓒ $y = -\frac{5}{2}(x - 2) + 2$
    Ⓓ $y = \frac{5}{2}(x + 2) - 2$

12. Select all the pairs of congruent triangles.

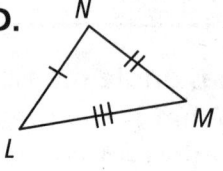

    ☐ A. 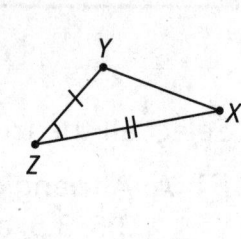 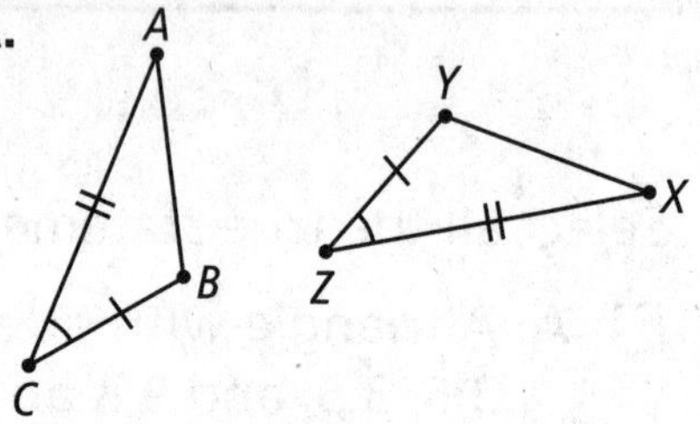
    ☐ B. 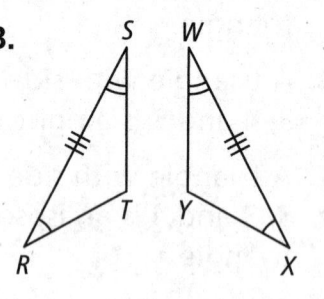
    ☐ C. 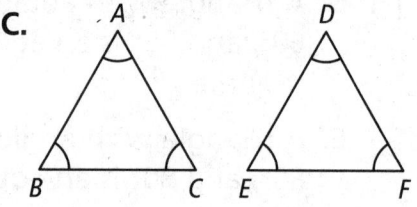
    ☐ D. 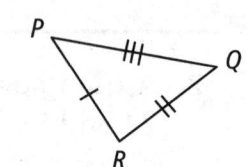
    ☐ E.

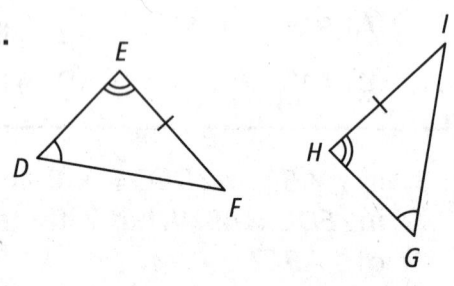

13. Segment PQ bisects ∠P and ∠Q, and $\overline{PQ} \cong \overline{PQ}$.

    How is △SPQ ≅ △RPQ?

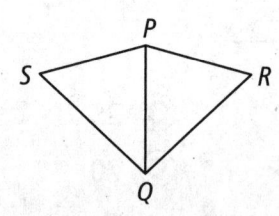

    Ⓐ AA   Ⓑ ASA   Ⓒ SAS   Ⓓ SSS

Name _____

5-1 Lesson Quiz

Perpendicular and Angle Bisectors

1. $\overline{DF}$ is the perpendicular bisector of $\overline{CE}$. If $CD = 12$ and $EF = 5$, what is the perimeter of $\triangle CDE$?

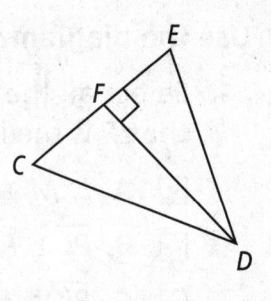

    Ⓐ 29
    Ⓑ 30
    Ⓒ 34
    Ⓓ 36

2. When constructing a perpendicular bisector of a segment, why should you make arcs with the same radius from each endpoint? Select the true statement.

    Ⓐ This makes the arcs perpendicular to each other.
    Ⓑ This makes the arcs equidistant from each other.
    Ⓒ This makes the intersections of the arcs equidistant from the endpoints.
    Ⓓ This makes the arcs parallel to the segment.

3. $\overline{PS}$ is the perpendicular bisector of $\overline{QR}$. Select all the statements about the figure that MUST be true.

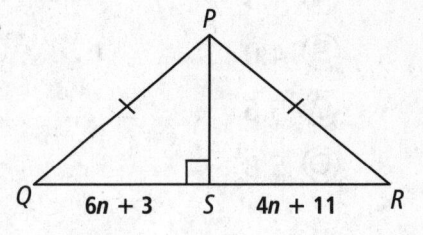

    ☐ A. $n = 7$
    ☐ B. $QS = 21$
    ☐ C. $SR = 27$
    ☐ D. $QR = 54$
    ☐ E. $PR = 15$
    ☐ F. $QP = 13$

4. If $m\angle XWY = 20$, $m\angle XWZ = 40$, and $XY = 16$, what is the value of YZ?

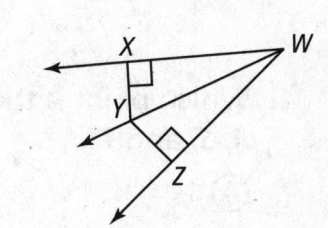

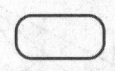

    ⬡

5. Select all the descriptions of the figure that MUST be true.

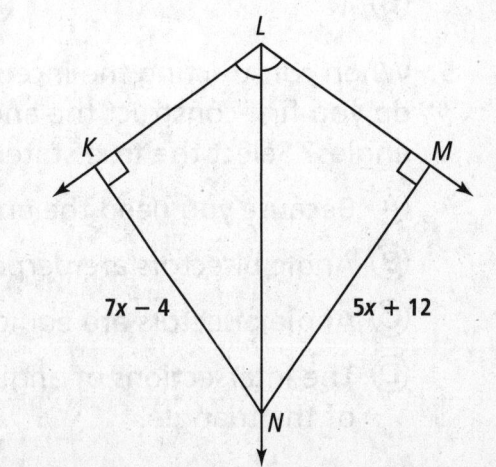

    ☐ A. $x = 8$
    ☐ B. $KN = 24$
    ☐ C. $MN = 52$
    ☐ D. $\overline{KL} \cong \overline{ML}$
    ☐ E. $\overline{LN} \cong \overline{LM}$

Name _____

5-2 Lesson Quiz
Bisectors in Triangles

Use the diagram shown for Items 1 and 2.

1. Select all the conditions that would be enough to prove that P is the incenter of △HJK.

   ☐ A. L, M, and N are the midpoints of $\overline{HK}$, $\overline{HJ}$ and $\overline{KJ}$.

   ☐ B. $\overline{PL} \cong \overline{PM} \cong \overline{PN}$

   ☐ C. $\overline{PK} \cong \overline{HP} \cong \overline{PJ}$

   ☐ D. △HJK is an acute triangle.

   ☐ E. $\overline{KP}$, $\overline{HP}$, and $\overline{JP}$ are angle bisectors of the triangle

2. Assume P is the incenter of △HJK. If $LP = 4x + 10$ and $MP = 8x - 2$, what is the radius of the inscribed circle of △HJK?

   Ⓐ 3   Ⓑ 12   Ⓒ 18   Ⓓ 22

3. What is the radius of the circumscribed circle of △ABC?

   Ⓐ 1.3
   Ⓑ 4.0
   Ⓒ 5.6
   Ⓓ 5.8

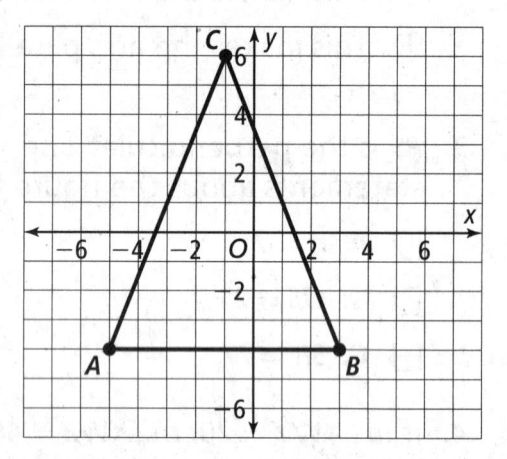

4. Which point is the center of a circle that contains R, S, and T?

   Ⓐ L   Ⓒ N
   Ⓑ M   Ⓓ P

5. When constructing the incenter of a triangle, why do you first construct the angle bisectors of two angles? Select the true statement.

   Ⓐ Because you need the angle bisectors of all the angles.

   Ⓑ Angle bisectors are perpendicular to each other.

   Ⓒ Angle bisectors are equidistant from the vertices of the triangle.

   Ⓓ The intersections of angle bisectors are equidistant from the sides of the triangle.

enVision® Geometry • Assessment Sourcebook

Name _____

5-3 Lesson Quiz
Medians and Altitudes

1. Select all the statements that are true for △ABC.
   - ☐ A. $\overline{AH}$ is an altitude.
   - ☐ B. $\overline{IH}$ is a median.
   - ☐ C. $\overline{JC}$ is a median.
   - ☐ D. The medians and altitudes intersect at the same point.
   - ☐ E. The altitudes intersect outside of the triangle.

2. In △ABC, the segment CJ = 18. If CG = BG, what is KJ?
   - Ⓐ 3
   - Ⓑ 6
   - Ⓒ 9
   - Ⓓ 12

For Items 3–4, use the coordinates J(7, 8), K(1, 2) and L(5, 2) for △JKL.

3. The centroid for △JKL is at point M. What is JM rounded to the nearest tenth?
   - Ⓐ 2.4
   - Ⓑ 4.3
   - Ⓒ 4.8
   - Ⓓ 7.2

4. The orthocenter for △JKL is at point N. What is KN rounded to the nearest tenth?
   - Ⓐ 2.7
   - Ⓑ 4.3
   - Ⓒ 6.0
   - Ⓓ 6.3

5. What is the relationship between a scalene triangle and the location of its centroid? Explain.
   - Ⓐ The centroid will always be inside the scalene triangle, since the centroid is always inside any type of triangle.
   - Ⓑ The centroid will always be outside the scalene triangle, since the centroid is always outside any type of triangle.
   - Ⓒ The centroid will always be on the scalene triangle, since the centroid is always on a triangle with no congruent side lengths.
   - Ⓓ The centroid will be inside, on, or outside the scalene triangle, depending on whether it is acute, right, or obtuse, respectively. The number of congruent sides does not affect the location of the centroid.

enVision® Geometry • Assessment Sourcebook

Name _____

5-4 Lesson Quiz

Inequalities in One Triangle

1. Select all the angle relationships in △ABC that are correct.

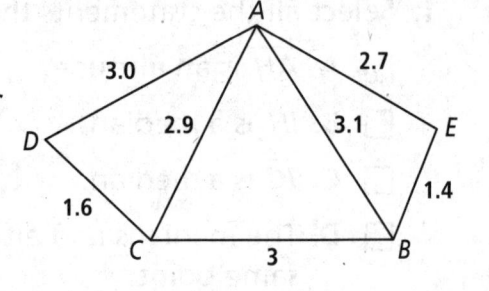

   ☐ A. m∠A < m∠C   ☐ D. m∠B < m∠A < m∠C
   ☐ B. m∠B = m∠C   ☐ E. m∠C < m∠A < m∠B
   ☐ C. m∠A < m∠B

   (Figure: pentagon with vertex A at top; sides AD = 3.0, AE = 2.7, DC = 2.9, AB = 3.1, EB = 1.4, DB = 1.6, CB = 3)

2. Select all the side-angle relationships in △ABC that are true.

   ☐ A. The largest angle is opposite the smallest side.
   ☐ B. The smallest angle is opposite the largest side.
   ☐ C. The smallest angle is opposite the smallest side.
   ☐ D. The largest angle is opposite the largest side.
   ☐ E. The side lengths and angle measures are not related.

3. In △XYZ, suppose XY < XZ. What inequality relates two angles in △XYZ?

   Ⓐ m∠X < m∠Y   Ⓒ m∠Y < m∠Z
   Ⓑ m∠X < m∠Z   Ⓓ m∠Z < m∠Y

4. What are the sides of △MNO listed from shortest to longest?

   Ⓐ $\overline{MO}, \overline{NO}, \overline{MN}$ Ⓒ $\overline{MN}, \overline{NO}, \overline{MO}$
   Ⓑ $\overline{MN}, \overline{MO}, \overline{NO}$ Ⓓ $\overline{NO}, \overline{MO}, \overline{MN}$

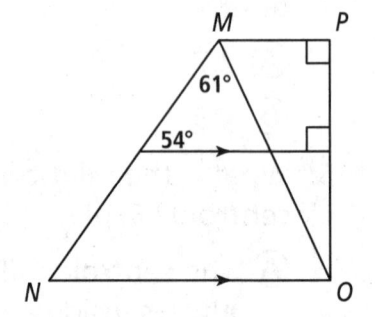

   (Figure: triangle MNO with angle at M = 61°, interior angle 54°, and right angle at P; MP ∥ NO)

5. A triangle has two sides measuring 8.5 cm and 15 cm. What is the greatest whole number length possible for the third side? Explain.

   Ⓐ 23; the third side length must be greater than 8.5 + 15 = 23.5. The smallest whole number greater than 23.5 is 23.

   Ⓑ 24; the third side length must be less than 8.5 + 15 = 23.5. The greatest whole number less than 23.5 is 24.

   Ⓒ 23; the third side length must be less than 8.5 + 15 = 23.5. The greatest whole number less than 23.5 is 23.

   Ⓓ 24; the third side length must be greater than 8.5 + 15 = 23.5. The smallest whole number greater than 23.5 is 24.

enVision® Geometry • Assessment Sourcebook

Name _____

5-5 Lesson Quiz

Inequalities in Two Triangles

1. Select all the inequalities that relate the sides of the figure shown. 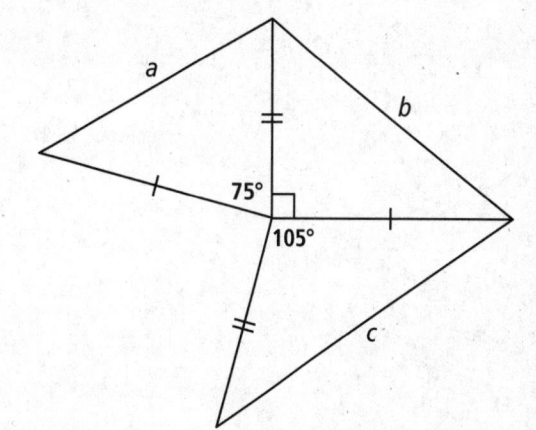
   - ☐ A. $b > a$
   - ☐ B. $c > a$
   - ☐ C. $b < c$
   - ☐ D. $a < b < c$
   - ☐ E. $c < b < a$

2. Select the inequality that relates KL and YZ in △JKL and △XYZ.

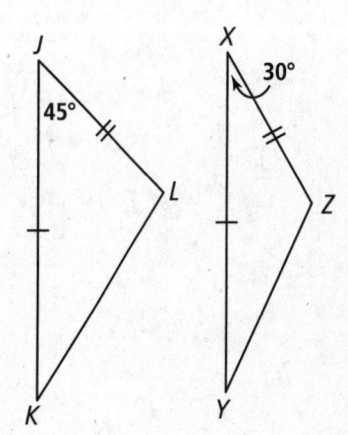

   KL $\begin{bmatrix} \square < \\ \square > \\ \square \leq \\ \square \geq \end{bmatrix}$ YZ

Use the diagram for Items 3–5.

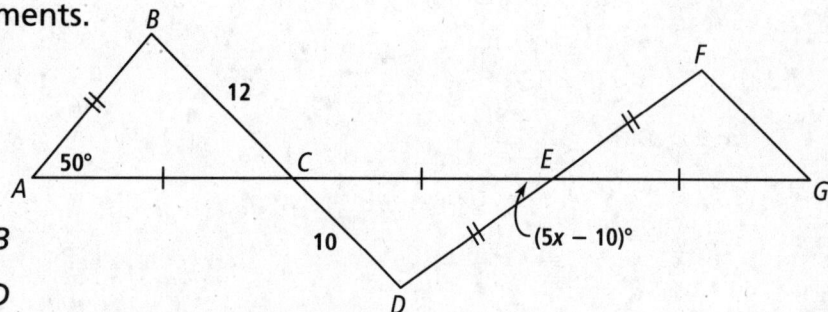

3. Select all the true statements.
   - ☐ A. $BC > FG$
   - ☐ B. $FG = 10$
   - ☐ C. $EG = 12$
   - ☐ D. $m\angle CED = m\angle CAB$
   - ☐ E. $m\angle CAB > m\angle CED$

4. Write an inequality to describe the possible values of x.

   ◯ $< x <$ ◯

5. Complete an equality or inequality that relates $m\angle B$ to $m\angle D$.

   $m\angle B$ $\begin{bmatrix} \square = \\ \square < \\ \square > \end{bmatrix}$ $\begin{bmatrix} \square \leq \\ \square \geq \end{bmatrix}$ $m\angle D$

enVision® Geometry • Assessment Sourcebook

Name _____

5 Topic Assessment Form A

1. To construct the circumscribed circle of a triangle, you must construct at least two of the

   ☐ altitudes
   ☐ angle bisectors
   ☐ medians
   ☐ perpendicular bisectors

   of the triangle and find their intersection point.

   Set your compass to the distance from the circumcenter to

   ☐ a point where a perpendicular bisector intersects the triangle.
   ☐ a vertex of the triangle.
   ☐ any point.

   Place the point of the compass on

   ☐ any vertex of the triangle
   ☐ the circumcenter

   and draw an arc with the compass.

2. Which statement is true?

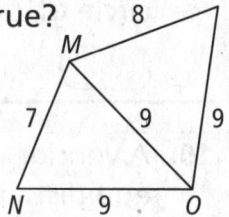

   Ⓐ $m\angle LOM < m\angle NOM$
   Ⓑ $\angle MLO \cong \angle LMO$
   Ⓒ $\angle MLO \cong \angle NMO$
   Ⓓ The circumcenter of each triangle is located outside the triangle.

For Items 3–5, a city planner is mapping out some new features for a triangular park. She sketches the park on grid paper. The coordinates of the vertices of the park are (1, 1), (1, 4), and (−3, 4).

3. The city planner wants to put recycling bins at the circumcenter of the park. What are the coordinates of the recycling bins?
   (☐ , ☐)

4. The city planner wants to plant a tree at the orthocenter of the park. What are the coordinates of the tree?
   (☐ , ☐)

5. The city planner wants to put a flower bed at the centroid of the park. What are the coordinates of the flower bed?
   (☐ , ☐)

For Items 6–7, use △DEF shown. M is the centroid.

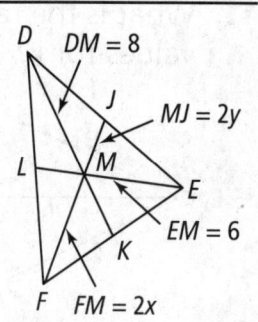

DM = 8, MJ = 2y, EM = 6, FM = 2x

6. What is EL?
   Ⓐ 9
   Ⓑ 4
   Ⓒ 3
   Ⓓ 12

7. What is an expression for FJ?
   Ⓐ $2x$
   Ⓑ $3x$
   Ⓒ $\frac{4}{3}x$
   Ⓓ $4x$

For Items 8–10, use △DEF shown.

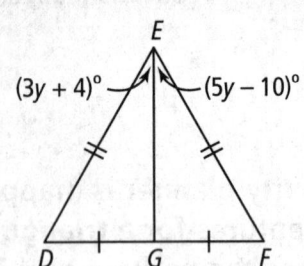

8. What is m∠DEF? ⬚

9. Select all the descriptions for $\overline{GE}$.
   - ☐ A. angle bisector
   - ☐ B. median
   - ☐ C. perpendicular bisector
   - ☐ D. altitude
   - ☐ E. hypotenuse

10. Select all the points that segment $\overline{GE}$ contains.
    - ☐ A. circumcenter
    - ☐ B. incenter
    - ☐ C. orthocenter
    - ☐ D. centroid
    - ☐ E. midpoint of edge DE

11. What is the range of possible values for x?

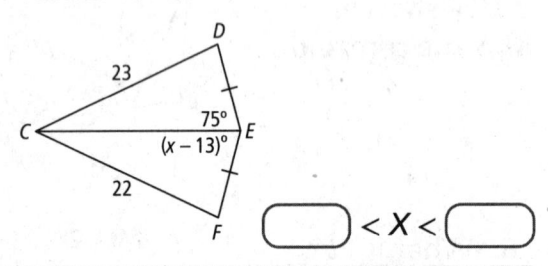

    ⬚ < X < ⬚

12. Suppose m∠ABH > m∠GHB in the figure. Select the inequality that relates AH and GB. 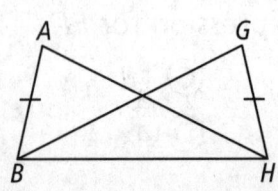
    - Ⓐ AH < GB
    - Ⓑ AH = GB
    - Ⓒ AH > GB

13. A triangular pendant has sides of length 23 mm and 31 mm. What are the possible lengths (in whole mm) for the third side?
    - Ⓐ 8 mm or less
    - Ⓑ between 9 mm and 53 mm
    - Ⓒ 54 mm or more
    - Ⓓ not possible

14. Select all the true statements.
    - ☐ A. A circumcenter is always inside of its triangle.
    - ☐ B. An incenter is always inside of its triangle.
    - ☐ C. An orthocenter is always inside of its triangle.
    - ☐ D. A centroid is always inside of its triangle.
    - ☐ E. A circumcenter, orthocenter, incenter, or centroid can be either inside or outside of its triangle.

15. In the figure, PQ = −2y + 15 and PS = 3y + 5. Find the radius of the inscribed circle of △LMN.

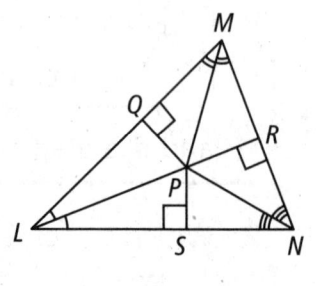

    ⬚

16. A vendor wants to be located equidistant from the entrances of a zoo and a park. She should locate her stand

    on
    - ☐ a perpendicular bisector.
    - ☐ an angle bisector.
    - ☐ a median.
    - ☐ an altitude.

Name _____

5 Topic Assessment Form B

1. To construct the inscribed circle of a triangle, you must construct at least two of the

   ☐ altitudes
   ☐ angle bisectors
   ☐ medians
   ☐ perpendicular bisectors

   of the triangle and find their intersection point. Draw a perpendicular line from this point and set your compass to measure

   ☐ the length of any side of the triangle.
   ☐ the length from the incenter to where the perpendicular line intersects the triangle.
   ☐ any length.

   Place the point of the compass on

   ☐ a vertex of the triangle
   ☐ the incenter of the triangle

   and draw an arc with the compass.

2. Which statement is true?

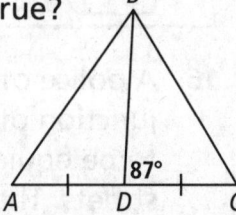

   Ⓐ $AB > BC$
   Ⓑ $AB < BC$
   Ⓒ $\overline{BD}$ bisects $\angle ABC$
   Ⓓ The circumcenter lies on $\overline{BD}$.

For Items 3–5, a school principal is mapping out some new features for a triangular playground. He sketches the playground on grid paper. The coordinates of the vertices of the playground are (1, 10), (−5, 2), and (7, 2).

3. The principal wants to plant a tree at the circumcenter of the playground. What are the coordinates of the tree?

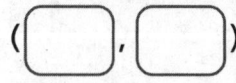

   (☐ , ☐)

4. The principal wants to put monkey bars at the orthocenter of the playground. What are the coordinates of the monkey bars?

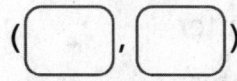

   (☐ , ☐)

5. The principal wants to put a slide at the centroid of the playground. What are the coordinates of the slide?

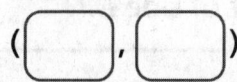

   (☐ , ☐)

For Items 6–7, use △AEC shown. F is the centroid.

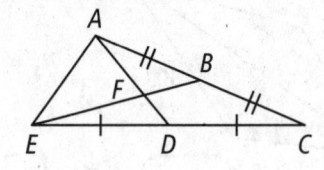

6. What is AD if $FD = 5$?

   Ⓐ 5   Ⓑ 10   Ⓒ 7.5   Ⓓ 15

7. Suppose $BE = 15x^2 + 3y$. What is EF?

   Ⓐ 3
   Ⓑ $10x^2 + 2y$
   Ⓒ $5x^2 + y$
   Ⓓ $10x^2 + y$

For Items 8–10, use △LMN shown.

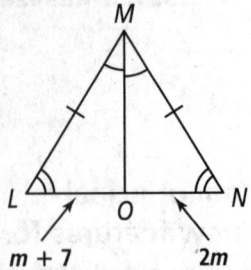

8. What is LN?

9. Select all the descriptions for $\overline{MO}$.
   - ☐ A. angle bisector
   - ☐ B. perpendicular bisector
   - ☐ C. median
   - ☐ D. altitude
   - ☐ E. hypotenuse

10. Select all the points that segment $\overline{MO}$ contains.
    - ☐ A. circumcenter
    - ☐ B. orthocenter
    - ☐ C. incenter
    - ☐ D. centroid
    - ☐ E. midpoint of side MN

11. What is a range of possible values for x?

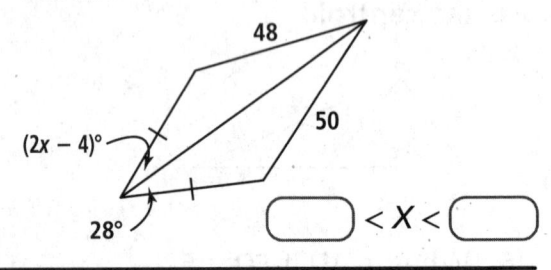

    ☐ < X < ☐

12. Suppose $AH < GB$ in the figure. Select the inequality that relates $m\angle ABH$ and $m\angle GHB$.
    - Ⓐ $m\angle ABH < m\angle GHB$
    - Ⓑ $m\angle ABH = m\angle GHB$
    - Ⓒ $m\angle ABH > m\angle GHB$

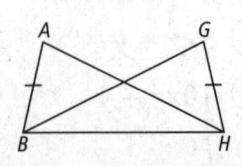

13. A triangular frame has sides of length 18 in. and 27 in. What are the possible lengths (in whole inches) for the third side?
    - Ⓐ 9 in. or less
    - Ⓑ 45 in. or more
    - Ⓒ between 10 in. and 44 in.
    - Ⓓ not possible

14. Select all the true statements.
    - ☐ A. A circumcenter can be outside of its triangle.
    - ☐ B. An incenter can be outside of its triangle.
    - ☐ C. An orthocenter can be outside of its triangle.
    - ☐ D. A centroid can be outside of its triangle.
    - ☐ E. A circumcenter, orthocenter, incenter, or centroid can be either inside or outside of its triangle.

15. In the figure, $XU = -4y + 20$ and $XW = 6y + 10$. Find the radius of the inscribed circle of △RST.

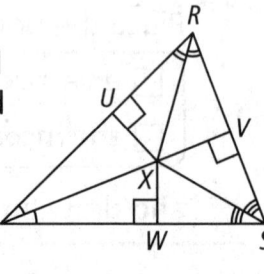

16. A police officer is parked at the junction of two streets. He wants to be equidistant from both streets. The police officer should be on
    - ☐ a perpendicular bisector.
    - ☐ an angle bisector.
    - ☐ a median.
    - ☐ an altitude.

enVision® Geometry   Assessment Sourcebook

5 Performance Assessment Form A

Lucy will go to college this fall. She is looking for the best location for her apartment. Most of her classes will be in Sawyer Hall. She currently works at the coffee shop. Use the diagrams for reference.

1. Campus housing has apartments at point A and point B. Which building should Lucy choose if she wants to live equidistant from Sawyer Hall and her work? Explain.

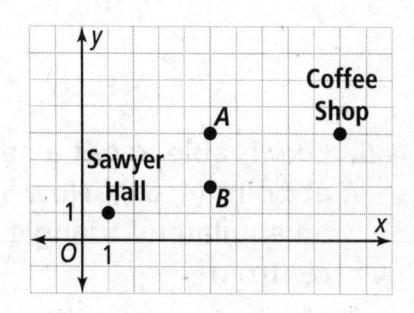

2. Lucy found Apartments C and D, which are equidistant from the coffee shop, as shown. If Lucy wants to minimize how far she travels, which apartment should she choose? How do the angles support your answer?

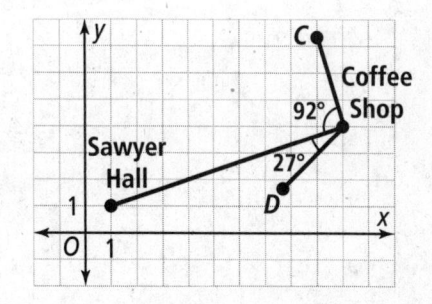

3. Lucy's parents live at point (7, 1). She has decided it is important to include her parents' house in her planning.

   ### Part A
   Construct the incenter and circumcenter for these three locations.

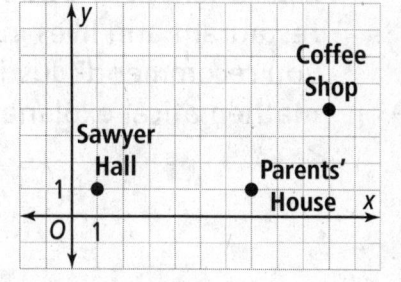

   ### Part B
   If Lucy's apartment were near the circumcenter of the triangle formed by the three locations, how would that affect the distance to each location?

   ### Part C
   Why would the incenter be a good location for Lucy's apartment compared to the circumcenter?

4. Suppose there are no housing options at the incenter nor at the circumcenter. What is another point Lucy could calculate if she wants to remain close to all three locations? Explain why that location would be helpful for Lucy.

5. Lucy is able to get a new job working at a restaurant. The restaurant is located at point (4, 6.2). Now Sawyer Hall, her parents' house, and her new job form an equilateral triangle. How does this impact the circumcenter, incenter, and centroid?

6. Lucy is deciding between two final options, both located at their respective centroids. In Option 1, Lucy works at the coffee shop and lives in Apartment E. In Option 2, Lucy works at the restaurant and lives in Apartment F. Which would you recommend? Justify your answer with a mathematical explanation.

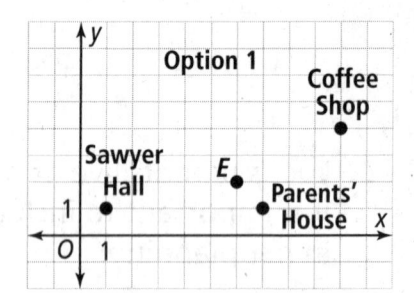

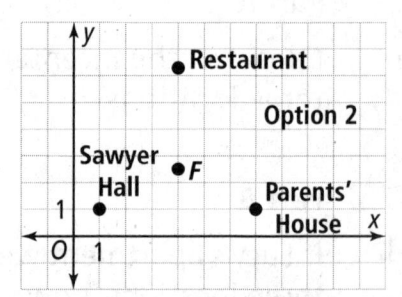

5 Performance Assessment Form B

A group of students from neighboring cities raised money to build a shared skate park. The students need to justify the location of the skate park to get approval from their city councils to build it.

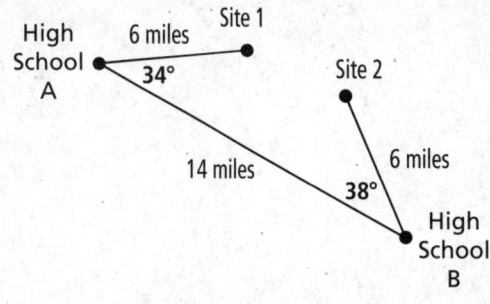

1. Two sites have been proposed, Site 1 and Site 2. Both sites are six miles from one of the high schools. Which site would be a fairer choice? Explain.

2. There are two main streets, one that goes through each city as shown. Explain how they could find a location that gives equal access to each main street.

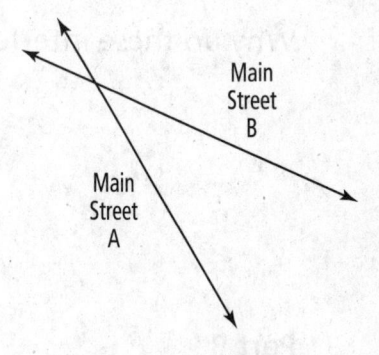

3. If students from a third city participate in funding the skate park, its main street crosses the other two at two separate points to form a triangle. Can you still use information from the previous answer to find a good location for all three cities? Explain.

4. If the students want to have the skate park equidistant from all three high schools, explain which point of concurrency they will use and how they would locate that point.

5. Suppose the high schools are arranged as shown. Use the coordinates of the centroid to help explain whether or not the centroid would be a fair location for all three cities.

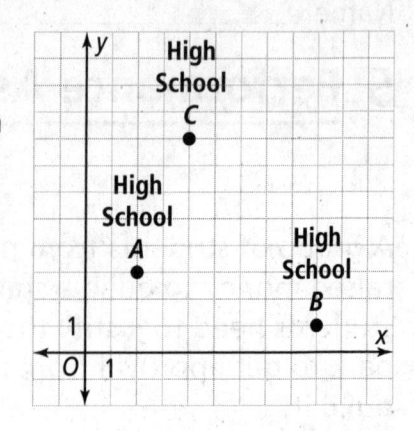

6. Suppose the distances between the three high schools are 14 miles, 28 miles, and 14 miles.

   Part A

   Why do these interfere with using a point of concurrency?

   Part B

   Suppose the high schools are arranged as shown. Could they use the perpendicular bisector, which goes through High School B, to find a location that is equidistant from all three schools? Explain your reasoning.

Name _____

6 Readiness Assessment

Use the figure shown for Items 1–4.
In the figure, $m\angle IJL = 0.5\ m\angle JIK$.

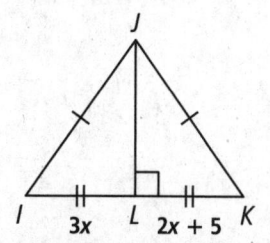

1. Select all the statements that must be true.

   ☐ A. $KL = 15$
   ☐ B. $\overline{JL}$ bisects $\overline{IK}$.
   ☐ C. $\triangle IJK$ is equilateral.
   ☐ D. $\overline{JL}$ is the perpendicular bisector of $\overline{IK}$.
   ☐ E. $JL = 2LK$

2. What is JL?

   ◯ $\sqrt{◯}$

3. What are the measures of the three angles in $\triangle IJK$?

   $m\angle IJK =$ ◯
   $m\angle JKI =$ ◯
   $m\angle KIJ =$ ◯

4. How many triangles congruent to $\triangle IJK$ can you fit around vertex J without overlaps or gaps?

   Ⓐ 4
   Ⓑ 5
   Ⓒ 6
   Ⓓ 7

Use the figure shown for Items 5–8.
In the figure, $m\angle 4 = 105$.

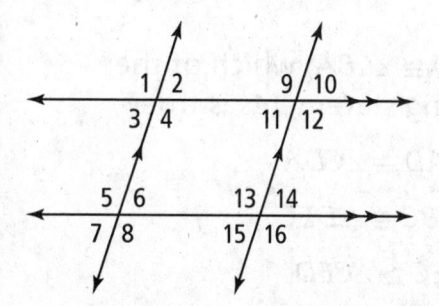

5. What is the measure of $m\angle 7$?

   ◯

6. Select all the angles that can be proven to be congruent to $\angle 4$ using **only** the Corresponding Angles Theorem.

   ☐ A. $\angle 8$ ☐ C. $\angle 12$ ☐ E. $\angle 1$
   ☐ B. $\angle 11$ ☐ D. $\angle 10$ ☐ F. $\angle 13$

7. Select all the angles that can be proven to be congruent to $\angle 6$ using **only** the Alternate Interior Angles Theorem.

   ☐ A. $\angle 13$ ☐ C. $\angle 1$ ☐ E. $\angle 11$
   ☐ B. $\angle 15$ ☐ D. $\angle 3$ ☐ F. $\angle 2$

8. Select all the statements that are true about $m\angle 4$ and $m\angle 6$.

   ☐ A. They are supplementary angles.
   ☐ B. They are same-side interior angles.
   ☐ C. $m\angle 4 + m\angle 6 = 180$
   ☐ D. They are complementary angles.
   ☐ E. $m\angle 4 + m\angle 6 = 90$

Use the figure shown for Items 9–12.
In the figure, $\overline{BC} \parallel \overline{AD}$.

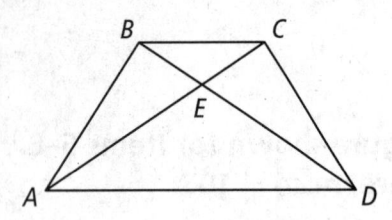

9. If $\angle BCD \cong \angle CBA$, which of the following statements is true?

  Ⓐ $\angle BAD \cong \angle CDA$
  Ⓑ $\triangle ABC \cong \triangle DEC$
  Ⓒ $\angle BEC \cong \angle CED$
  Ⓓ $\frac{1}{2} AD = BC$

10. What is $m\angle BCD + m\angle CDB + m\angle DBC$?

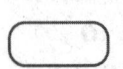

11. What is $m\angle ABD + m\angle BDA + m\angle DAB$?

12. Part A

    Why is $\angle BEC \cong \angle AED$?

    Ⓐ complementary angles
    Ⓑ alternate interior angles
    Ⓒ corresponding angles
    Ⓓ vertical angles

    Part B

    Using the same theorem, complete the statement.

    $\angle BEA \cong$ ☐ $\angle DEA$ / ☐ $\angle AEB$ / ☐ $\angle CED$

Use the figure shown for Items 13–17.
In the figure, $\overline{KM}$ is perpendicular to $\overline{JL}$. Point P is the midpoint of $\overline{JL}$.

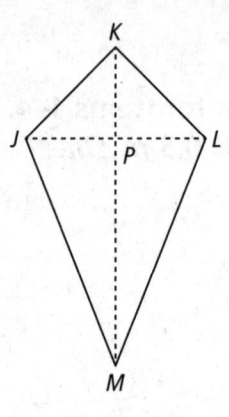

13. Why is $\triangle JPK \cong \triangle LPK$?

    Ⓐ SAS   Ⓒ SSA
    Ⓑ ASA   Ⓓ AAS

14. Complete the statement to answer why $\overline{JM} \cong \overline{LM}$ by CPCTC.

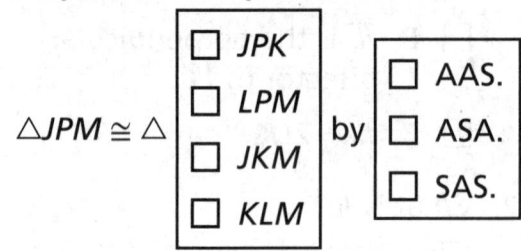

    $\triangle JPM \cong \triangle$ ☐ JPK / ☐ LPM / ☐ JKM / ☐ KLM by ☐ AAS. / ☐ ASA. / ☐ SAS.

15. Given $\triangle JPK \cong \triangle LPK$ and $\triangle JPM \cong \triangle LPM$, which criterion can be directly applied to show that $\triangle KJM \cong \triangle KLM$?

    Ⓐ SAS   Ⓒ HL
    Ⓑ ASA   Ⓓ SSS

16. If $m\angle JKL = 90$ and $m\angle JML = 60$, what is $m\angle KLM$?

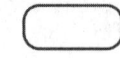

17. What is the sum of the measures of all the interior angles in quadrilateral JKLM?

Name _____

6-1 Lesson Quiz

The Polygon Angle-Sum Theorems

1. What is m∠B? 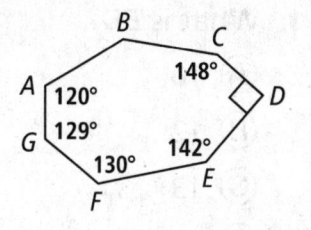
   - Ⓐ 51
   - Ⓑ 129
   - Ⓒ 134
   - Ⓓ 141

2. A convex polygon has ☐ 13 ☐ 17 ☐ 15 ☐ 19 sides when the interior angle sum is 1980°.

3. Each exterior angle in a regular polygon has a measure of 18. How many sides does the polygon have? What is the sum of the measures of the interior angles?
   - Ⓐ 10; 1,440
   - Ⓑ 18; 2,880
   - Ⓒ 20; 3,240
   - Ⓓ 36; 6,120

4. Refer to the figure at the right. What is m∠P?

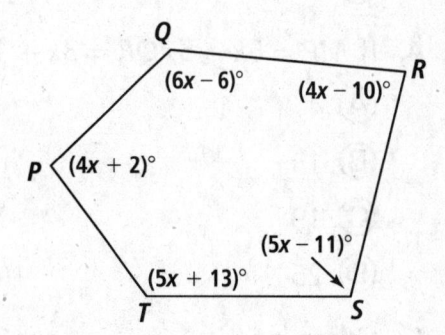

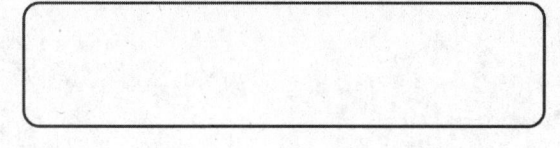

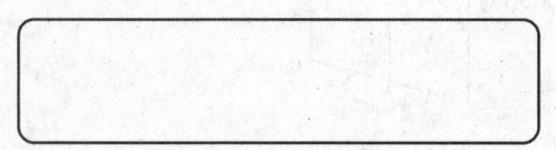

5. If ∠1 ≅ ∠2 ≅ ∠3, ∠4 ≅ ∠5, and m∠4 = m∠3 + 10, what is m∠5?

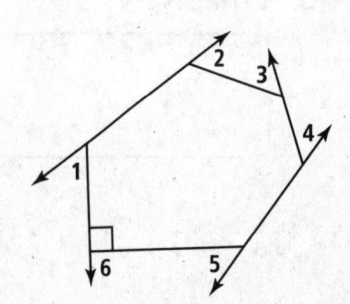

Name _____

6-2 Lesson Quiz

Kites and Trapezoids

1. What is BD?
   - Ⓐ 10
   - Ⓑ 12
   - Ⓒ 13
   - Ⓓ 14

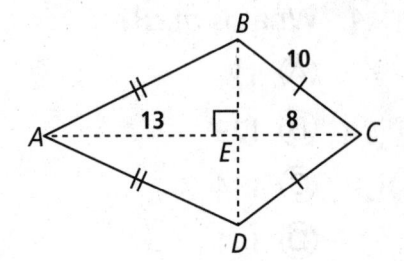

Use the figure shown for Items 2–4.

2. If $m\angle MNP = 107$, what is $m\angle NMQ$?

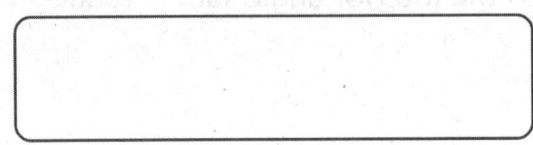

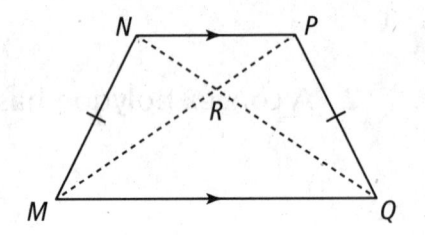

3. What can be concluded about the base angles of the trapezoid?
   - Ⓐ The base angles are complementary.
   - Ⓑ The base angles are congruent.
   - Ⓒ The base angles are supplementary.
   - Ⓓ The base angles are opposite angles.

4. If $MP = 6x - 5$, $QR = 3x + 1$, and $RN = 6$, what is QN?
   - Ⓐ 4
   - Ⓑ 13
   - Ⓒ 19
   - Ⓓ 25

5. What is HL?

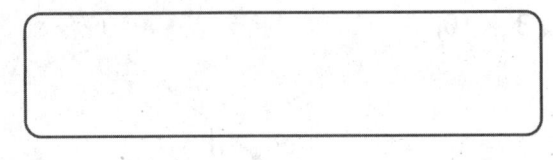

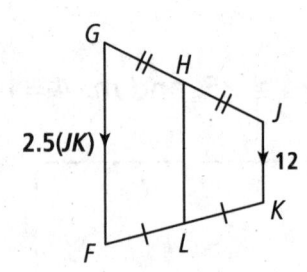

6-3 Lesson Quiz

Properties of Parallelograms

Use the figure shown for Items 1–2.

1. If $AB = 9$ and $\overline{AB} \parallel \overline{DC}$, what is the perimeter of $ABCD$?

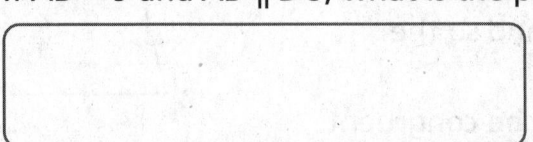

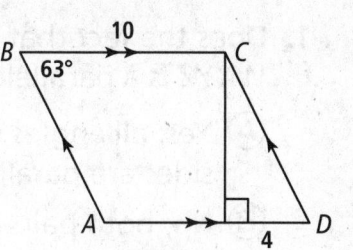

2. What is the measure of the exterior angle at D when $\overline{AD}$ is extended?

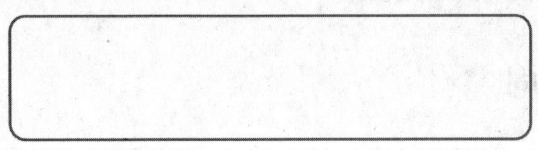

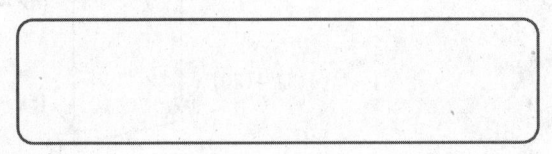

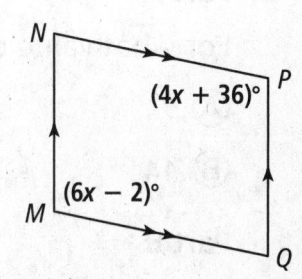

3. What is $m\angle N$?

Use the figure shown for Items 4–5.

4. If $WY + XZ = 28$, what is PZ?

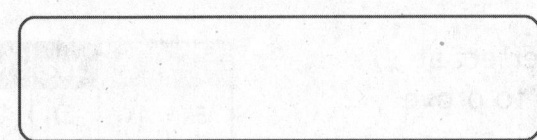

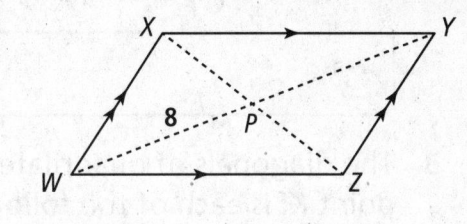

5. If $XZ = 7x + 1$ and $PZ = 4x - 1$, what is XP?
   - Ⓐ 11
   - Ⓑ 12
   - Ⓒ 19
   - Ⓓ 22

6-4 Lesson Quiz

Proving a Quadrilateral Is a Parallelogram

1. Does the fact that YZ = WX lead to the proof that WXYZ is a parallelogram? Why or why not?

   Ⓐ Yes; all angles will be right angles, and so the sides are parallel.

   Ⓑ No; both pairs of opposite sides can be congruent without being parallel.

   Ⓒ Yes; if both pairs of opposite sides are congruent they must also be parallel.

   Ⓓ No; opposite angles may not be equal.

2. **Part A**

   For what value of x is JKLM a parallelogram?

   Ⓐ 7 Ⓒ 21
   Ⓑ 14 Ⓓ 28

   Part B

   If JKLM is a parallelogram, what is m∠K?

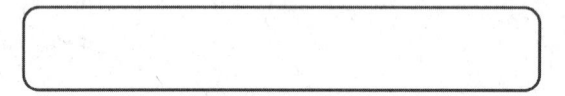

3. The diagonals of quadrilateral ABCD intersect at point K. Is each of the following needed to prove that ABCD is a parallelogram?

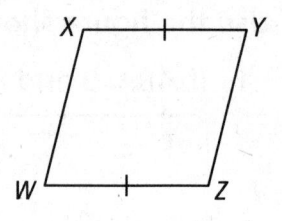

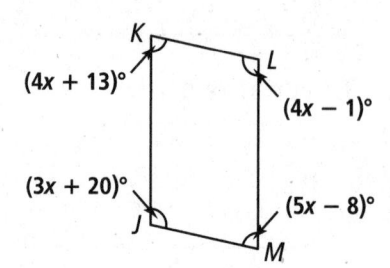

	Yes	No
BK = AK	☐	☐
BK = DK	☐	☐
CK = AK	☐	☐
CK = DK	☐	☐

4. In quadrilateral PQRS, the exterior angle at Q when $\overline{PQ}$ is extended measures 155 and PS = QR. What measure of ∠PSR would confirm that PQRS is a parallelogram?

5. Which condition is sufficient to show that quadrilateral DEFG is a parallelogram?

   Ⓐ ∠GDE is supplementary to ∠DEF

   Ⓑ ∠GDE is supplementary to ∠EFG

   Ⓒ ∠GDE is supplementary to ∠DEF and ∠EFG

   Ⓓ ∠GDE is congruent to ∠FGD

6-5 Lesson Quiz

Properties of Special Parallelograms

1. What is the most precise term for each parallelogram described below?

   A parallelogram with diagonals that are congruent and perpendicular is a ☐ rhombus. ☐ square.

   A parallelogram with diagonals that are perpendicular, but not always congruent, is a ☐ rhombus. ☐ square.

2. What is the measure of ∠WZX in rhombus WXYZ?
   - Ⓐ 38.5
   - Ⓑ 51.5
   - Ⓒ 77
   - Ⓓ 103

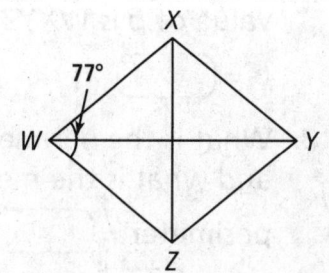

3. **Part A**

   In rhombus ABCD, diagonals $\overline{BD}$ and $\overline{AC}$ intersect at point E. If $BE = 4n - 3$ and $EC = 2n + 5$, which expression can be used to represent AD?

   - Ⓐ $(2n + 5)^2 + (4n - 3)^2$
   - Ⓑ $2(2n + 5) + 2(4n - 3)$
   - Ⓒ $\sqrt{(2n + 5) + (4n - 3)}$
   - Ⓓ $\sqrt{(2n + 5)^2 + (4n - 3)^2}$

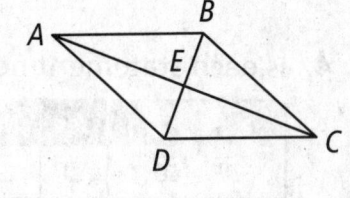

   Part B

   If $AC = 14$, what is the measure of BD?
   $BD = \boxed{}$

4. In rectangle PQRS, the diagonals intersect each other at point T. If $PR = 9$ and $PQ = 7$, what is the area of △PQR? Round to the nearest tenth.

   $\boxed{}$ square units

5. A rectangle with area 5000 square cm is 2 times as long as it is wide. What is the sum of the diagonals? Round to the nearest tenth.
   - Ⓐ 55.9 cm
   - Ⓑ 111.8 cm
   - Ⓒ 223.6 cm
   - Ⓓ 300.0 cm

6-6 Lesson Quiz

Conditions of Special Parallelograms

1. Describe a method to test whether a parallelogram is a rectangle, if you do not know the angle measures.

   To prove that a particular parallelogram is a rectangle, you can check if the
   - ☐ opposite angles
   - ☐ diagonals
   - ☐ opposite sides

   - ☐ are congruent.
   - ☐ bisect each other.

2. The expressions $\frac{10}{12}\left(\frac{24}{5}b - \frac{36}{5}\right)$ and $\frac{2}{3}(3b + 6)$ represent the lengths of the diagonals of parallelogram WXYZ. For what value of b is WXYZ a rectangle?

   b = ☐

3. What is the perimeter of parallelogram ABCD, and what is the measure of AC?

   perimeter = ☐

   AC = ☐

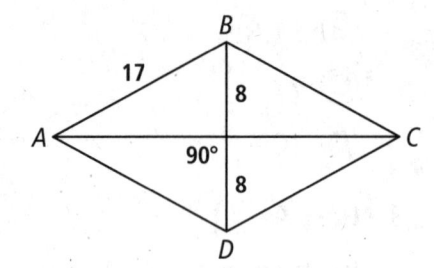

4. Is each statement necessarily true for parallelogram DEFG?

	Yes	No
$\overline{DF} \cong \overline{EG}$	☐	☐
$\overline{EF} \cong \overline{DG}$	☐	☐
$\angle DEG \cong \angle FGE$	☐	☐
$\angle EDF \cong \angle GDF$	☐	☐

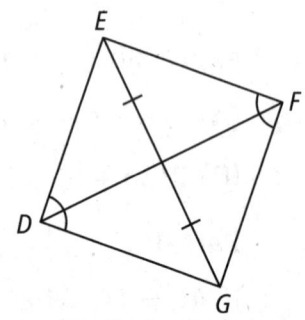

5. Which expression can be used to represent the area of parallelogram PQRS?

   Ⓐ 50
   Ⓑ 50x
   Ⓒ $25x^2$
   Ⓓ $50x^2$

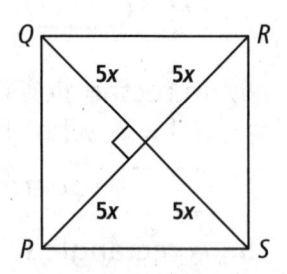

Name _____

6 Topic Assessment Form A

1. What is the value of x?

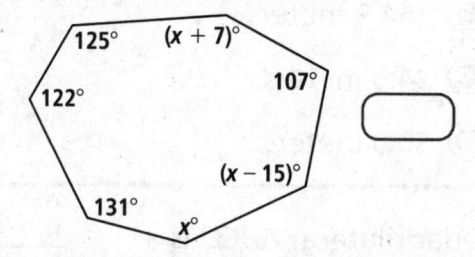

   (Heptagon with angles: 125°, (x + 7)°, 107°, (x − 15)°, x°, 131°, 122°)

Use Quadrilateral PQRS for Items 2–3.

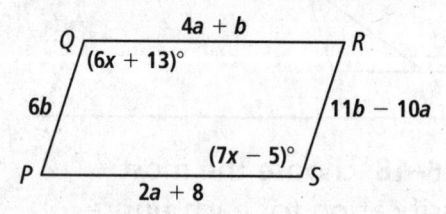

(Quadrilateral PQRS with: QR = 4a + b, angle Q = (6x + 13)°, PQ = 6b, RS = 11b − 10a, angle S = (7x − 5)°, PS = 2a + 8)

2. What must m∠QPS be for PQRS to be a parallelogram?

   Ⓐ 18
   Ⓑ 59
   Ⓒ 121
   Ⓓ not enough information

3. What must the values of a and b be for PQRS to be a parallelogram?

   a = ☐   b = ☐

4. The diagonals of parallelogram ABCD intersect at P. Select all the statements that must be true.

   ☐ A. $\overline{AP} \cong \overline{CP}$
   ☐ B. $\overline{BC} \cong \overline{AD}$
   ☐ C. m∠ABC = 90
   ☐ D. ∠CAD ≅ ∠ACB
   ☐ E. ∠BPC ≅ ∠APD

5. Given parallelogram ABCD, in order to prove that opposite sides are congruent, what additional segments or points will you need?

   Ⓐ both diagonals
   Ⓑ one diagonal
   Ⓒ the midpoints of each side
   Ⓓ none of the above

6. The diagonals of quadrilateral WXYZ intersect at R. If R is the midpoint of $\overline{WY}$ and $\overline{XZ}$, and WR = XR, what is the most specific quadrilateral that WXYZ can be?

   Ⓐ parallelogram   Ⓒ trapezoid
   Ⓑ rhombus   Ⓓ rectangle

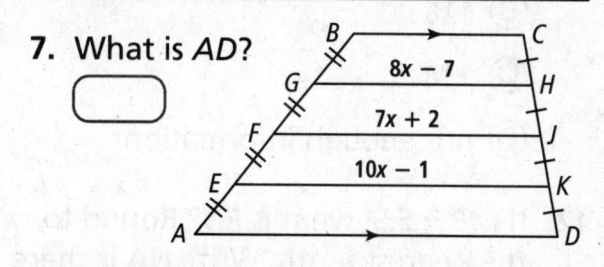

7. What is AD?

   ☐

   (Trapezoid ABCD with parallel segments; BC = 8x − 7, GH = 7x + 2, FJ (middle) labeled, EK = 10x − 1, AD is bottom)

8. What is the perimeter of FGHJ?

   (Rhombus-like quadrilateral FGHJ with diagonals; segments labeled 9, 4, 4, 6)

   Ⓐ $4\sqrt{13} + 2\sqrt{97}$
   Ⓑ 34
   Ⓒ $8\sqrt{2} + 6\sqrt{13}$
   Ⓓ not enough information

Use Parallelogram ABCD for Items 9–10.

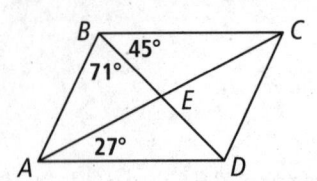

9. What is m∠BAC? ☐

10. If BE = 2x + 2, BD = 5x − 3, and AE = 4x − 6, what are the values of x and AC?

    x = ☐   AC = ☐

Use Quadrilateral MNPQ for Items 11–12.

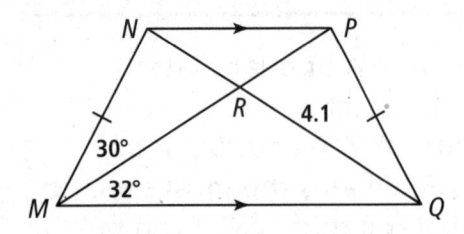

11. What is m∠NPQ?

    Ⓐ 62
    Ⓑ 116
    Ⓒ 118
    Ⓓ not enough information

12. If MP = 5.9, what is RN? Round to the nearest tenth. Write NA if there is not enough information given.

    RN = ☐

13. Select all the statements that are true about square EFGH.

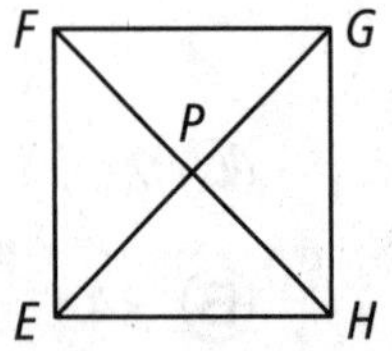

    ☐ A. FP = 2(EG)
    ☐ B. EP = EH
    ☐ C. EP = GP
    ☐ D. GP = HP
    ☐ E. m∠EFH = 45

14. A rectangle with area 1800 sq m is 3 times as long as it is wide. What is the sum of the diagonals? Round to the nearest tenth.

    Ⓐ 77.5 meters
    Ⓑ 154.9 meters
    Ⓒ 24.5 meters
    Ⓓ 50.0 meters

15. Quadrilateral ABCD is a parallelogram. What is BC? ☐

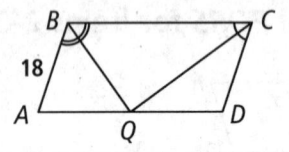

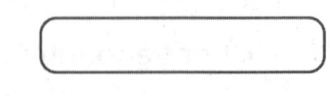

For Items 16–18, choose the most precise classification for each figure.

(parallelogram) (quadrilateral)
(rectangle)   (rhombus)
(square)   (trapezoid)

16. 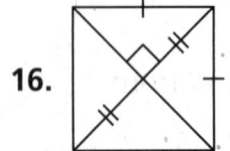 ☐

17. 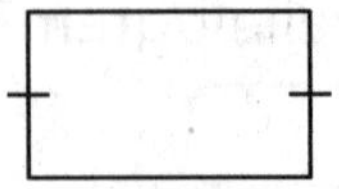 ☐

18. 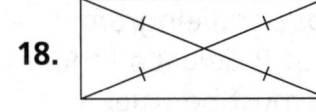 ☐

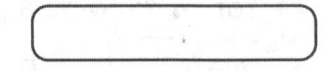

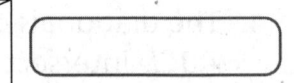

19. What is the measure of an interior angle of a regular 10-gon?

    Ⓐ 80   Ⓒ 216
    Ⓑ 36   Ⓓ 144

Name _____

6 Topic Assessment Form B

1. What is the value of x?

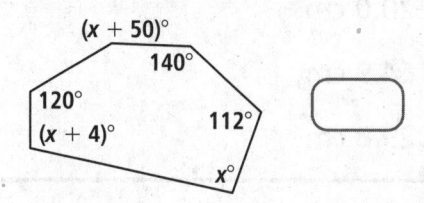

   (x + 50)°, 140°, 120°, (x + 4)°, 112°, x°

   ☐

Use Quadrilateral ABCD for Items 2–3.

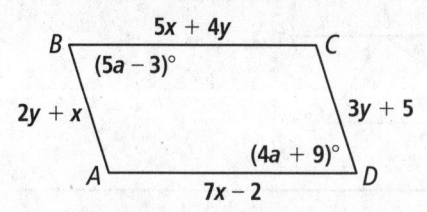

   B — 5x + 4y — C
   (5a − 3)°
   2y + x
   3y + 5
   A — 7x − 2 — D
   (4a + 9)°

2. What must m∠BCD be for ABCD to be a parallelogram?

   Ⓐ 12
   Ⓑ 57
   Ⓒ 123
   Ⓓ not enough information

3. What must the values of x and y be for ABCD to be a parallelogram?

   x = ☐   y = ☐

4. The diagonals of parallelogram WXYZ intersect at D. Select all the statements that must be true.

   ☐ A. $\overline{XD} \cong \overline{YD}$
   ☐ B. $\overline{XD} \cong \overline{ZD}$
   ☐ C. ∠WXZ ≅ ∠YZX
   ☐ D. $\overline{XZ} \cong \overline{WY}$
   ☐ E. ∠XDY ≅ ∠WDZ

5. Given trapezoid ABCD, in order to prove that there are two distinct pairs of supplementary angles, what additional segments or points will you need?

   Ⓐ both diagonals
   Ⓑ one diagonal
   Ⓒ the midpoints of each side
   Ⓓ none of the above

6. The diagonals of quadrilateral JKLM intersect at A. If $\overline{KL} \cong \overline{JM}$, $\overline{JK} \cong \overline{LM}$, $\overline{KA} \cong \overline{MA}$, and $\overline{KM} \perp \overline{JL}$, what is the most specific quadrilateral that JKLM can be?

   Ⓐ kite   Ⓒ parallelogram
   Ⓑ rectangle   Ⓓ rhombus

7. What is WZ? ☐

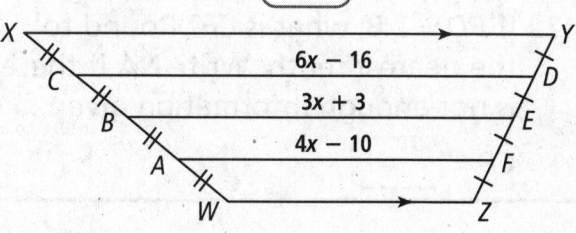

   X ————————————— Y
   C   6x − 16   D
   B   3x + 3   E
   A   4x − 10   F
   W ————————————— Z

8. What is the perimeter of PQRS?

   Q, 5, 12, 9, P, R, 5, S

   Ⓐ 119
   Ⓑ 26 + 2√106
   Ⓒ 13 + √106
   Ⓓ not enough information

Use Parallelogram JKLM for Items 9–10.

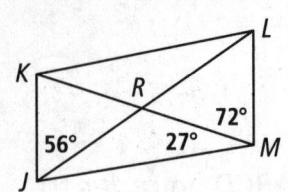

9. What is m∠LJM? ☐

10. If KR = x + 7, KM = 3x − 5, and JL = 4x − 10, what are the values of x and JR?

    x = ☐   JR = ☐

Use Quadrilateral ABCD for Items 11–12.

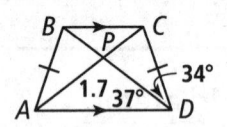

11. What is m∠ABC?
    - Ⓐ 71
    - Ⓑ 109
    - Ⓒ 106
    - Ⓓ not enough information

12. If BD = 2.8, what is CP? Round to the nearest tenth. Write NA if there is not enough information given.

    CP = ☐

13. Select all the statements that are true about rhombus MNPQ. 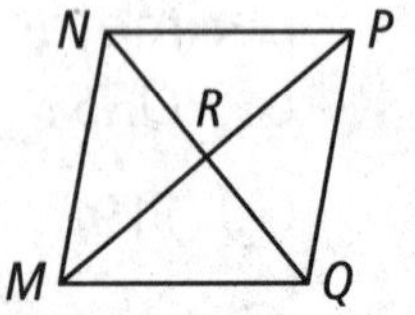
    - ☐ A. NP = MQ
    - ☐ B. NR = QR
    - ☐ C. NR = NP
    - ☐ D. ∠MNQ ≅ ∠PNQ
    - ☐ E. NQ = MP

14. A rectangle with area 6400 sq cm is 4 times as long as it is wide. What is the sum of the diagonals? Round to the nearest tenth.
    - Ⓐ 160 cm
    - Ⓑ 320.0 cm
    - Ⓒ 164.9 cm
    - Ⓓ 329.8 cm

15. WXYZ is a parallelogram. What is m∠DZW? ☐

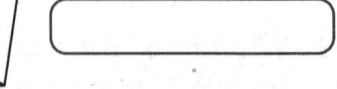

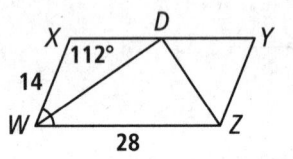

For Items 16–18, choose the most precise classification for each figure.

parallelogram   quadrilateral
rectangle   rhombus
square   trapezoid

16. 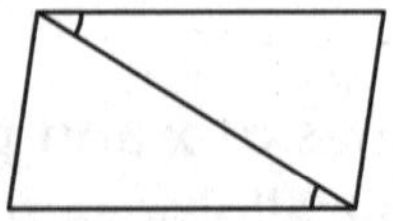 ☐

17. 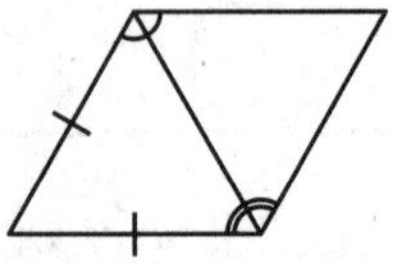 ☐

18. 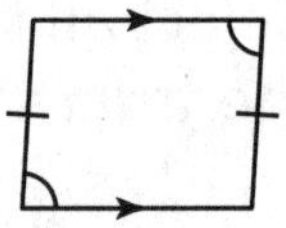 ☐

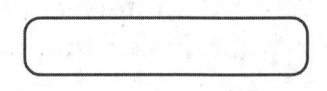

19. What is the measure of an interior angle of a regular 12-gon?
    - Ⓐ 112.5
    - Ⓑ 216
    - Ⓒ 30
    - Ⓓ 150

6 Performance Assessment Form A

Kimberly, Richard, and Cindy are helping design a tiled entrance and the parking lot for a new building.

Kimberly selected the tile shown in the diagram, with measurements in inches.

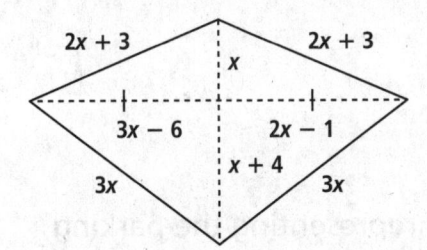

```
         2x + 3          2x + 3
                  x
      ---+------+------+---
         3x − 6    2x − 1
                  x + 4
         3x              3x
```

1. What is the most descriptive name for the tile? Justify your answer.

2. Find x.

3. What is the length of each longer side? What is the length of each shorter side?

Richard could not decide on one tile, so he selected several, all of which can be modeled as quadrilateral ABCD.

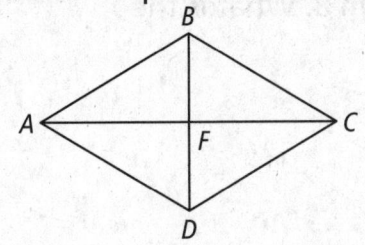

```
            B
        A ──F── C
            D
```

4. Suppose one of the selected tiles represented as ABCD is a parallelogram. How can you prove ABCD is a rectangle by comparing another segment to $\overline{BD}$?

5. Suppose one of the selected tiles represented as ABCD is a rhombus. How can you prove that ABCD is a square using the segment $\overline{AD}$?

For the parking lot, Kimberly, Richard, and Cindy decide to angle the parking spaces, as shown in the diagram, with lengths measured in feet. Cindy wants to find the size of a parking space.

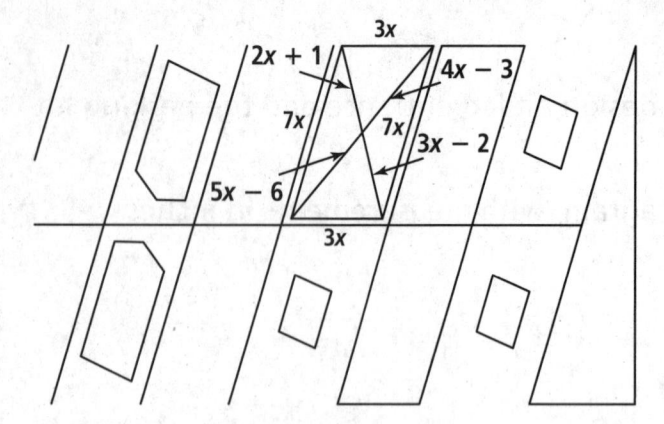

6. What is the most descriptive name for the figure representing the parking space? Explain.

7. Find x.

8. What is the length of the longer side? What is the length of the shorter side?

9. Cindy wants to know the measure of the angle that the sides of the parking space make with the center dividing line. She finds a table of dimension specifications. Use the table and your answers to Item 8. What is the parking angle?

Parking Angle	Space Width	Space Length
90°	9'	18'0"
60°	9'	21'0"
45°	9'	19'10"
30°	9'	16'10"

Name _____

6 Performance Assessment Form B

Tyler found this diagram of a tiered, raised-bed garden in a book. From the diagram, Tyler thinks that both ACEG and BDFH are parallelograms.

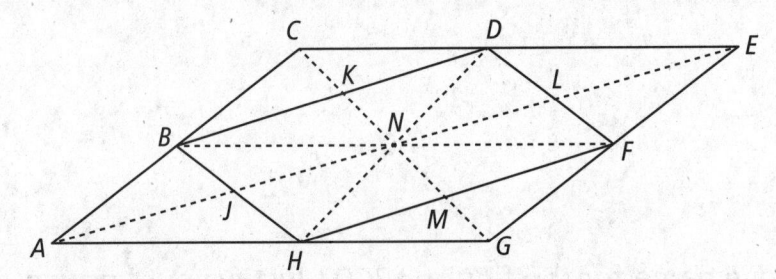

1. If BDFH is a parallelogram, what is true about $\overline{KN}$ and $\overline{MN}$? Explain.

2. If ACEG is a parallelogram, how could you show that ACEG is a square? Explain.

3. If ACEG is a parallelogram, how could you show that ACEG is a rhombus? Explain.

Tyler makes another drawing by rotating the inner quadrilateral. He likes his new garden diagram better. The ratio of each outer side to the corresponding inner side is 5 to 2, and the labels represent the lengths of the sides, measured in inches.

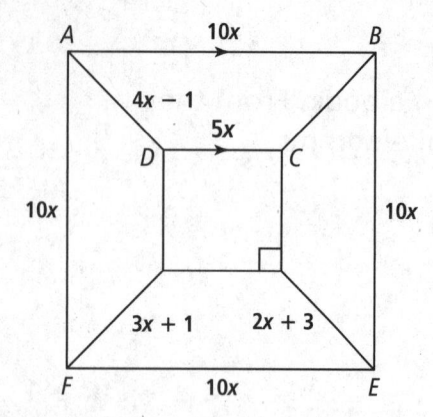

4. What is the most descriptive name for the figure ABCD? Justify your answer.

5. Find x.

6. What is AB? What is CD?

7. What is the most descriptive name of ABEF? Justify your answer.

8. What is true of the diagonals of ABEF?

9. What is the measure of the angle in each pair of base angles of ABCD? How are these two angles related?

10. How could you fit two trapezoid tiles together to make a parallelogram? How do you know you've made a parallelogram?

Name _____

Benchmark Assessment 3

1. The perpendicular bisector of $\overline{FN}$ is $\overline{AB}$. What is the length of $\overline{AN}$?

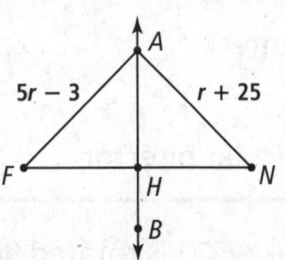

   (Triangle with A at top, F and N at base, H on FN, B below. $5r - 3$ on AF, $r + 25$ on AN.)

   Ⓐ 7   Ⓑ 11   Ⓒ 32   Ⓓ 57

2. [parallel] [perpendicular] [congruent]

   $\overline{AB}$ is parallel to $\overline{XY}$. $\overline{AB}$ and $\overline{XY}$ are reflected over the x-axis to form $\overline{A'B'}$ and $\overline{X'Y'}$. Complete the statement.

   $\overline{A'B'}$ is [ ] to $\overline{X'Y'}$.

3. Point C is $\frac{3}{4}$ of the way from point $A(-4, -2)$ to point $B(8, 6)$. What are the coordinates of C?

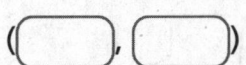

   ([ ] , [ ])

4. Transversal t passes through parallel lines p and s. What is the value of a?

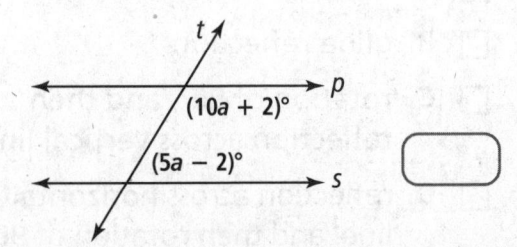

   (Figure showing transversal with angles $(10a + 2)°$ and $(5a - 2)°$)

5. Select all the true statement about the figure below.

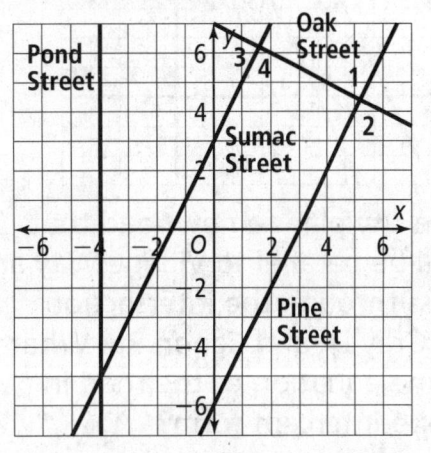

   (Graph showing Pond Street, Oak Street, Sumac Street, Pine Street with angles 1, 2, 3, 4)

   ☐ A. Sumac Street and Pine Street are parallel.
   ☐ B. Pond Street and Pine Street are parallel.
   ☐ C. ∠1 and ∠4 have the same measure.
   ☐ D. ∠1 and ∠2 have the same measure.
   ☐ E. ∠1 and ∠3 have the same measure.

6. Quadrilateral PQRS is a parallelogram. What is $m\angle KSP$?

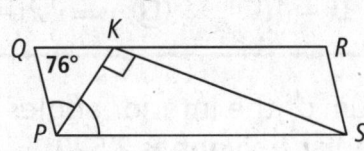

   (Parallelogram PQRS with K on QR, angle at Q is 76°, right angle at K)

   Ⓐ 38
   Ⓑ 52
   Ⓒ 76
   Ⓓ 104

For Items 7–8, use the map shown.

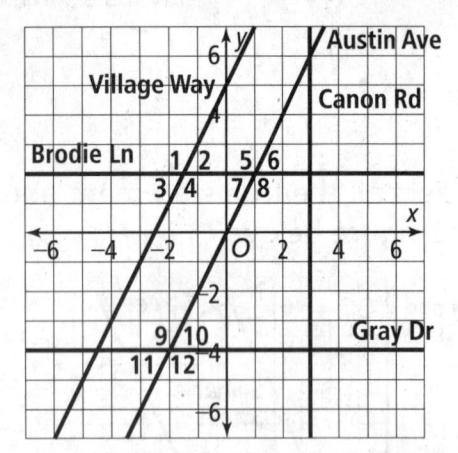

7. The city plans a new road that will be parallel to Village Way and pass through the intersection of Gray Dr and Canon Rd. What is the equation of the road in slope-intercept form?

   y = ☐ x − ☐

8. Let $m\angle 1 = x$. Select all the angles that have a measure of $180 - x$.
   - ☐ A. $\angle 3$
   - ☐ B. $\angle 4$
   - ☐ C. $\angle 5$
   - ☐ D. $\angle 10$
   - ☐ E. $\angle 11$

9. What is the equation of a line that is perpendicular to the line $y = -3x + 2$ and passes through the point (6, 8)?
   - Ⓐ $y = 3x + 2$
   - Ⓑ $y = 3x - 10$
   - Ⓒ $y = \frac{1}{3}x + 2$
   - Ⓓ $y = \frac{1}{3}x + 6$

10. If the sum of the interior angles of a regular polygon is 2,520°, how many sides does the polygon have? What is the measure of one interior angle?
    - Ⓐ 158 sides; 16.0
    - Ⓑ 112 sides; 22.5
    - Ⓒ 16 sides; 157.5
    - Ⓓ 12 sides; 205.7

11. What is being constructed in the sketch? 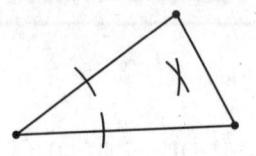
    - Ⓐ angle bisector
    - Ⓑ circumcenter
    - Ⓒ median
    - Ⓓ perpendicular bisector

12. Quadrilateral ABCD is rotated 90° clockwise to produce A'B'C'D'. Is each statement true?

	Yes	No
$AB = A'B'$	☐	☐
If $\overline{AC} \parallel \overline{BD}$, then $\overline{A'C'} \parallel \overline{B'D'}$.	☐	☐
$m\angle ABC < m\angle A'B'C'$	☐	☐

13. Represent the reflection across the y-axis using coordinates.

    $(x, y) \longrightarrow ($ ☐ $x,$ ☐ $y)$

14. Select all the rigid transformations that describe the preimage and image shown.

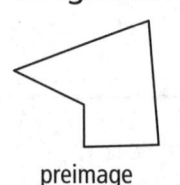

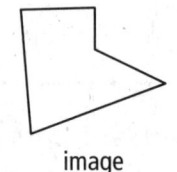

    preimage   image

    - ☐ A. rotation of 180°
    - ☐ B. glide reflection
    - ☐ C. rotation of 90°, and then reflection across vertical line
    - ☐ D. reflection across horizontal line, and then rotation of 90°
    - ☐ E. reflection across vertical line, and then reflection across horizontal line

15. The rule $T_{\langle -3, 1 \rangle}$ is applied to point (2, −7). In which part of the coordinate system is the translated point located?

Ⓐ quadrant I Ⓒ quadrant III
Ⓑ quadrant II Ⓓ quadrant IV

16. Part A

Which triangle is congruent to $\triangle PQR$?

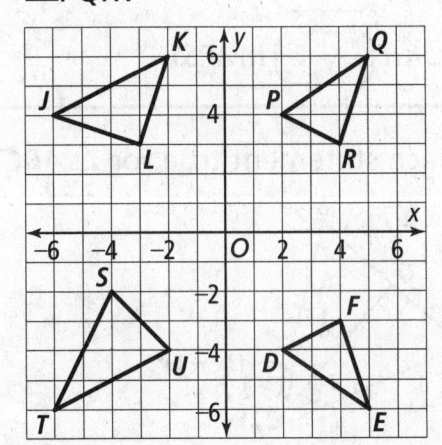

Ⓐ $\triangle STU$ Ⓒ $\triangle DEF$
Ⓑ $\triangle JKL$ Ⓓ none

Part B

State which measures are equal.

PQ = ☐ DE ☐ DF ☐ JL ☐ SU

QR = ☐ KL ☐ ST ☐ JL ☐ EF

RP = ☐ JL ☐ SU ☐ DF ☐ KL

17. Are $\overline{QP}$ and $\overline{ST}$ parallel? Why or why not?

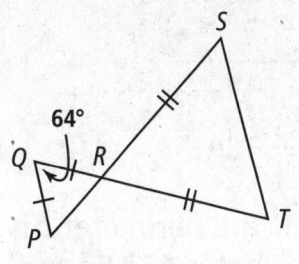

Ⓐ No; $m\angle P \neq m\angle T$
Ⓑ No; $m\angle S \neq m\angle P$ and $m\angle Q \neq m\angle T$
Ⓒ Yes; $m\angle S = m\angle P$ and $m\angle Q = m\angle T$
Ⓓ Yes; $m\angle P = m\angle T$

18. What value of x would support the conclusion that $\triangle JKL \cong \triangle LMJ$ by AAS?

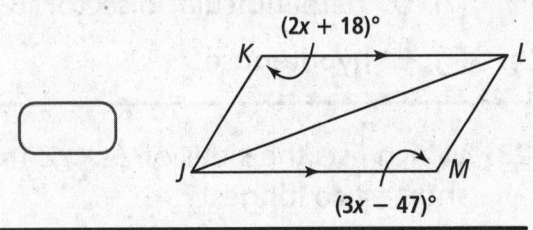

19. By which theorem can you conclude $\triangle DHF \cong \triangle EHG$?

Ⓐ ASA
Ⓑ HL
Ⓒ SAS
Ⓓ SSS

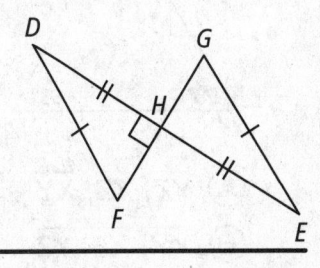

20. Which theorem of triangle congruence shows that $\triangle TUV \cong \triangle WVU$?

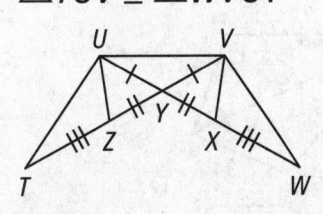

Ⓐ AAS   Ⓒ SAS
Ⓑ ASA   Ⓓ SSS

For Items 21–22, use △DEF.

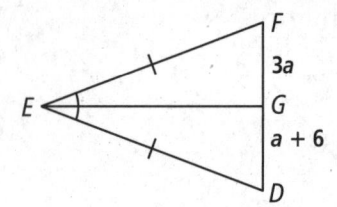

(Triangle DEF with F at top, D at bottom, E at left. G on segment FD with FG = 3a and GD = a + 6. Tick marks on EF and ED.)

21. What is DF? If the perimeter of △DEF is 58, what is EG? Round answers to the nearest tenth if necessary.

    DF = ☐   EG = ☐

22. Select all the statements that describe $\overline{EG}$.
    - ☐ A. median
    - ☐ B. angle bisector
    - ☐ C. altitude
    - ☐ D. perpendicular bisector
    - ☐ E. hypotenuse

23. Which lists the sides of △XYZ from shortest to longest?

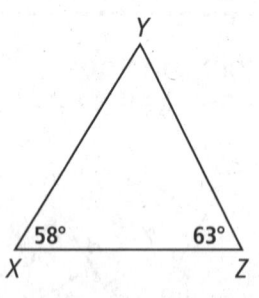

    (Triangle XYZ with angle X = 58°, angle Z = 63°.)

    Ⓐ $\overline{YZ}, \overline{XZ}, \overline{XY}$ Ⓒ $\overline{XZ}, \overline{YZ}, \overline{XY}$
    Ⓑ $\overline{XY}, \overline{XZ}, \overline{YZ}$ Ⓓ $\overline{XY}, \overline{YZ}, \overline{XZ}$

24. What is the range of possible values of x?

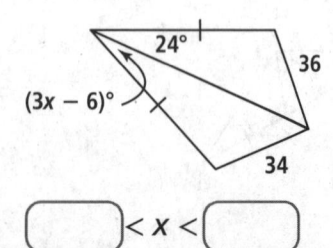

    (Quadrilateral-like figure with sides 36, 34, angle 24°, and angle $(3x-6)°$.)

    ☐ < x < ☐

25. Given KR < JS, complete the comparisons.

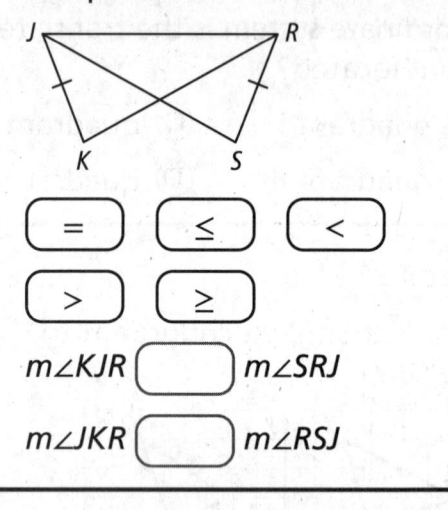

    (Figure with J and R at top, K and S at bottom, segments JS and KR crossing.)

    Options: =, ≤, <, >, ≥

    m∠KJR ☐ m∠SRJ

    m∠JKR ☐ m∠RSJ

26. Is each statement true for △ABC?

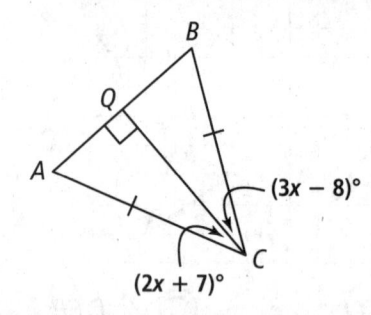

    (Triangle ABC with point Q inside, segments from Q forming right angle at Q on AB, angles $(3x-8)°$ and $(2x+7)°$ at C.)

	Yes	No
x = 15	☐	☐
$\overline{CQ}$ bisects ∠ACB.	☐	☐
$\overline{CQ}$ is the perpendicular bisector of $\overline{AB}$.	☐	☐
m∠QCB = 26	☐	☐

27. A triangle has vertices at (–4, 0), (2, 8), and (8, 0). Complete the table. Write answers as decimals rounded to the nearest hundredth, when necessary.

	x	y
coordinates of centroid	☐	☐
coordinates of circumcenter	☐	☐
coordinates of orthocenter	☐	☐

28. A triangle has two sides with lengths 31 centimeters and 39 centimeters. Which best describes the length of the third side?

   Ⓐ less than 8 cm
   Ⓑ greater than 70 cm
   Ⓒ less than 8 cm or greater than 70 cm
   Ⓓ greater than 8 cm and less than 70 cm

29. In order to construct a circumscribed triangle, you must find the

   ☐ centroid
   ☐ circumcenter   of the triangle.
   ☐ incenter
   ☐ orthocenter

   To do that you must construct two of the

   ☐ altitudes
   ☐ angle bisectors
   ☐ medians
   ☐ perpendicular bisectors

   of the triangle.

30. What are the perimeter and area of △XYZ?

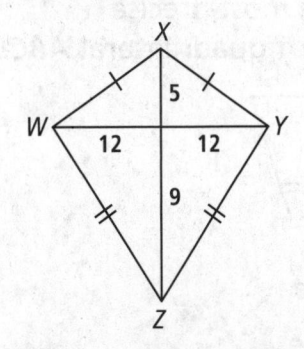

   Ⓐ $P = 28$; $A = 540$
   Ⓑ $P = 42$; $A = 84$
   Ⓒ $P = 50$; $A = 216$
   Ⓓ $P = 54$; $A = 57$

31. Quadrilateral JKLM is an isosceles trapezoid. Write each length or angle measure.

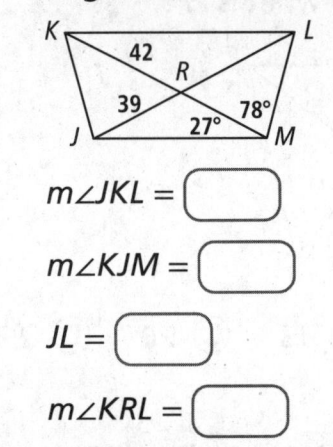

   $m\angle JKL = \boxed{}$

   $m\angle KJM = \boxed{}$

   $JL = \boxed{}$

   $m\angle KRL = \boxed{}$

32. Match each figure to the type of symmetry it has. A figure may have one type of symmetry, both types of symmetry, or neither types of symmetry.

	Reflectional	Rotational
	☐	☐
	☐	☐
	☐	☐
	☐	☐

33. What is the value of a?

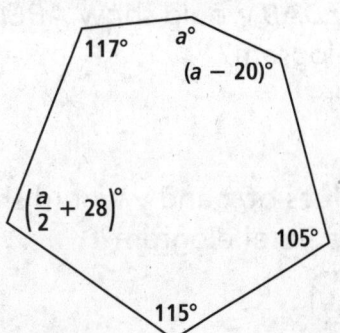

   Ⓐ 113
   Ⓑ 150
   Ⓒ 210
   Ⓓ 330

34. Part A

Given parallelogram DEFG, if DF = 5x + 1, what is PF?

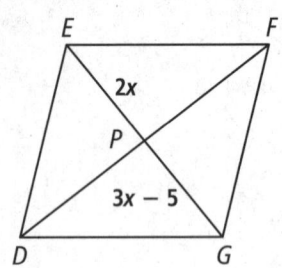

(diagram: parallelogram DEFG with diagonals intersecting at P; EP segment labeled 2x, PG labeled 3x − 5)

Ⓐ 10   Ⓑ 13   Ⓒ 20   Ⓓ 26

Part B

Is EG ⊥ DF? Why or why not?

Ⓐ No; the diagonals are not congruent, so DEFG is not a rhombus.

Ⓑ Yes; the diagonals are congruent, so DEFG is a rhombus.

Ⓒ Yes; diagonals are always perpendicular in parallelograms.

Ⓓ Impossible to tell; not enough information is given.

For Items 35–36, use quadrilateral ABCD.

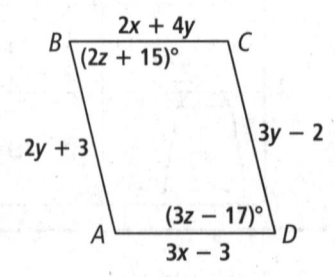

(diagram: quadrilateral ABCD with BC = 2x + 4y, angle B = (2z + 15)°, CD = 3y − 2, angle D = (3z − 17)°, AD = 3x − 3, AB = 2y + 3)

35. What m∠DAB would show ABCD is a parallelogram?

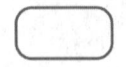

☐

36. What values of x and y would show ABCD is a parallelogram?

x = ☐

y = ☐

---

37. Is the statement true for all rectangles?

	Yes	No
Diagonals are congruent.	☐	☐
Diagonals bisect opposite angles.	☐	☐
Diagonals are perpendicular.	☐	☐

38. Which expression represents the perimeter of a rhombus with diagonal lengths 8a and 10a?

Ⓐ $3\sqrt{a}$

Ⓑ $a\sqrt{41}$

Ⓒ $12\sqrt{a}$

Ⓓ $4a\sqrt{41}$

39. If XZ ⊥ WY, XE = 4, and WY = 7, what is the perimeter of WXYZ, rounded to the nearest tenth?

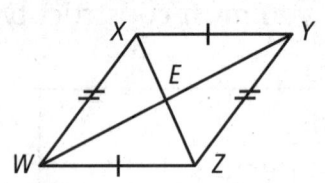

(diagram: rhombus WXYZ with diagonals meeting at E)

Ⓐ 5.3

Ⓑ 8.1

Ⓒ 21.3

Ⓓ 32.2

40. Which is the most precise description of quadrilateral ABCD?

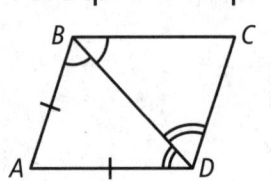

(diagram: quadrilateral ABCD)

Ⓐ rhombus

Ⓑ rectangle

Ⓒ quadrilateral

Ⓓ parallelogram

7 Readiness Assessment

1. Given $A(5, -2)$, what are the coordinates of the image of A after a reflection across the x-axis?
   - Ⓐ $(-2, 5)$
   - Ⓑ $(-5, 2)$
   - Ⓒ $(-5, -2)$
   - Ⓓ $(5, 2)$

2. On a map, the scale is 1 inch = 12 miles. If the distance between two towns on the map is 4.5 inches, what is the actual distance between the two towns?
   - Ⓐ 30 miles
   - Ⓑ 45 miles
   - Ⓒ 54 miles
   - Ⓓ 60 miles

3. Six out of every 9 households have a guest room. Margaret asked x households in her neighborhood if they have a guest room, and 24 said yes. Find x.
   - Ⓐ 16
   - Ⓑ 30
   - Ⓒ 36
   - Ⓓ 40

4. A dilation with center $(0, 0)$ and scale factor 2 maps $\triangle ABC$ to $\triangle DEF$. Which best compares $m\angle B$ to $m\angle E$?
   - Ⓐ $m\angle B = 2(m\angle E)$
   - Ⓑ $m\angle E = 2(m\angle B)$
   - Ⓒ $m\angle B = m\angle E$
   - Ⓓ $m\angle E = 180 - m\angle B$

5. Triangle DEF has coordinates $D(1, 1)$, $E(1, 5)$, and $F(5, 1)$. Triangle $D'E'F'$ is the image of $\triangle DEF$ by a dilation with center $(0, 0)$ and scale factor of 7. What is $D'F'$? ⬚

6. A rigid transformation preserves ⬚ and ⬚.

7. A 90° rotation about the origin followed by a reflection across the line $x = 3$ maps $\triangle JKL$, with coordinates $J(-2, 2)$, $K(-2, 6)$, and $L(-8, 2)$, to $\triangle PQR$. Find the area of $\triangle PQR$. ⬚ square units

8. In triangle $\triangle ABC$, $m\angle A = 50$, $AB = 4.5$ cm, and $m\angle B = 73$. $\triangle ABC$ is ASA congruent with $\triangle DEF$. Find each measure.
   $DE = $ ⬚ cm $m\angle F = $ ⬚

9. In the figure shown, $m\angle 1 = 5x - 9$ and $m\angle 2 = 2x - 6$.

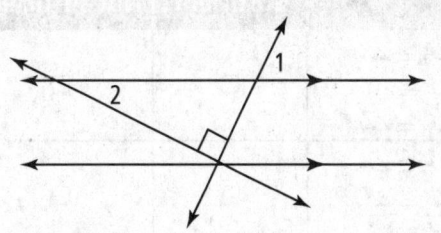

   Find the measures of $\angle 1$ and $\angle 2$.
   $m\angle 1 = $ ⬚ $m\angle 2 = $ ⬚

10. Triangles ABC and $A'B'C'$ are similar, but not congruent. Which transformation(s) could map $\triangle ABC$ to $\triangle A'B'C'$?

Transformation	Yes	No
dilation with factor 2	☐	☐
reflection	☐	☐
rotation	☐	☐
translation	☐	☐

11. Quadrilateral *RSTU* is graphed. Its image (partially graphed) is a rotation 180° about point *T*. What are the coordinates of *S'*?

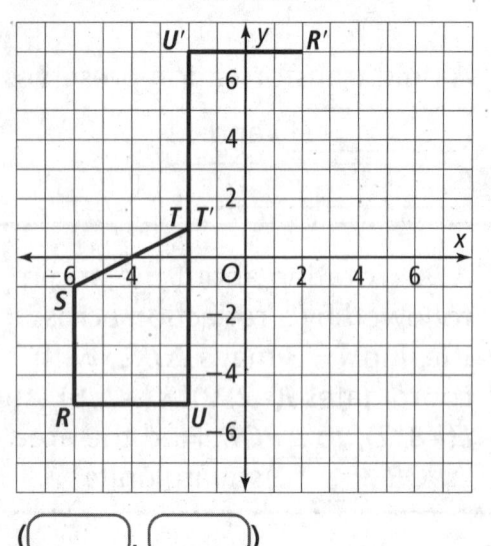

(◯ , ◯)

12. △*ABC* has been transformed through rigid transformations and its image is compared to △*XYZ*. Determine whether each set of given information is sufficient to make △*ABC* ≅ △*XYZ*.

	Sufficient	Not sufficient
∠A ≅ ∠X, ∠B ≅ ∠Y, ∠C ≅ ∠Z	☐	☐
∠A ≅ ∠X, ∠B ≅ ∠Y, $\overline{BC}$ ≅ $\overline{YZ}$	☐	☐
∠C ≅ ∠Z, $\overline{AB}$ ≅ $\overline{XY}$, $\overline{BC}$ ≅ $\overline{YZ}$	☐	☐

13. What is the value of *p*?
$\frac{45}{20} = \frac{40.5}{p}$ ◯

14. A translation followed by a rotation maps quadrilateral *ABCD* to quadrilateral *EFGH*. If m∠*BCD* = 27.9, what is m∠*FGH*?

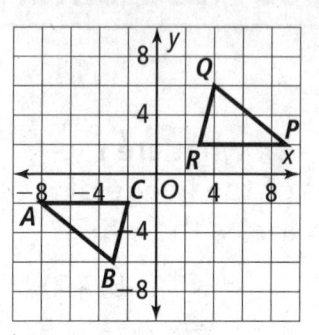

◯

15. Consider △*ABC* and △*PQR* in the figure.

The two triangles are congruent because there exists a sequence of rigid transformations that maps one triangle to the other triangle.

Select the two transformations that combine to map △*ABC* to △*PQR*.

☐ A. translation 1 unit up

☐ B. rotation of 180° about the origin

☐ C. reflection across the *x*-axis

☐ D. reflection across the *y*-axis

☐ E. translation 1 unit to the right

☐ F. rotation of 90° about the origin

16. △*ABC* is an isosceles triangle. Each horizontal line is the bisector of two sides of a triangle. How long is $\overline{MN}$?

◯ cm

Name _____

7-1 Lesson Quiz
Dilations

1. Given that △A'B'C' is a dilation of △ABC, how are the angles and side lengths of the preimage related to the angles and side lengths of the image?

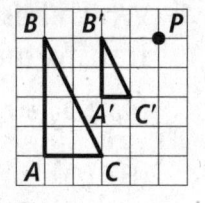

   Ⓐ The angles are congruent and the side lengths are congruent.

   Ⓑ The angles are congruent and the side lengths are proportional.

   Ⓒ The angles are proportional and the side lengths are congruent.

   Ⓓ The angles are proportional and the side lengths are proportional.

2. What is the scale factor of the dilation shown?

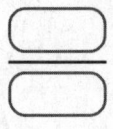

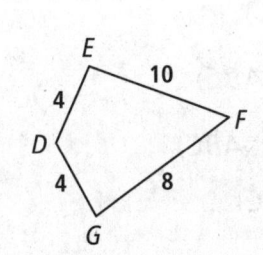

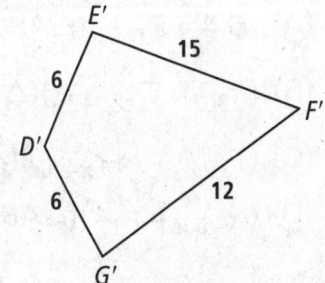

   ▢/▢

3. What are the coordinates of R' for the dilation $D_{(0.5, P)}(\square PQRS)$?

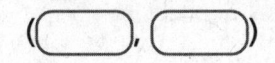

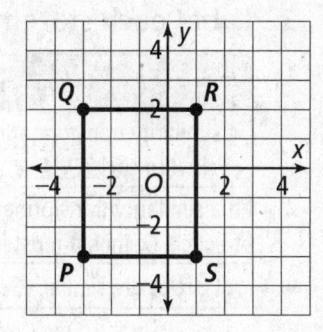

   (▢, ▢)

4. The vertices of △JKL are J(−3, −2), K(1, 4), and L(4, 2). Find the coordinate pairs of the vertices of D_5(△JKL).

   J' = (▢, ▢)

   K' = (▢, ▢)

   L' = (▢, ▢)

5. Graph $D_{\frac{1}{3}}$(WXYZ).

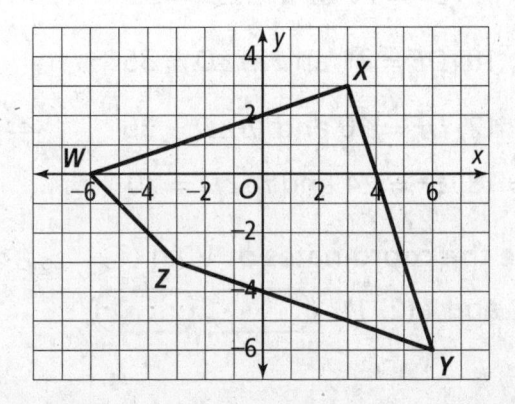

Name _____

7-2 Lesson Quiz

Similarity Transformations

1. Which best describes the composition of transformations that maps *JKLM* to *PQRS*?

    Ⓐ $(D_3 \circ r_n)(JKLM)$

    Ⓑ $(D_{\frac{1}{3}} \circ r_n)(JKLM)$

    Ⓒ $(D_3 \circ T_{<-2, -5>})(JKLM)$

    Ⓓ $(D_{\frac{1}{3}} \circ T_{<-2, -5>})(JKLM)$

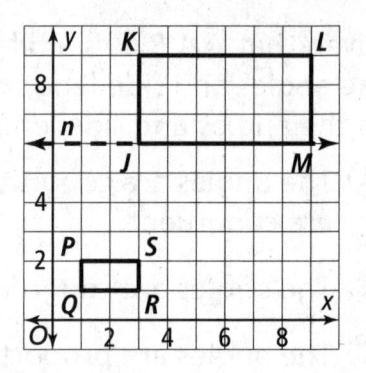

2. Which maps △*ABC* to a similar, but not congruent, triangle?

    Ⓐ $(D_4 \circ R_{180°})(\triangle ABC)$

    Ⓑ $(R_{90°} \circ T_{<2, -2>})(\triangle ABC)$

    Ⓒ $(T_{<2, -2>} \circ r_{x\text{-axis}})(\triangle ABC)$

    Ⓓ $(r_{x\text{-axis}} \circ r_{90°})(\triangle ABC)$

3. Label each statement True or False.

	True	False
A similarity transformation exists that maps circle *P* to circle *Q*.	❑	❑
If a similarity transformation maps circle *A* to circle *Q*, then it must include a rotation.	❑	❑
All circles are similar.	❑	❑

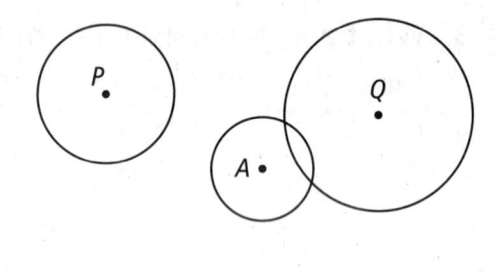

4. The triangles △*ABC* and △*DEF* appear to be similar.

    Which set of measurements prove that the two triangles are similar?

    Ⓐ $DE = 15$, $EF = 20$ and $m\angle D = 35$

    Ⓑ $DE = 16$, $DF = 21$ and $m\angle D = 35$

    Ⓒ $DE = 12$, $DF = 16$ and $m\angle D = 35$

    Ⓓ $DE = 18$, $EF = 24$ and $m\angle D = 70$

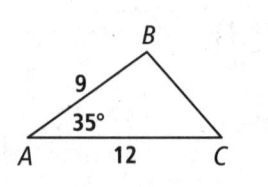

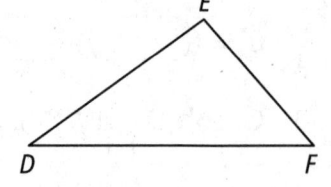

5. What are the coordinates of *V'* in $(T_{<3, -2>} \circ D_5)(\triangle TUV)$ if $T(-1, -1)$, $U(-1, 2)$, and $V(2, 1)$? (____ , ____)

enVision® Geometry • Assessment Sourcebook

7-3 Lesson Quiz

Proving Triangles Similar

1. For what value of x is △ABC ~ △DEF?

   x = ☐

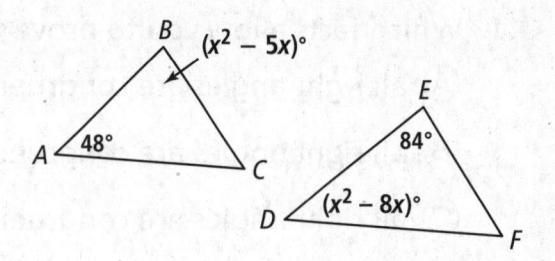

2. Which condition would prove △JKL ~ △XYZ?

   Ⓐ $\frac{JK}{XY} = \frac{1}{8}$ Ⓒ $\frac{KL}{YZ} = 8$

   Ⓑ $\frac{JL}{XZ} = \frac{1}{8}$ Ⓓ $\frac{JL}{XZ} = 8$

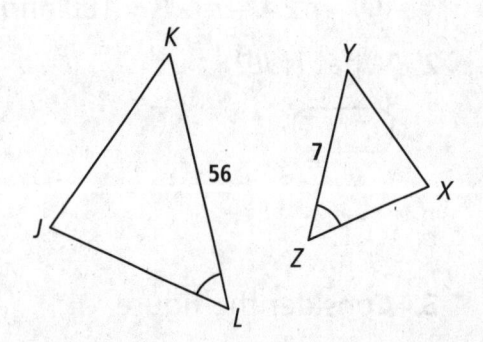

3. Given △FGH ~ △LMN, select all the statements that are true.

   ☐ A. $\frac{FG}{LM} = \frac{FH}{LN}$

   ☐ B. FH ~ LN

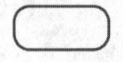

   ☐ C. $\frac{m\angle F}{m\angle L} = \frac{m\angle G}{m\angle M}$

   ☐ D. GH = MN

   ☐ E. m∠H = m∠N

4. Given △ACD ~ △CDF, what is FD?

   ☐

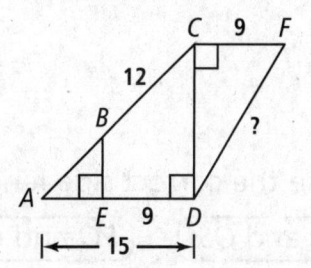

5. Given △PQR ~ △STU, find the missing measures in △STU.

SU	ST	TU	m∠S	m∠T	m∠U
6	☐	☐	☐	☐	☐

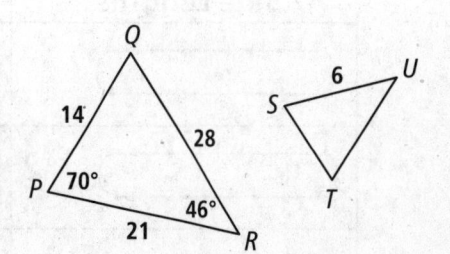

Name _____

7-4 Lesson Quiz

Similarity in Right Triangles

1. Which facts allow you to prove that △ABC ~ △CBD by AA~?

   Ⓐ all right angles are congruent and ∠C ≅ ∠C

   Ⓑ all right angles are congruent and ∠A ≅ ∠B

   Ⓒ all right angles are congruent and ∠B ≅ ∠B

   Ⓓ m∠A + m∠B = 180 and ∠B ≅ ∠B

2. What is JL?

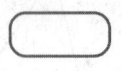

3. Consider the figure.

   What values should x and y have to complete the proportion $\frac{x}{a} = \frac{a}{y}$?

   x = ☐   y = ☐

4. Which triangles are similar to △ABE?

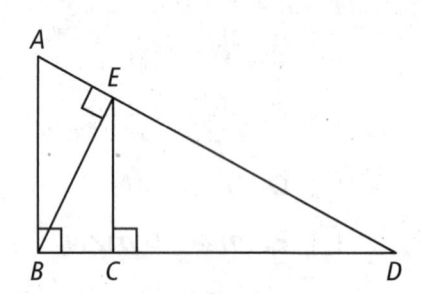

	Yes	No
△ADB	☐	☐
△EDC	☐	☐
△BEC	☐	☐
△BDE	☐	☐

5. Given △PQR, choose the correct side lengths to complete the table.

   (PS and QS)   (PR and QS)   (PQ and QS)   (PQ and PS)   (QR and QS)

Side Lengths	Geometric Mean
	RS
	PR
	QR

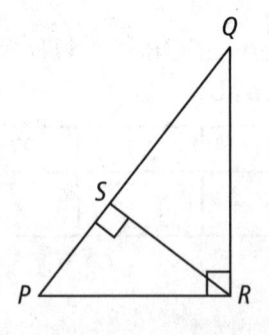

Name _____

7-5 Lesson Quiz

Proportions in Triangles

1. If LM = 6, what is the perimeter of △PKQ?

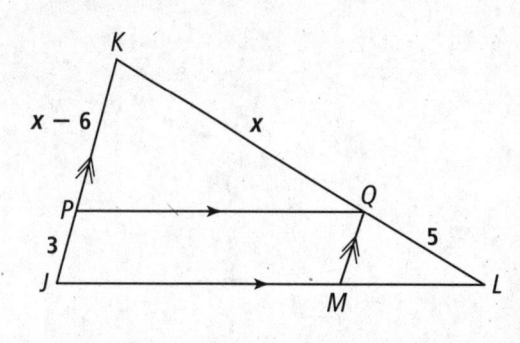

2. Find the perimeter, in inches, of ABHG. Round your answer to the nearest hundredth.

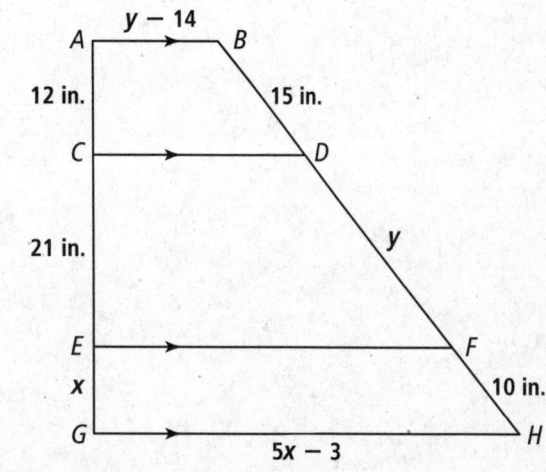

3. What is BD?

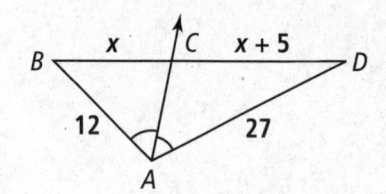

4. $\overline{YQ}$ and $\overline{XP}$ are altitudes to the congruent sides of isosceles triangle △WXY.

   Select all the true statements.

   ☐ A. $\dfrac{WQ}{XQ} = \dfrac{WY}{XY}$ ☐ D. $\dfrac{WQ}{QX} = \dfrac{WP}{PY}$

   ☐ B. YQ = XP ☐ E. $\overline{PQ}$ is parallel to $\overline{XY}$

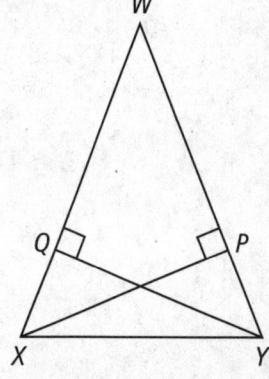

   ☐ C. m∠WXY = m∠WYX ☐ F. m∠PXY = m∠QYX

5. Given EP = FP and GQ = FQ, what is the perimeter of △EFG?

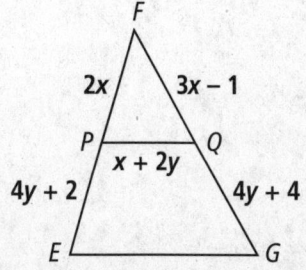

enVision® Geometry • Assessment Sourcebook

Name _____

7 Topic Assessment Form A

1. $D_{\frac{1}{3}}(\triangle ABC) = \triangle A'B'C'$ and $D_{\frac{3}{2}}(\triangle A'B'C') = \triangle A''B''C''$. What is the scale factor of the dilation between $\triangle ABC$ and $\triangle A''B''C''$?

   Ⓐ $\frac{2}{9}$ Ⓑ $\frac{1}{2}$ Ⓒ 2   Ⓓ $\frac{9}{2}$

2. Does the transformation preserve distance? Select Yes or No.

Transformation	Yes	No
Dilation by factor 2	☐	☐
Reflection across x-axis	☐	☐
Rotation about (0, 0)	☐	☐

3. What are the coordinates of the image of (1, 3), where $R(-3, 5)$ is the center of dilation with scale factor 0.5? (☐, ☐)

4. Graph $D_{\frac{1}{2}}(\triangle XYZ)$.

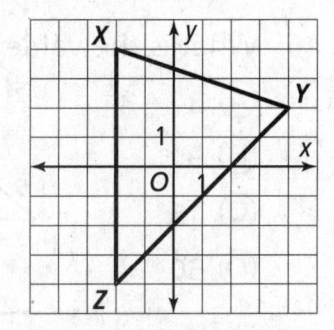

5. Pentagon EQUAL is similar to pentagon POINT.

   Since the pentagons are similar, there exists a
   ☐ dilation
   ☐ reflection
   ☐ rotation
   ☐ translation
   that maps EQUAL onto POINT.

6. Which best describes the sequence of transformations that maps $\triangle LMN$ to $\triangle L'M'N'$?

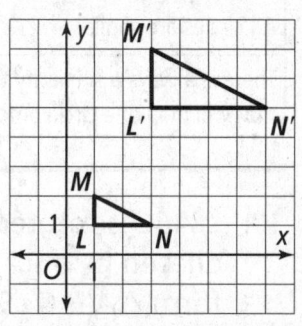

   ☐ dilation center O, scale factor 2
   ☐ dilation center O, scale factor $\frac{1}{2}$
   ☐ translation right 1 and up 3
   ☐ translation left 1 and down 2

   then

   ☐ dilation center O, scale factor 2
   ☐ dilation center O, scale factor $\frac{1}{2}$
   ☐ translation right 1 and up 3
   ☐ translation left 1 and down 2

   The triangles are ☐ congruent.
   ☐ similar.

7. What are the coordinates of X' for the transformation $(T_{\langle -3, 1 \rangle} \circ D_4)(\triangle TUX)$ of $T(-7, -6)$, $U(-8, 3)$, and $X(2, 1)$? (☐, ☐)

8. Which conclusion does the diagram support?

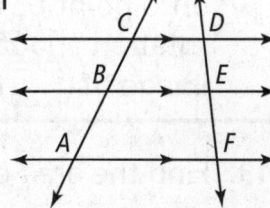

   Ⓐ $AF = \frac{1}{2}CD$
   Ⓑ $BE = \frac{1}{2}CD$
   Ⓒ $\frac{AB}{BC} = \frac{FE}{ED}$
   Ⓓ $\frac{BE}{CD} = \frac{AF}{BE}$

9. Select true or false.

	True	False
A similarity transformation that maps one circle onto another must include a rotation.	❏	❏
All circles are similar.	❏	❏
There is always a similarity transformation that will map one circle onto another.	❏	❏

10. △ABC is rotated 90° and then dilated by a scale factor of $\frac{1}{2}$ to form △A'B'C'. Select all that apply.

☐ A. ∠B ~ ∠B'
☐ B. ∠A ≅ ∠A'
☐ C. △ABC ~ △A'B'C'
☐ D. $\overline{AC}$ ~ $\overline{A'B'}$
☐ E. AB = 2A'B'

11. Which condition would prove △DEF ~ △JKL?

Ⓐ DE : JK = 1 : 3
Ⓑ DF : JL = 1 : 3
Ⓒ EF : KL = 3 : 1
Ⓓ DF : JL = 3 : 1

12. Complete the sentences.

[C] [D] [G] [J] [$\overline{CD}$] [$\overline{DE}$]

Given that $\frac{CD}{GH} = \frac{DE}{HJ} = \frac{CE}{GJ}$, you can prove △CDE ~ △GHJ by applying a translation that maps point ◯ onto point G. Then apply a rotation about ◯ that maps the image of ◯ onto $\overline{GH}$.

13. Find the area of △LKJ.

Ⓐ 108 sq. units
Ⓑ 300 sq. units
Ⓒ 165 sq. units
Ⓓ 150 sq. units

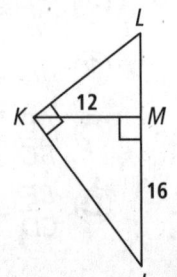

14. Select true or false.

	True	False
A dilation is the only transformation that results in congruent corresponding angles.	❏	❏
A dilation is a similarity transformation in which the corresponding sides are proportional.	❏	❏
A dilation is a similarity transformation in which the corresponding angles are proportional.	❏	❏

15. Which triangles are similar?

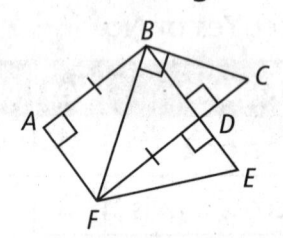

	True	False
△ABF ~ △DBC	❏	❏
△FBC ~ △FDE	❏	❏
△ABF ~ △FDE	❏	❏
△FDE ~ △DBC	❏	❏

16. What is the value of x?

Ⓐ 3
Ⓑ 9
Ⓒ 15
Ⓓ 30

17. The area of △QRS is 14 sq. ft. What is the area, in sq. ft, of the image of △QRS after dilation with scale factor 2? ◯

18. What is EG?

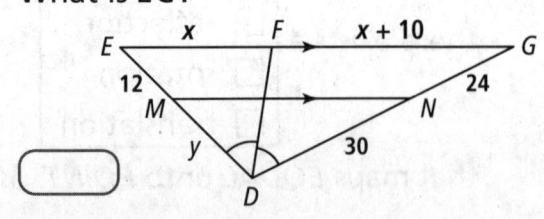

◯

Name _____

7 Topic Assessment Form B

1. $D_{\frac{2}{5}}(\triangle ABC) = \triangle A'B'C'$ and $D_{\frac{5}{3}}(\triangle A'B'C') = \triangle A''B''C''$. What is the scale factor of the dilation between $\triangle ABC$ and $\triangle A''B''C''$?

   Ⓐ $\frac{6}{25}$ Ⓑ $\frac{31}{15}$ Ⓒ $\frac{2}{3}$ Ⓓ $\frac{3}{2}$

2. Does the transformation preserve distance? Select Yes or No.

Transformation	Yes	No
Rotation about (2, 3)	☐	☐
Reflection across line $y = x$	☐	☐
Dilation by factor 0.5	☐	☐

3. What are the coordinates of the image of (2, 4), where $R(6, -2)$ is the center of dilation with scale factor 0.5? (☐ , ☐)

4. Graph $D_2(\triangle XYZ)$.

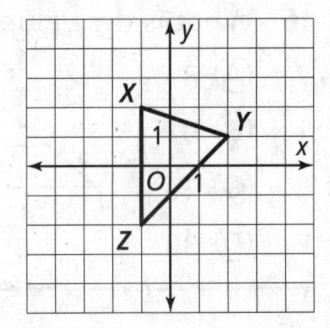

5. Quadrilateral QUAD is similar to quadrilateral PENT.

   Since the quadrilaterals are similar, there exists a
   ☐ reflection
   ☐ rotation
   ☐ dilation
   ☐ translation

   that maps QUAD onto PENT.

6. Which best describes the sequence of transformations that maps $\triangle LMN$ to $\triangle L'M'N'$?

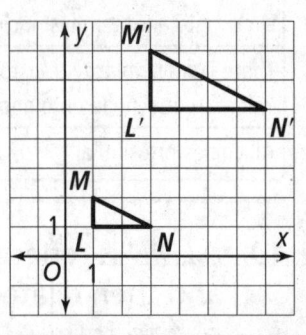

   ☐ translation right 1 and up 3
   ☐ translation left 1 and down 2
   ☐ dilation center O, scale factor 2
   ☐ dilation center O, scale factor $\frac{1}{2}$

   then

   ☐ translation right 1 and up 3
   ☐ translation left 1 and down 2
   ☐ dilation center O, scale factor 2
   ☐ dilation center O, scale factor $\frac{1}{2}$

   The triangles are ☐ similar.
   ☐ congruent.

7. What are the coordinates of U' for the transformation $(T_{\langle -3, 1 \rangle} \circ D_4)(\triangle TUV)$ of $T(-7, -6)$, $U(-8, 3)$, and $V(2, 1)$? (☐ , ☐)

8. Which conclusion does the diagram support?

   Ⓐ $\frac{BC}{AB} = \frac{ED}{FE}$

   Ⓑ $\frac{AB}{BC} = \frac{ED}{FE}$

   Ⓒ $\frac{BE}{CD} = \frac{AF}{BE}$

   Ⓓ $BE = \frac{1}{2}CD$

9. Select whether each statement is true or false.

	True	False
A similarity transformation that maps one circle onto another must include a reflection.	☐	☐
There is no similarity transformation that will map one circle onto another.	☐	☐
All circles are similar.	☐	☐

10. $\triangle LMN$ is reflected over the x-axis and then dilated by a scale factor of $\frac{2}{3}$ to form $\triangle L'M'N'$. Select all that apply.

☐ A. $\triangle LMN \sim \triangle L'M'N'$
☐ B. $\angle M \sim \angle M'$
☐ C. $\overline{MN} \sim \overline{L'M'}$
☐ D. $\angle L \cong \angle L'$
☐ E. $2LM = 3L'M'$

11. Which condition would prove $\triangle DEF \sim \triangle JKL$?

Ⓐ $EF : KL = 2 : 1$
Ⓑ $DF : JL = 2 : 1$
Ⓒ $DE : JK = 1 : 2$
Ⓓ $DF : JL = 1 : 2$

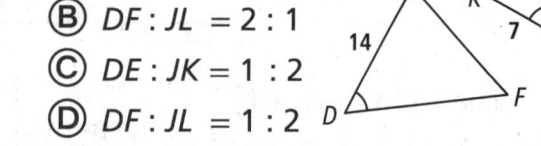

12. Complete the sentences.

[L] [M] [P] [R] [$\overline{LM}$] [$\overline{MN}$]

Given that $\frac{LM}{PQ} = \frac{MN}{QR} = \frac{LN}{PR}$, you can prove $\triangle LMN \sim \triangle PQR$ by applying a translation that maps point ◯ onto point P. Then apply a rotation about ◯ that maps the image of ◯ onto $\overline{PQ}$.

13. Find the area of $\triangle LKJ$.

Ⓐ 18.75 sq. units
Ⓑ 13.5 sq. units
Ⓒ 24 sq. units
Ⓓ 37.5 sq. units

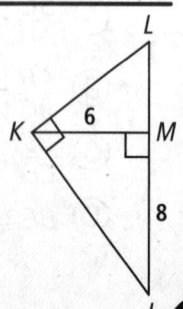

14. Select true or false.

	True	False
A dilation is a similarity transformation in which the corresponding angles are congruent.	☐	☐
A dilation is a similarity transformation in which the corresponding sides are congruent.	☐	☐
A dilation is the only transformation that results in congruent corresponding angles.	☐	☐

15. Which triangles are similar?

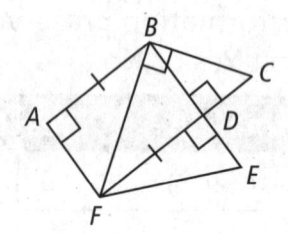

	True	False
$\triangle ABF \sim \triangle BFC$	☐	☐
$\triangle FBC \sim \triangle CDB$	☐	☐
$\triangle ABF \sim \triangle DBC$	☐	☐
$\triangle BCF \sim \triangle DBC$	☐	☐

16. What is the value of x?

Ⓐ 3
Ⓑ 9
Ⓒ 15
Ⓓ 30

17. The area of $\triangle QRS$ is 21 sq. ft. What is the area, in sq. ft, of the image of $\triangle QRS$ after dilation with scale factor 2? ◯

18. What is EG?

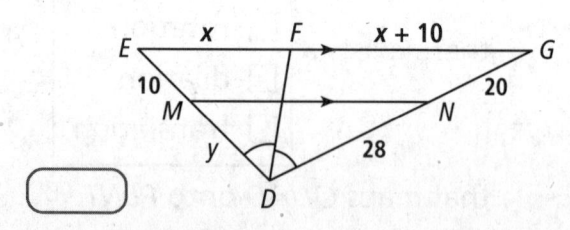

◯

Name _____

7 Performance Assessment Form A

Arthur's mother is a mechanical engineer. She is designing rectangular carts for moving finished goods from a factory's manufacturing floor to the loading dock, where the goods are placed on trucks.

She made a drawing showing where the carts must turn from a hallway 48 inches wide to pass through a doorway 36 inches wide. The drawing shows the longest cart that will pass through the doorway.

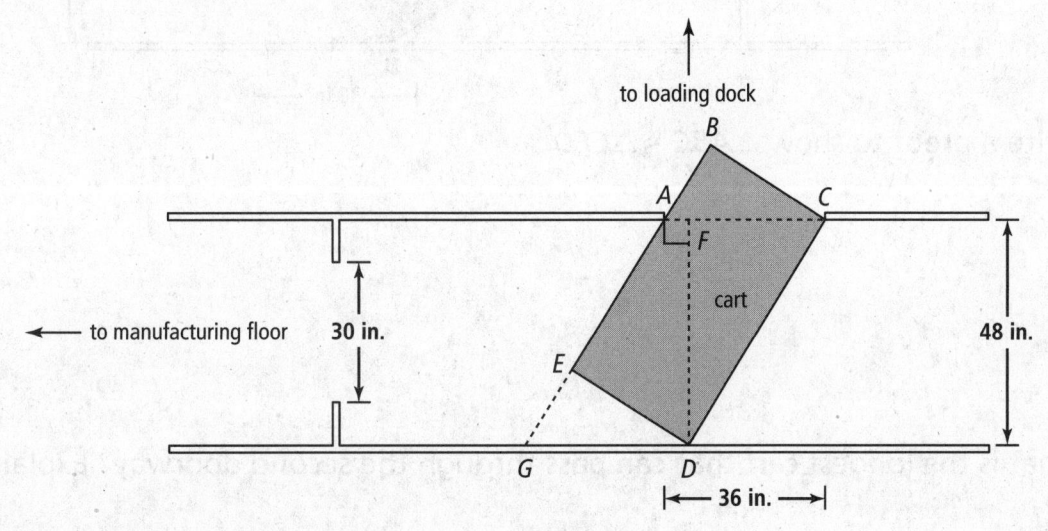

1. What kind of triangles are △ABC and △CFD?

2. In the drawing, one sixth of an inch represents 1 foot. What is the scale factor of the drawing? Explain.

The carts need to be as wide as possible. The widest cart that will pass through the doorway between the manufacturing floor and the loading dock is 30 inches wide. The carts also should be as long as possible so they can carry the largest quantity of finished goods per trip. Arthur tells his mother she can solve the problem using similarity.

3. The first similarity that Arthur's mother needs to determine is the similarity of △ABC and △GED. Write a proof to show △ABC ~ △GED.

4. What is the scale factor for △ABC ~ △GED? Are the triangles congruent? Explain.

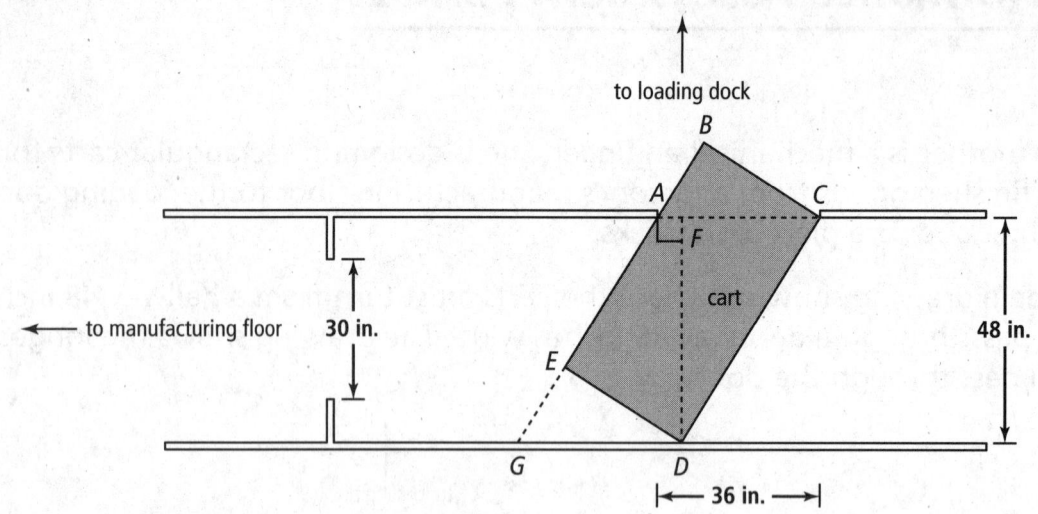

5. Write a proof to show △ABC ~ △CFD.

6. What is the longest cart that can pass through the second doorway? Explain.

Some of the factory's products are long fragile rods that are carried through the door by hand. The first door is 72 inches west of the start of the second door. Assume the rod has zero width and BA = 13 in.

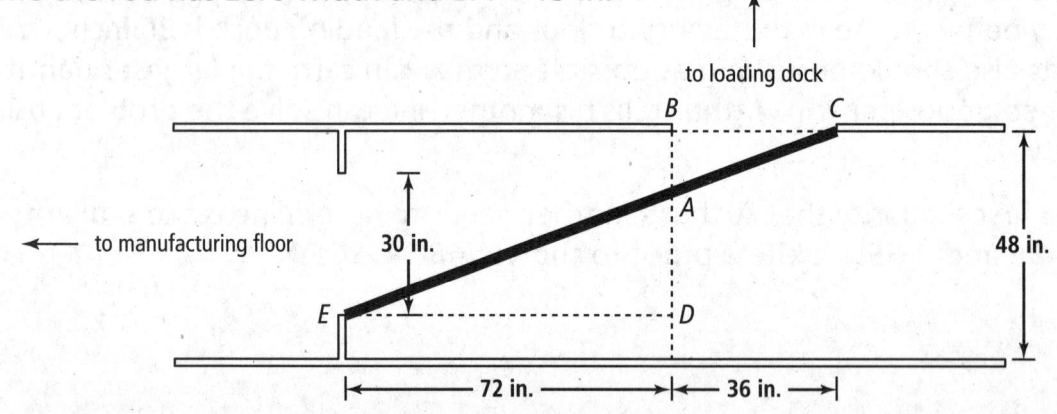

7. What is the longest rod that can be carried to the loading dock? Round to the nearest tenth of an inch.

Name _____

7 Performance Assessment Form B

Jamie is helping his aunt make kites to sell at a craft fair. Jamie's aunt gave him stacks of four different sizes of nylon triangles. She asked him to sew them into kites. She told him that he needs to use at least four triangles for each kite, and the kites must meet the requirements shown in the figure.

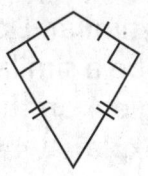

He also needs to make pockets on the back of the kite so he can secure rods along the diagonals of the kite for structure. Then he needs to sew reflective trim around the perimeter of the kite.

Jamie took a few measurements from these four triangle shapes:

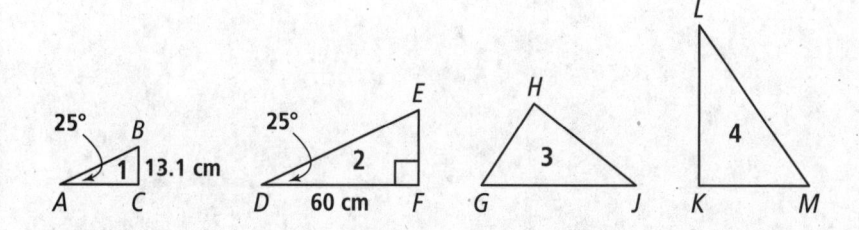

25° B
∠1 13.1 cm
A   C

25° E
  2
D 60 cm F

H
3
G   J

L
4
K   M

1. After trying different arrangements, Jamie discovered that he can arrange two of Triangle 1 and two of Triangle 2 as shown to meet his aunt's requirements.

    a. What lengths of rods does Jamie need to cut? Round to the nearest tenth. Explain.

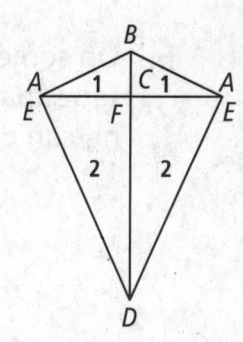

    B
    A 1 C 1 A
    E   F   E
      2   2
        D

    b. How much reflective tape does he need for the perimeter? Round UP to the nearest centimeter.

2. Jamie continued to find other ways to form kites. He discovered he can make a larger kite by attaching more triangles to the first arrangement.

   a. Jamie said that because both arrangements meet his aunt's requirements, the four triangles must all be similar. Do you agree? If so, explain and describe a similarity transformation that maps Triangle 4 on the left to Triangle 2 on the right. If not, explain why not.

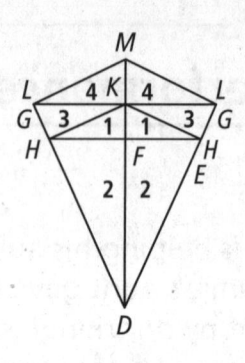

   b. On some of the kites, Jamie needs to sew a second outline with reflective tape that is the same shape as the kite but half the perimeter. Describe how he can do that for the kite shown.

3. Jamie needs to make a different-sized kite that is larger than the first kite and smaller than the second kite. Draw a diagram to show how Jamie can construct the third kite.

Name _____

8 Readiness Assessment

1. Which conclusion does the proportion support?

   $\dfrac{3}{9} = \dfrac{9}{27}$

   Ⓐ The average of 3 and 27 is 9.

   Ⓑ The numbers 3, 9, and 27 are prime.

   Ⓒ The geometric mean of 3 and 27 is 9.

   Ⓓ The sides of a triangle could be 3, 9, and 27.

2. Joe saves $5 for every $8 he earns. Joe made a total of $20 in his first day of work. How much did he save on day 1?

   Ⓐ $2.50   Ⓒ $14.00
   Ⓑ $12.50 Ⓓ $32.00

3. The lengths of the legs of a right triangle are 6 and 10. What is the length of the hypotenuse to the nearest tenth?

   [ ]

4. Select all the true statements about △ABC.

   ☐ A. $\overline{AE}$ is a bisector of ∠ABC.

   ☐ B. $\dfrac{AB}{AD} \neq \dfrac{AC}{CE}$

   ☐ C. $\dfrac{AB}{AD} = \dfrac{BC}{CD}$

   ☐ D. m∠CBA = 90

   ☐ E. $\overline{BD}$ is an altitude of △ABC.

5. Given the equation $x^2 + y^2 = 4z$, which expression is equivalent to a positive value of x?

   Ⓐ $y - 2\sqrt{z}$ Ⓒ $\sqrt{y^2 - 4z}$
   Ⓑ $2\sqrt{z} - y$ Ⓓ $\sqrt{4z - y^2}$

6. In △ABC, m∠A = 45° and m∠B = 90°. In △DEF, m∠D = 45° and m∠F = 45°. Select all of the statements that must be true.

   ☐ A. △ABC is congruent to △DEF
   ☐ B. m∠B = m∠E
   ☐ C. AC = EF
   ☐ D. BC = AB
   ☐ E. △ABC is similar to △DEF

7. A rectangle is 15 in. long and 4 in. wide. A similar rectangle is 21 in. long. What is its width, in inches?

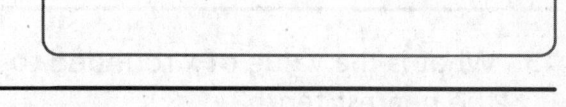

   [ ]

8. Which could be the lengths of the sides of a right triangle?

   Ⓐ 5, 12, 169   Ⓒ 31, 32, 63
   Ⓑ 28, 45, 53   Ⓓ 36, 49, 64

9. Given △XYZ, which expression is equivalent to a?

   Ⓐ $3^2 + 7^2$
   Ⓑ $7^2 - 3^2$
   Ⓒ $\sqrt{3^2 + 7^2}$
   Ⓓ $\sqrt{7^2 - 3^2}$

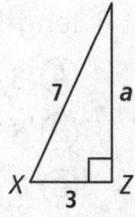

10. In a right triangle, the altitude q from the right angle to the hypotenuse divides the hypotenuse into 4 cm and 16 cm segments. Find the length of q, in cm.

11. Given the equation shown, write an expression that is equivalent to a positive value of b.

$c^2 = b^2 + d^2 - 2cd$

Ⓐ $\sqrt{(c^2 + d^2 - 2cd)}$
Ⓑ $\sqrt{(c^2 + d^2 + 2cd)}$
Ⓒ $\sqrt{(c^2 - d^2 - 2cd)}$
Ⓓ $\sqrt{(c^2 - d^2 + 2cd)}$

12. Find the length of the hypotenuse in an isosceles right triangle if each of the legs measures 4 inches. Round to the nearest hundredth inch.

13. What is the value of x rounded to the nearest tenth?

$x + x\sqrt{2} = 10$

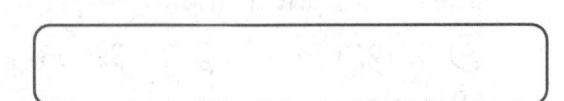

14. The hypotenuse of a right triangle measures 25. Which could be the lengths of the legs?

Ⓐ 3 and 4
Ⓑ 5 and 5
Ⓒ 7 and 24
Ⓓ 10 and 15

15. Which are possible measures of x and y?

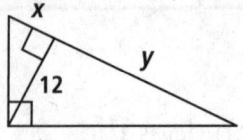

Ⓐ $x = 8, y = 16$ Ⓒ $x = 7, y = 18$
Ⓑ $x = 9, y = 16$ Ⓓ $x = 5, y = 18$

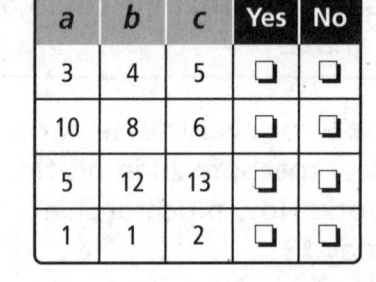

16. Which could be values of a, b, and c in $\triangle ABC$?

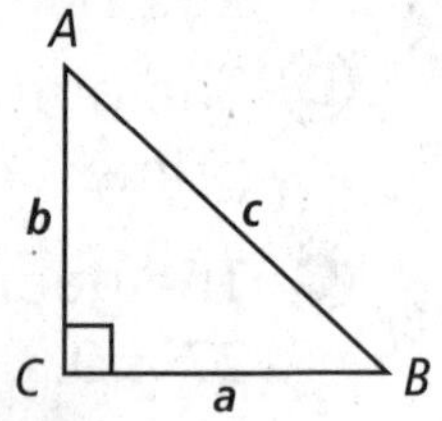

a	b	c	Yes	No
3	4	5	❏	❏
10	8	6	❏	❏
5	12	13	❏	❏
1	1	2	❏	❏

17. Maria makes a quilting pattern with two similar isosceles triangles. In one triangle, the base is 1.4 in. and the other side lengths are each 3.2 in. Find the length of each side, r, of the other triangle if its base is 4.48 in.

18. Which of the following is true for the figure shown?

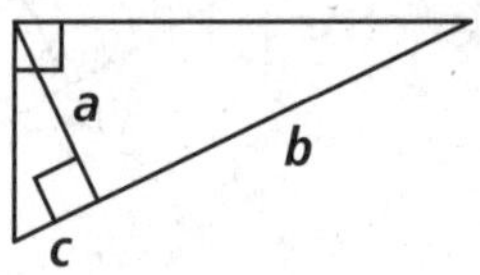

Ⓐ $\frac{b}{a} = \frac{a}{c}$ Ⓒ $a^2 + b^2 = c^2$
Ⓑ $a = \frac{b+c}{2}$ Ⓓ $a = \frac{1}{2}bc$

8-1 Lesson Quiz

Right Triangles and the Pythagorean Theorem

1. The diagram shows Pete's plans for a kite, with vertices ABCD. How much material, in square inches, does he need to cover one side of the kite?

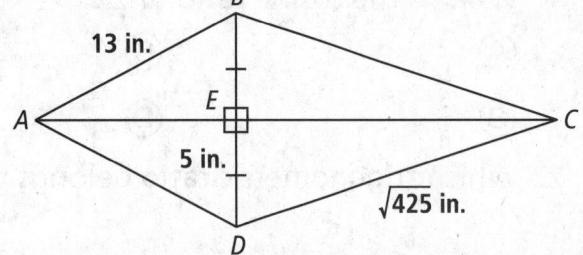

   [_____]

2. Jin's quilting project uses rectangles and right triangles of fabric to make blocks of different sizes. Select whether each combination of side lengths, in cm, could make a triangle for the quilt.

	Yes	No
12, 35, 37	☐	☐
16, 30, 34	☐	☐
18, 24, 42	☐	☐
20, 21, 29	☐	☐

3. Adaline is designing a garden in the shape of a 45°-45°-90° triangle, with an area of 32 ft². To the nearest foot, how much fencing will she need to enclose the garden?

   Ⓐ 24 feet   Ⓒ 32 feet
   Ⓑ 27 feet   Ⓓ 75 feet

4. Ben made a sundial in his backyard by placing a stick with height 6 in. straight into the ground, and marking the hours in the grass. To test it, he checks the time each day when the sun makes an angle of 30° or 60° with the ground. Select all the possible lengths of the shadow when Ben checks the sundial.

   ☐ A. $2\sqrt{2}$ in.   ☐ D. $6\sqrt{3}$ in.
   ☐ B. $2\sqrt{3}$ in.   ☐ E. 12 in.
   ☐ C. 8 in.

5. A new park design uses part of a city block, but there is already a building in the northwest corner of the block. If the park uses all of the space in the block from $\overline{AC}$ to the right, what is the area of the park in the blueprint, rounded to the nearest square cm?

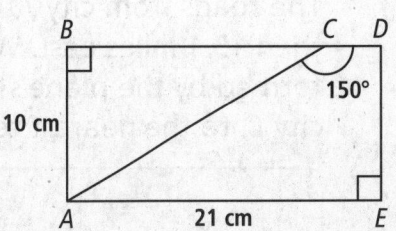

   Ⓐ 87 cm²   Ⓒ 123 cm²
   Ⓑ 105 cm²   Ⓓ 210 cm²

8-2 Lesson Quiz

Trigonometric Ratios

1. What is the cosine ratio of ∠Z?

   Ⓐ $\frac{3}{5}$ Ⓒ $\frac{4}{5}$

   Ⓑ $\frac{3}{4}$ Ⓓ $\frac{5}{3}$

2. Which trigonometric ratio belongs with each value?

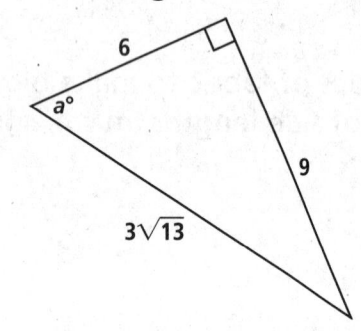

   | tan 90° | sin 90° | tan a° | sin a° | cos 90° | cos a° |

   [ ] = $\frac{3}{2}$ [ ] = $\frac{2\sqrt{13}}{13}$ [ ] = $\frac{3\sqrt{13}}{13}$

3. Select all the trigonometric values that are equivalent to $\frac{1}{2}$.

   ☐ A. sin 30°
   ☐ B. sin 45°
   ☐ C. cos 45°
   ☐ D. cos 60°
   ☐ E. tan 30°
   ☐ F. tan 45°

4. What is the perimeter of △DEF to the nearest tenth?

   Ⓐ 19.4   Ⓒ 25.3

   Ⓑ 20.1   Ⓓ 43.3

5. A plane flies in a straight line path over city J and city K. The roads from city J to city K run 9.4 miles south and then 15.1 miles east. What is the measure of the angle formed by the plane's path and the road from city J to city L, to the nearest tenth?

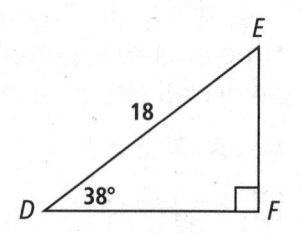

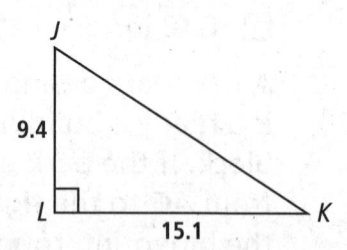

   [ ]

Name _____

8-3 Lesson Quiz

Law of Sines

1. Select all the true statements about △ABC. 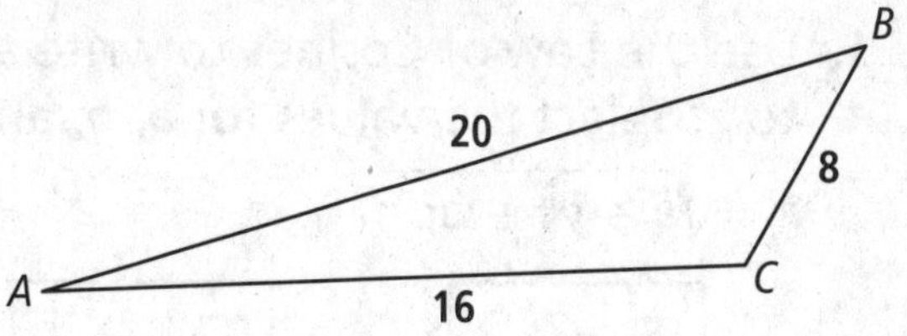
   ☐ A. sin(A) + sin(B) = 1.2 sin(C)
   ☐ B. sin(A) − sin(B) = 0.4 sin(C)
   ☐ C. sin(A) = 2 sin(B)
   ☐ D. sin(C) = 2.5 sin(A) = 1.25 sin(B)
   ☐ E. sin(A) + sin(C) = 1.75 sin(B)

2. Find the value of x to the nearest tenth.

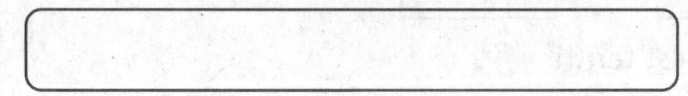

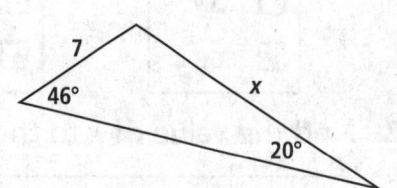

3. Use the Law of Sines to write an expression that represents angle measure x. Select the values for A, B, and C in the expression.

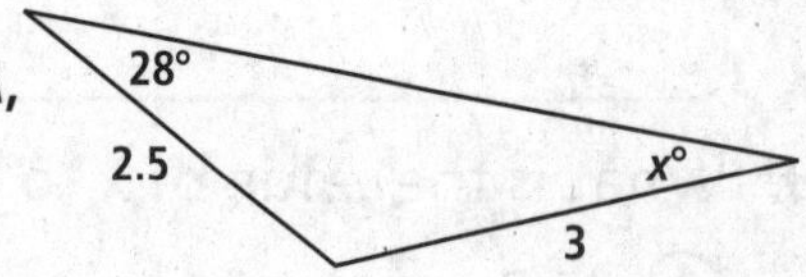

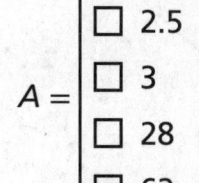

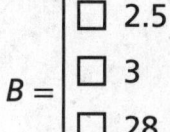

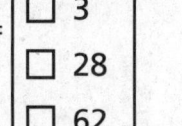

   $x = \sin^{-1}\left(\dfrac{A \cdot \sin B°}{C}\right)$

   $A = \begin{bmatrix} \square\ 2.5 \\ \square\ 3 \\ \square\ 28 \\ \square\ 62 \end{bmatrix}$ $B = \begin{bmatrix} \square\ 2.5 \\ \square\ 3 \\ \square\ 28 \\ \square\ 62 \end{bmatrix}$ $C = \begin{bmatrix} \square\ 2.5 \\ \square\ 3 \\ \square\ 28 \\ \square\ 62 \end{bmatrix}$

4. What is the perimeter of △ABC to the nearest whole number? 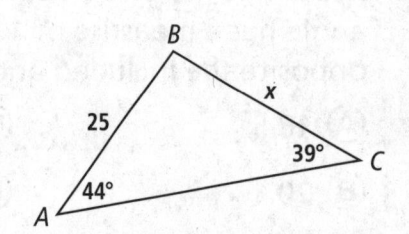
   Ⓐ 53
   Ⓑ 92
   Ⓒ 108
   Ⓓ 180

5. What is the value of x to the nearest tenth? 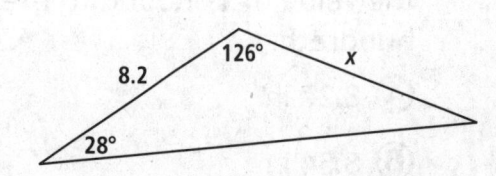
   Ⓐ 4.8   Ⓒ 8.8
   Ⓑ 7.7   Ⓓ 14.1

Name _____

8-4 Lesson Quiz

Law of Cosines

1. Use the Law of Cosines to write an expression equivalent to z. Select the values for a, b, and c in the expression.

   $z = \sqrt{a + y^2 - bc}$

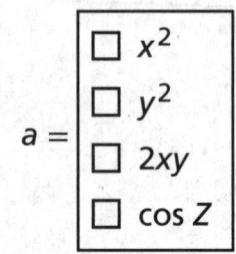

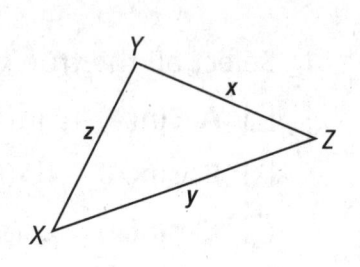

   $a = \begin{bmatrix} \square \ x^2 \\ \square \ y^2 \\ \square \ 2xy \\ \square \ \cos Z \end{bmatrix}$ $b = \begin{bmatrix} \square \ x^2 \\ \square \ y^2 \\ \square \ z^2 \\ \square \ 2xy \end{bmatrix}$ $c = \begin{bmatrix} \square \ x^2 \\ \square \ y^2 \\ \square \ z^2 \\ \square \ \cos Z \end{bmatrix}$

2. Find the value of x to the nearest tenth.

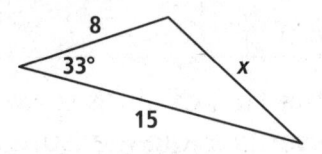

   [_____]

3. What is the value of x to the nearest tenth?

   Ⓐ 25.7

   Ⓑ 43.2

   Ⓒ 88.8

   Ⓓ 89.7

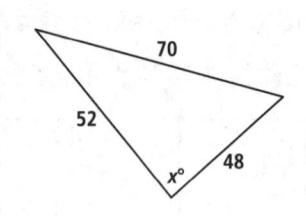

4. A triangle has two sides measuring 16 and 21. The included angle has a measure of 116°. What is the length of the side opposite the included angle?

   Ⓐ 18.5   Ⓒ 26.4

   Ⓑ 20.1   Ⓓ 31.5

5. Mr. Katz is designing a flower garden in the shape of a trapezoid. What is the value of x? Round to the nearest hundreth.

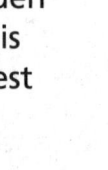

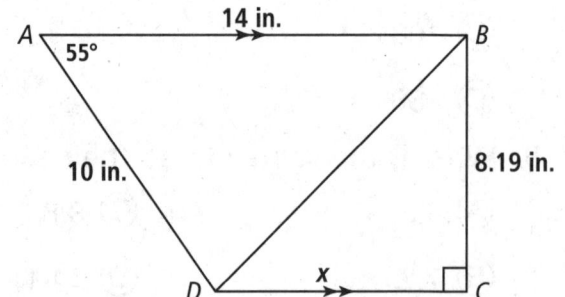

   Ⓐ 8.27 in.

   Ⓑ 8.54 in.

   Ⓒ 10.73 in.

   Ⓓ 12.19 in.

enVision® Geometry • Assessment Sourcebook

Name _____

8-5 Lesson Quiz

Problem Solving with Trigonometry

1. A 500-foot cable is attached to the top of a tower and is stretched tight to a point 350 feet away from the base of the tower. What is the angle of depression formed by the cable?

    Ⓐ 34.9°

    Ⓑ 35.3°

    Ⓒ 44.4°

    Ⓓ 45.6°

2. The angle of elevation from a viewer to the center of a fireworks display is 55°. If the viewer is 75 yards away from where the fireworks are launched, at what height is the center of the display? Round to the nearest whole yard.

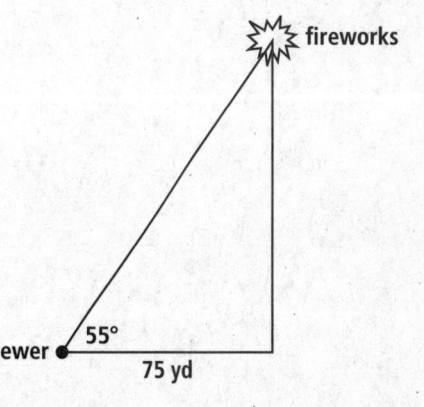

    [   ]

3. What is the angle of elevation from the ground to the top of a 45-foot tree from 65 feet away? Round to the nearest tenth of a degree.

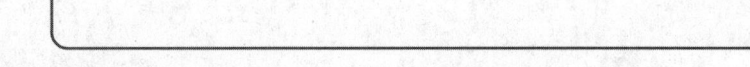

    [   ]

4. What is the area of △JKL in square units?

    Ⓐ 215.7

    Ⓑ 431.4

    Ⓒ 490.8

    Ⓓ 981.6

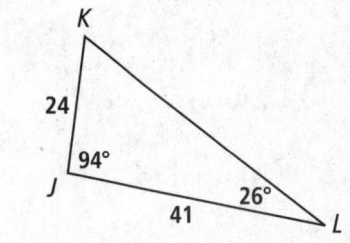

5. Given that the area of △PQR is A, write an expression you could use to find the measure of ∠R.

    Ⓐ $\sin^{-1} \frac{2A}{pq}$

    Ⓑ $\sin^{-1} \frac{pq}{2A}$

    Ⓒ $\cos^{-1} \frac{2A}{pq}$

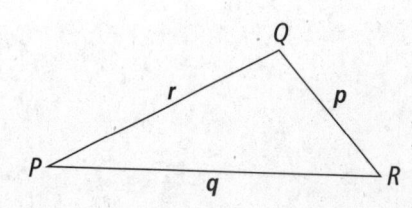

    Ⓓ $\cos^{-1} \frac{2A}{pq}$

Name _____

8 Topic Assessment Form A

1. A sketch of a wheelchair ramp is shown. What is the horizontal distance of the ramp, in inches? Round to the nearest tenth.

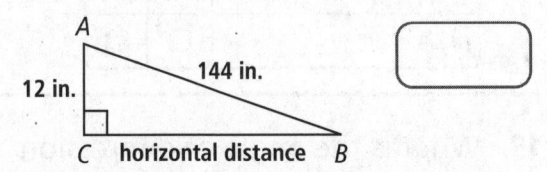

   Triangle with A at top, C at bottom-left (right angle), B at bottom-right. AC = 12 in., AB = 144 in., CB = horizontal distance.

2. John is designing a shelf in the shape of a right triangle. He records possible side lengths of the shelf below. Will the side lengths form the shelf?

	Yes	No
9, 40, 41	☐	☐
11, 60, 62	☐	☐
48, 55, 73	☐	☐

3. A 30°–60°–90° triangle is shown. Prove that if the shortest side length is s, the others are $s\sqrt{3}$ and $2s$.

   Which shows how to find the length of the longer leg, x?

   Ⓐ $\tan 30° = \frac{x}{s}$; $x = s\sqrt{3}$
   Ⓑ $\tan 60° = \frac{x}{s}$; $x = s\sqrt{3}$
   Ⓒ $\sin 60° = \frac{x}{s}$; $x = 2s$
   Ⓓ $\cos 30° = \frac{x}{s}$; $x = s\sqrt{3}$

   Which shows how to find the length of the hypotenuse, c?

   Ⓐ $\tan 30° = \frac{s}{c}$; $c = s\sqrt{3}$
   Ⓑ $\sin 60° = \frac{s}{c}$; $c = 2s\sqrt{3}$
   Ⓒ $\cos 30° = \frac{c}{s}$; $c = 2s$
   Ⓓ $\sin 60° = \frac{s}{c}$; $c = 2s$

4. If $\sin(x) = \cos(y)$ for acute angles x and y, how are the angles related?

   Ⓐ congruent
   Ⓑ complementary
   Ⓒ supplementary
   Ⓓ not enough information

5. A sketch of a rectangular patio is shown. A concrete triangular section is planned for an outdoor fireplace. What is the area of the concrete section, in square units?

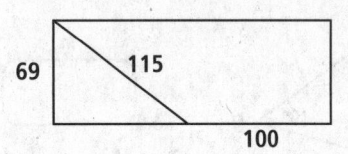

   Rectangle with triangle inside: sides labeled 69, 115, 100.

   Ⓐ 517.5
   Ⓑ 1,587
   Ⓒ 3,174
   Ⓓ 7,935

6. The diagram shows a building and two beams, located on top and to the right of the building, respectively. Angle x is formed between the tops of the two beams as shown. Find x, to the nearest tenth of a degree.

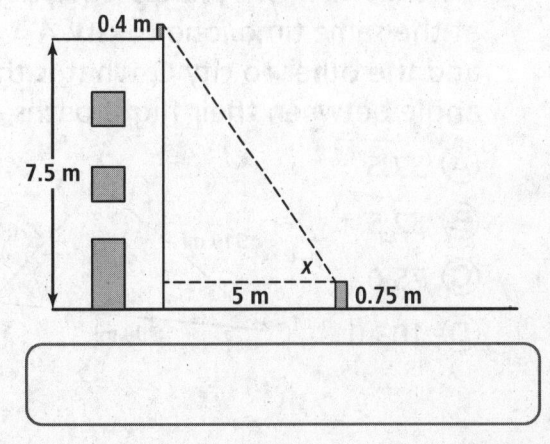

   Diagram: building height 7.5 m, top beam 0.4 m, horizontal distance 5 m, right beam 0.75 m.

enVision® Geometry   Assessment Sourcebook

7. Find the value of x to the nearest tenth.

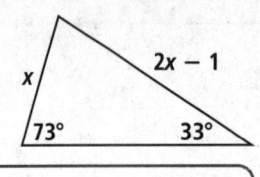

   (triangle with angles 73°, 33°, sides x and 2x − 1)

8. What is the measure of ∠ABC?
   Ⓐ 72.72 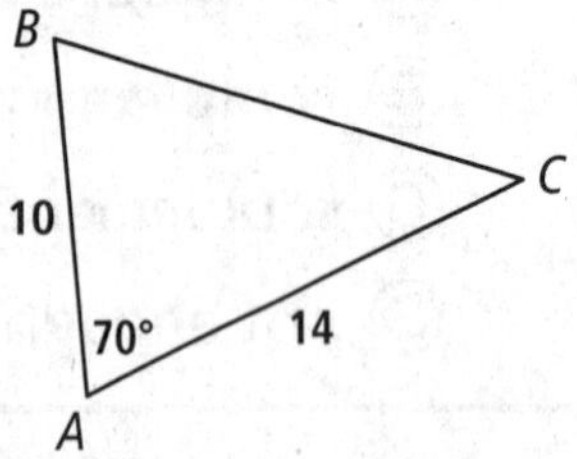
   Ⓑ 71.76
   Ⓒ 68.39
   Ⓓ 65.48

   (triangle with B, C, A; sides 10, 14, angle 70° at A)

9. Mary is building a fence around her triangular garden. How much fencing, in feet, does she need? Round to the nearest foot.

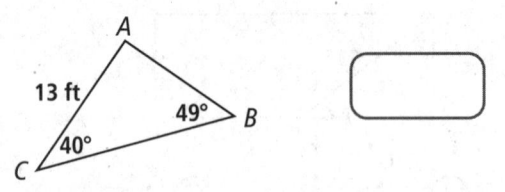

   (triangle with A, B, C; side 13 ft, angles 49°, 40°)

10. Find CD to the nearest tenth.

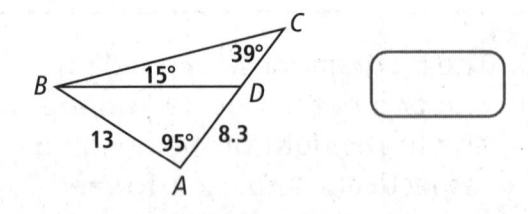

    (triangle with B, D, C, A; angles 15°, 39°, 95°, sides 13, 8.3)

11. The distances between three cities are shown. If two planes leave city B at the same time, one to city A and the other to city C, what is the angle between their flight paths, x?
    Ⓐ 37.5
    Ⓑ 52.5
    Ⓒ 75.0
    Ⓓ 103.0

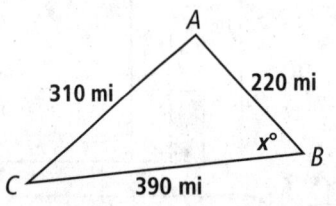

    (triangle: A, B, C with sides 310 mi, 220 mi, 390 mi, angle x° at B)

12. Which measurements of △ABC are correct?

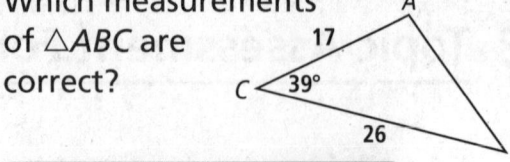

    (triangle with A, B, C; side 17, 26, angle 39° at C)

	Yes	No
AB ≈ 16.67 units	☐	☐
Area of △ABC ≈ 139.08 square units	☐	☐
m∠A ≈ 24.30	☐	☐

13. What is the angle of depression from the start of a 6-foot-high access ramp that ends at a point 40 feet away along the ground?
    Ⓐ 0.15°
    Ⓑ 8.2°
    Ⓒ 8.5°
    Ⓓ 45.6°

14. The angle of elevation from a viewer to the top of a flagpole is 50°. If the viewer is 40 ft away and their eyes are 5.5 ft from the ground, how high is the pole, to the nearest tenth of a foot?

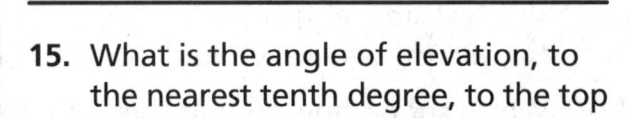

15. What is the angle of elevation, to the nearest tenth degree, to the top of a 35-m tree from 75 m away?

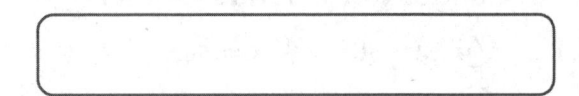

16. The area of the tabletop shown is D square units. Which expression represents the measure of ∠C?
    Ⓐ $\sin^{-1} \frac{2D}{ab}$
    Ⓑ $\sin^{-1} \frac{ab}{2D}$
    Ⓒ $\cos^{-1} \frac{ab}{2D}$
    Ⓓ $\cos^{-1} \frac{2D}{ab}$

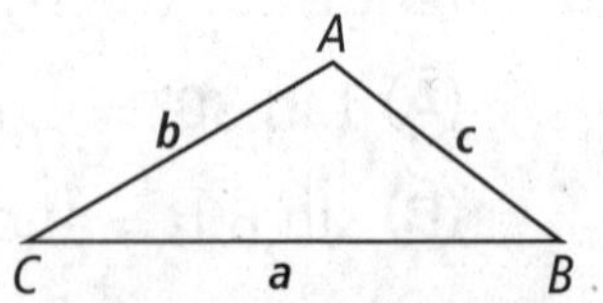

    (triangle with vertices A, B, C and sides a, b, c)

8 Topic Assessment Form B

1. A sketch of a skateboard ramp is shown. What is the horizontal distance of the ramp, in inches?

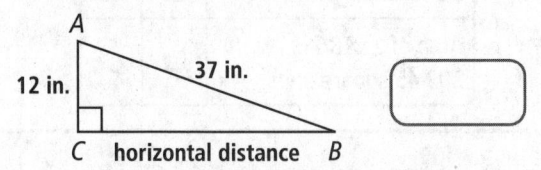

   A
   12 in.   37 in.
   C horizontal distance B

2. Martin is making a lean-to for his dog in the shape of a right triangle. He records possible side lengths of the lean-to below. Will the side lengths form the lean-to?

	Yes	No
28, 45, 53	☐	☐
33, 56, 64	☐	☐
36, 77, 85	☐	☐

3. A 45°–45°–90° triangle is shown. Prove that if one side length is s, the others are s and $s\sqrt{2}$.

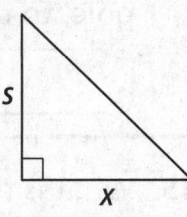

   Which shows how to find x?

   Ⓐ $\sin 45° = \frac{s}{x}$; $x = s$

   Ⓑ $\sin 45° = \frac{s}{x}$; $x = s\sqrt{2}$

   Ⓒ $\sin 90° = 2(45)°$, $x = s\sqrt{2}$

   Ⓓ since the acute angles are the same, $x = s$

   Which shows how to find the length of the hypotenuse, c?

   Ⓐ $\sin 45° = \frac{s}{c}$; $c = s$

   Ⓑ $\sin 45° = \frac{s}{c}$; $c = s\sqrt{2}$

   Ⓒ $\tan 45° = \frac{c}{s}$; $c = s$

   Ⓓ $\tan 45° = \frac{s}{c}$; $c = s\sqrt{2}$

4. If $\sin(x) = \tan(y)$ for acute angles x and y, how are the angles related?

   Ⓐ congruent

   Ⓑ complementary

   Ⓒ supplementary

   Ⓓ not enough information

5. A sketch of a rectangular garden plot is shown. The triangular section will be for flowers, and the rest will be for vegetables. What is the area of the vegetable garden, in sq units?

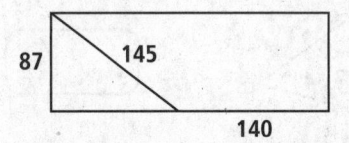

   87   145
              140

   Ⓐ 22,272   Ⓒ 24,795

   Ⓑ 12,180   Ⓓ 17,226

6. The diagram shows a building and two beams, located on top and to the right of the building, respectively. Angle x is formed between the tops of the two beams as shown. Find x, to the nearest tenth of a degree.

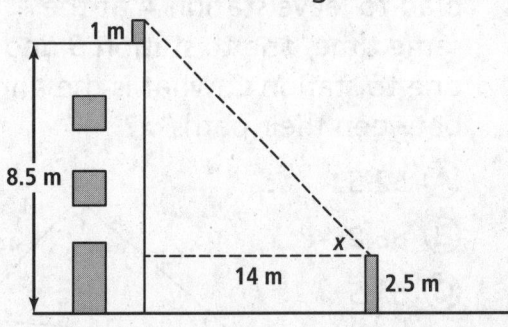

   1 m
   8.5 m
   14 m   2.5 m

7. Find the value of x to the nearest hundreth.

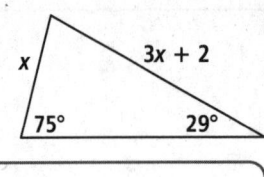

   (triangle with sides x, 3x + 2, angles 75°, 29°)

8. What is the measure of ∠KHJ?
   Ⓐ 13.38
   Ⓑ 25.82
   Ⓒ 43.30
   Ⓓ 88.70

   (triangle HJK with HK = 12, JK = 18, ∠K = 48°)

9. Luciano is lining his triangular pool with vinyl. How much vinyl, in feet, does he need? Round to the nearest foot.

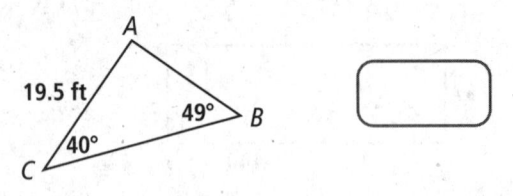

   (triangle ABC with AC = 19.5 ft, ∠B = 49°, ∠C = 40°)

10. Find AD to the nearest hundreth.

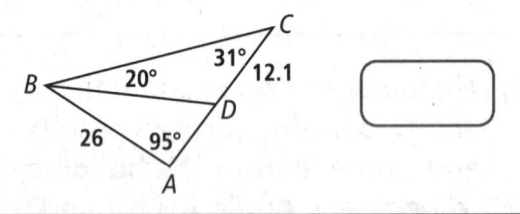

    (triangle with CD = 12.1, ∠C = 31°, ∠ABD = 20°, BA = 26, ∠A = 95°)

11. The distances between three train stations are shown. If two trains plan to leave station A at the same time, one to station B and one to station C, what is the angle between their paths, x?
    Ⓐ 52.5
    Ⓑ 86.8
    Ⓒ 51.5
    Ⓓ 89.7

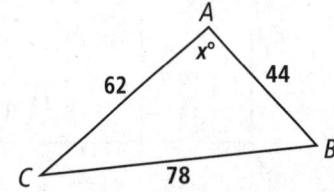

    (triangle ABC with AC = 62, AB = 44, CB = 78, angle x° at A)

12. Which measurements of △ABC are correct?

    (triangle ABC with ∠B = 39°, CA = 17, BA = 26)

	Yes	No
m∠C ≈ 67°	☐	☐
BC ≈ 24.87 units	☐	☐
Area of △ABC ≈ 203.45 square units	☐	☐

13. What is the angle of depression from the start of a 3-foot-high access ramp that ends at a point 25 feet away along the ground?
    Ⓐ 0.15°
    Ⓑ 1°
    Ⓒ 6.8°
    Ⓓ 83.1°

14. The angle of elevation from a viewer to the top of a flagpole is 50°. If the viewer is 20 feet away and the viewer's eyes are 5 feet from the ground, how high is the pole, to the nearest tenth of a foot?

15. What is the angle of elevation, to the nearest tenth of a degree, to the top of a 45-foot building from 85 feet away?

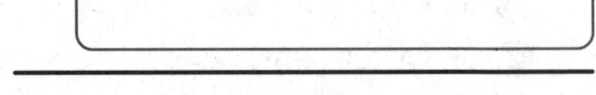

16. Given that the area of △ABC is D, write an expression you could use to find the measure of ∠A.
    Ⓐ $\sin^{-1} \frac{bc}{2D}$
    Ⓑ $\cos^{-1} \frac{2D}{bc}$
    Ⓒ $\cos^{-1} \frac{bc}{2D}$
    Ⓓ $\sin^{-1} \frac{2D}{bc}$

    (triangle ABC with sides a, b, c)

8 Performance Assessment Form A

An outdoor enclosure at a wildlife sanctuary has an observation tower at each vertex. Anna, Benito, Charlie, and Deon want to determine information about the enclosure. Each friend goes to the top of an observation tower and uses an elevation app to determine his or her elevation above sea level. The first table shows their elevations. Anna measures the angles of elevation of her sight lines to Benito and Deon, and Charlie measures the angle of depression of his sight line to Benito. This information is shown in the second table. The diagram shows an overhead view of the enclosure.

Elevations	
Anna	690 ft
Benito	713 ft
Charlie	743 ft
Deon	725 ft

Sight Line Angles of Depression and Elevation	
Anna to Benito	2° angle of elevation
Anna to Deon	3° angle of elevation
Charlie to Benito	5° angle of depression

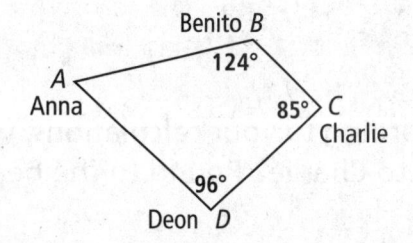

1. What are AB, BC, and AD? Round to the nearest tenth. Explain.

2. What is BD? Round to the nearest tenth. Explain.

3. What is the perimeter of the enclosure? Round to the nearest tenth. Explain.

4. According to your calculations, what is the angle of elevation of Anna's sight line to Charlie? Round to the nearest tenth. Explain.

5. What is the area of the enclosure, to the nearest square foot?

Name _____

8 Performance Assessment Form B

Venetta leads walking tours through part of her city. She needs to determine the length of her route but her city map shows only some distances. Venetta took some additional angle measurements to determine the remaining distances. The known distances and angle measurements are shown in the diagram. The darker lines in the diagram show the route she follows.

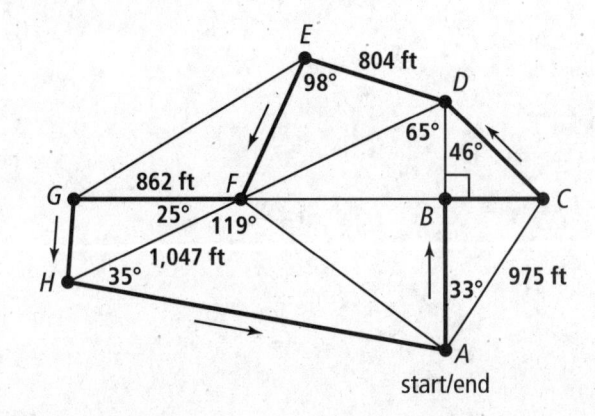

1. How far is the portion of her route from A to D? Round to the nearest whole number. Explain.

2. For the next two weeks, the monument at point E will be closed, so the tour walks directly to point F from point D. The distance from E to F is the same as from point D to point E. How much shorter is the route if the tour walks the direct distance from D to F?

3. Venetta assumes that the map shows a right angle at G to get a close estimate for the distance from point G to point H. Using this strategy, what is this estimated distance?

4. How far is the portion of her route from H to A?

5. What is the total length of her route in miles? Round each distance to the nearest whole foot. (1 mile = 5,280 feet)

6. Some customers have requested a shorter tour with fewer stops. All her tours need to start and end at point A. Suggest a shorter route that eliminates two or three stops from her current route. What is the length, in miles, of the route you suggest?

Benchmark Assessment 4

Name _____

1. What is $m\angle DBC$?

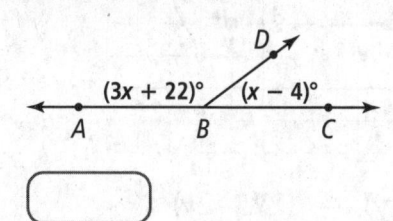

   $(3x + 22)°$ at $\angle ABD$, $(x - 4)°$ at $\angle DBC$, with points A, B, C collinear and D above B.

   [   ]

2. Select whether each statement is true or false.

	True	False
All circles are similar.	☐	☐
If two circles are similar, then their areas are congruent.	☐	☐
All right triangles are similar.	☐	☐
If two triangles are similar, then their corresponding angles are congruent.	☐	☐

3. Select all the angles that are congruent to $\angle 8$.

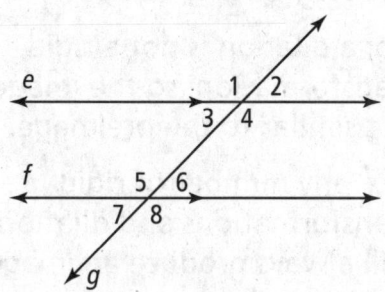

   (Figure with lines e, f, g and angles 1–8)

   ☐ A. $\angle 1$
   ☐ B. $\angle 2$
   ☐ C. $\angle 3$
   ☐ D. $\angle 4$
   ☐ E. $\angle 5$

For Items 4 and 5, use quadrilateral JKLO.

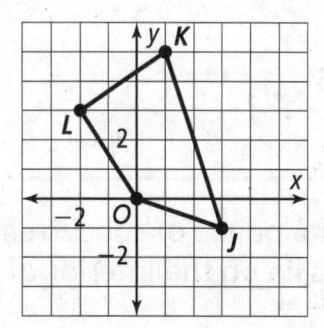

(Graph showing quadrilateral JKLO)

4. What are the coordinates of the vertices of the image after a reflection across the y-axis?

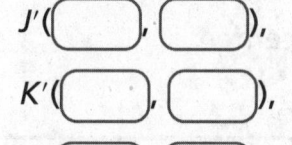

   J'([ ] , [ ]),
   K'([ ] , [ ]),
   L'([ ] , [ ]),
   O'([ ] , [ ])

5. What are the coordinates of the vertices of the image after rotation 90° clockwise about the origin?

   J'([ ] , [ ]),
   K'([ ] , [ ]),
   L'([ ] , [ ]),
   O'([ ] , [ ])

6. What is the perimeter of quadrilateral MNPQ?

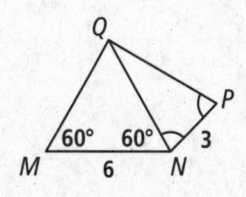

   (Figure with triangle MNQ having 60° angles at M and N, MN = 6, and triangle NPQ with NP = 3)

   [   ]

7. $\overline{SU}$ and $\overline{RT}$ bisect each other at point V, and $\overline{UT} \cong \overline{RS}$. Select all the theorems that can be used to show that $\triangle RSV \cong \triangle TUV$.

   ☐ A. ASA
   ☐ B. SSS
   ☐ C. SAS
   ☐ D. AAS
   ☐ E. HL

8. Select all the points of concurrency that always lie on the interior of a triangle.

   ☐ A. centroid
   ☐ B. circumcenter
   ☐ C. incenter
   ☐ D. orthocenter
   ☐ E. vertex

9. The length of one of the diagonals of a rhombus is 6, and the perimeter is 20. What is the length of the other diagonal?

   ☐

10. If $\sin(x) = \frac{12}{13}$ and $\cos(y) = \frac{12}{13}$, then x and y are

    ☐ complementary
    ☐ supplementary   angles.
    ☐ congruent
    ☐ right

11. Describe the transformations that show Figure A is similar to Figure B.

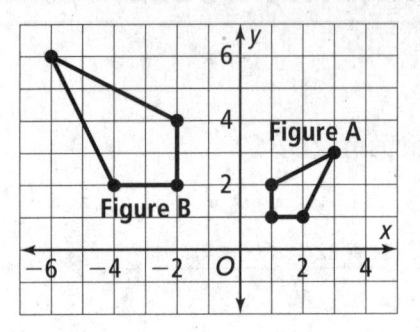

    Ⓐ $(x, y) \longrightarrow (2x, -2y)$
    Ⓑ $(x, y) \longrightarrow (-\frac{1}{2}x, \frac{1}{2}y)$
    Ⓒ $(x, y) \longrightarrow (-2y, -2x)$
    Ⓓ $(x, y) \longrightarrow (-x - 1, -y + 1)$

12. Given A(2, 4), what are the coordinates of A' for the dilation with scale factor 1.5 and center at the origin?

    A'(☐, ☐)

13. A figure undergoes a translation, reflection, and dilation. Will the image be similar to the original figure? Why or why not?

    Ⓐ No; a dilation is not a rigid transformation, so the image is not similar to the preimage.
    Ⓑ Yes; any number of rigid transformations and dilations will always produce an image similar to the preimage.
    Ⓒ No; when more than one transformation is applied, the image is not similar to the preimage.
    Ⓓ Yes; since only 3 transformations were applied, the image will be similar to the preimage.

14. Given C(2, −8), D(−6, 4), E(0, 4), U(1, −4), V(−3, 2), and W(0, 2), and that △CDE is the preimage of △UVW, represent the transformation algebraically.

(x, y) ⟶ (☐ x, ☐ y)

---

15. △GHJ is dilated and then reflected to form △G'H'J'. Select all the statements that must be true.

☐ A. Each angle in △GHJ is similar to its corresponding angle in △G'H'J'.

☐ B. HJ = LM

☐ C. $\frac{GH}{KL} = \frac{GJ}{KM}$

☐ D. Each angle in △GHJ is congruent to its corresponding angle in △G'H'J'.

☐ E. $\frac{m\angle G}{m\angle K} = \frac{m\angle H}{m\angle L}$

---

16. Given △HJK and △RST, what is cos T?

Ⓐ $\frac{2\sqrt{14}}{9}$

Ⓑ $\frac{5}{9}$

Ⓒ $\frac{9}{5}$

Ⓓ $\frac{5\sqrt{14}}{28}$

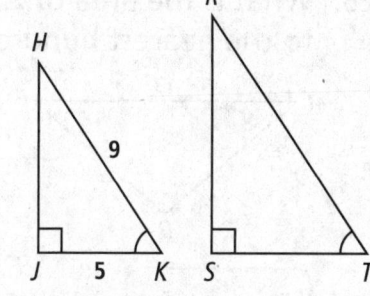

17. What are HK and GH?

Ⓐ HK = 5; GH = $\sqrt{29}$

Ⓑ HK = 4; GH = $2\sqrt{5}$

Ⓒ HK = $2\sqrt{5}$; GH = $2\sqrt{6}$

Ⓓ HK = $\sqrt{5}$; GH = 3

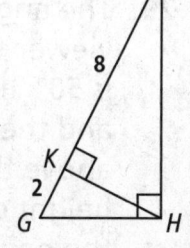

---

18. Is the triangle similar to △PQR?

	Yes	No
△RQS	☐	☐
△QSR	☐	☐
△PRS	☐	☐

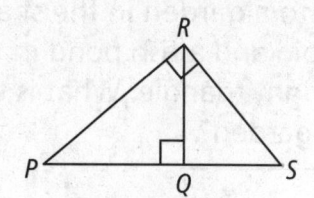

---

19. Which conclusion does the diagram support?

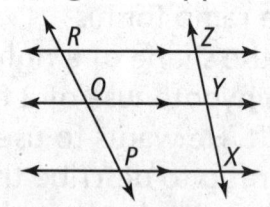

Ⓐ $\frac{PQ}{QR} = \frac{XY}{YZ}$

Ⓑ PX = $\frac{1}{2}$RZ

Ⓒ $\frac{QY}{RZ} = \frac{PX}{QY}$

Ⓓ QY = $\frac{1}{2}$PX

---

20. In △ABC, point P is the midpoint of $\overline{AB}$, and point Q is the midpoint of $\overline{BC}$. Select the statement that could be **false**.

Ⓐ m∠BAC = m∠BCA

Ⓑ AC ∥ PQ

Ⓒ m∠BPQ = m∠BAC

Ⓓ m∠PQC + m∠QCA = 180

---

21. A triangle with area 5 cm² is dilated with a scale factor of 3. What is the area of the image, in square centimeters?

☐

22. Bella is splitting her rectangular backyard into a garden in the shape of a trapezoid and a fish pond in the shape of a right triangle. What is the area of the garden?

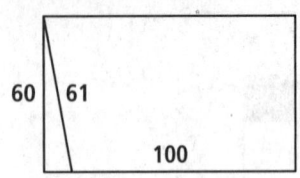

[Trapezoid diagram: left side 60, slanted side 61, bottom 100]

Ⓐ 6,000 units²

Ⓑ 6,330 units²

Ⓒ 6,660 units²

Ⓓ 660 units²

23. Garret makes a ramp for his skateboard in the shape of a right triangle with a hypotenuse of 2 ft, and a leg of 1 ft. He wants to use a trigonometric ratio to describe the relationship between these two sides. Select all of the expressions that he could use.

☐ A. sin 30°

☐ B. cos 45°

☐ C. tan 30°

☐ D. sin 45°

☐ E. cos 60°

☐ F. tan 45°

24. Point P is plotted at (2, −6). What are the coordinates of P´ for the transformation $(D_{\frac{1}{2}} \circ R_{x\text{-axis}})(P)$.

(☐, ☐)

25. What is the value of x? Round to the nearest tenth.

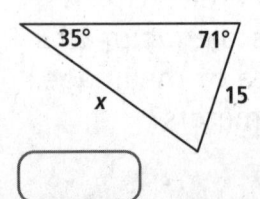

[Triangle with angles 35° and 71°, side 15 opposite to 35°, side x]

☐

26. What is the perimeter of △DEF? Round to the nearest whole number.

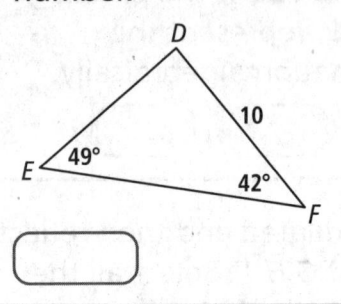

[Triangle DEF with angle E = 49°, angle F = 42°, side DF = 10]

☐

27. Javi bikes 2.4 miles from his home to the library. He then makes a 43° turn and bikes 3.9 more miles to school. How far away from the school does Javi live? Round to the nearest tenth of a mile.

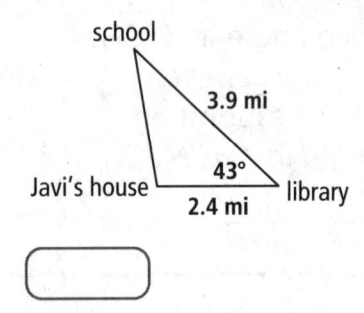

[Triangle: Javi's house to library = 2.4 mi, library to school = 3.9 mi, angle at library = 43°]

☐

28. What is the area of △DEF? Round to the nearest hundredth.

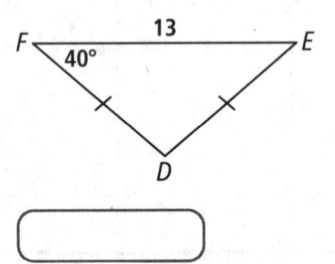

[Isosceles triangle with F angle = 40°, FE = 13, FD = ED (tick marks)]

☐

29. The angle of elevation from a viewer to the top of a building is 50°. If the viewer is 80 ft away and the viewer's eyes are 5.5 ft above the ground, what is the height of the building? Round to the nearest tenth of a foot.

☐

30. △RST shows a city's plan for a new building. Given that the area of △RST is x, select an expression for m∠T.

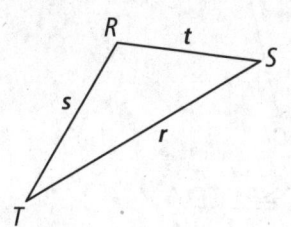

Ⓐ $\frac{1}{2}rs \sin T$

Ⓑ $\sin\left(\frac{2x}{rs}\right)$

Ⓒ $\sin^{-1}\left(\frac{2x}{rs}\right)$

Ⓓ $\sin^{-1}\left(\frac{rs}{2x}\right)$

---

31. Order the steps to prove that any two circles are similar.

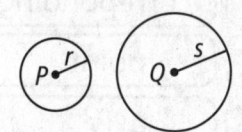

☐ 1 ☐ 2 ☐ 3 ☐ 4

☐	Since a similarity transformation exists, ⊙P ~ ⊙Q.
☐	Translate P to Q so P′ coincides with Q.
☐	Let $k = \frac{s}{r}$. Then the translation followed by a dilation centered at Q with scale factor k maps ⊙P onto ⊙Q.
☐	Find a scale factor that dilates ⊙P′ to the circle with radius s.

---

32. What are the coordinates of the vertices of the dilation of △ABC with center A and scale factor 3 for A(0, 4), B(−2, 5), and C(3, 7)? Does the area increase or decrease?

Ⓐ A′(0, 12), B′(−6, 15), C′(9, 21); The area decreases.

Ⓑ A′(0, 15), B′(−6, 18), C′(9, 24); The area increases.

Ⓒ A′(0, 9), B′(−6, 12), C′(9, 18); The area decreases.

Ⓓ A′(0, 4), B′(−6, 7), C′(9, 13); The area increases.

---

33. Find the value of x to the nearest tenth of a unit.

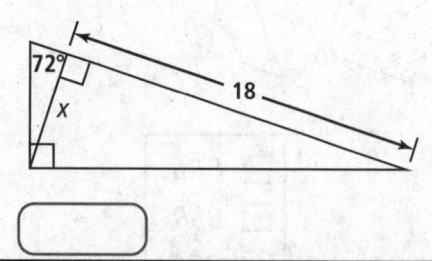

☐

---

34. In △TJB and △DSP, $\overline{JB} \cong \overline{SP}$ and ∠B ≅ ∠P. Which additional piece(s) of information is needed to prove that the triangles are congruent by each given theorem?

	∠T ≅ ∠D	∠J ≅ ∠S	$\overline{JT} \cong \overline{SD}$	$\overline{TB} \cong \overline{DP}$
ASA	☐	☐	☐	☐
SSS	☐	☐	☐	☐
SAS	☐	☐	☐	☐
AAS	☐	☐	☐	☐

35. Jack's eyes are 5 feet above the ground. He is standing 400 feet from the base of a building. His line of sight forms a 67° angle with the top of the building. About how tall is the building?

Ⓐ 161 ft
Ⓑ 175 ft
Ⓒ 373 ft
Ⓓ 947 ft

36. Complete the congruence statement.

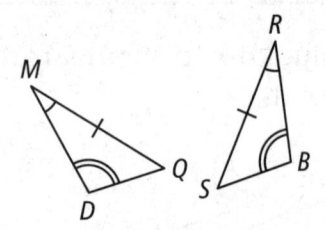

△DMQ ≅ △
☐ BRS
☐ BSR
☐ RBS
☐ RSB
☐ SBR
☐ SRB

37. Point N'(7, −8) is the image of point N(7, 8) under a reflection. What is the image of (−4, −10) under the same reflection?

Ⓐ (−4, 10)
Ⓑ (4, −10)
Ⓒ (4, 10)
Ⓓ (−4, −10)

38. Select all the statement that are always true about ABCD.

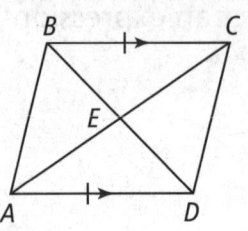

☐ A. ∠ABC ≅ ∠CDA
☐ B. $\overline{BD} \perp \overline{AC}$
☐ C. $\overline{BE} \cong \overline{ED}$
☐ D. m∠ABC + m∠BCD = 180
☐ E. $\overline{AB} \cong \overline{CD}$

39. Complete the sentences with the words below.

intersect	supplementary
plane	correponding
reflect	point
congruent	axis

Parallel lines are in the same ☐ but they do not ☐.

When a transversal crosses parallel lines, alternate interior angles are ☐.

9 Readiness Assessment

1. On a number line, what is the midpoint between −2 and 7?

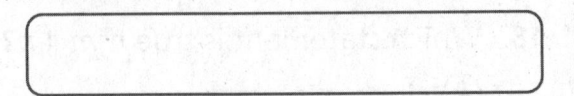

2. On a number line, what is the distance between −14 and −3?

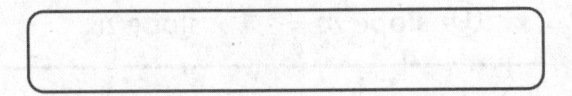

For Items 3–8, use the graph.

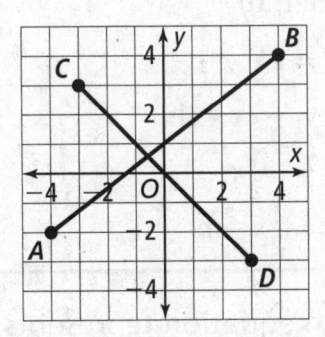

3. Select all the expressions that represent AB.
   - A. $\sqrt{(x_A - x_B)^2 + (y_A - y_B)^2}$
   - B. $\sqrt{(-4-4)^2 + (-2-4)^2}$
   - C. $\sqrt{(-4--2)^2 + (4-4)^2}$
   - D. $\sqrt{8^2 + 6^2}$
   - E. $\sqrt{2^2 + 0^2}$

4. What is AB?

5. What are the coordinates of the point $\frac{1}{4}$ of the way from A to B?

6. What is the midpoint of $\overline{CD}$?

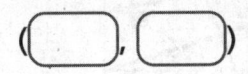

7. What is the length of $\overline{CD}$? Round to the nearest hundredth.

8. What are the coordinates of the point $\frac{1}{3}$ of the distance from D to C?

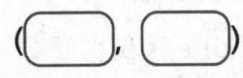

9. Select all the expressions that represent the distance between (x_1, y_1) and (x_2, y_2).
   - A. $d = \sqrt{(x_2 + x_1)^2 + (y_2 + y_1)^2}$
   - B. $d = \sqrt{|x_2 - x_1|^2 + |y_2 - y_1|^2}$
   - C. $d = \sqrt{(x_1 - x_2)^2 + (y_1 - y_2)^2}$
   - D. $d = \sqrt{(x_2 - x_1)^2 + (y_2 - y_1)^2}$
   - E. $d = \sqrt{(x_2 - x_1)^2 - (y_2 - y_1)^2}$

10. Which represents the distance between the point $P(x, y)$ and the origin?
    - Ⓐ $d = \sqrt{y^2 - x^2}$
    - Ⓑ $d = \sqrt{x^2 + y^2}$
    - Ⓒ $d = \sqrt{x^2 - y^2}$
    - Ⓓ $d = 0$

For Items 11–16, use the graph.

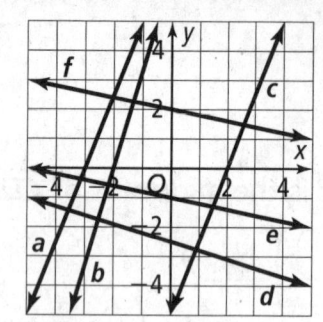

11. Select all the slopes that are correct.
    ☐ A. The slope of f is $-\frac{1}{5}$.
    ☐ B. The slope of d is $-\frac{1}{5}$.
    ☐ C. The slope of a is $\frac{5}{2}$.
    ☐ D. The slope of b is $-\frac{5}{2}$.
    ☐ E. The slope of e is 5.

12. Which statement is true?
    Ⓐ $a \perp d$　　Ⓒ $d \parallel f$
    Ⓑ $b \perp d$　　Ⓓ $a \parallel c$

13. What is the equation of d, in slope-intercept form?
    $y = \boxed{}x - \boxed{}$

14. Find the missing y-values and the slope for c.
    (2, ☐), (4, ☐),
    slope = ☐

15. Find the missing y-values and the slope for e.
    (0, ☐), (−5, ☐),
    slope = ☐

16. Find the missing y-values and the slope for d.
    (5, ☐) (−5, ☐),
    slope = ☐

17. Which statement is true if $m \perp n$?
    Ⓐ slope m = slope n
    Ⓑ slope m = −1 ÷ slope n
    Ⓒ slope m = 1 ÷ slope n
    Ⓓ slope m = −1 × slope n

18. Which statement is true if $m \parallel n$?
    Ⓐ slope m = slope n
    Ⓑ slope m = −1 ÷ slope n
    Ⓒ slope m = 1 ÷ slope n
    Ⓓ slope m = −1 × slope n

19. Which equation represents a line parallel to the line through A(0, 2) and B(1, 0)?
    Ⓐ $y = 2x + 1$
    Ⓑ $y = -2x + 1$
    Ⓒ $y = -\frac{1}{2}x - 1$
    Ⓓ $y = \frac{1}{2}x - 1$

20. Which equation represents a line perpendicular to the line through A(0, 3) and B(5, 1)?
    Ⓐ $y = \frac{5}{2}x + 2$
    Ⓑ $y = -\frac{2}{5}x - 2$
    Ⓒ $y = -\frac{5}{2}x - 2$
    Ⓓ $y = \frac{2}{5}x + 2$

Name _____

9-1 Lesson Quiz

Polygons in the Coordinate Plane

△ABC maps the outline of a new park. Use △ABC for Items 1 and 2.

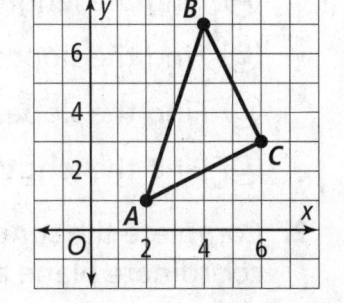

1. Select all the types of triangles that describe the park.
   - ☐ A. scalene
   - ☐ B. right
   - ☐ C. isosceles
   - ☐ D. equilateral
   - ☐ E. acute

2. What is the area of the park, in square units?
   - Ⓐ $2\sqrt{5}$
   - Ⓑ $4\sqrt{5}$
   - Ⓒ 10
   - Ⓓ 20

DEFG models the shape of a pig pen on a farm. Use *DEFG* for Items 3–5.

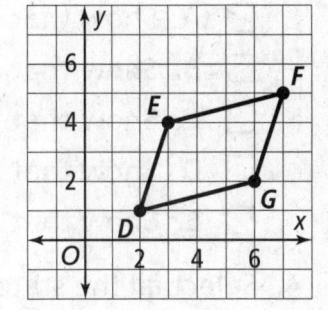

3. What is the perimeter of the pen, in units?
   - Ⓐ $\sqrt{8} + 3$
   - Ⓑ $\sqrt{8} + 9$
   - Ⓒ $\sqrt{10} + \sqrt{17}$
   - Ⓓ $2\sqrt{10} + 2\sqrt{17}$

4. Select all the correct descriptions of the relationship between $\overline{DE}$ and $\overline{FG}$.
   - ☐ A. parallel
   - ☐ B. perpendicular
   - ☐ C. proportional
   - ☐ D. equal length
   - ☐ E. collinear

5. What type of quadrilateral is *DEFG*? How do you know?
   - Ⓐ Square; all sides are congruent and opposite angles are equal.
   - Ⓑ Rhombus; all sides are congruent and opposite angles are equal.
   - Ⓒ Trapezoid; opposite sides are parallel and opposite angles are equal.
   - Ⓓ Parallelogram; opposite sides are parallel and opposite angles are equal.

Name _____

9-2 Lesson Quiz

Proofs Using Coordinate Geometry

1. Which is a plan to show that line *m* and line *n* are perpendicular?
   - Ⓐ Find the lengths of *m* and *n*, and show that length *m* = length *n*.
   - Ⓑ Find the slopes of *m* and *n*, and show that slope *m* = −1 × slope *n*.
   - Ⓒ Find the slopes of *m* and *n*, and show that slope *m* = −1 ÷ slope *n*.
   - Ⓓ Find the lengths of *m* and *n*, and show that length *m* = −1 ÷ length *n*.

2. Complete the sentence to explain how to show that points *A*, *B*, and *C* on the coordinate plane are collinear.

   Find the equation of [ ] $\overleftrightarrow{AB}$ / [ ] $\overleftrightarrow{BC}$ / [ ] $\overleftrightarrow{AC}$ and show that *C* is [ ] a solution / [ ] not a solution of the equation.

3. Select all the statements that would show that *DEFG* is a parallelogram.
   - [ ] A. Show that $\overline{DE} \cong \overline{FG}$ and $\overline{DE} \parallel \overline{FG}$.
   - [ ] B. Show that $\overline{DE} \cong \overline{FG}$ and $\overline{DE} \perp \overline{FG}$.
   - [ ] C. Show that $DE = FG$ and $\overline{DE} \parallel \overline{FG}$.
   - [ ] D. Show that $DE = FG$ and $\overline{DE} \perp \overline{FG}$.
   - [ ] E. Show that $DE = FG$ and $m\angle DEF = 90$.

4. Select all the statements that would show that the diagonals of *HJKL* are perpendicular.
   - [ ] A. $\overline{HJ} \perp \overline{KL}$
   - [ ] B. $\overline{HK} \perp \overline{JL}$
   - [ ] C. slope $\overline{HJ}$ = −1 ÷ slope $\overline{KL}$
   - [ ] D. slope $\overline{HK}$ = −1 ÷ slope $\overline{JL}$
   - [ ] E. $\overline{HJ} \parallel \overline{KL}$

5. Complete the sentences to explain how to show that all squares are similar.
   Draw a square on a coordinate plane with vertices at
   (0, 0), (0, [   ]), (*a*, *a*), and (*a*, [   ]).

   Draw another square with vertices at
   (0, 0), (0, [   ]), (*b*, *b*), and (*b*, [   ]).

   Explain that these two squares can represent any two squares. Then show that there is a dilation that maps one square to the other, so all squares are similar.

enVision® Geometry • Assessment Sourcebook

Name _____

9-3 Lesson Quiz

Circles in the Coordinate Plane

1. Use the numbers and operators to complete the equation for ⊙A.

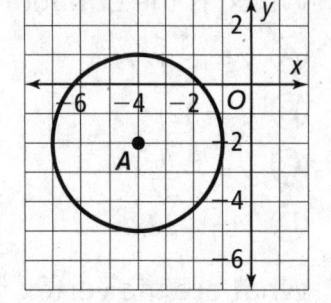

   (+) (−) (2) (4) (9) (16)

   $(x \;\square\; \square)^2 + (y \;\square\; \square)^2 = \square$

2. Which are the center and radius of the circle with equation $(x + 5)^2 + (y - 4)^2 = 9$?

   Ⓐ $(-5, -4); r = 3$ Ⓒ $(-5, 4); r = 3$
   Ⓑ $(5, -4); r = 9$ Ⓓ $(5, 4); r = 9$

3. Which is the equation of the circle with center (6, 2) and radius 8?

   Ⓐ $(x + 6)^2 + (y + 2)^2 = 64$
   Ⓑ $(x - 6)^2 + (y - 2)^2 = 64$
   Ⓒ $(x - 6)^2 - (y - 2)^2 = 64$
   Ⓓ $(x - 6)^2 + (y - 2)^2 = 8$

4. Which is the equation of ⊙B?

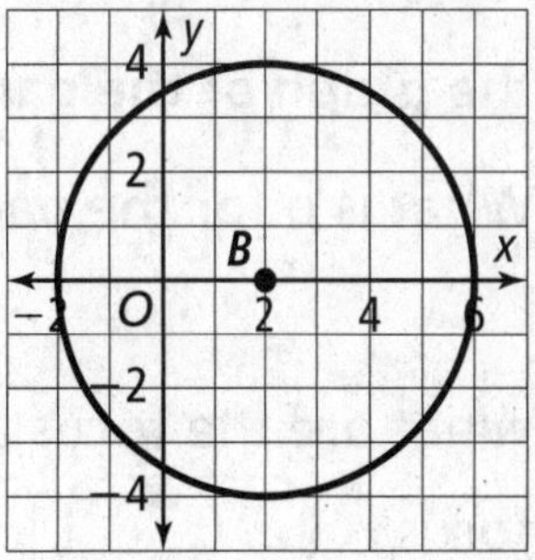

   Ⓐ $(x - 2)^2 + y^2 = 16$
   Ⓑ $(x + 2)^2 + y^2 = 16$
   Ⓒ $(x - 2)^2 - y^2 = 16$
   Ⓓ $(x + 2)^2 - y^2 = 16$

5. Is the point (−11, 2) on the circle with radius 5 and center (−7, 4)? Complete the sentences to explain.

   An equation of the circle is $(x + \square)^2 + (y + \square)^2 = \square$.

   Substitute (−11, 2) into the expression on the left side to get

   $(-4)^2 + (-2)^2$, which is $\square$. Because this value ☐ does / ☐ does not equal 25,

   the point (−11, 2) ☐ is / ☐ is not on the circle.

9-4 Lesson Quiz

Parabolas in the Coordinate Plane

1. Which is the equation of the parabola with focus (0, 8) and directrix $y = -8$?
   - Ⓐ $y = \frac{1}{32}x^2$
   - Ⓑ $y = 32x^2$
   - Ⓒ $y = -\frac{1}{32}x^2$
   - Ⓓ $y = -32x^2$

2. What are the vertex, focus, and directrix of the parabola with equation $y - 8 = \frac{1}{4}(x - 2)^2$?

   vertex = (⬚ , ⬚)

   focus = (⬚ , ⬚)

   directrix: $y = $ ⬚

3. Which is the equation of the parabola with focus (6, 2) and vertex (6, −4)?
   - Ⓐ $(y - 6) = \frac{1}{24}(x + 4)^2$
   - Ⓑ $(y - 4) = \frac{1}{24}(x + 6)^2$
   - Ⓒ $(y + 4) = \frac{1}{24}(x - 6)^2$
   - Ⓓ $(y + 6) = \frac{1}{24}(x - 4)^2$

Use the graph of the parabola to answer Items 4 and 5.

4. What is p for the parabola?

5. What are the focus and directrix of the parabola?

   focus = (⬚ , ⬚)

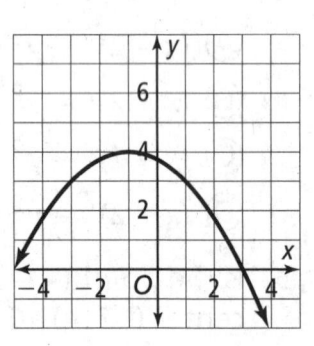

   directrix: $y = $ ⬚

Name _____

9 Topic Assessment Form A

Use DEFG for Items 1–3.

1. Select all the correct descriptors for the relationship between $\overline{EF}$ and $\overline{DG}$.

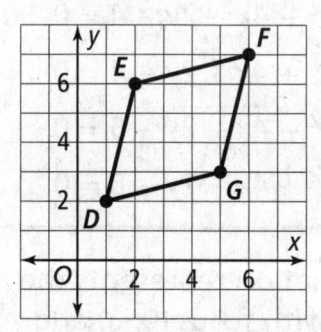

   ☐ A. perpendicular
   ☐ B. bisect each other
   ☐ C. parallel
   ☐ D. congruent
   ☐ E. collinear

2. Select all the types of quadrilaterals that describe DEFG.

   ☐ A. parallelogram
   ☐ B. rhombus
   ☐ C. square
   ☐ D. trapezoid
   ☐ E. rectangle

3. DEFG maps out Caroline's running route. If she does one complete loop, how far does she run?

   Ⓐ $8\sqrt{5}$
   Ⓑ $4\sqrt{17}$
   Ⓒ 17
   Ⓓ $4\sqrt{73}$

4. Given △ABD with midpoints E and F, complete part of a coordinate proof of the Triangle Midsegment Theorem.

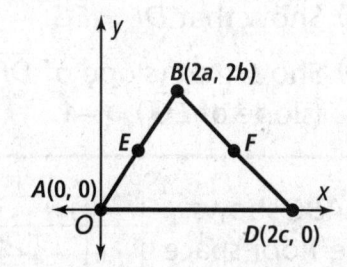

   [B(2a, 2b), E, F, A(0,0), D(2c, 0)]

   $\boxed{\dfrac{b}{a}}$ $\boxed{\text{parallel}}$ $\boxed{\text{perpendicular}}$

   $\boxed{c}$ $\boxed{b}$ $\boxed{\dfrac{a}{b}}$ $\boxed{0}$ $\boxed{a}$

   By the Midpoint Formula, the coordinates of the midpoints are E(☐, b) and F(a + c, ☐).

   The slope of $\overline{EF}$ = ☐ and the slope of $\overline{AD}$ = ☐, so $\overline{EF}$ is ☐ to $\overline{AD}$.

5. Select all the statements that would show that quadrilateral LMNP on the coordinate plane is a parallelogram.

   ☐ A. Show that the midpoint of $\overline{LN}$ is the same as the midpoint of $\overline{MP}$.
   ☐ B. Show that LN = MP.
   ☐ C. Show that LM = NP and MN = LP.
   ☐ D. Show that (slope of $\overline{LN}$) × (slope of $\overline{MP}$) = −1.
   ☐ E. Show that MN = LP.

6. Which of the following would show that the diagonals of quadrilateral DEFG on the coordinate plane are perpendicular?

   Ⓐ Show that slope of $\overline{DF}$ = slope of $\overline{EG}$.

   Ⓑ Show that midpoint of $\overline{DF}$ is the same as midpoint of $\overline{EG}$.

   Ⓒ Show that $DF = EG$.

   Ⓓ Show that (slope of $\overline{DF}$) × (slope of $\overline{EG}$) = –1.

7. △ABC shows the floor space that a corner cabinet takes up. What is the area in square units?

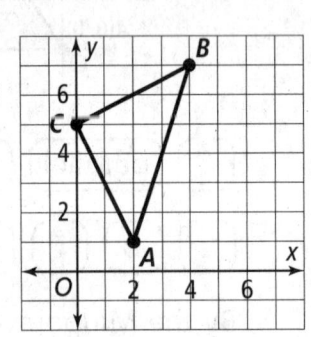

   Ⓐ 20
   Ⓑ 10
   Ⓒ $4\sqrt{5}$
   Ⓓ $2\sqrt{5}$

8. Complete the equation for a circle with center (2, 4) and radius 7.

   $(x + \square)^2 + (y + \square)^2 = \square$

9. Complete the equation for ⊙A.

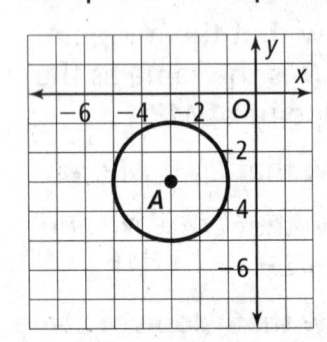

   $(x + \square)^2 + (y + \square)^2 = \square$

10. Which equation represents ⊙B?

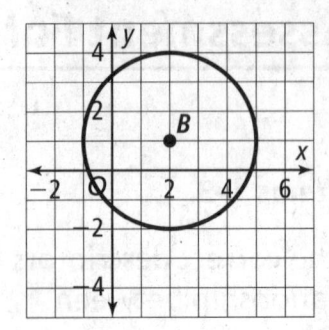

    Ⓐ $x^2 + y^2 - 4x - 2y - 4 = 0$
    Ⓑ $x^2 + y^2 + 4x + 2y - 4 = 0$
    Ⓒ $x^2 - y^2 - 4x + 2y - 6 = 0$
    Ⓓ $x^2 - y^2 + 4x - 2y - 6 = 0$

11. Which equation represents the parabola with focus (0, 6) and directrix $y = 2$?

    Ⓐ $y = 8x^2$
    Ⓑ $y = -\frac{1}{8}x^2$
    Ⓒ $(y - 4) = \frac{1}{8}x^2$
    Ⓓ $y = -8x^2$

12. △DEF as vertices D(0, 2) and F(6, 2). If △DEF has an area of 12 square units, select all the possible coordinates for E.

    ☐ A. (3, 4)   ☐ E. (6, –2)
    ☐ B. (3, –2)   ☐ F. (0, 0)
    ☐ C. (6, 0)   ☐ G. (0, 6)
    ☐ D. (3, 6)

13. Which equation represents the parabola with focus (8, 4) and vertex (8, –2)?

    Ⓐ $(y - 8) = \frac{1}{24}(x + 2)^2$
    Ⓑ $(y - 2) = \frac{1}{24}(x + 8)^2$
    Ⓒ $(y + 8) = \frac{1}{24}(x - 2)^2$
    Ⓓ $(y + 2) = \frac{1}{24}(x - 8)^2$

9 Topic Assessment Form B

Use DEFG for Items 1–3.

1. Select all the correct descriptors for the relationship between $\overline{EG}$ and $\overline{DF}$.

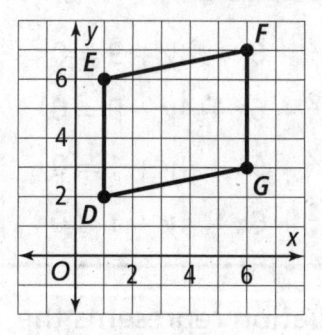

   ☐ A. parallel
   ☐ B. perpendicular
   ☐ C. bisect each other
   ☐ D. congruent
   ☐ E. coplanar

2. Select all the terms that describe DEFG.

   ☐ A. square
   ☐ B. quadrilateral
   ☐ C. parallelogram
   ☐ D. rhombus
   ☐ E. rectangle

3. DEFG maps out Carrie's dog walking route. If she does one complete loop, how far does she walk with the dogs?

   Ⓐ $8 + 4\sqrt{26}$
   Ⓑ $12\sqrt{26}$
   Ⓒ $8 + 2\sqrt{26}$
   Ⓓ $12 + \sqrt{26}$

4. Given $\triangle ABD$ with midpoints E and F, complete part of a coordinate proof of the Triangle Midsegment Theorem.

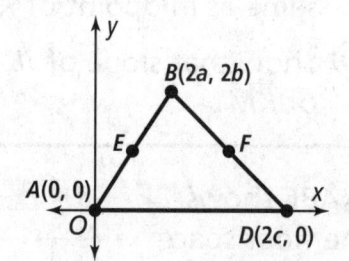

   ⓐ ⓑ ⓒ ⓐ+ⓒ ⓑ+ⓒ

   ⓐ+ⓑ ⓵⁄₂ ⓶ⓐ ⓶ⓑ ⓶ⓒ

   By the Midpoint Formula, the coordinates of the midpoints are

   $E(\boxed{}, b)$ and $F(\boxed{}, b)$.

   $EF = \boxed{}$ and $AD = \boxed{}$,

   so $EF = \boxed{}$.

5. Select all the statements that would show that quadrilateral PQRS on the coordinate plane is a parallelogram.

   ☐ A. Show that slope of $\overline{PQ}$ = slope of $\overline{RS}$ and $PS = QR$.
   ☐ B. Show that slope of $\overline{PQ}$ = slope of $\overline{RS}$ and $PQ = RS$.
   ☐ C. Show that midpoint of $\overline{PR}$ is the same as midpoint of $\overline{QS}$.
   ☐ D. Show that (slope of $\overline{PR}$) × (slope of $\overline{QS}$) = -1.
   ☐ E. Show that $PR = RS$.

6. Which of the following would show that the diagonals of quadrilateral JKLM on the coordinate plane are congruent?

Ⓐ Show that JL = KM.
Ⓑ Show that (slope of $\overline{JL}$) × (slope of $\overline{KM}$) = −1.
Ⓒ Show that midpoint of $\overline{JL}$ is the same as midpoint of $\overline{KM}$.
Ⓓ Show that slope of $\overline{JL}$ = slope of $\overline{KM}$.

7. △ABC shows the floor space that a corner cabinet takes up. What is the area in square units?

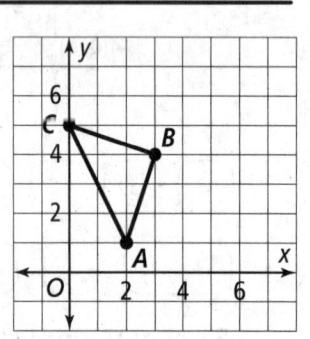

Ⓐ 10
Ⓑ 5
Ⓒ $2\sqrt{10}$
Ⓓ $\sqrt{10}$

8. Complete the equation for a circle with center (4, 8) and radius 2.

$(x + \boxed{})^2 + (y + \boxed{})^2 = \boxed{}$

9. Complete the equation for ⊙A.

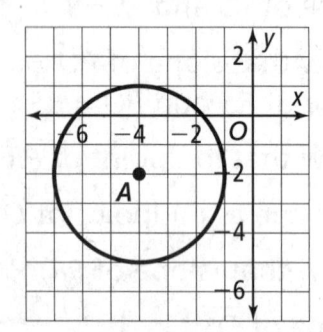

$(x + \boxed{})^2 + (y + \boxed{})^2 = \boxed{}$

10. Which equation represents ⊙B?

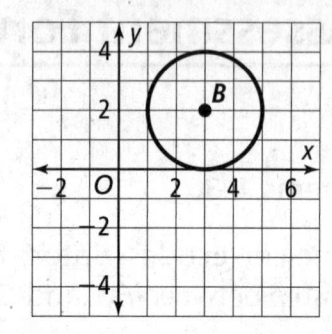

Ⓐ $x^2 + y^2 − 6x − 4y + 9 = 0$
Ⓑ $x^2 + y^2 + 6x + 4y + 9 = 0$
Ⓒ $x^2 − y^2 − 6x + 4y + 1 = 0$
Ⓓ $x^2 − y^2 + 6x − 4y + 1 = 0$

11. Which equation represents the parabola with focus (0, 4) and directrix y = 2?

Ⓐ $(y − 3) = \frac{1}{4}x^2$
Ⓑ $y = 4x^2$
Ⓒ $y = -\frac{1}{4}x^2$
Ⓓ $y = -4x^2$

12. △LMN as vertices L(0, 4) and N(8, 4). If △LMN has an area of 16 square units, select all the possible coordinates for M.

☐ A. (8, 8)   ☐ E. (0, 6)
☐ B. (8, 2)   ☐ F. (4, 8)
☐ C. (0, 0)   ☐ G. (4, 2)
☐ D. (4, 0)

13. Which equation represents the parabola with focus (−6, 4) and vertex (−6, 1)?

Ⓐ $(y − 6) = \frac{1}{12}(x + 1)^2$
Ⓑ $(y − 1) = \frac{1}{12}(x + 6)^2$
Ⓒ $(y + 1) = \frac{1}{12}(x − 6)^2$
Ⓓ $(y + 6) = \frac{1}{12}(x − 1)^2$

Name _____

9 Performance Assessment Form A

A landscape architect is planning a rose garden. The garden will have a circular fountain with a diameter of 10 meters centered at the point of intersection of the diagonals of the rose garden. The vertices of the rose garden will be placed at points A, B, C, and D. Each unit in the diagram represents 10 meters.

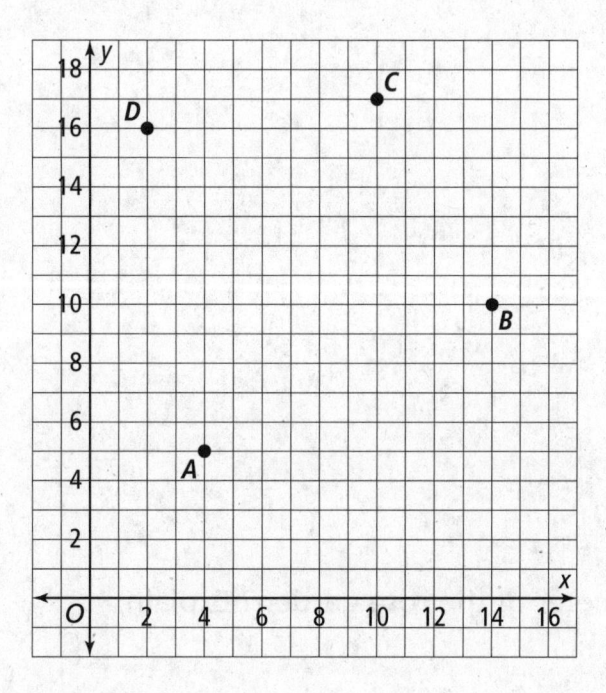

1. Find the lengths and slopes of the sides of the rose garden. What shape is the best description of the rose garden? Explain.

2. What equation represents the fountain? Explain.

3. What is the perimeter of the rose garden? Explain.

4. What is the total area covered by the rose garden? Explain.

Name _____

9 Performance Assessment Form B

The owner of a large campground wants to increase the number of recycling and composting bins that are available for guests and reorganize the distribution of the bins throughout the campground. The plan is for each small group of campsites to have a designated recycling and composting center.

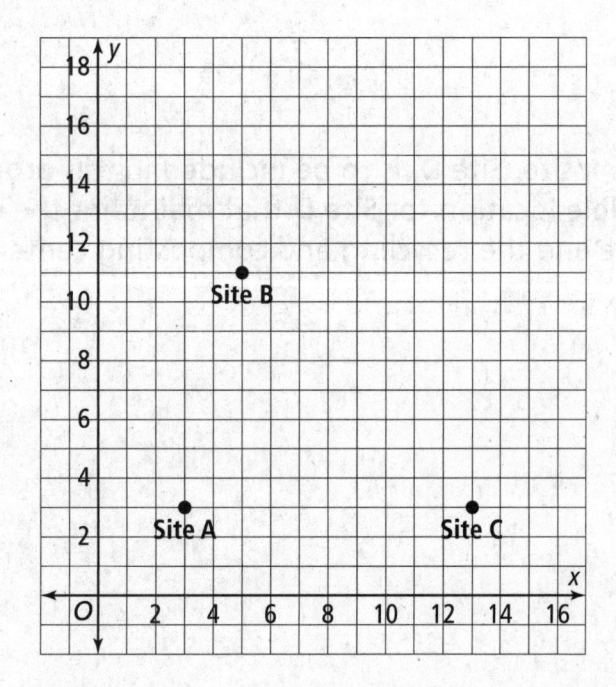

1. The recycling and composting center needs to be equidistant from the campsites in each group. Where should the center be located for Sites A, B, and C? Explain.

2. Show evidence that your location for the recycling and composting center is equidistant from Sites A, B, and C.

3. Suppose a 4th campsite, Site D, is to be included in this group of campsites. What is one possible location for Site D that maintains the equal distance between each site and the recycling and composting center? Explain.

4. What geometric figure would show all possible locations for campsites that are the same distance from the recycling and composting center as Sites A, B, and C? What is an equation for that figure?

Name _____

10 Readiness Assessment

1. What is the area of ⊙X expressed in terms of π?

    Ⓐ 4.5π
    Ⓑ 9π
    Ⓒ 20.25π
    Ⓓ 81π

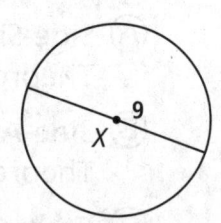

2. Rachael's grandpa's age is 19 more than 7 times Rachael's age. Her grandma's age is 9 times Rachael's age, plus 3. If Rachael's grandma and grandpa are the same age, what is Rachael's age?

    _____

3. The lengths of the legs of a right triangle are 20 and 21. What is the length of the hypotenuse?

    _____

4. Given isosceles trapezoid ABCD, what are m∠B, m∠C, and m∠D?

    Ⓐ m∠B = 124°, m∠C = 56°, m∠D = 56°
    Ⓑ m∠B = 56°, m∠C = 56°, m∠D = 124°
    Ⓒ m∠B = 56°, m∠C = 124°, m∠D = 56°
    Ⓓ m∠B = 124°, m∠C = 112°, m∠D = 112°

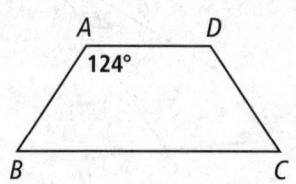

5. Which additional fact would prove △PQR ≅ △STU?

    Ⓐ ∠P ≅ ∠S   Ⓒ ∠R ≅ ∠S
    Ⓑ ∠Q ≅ ∠T   Ⓓ ∠R ≅ ∠U

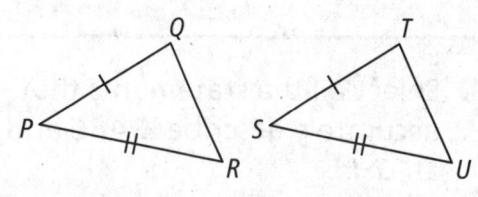

6. The circumference of a circle is 64π. What is the radius of the circle?

    Ⓐ 32   Ⓑ 64   Ⓒ 80   Ⓓ 128

7. If Lucas makes $8 an hour, and made $42 in one day, how many hours did he work that day?

    _____

8. Which could be the lengths of the sides of a right triangle?

    Ⓐ 8, 15, 17   Ⓒ 4, 7, 22
    Ⓑ 6, 12, 18   Ⓓ 3, 5, 34

9. In parallelogram ABCD, what is m∠A?

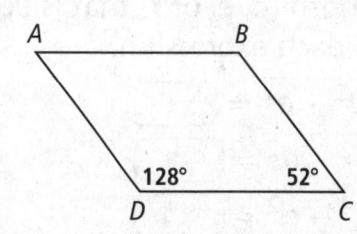

    Ⓐ 360°
    Ⓑ 180°
    Ⓒ 128°
    Ⓓ 52°

10. Four people's ages are related by the following equation. Solve the equation for p.

$(q + p)q = (s + r)s$

$\boxed{} = \dfrac{(\boxed{} + \boxed{})\boxed{}}{\boxed{}} - \boxed{}$

11. Select all the statements that accurately describe △ABC and △FGH.

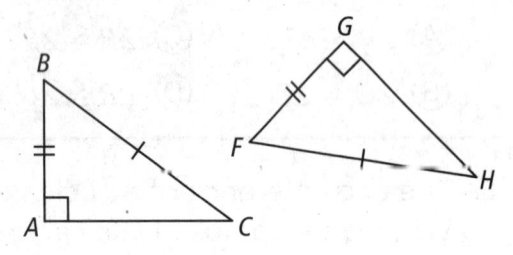

☐ **A.** $\overline{AC} \cong \overline{GH}$
☐ **B.** $\angle B \cong \angle H$
☐ **C.** $\overline{GH} \cong \overline{BC}$
☐ **D.** $\angle F \cong \angle B$
☐ **E.** $m\angle H + m\angle B = 90$

12. If the area of a circle is 12π, what is the circumference of the circle expressed in terms of π?

$\boxed{}\sqrt{\boxed{}}\pi$

13. A right triangle has legs with lengths d and e, and a hypotenuse with length f. Write a single side length (d, e, or f) that is equivalent to each expression.

$\sqrt{d^2 + e^2} = \boxed{}$
$\sqrt{f^2 - d^2} = \boxed{}$
$\sqrt{f^2 - e^2} = \boxed{}$

14. Which best describes a triangle with sides 65, 72, and 97?

Ⓐ right scalene   Ⓒ right isosceles
Ⓑ acute scalene Ⓓ obtuse isosceles

15. Which best describes the reason why $\angle A \cong \angle R$ in the triangles shown?

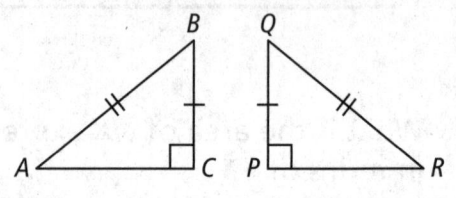

Ⓐ Side-Side-Side Congruence Theorem

Ⓑ Side-Angle-Side Congruence Theorem

Ⓒ Corresponding parts of congruent triangles are congruent.

Ⓓ The square of the hypotenuse is equal to the sum of the squares of the legs.

16. Write an expression in terms of π to represent the area of circle P.

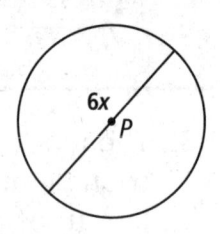

$\boxed{}\boxed{}^2(\pi)$

17. Is $m\angle BCD = m\angle CAB + m\angle ABC$? Why or why not?

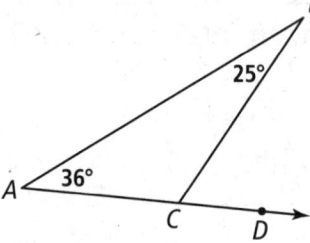

Ⓐ Yes; it is true in this case, but not for all possible cases.

Ⓑ No; $m\angle BCD = m\angle CAB$ because corresponding angles are congruent.

Ⓒ Yes; the measures of the angles in a triangle add to 180, as do supplementary angles.

Ⓓ No; this case does not work, but it would if ABC were a right triangle.

Name _____

10-1 Lesson Quiz
Arcs and Sectors

enVision Geometry
SavvasRealize.com

1. Given ⊙N, what is m$\widehat{ABC}$? 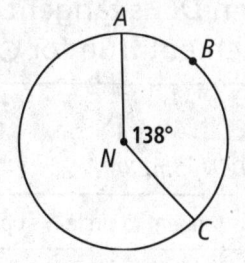
   - Ⓐ 111
   - Ⓑ 138
   - Ⓒ 222
   - Ⓓ 276

2. In ⊙Z, m∠PZR is 120°. What is the length of $\widehat{PR}$? 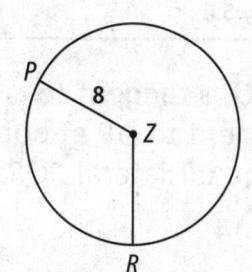
   - Ⓐ $\frac{2}{3}\pi$
   - Ⓒ $\frac{4}{3}\pi$
   - Ⓑ $\frac{8}{3}\pi$
   - Ⓓ $\frac{16}{3}\pi$

3. If the arc length of $\widehat{NMP}$ is $\frac{11}{2}\pi$, what is the length of $\widehat{MNP}$ expressed in terms of π? 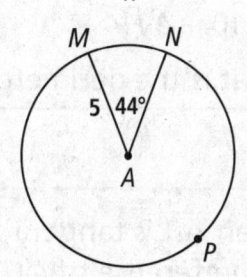
   - Ⓐ 54π
   - Ⓑ 108π
   - Ⓒ $\frac{10}{18}\pi$
   - Ⓓ $\frac{108}{9}\pi$

4. Calculate each value for ⊙P.

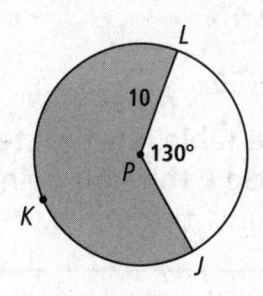

   m$\widehat{JKL}$ = ☐

   area of shaded sector = $\frac{\square}{\square}\pi$

   area of unshaded sector = $\frac{\square}{\square}\pi$

5. Which is an expression in square units that represents the area of the shaded segment of ⊙C? 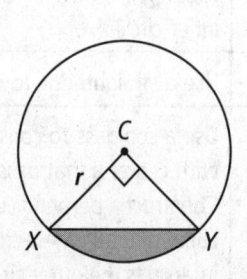
   - Ⓐ $\frac{1}{4}r^2(\pi - 4)$
   - Ⓑ $\frac{1}{4}\pi r^2$
   - Ⓒ $\frac{1}{4}\pi r^2 - 2r^2$
   - Ⓓ $\frac{1}{2}r^2\left(\frac{1}{2}\pi - 1\right)$

enVision® Geometry • Assessment Sourcebook

10-2 Lesson Quiz

Lines Tangent to a Circle

1. Given $\overrightarrow{DC}$ is tangent to ⊙N at point C, is each statement true for ⊙N?

	Yes	No
m∠DCN < m∠BAN	☐	☐
$\overrightarrow{BA}$ is tangent to circle N at point A.	☐	☐
NB ≈ 6.4	☐	☐

2. If $\overline{PQ}$ is tangent to circle R at point Q and $\overline{PS}$ is tangent to ⊙R at point S, what is the perimeter of quadrilateral PQRS?

   Ⓐ 14 Ⓒ $5 + 4\sqrt{14}$
   Ⓑ $10 + 4\sqrt{14}$ Ⓓ 28

3. What is the perimeter of △XYZ?

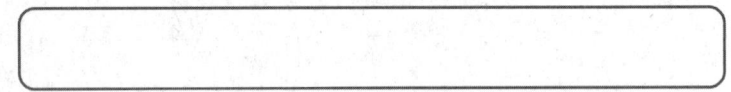

   [ ]

4. Given $\overline{AB}$ is tangent to ⊙C at point B, what is the circumference of ⊙C?

   Ⓐ 16π Ⓒ 34π
   Ⓑ 30π Ⓓ 64π

5. The table lists the steps to construct a tangent to circle P through point T. Label the steps in order from 1 through 4.

	Use a straightedge to construct $\overline{BP}$. Label point C where $\overline{BP}$ intersects the inner circle.
	Use a straightedge to construct $\overline{TC}$.
	Use a compass to construct a circle with center P that passes through T. Construct a perpendicular to $\overline{TP}$ at A. Label point B where the perpendicular intersects the outer circle.
	Use a straightedge to draw $\overline{PT}$. Label point A where $\overline{PT}$ intersects the circle.

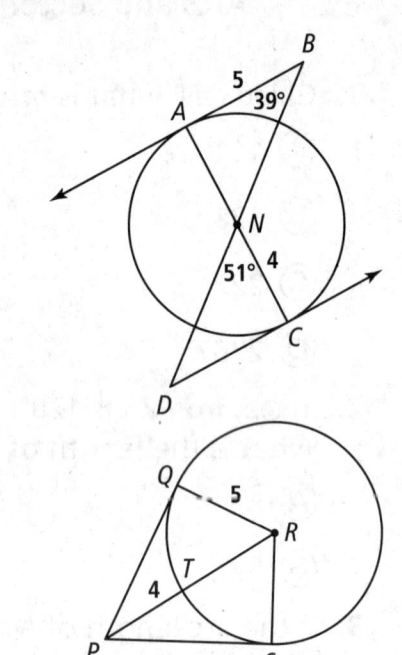

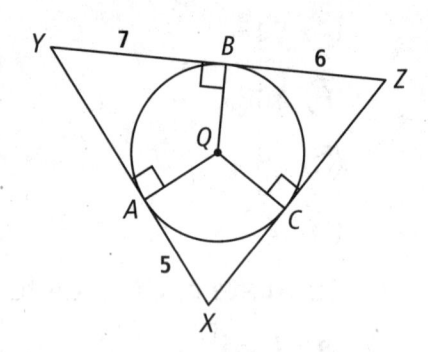

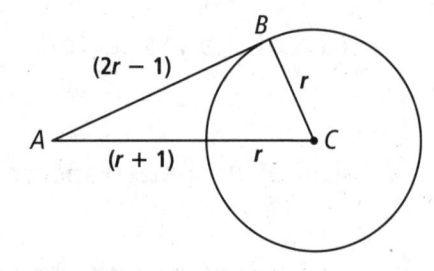

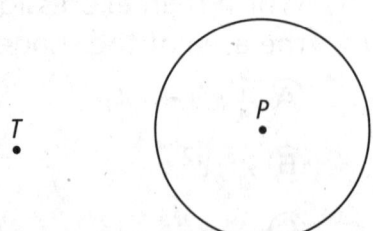

10-3 Lesson Quiz
Chords

1. Is each statement true for ⊙A?

	Yes	No
$\overline{KA} \cong \overline{MA}$	☐	☐
∠JKA ≅ ∠MLA	☐	☐
∠LAK ≅ ∠MAJ	☐	☐

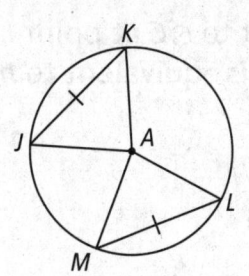

2. Use ⊙Q, DE = FG. Select all of the statements that must be true.
   - ☐ A. $\overline{DE} \cong \overline{FG}$
   - ☐ B. $\overline{EF} \cong \overline{QD}$
   - ☐ C. △DQE ≅ △FQE
   - ☐ D. △FQE ≅ △FQG
   - ☐ E. ∠DQE ≅ ∠GQF

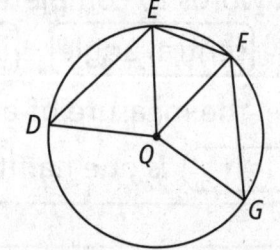

3. Given TU = 7.4, what is PS in ⊙C?

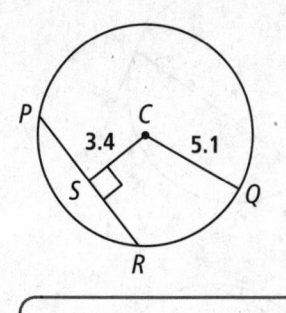

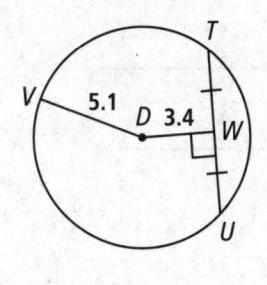

   ☐

4. In ⊙Z, chords $\overline{JK}$ and $\overline{LM}$ are congruent. Which must be equivalent to the distance from $\overline{JK}$ to point Z?

   Ⓐ the distance from $\overline{JK}$ to $\overline{LM}$

   Ⓑ the distance from $\overline{LM}$ to point Z

   Ⓒ the distance from point K to $\overline{LM}$

   Ⓓ the distance from point J to point Z

5. Given ⊙N with chord $\overline{AB}$, which point lies on the perpendicular bisector of $\overline{AB}$?

   Ⓐ A   Ⓒ N

   Ⓑ B   Ⓓ none of these points

10-4 Lesson Quiz

Inscribed Angles

1. Given $\overleftrightarrow{LM}$ tangent to $\odot C$ at point L, which expression is equivalent to $m\widehat{JK}$?

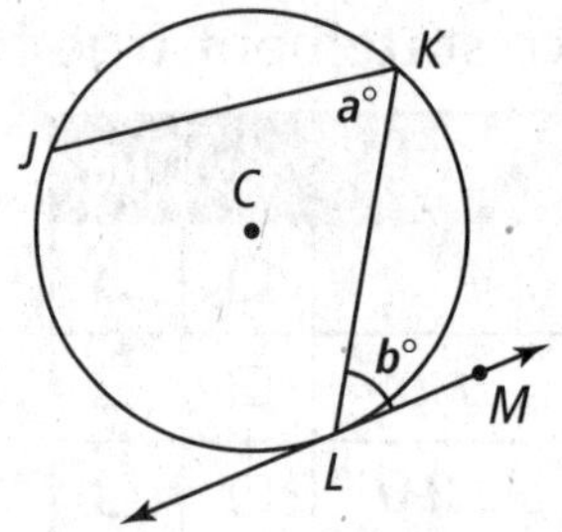

   Ⓐ $360 - (a + b)$

   Ⓑ $360 - 2(a + b)$

   Ⓒ $360 - (2a + b)$

   Ⓓ $360 + (2a + b)$

2. Select the correct words to complete the statement.

   [intercepted arc] [central angle] [inscribed angle]

   In any given circle, the measure of a(n) _____ is one half the measure of the _____.

3. Given $\overleftrightarrow{YZ}$ tangent to $\odot J$ at point Y and $m\angle WYZ = 104$, what is $m\widehat{WXY}$?

   _____

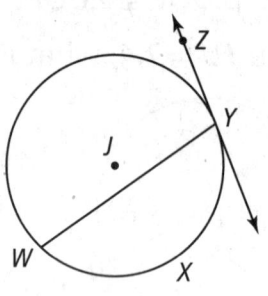

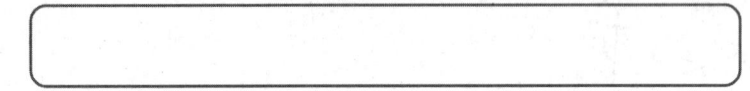

For Items 4 and 5, use $\odot Z$.

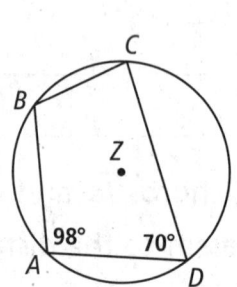

4. What is $m\widehat{BC}$?

   Ⓐ 28

   Ⓑ 56

   Ⓒ 70

   Ⓓ 140

5. What is $m\angle BCD$?

   Ⓐ 82

   Ⓑ 168

   Ⓒ 192

   Ⓓ 220

Name _____

10-5 Lesson Quiz

Secant Lines and Segments

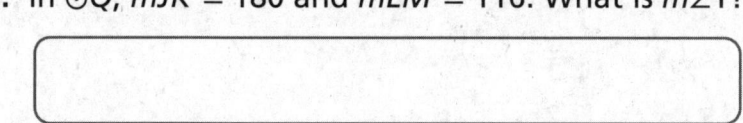

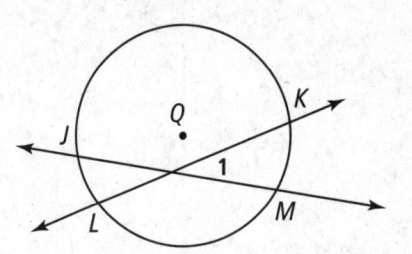

1. In ⊙Q, $m\widehat{JK} = 180$ and $m\widehat{LM} = 116$. What is $m\angle 1$?

   [   ]

2. Select the correct words to complete the statement.

   [half]   [twice]   [sum]   [difference]

   The measure of the angle formed by two lines that intersect outside a circle is [   ] the measure of the [   ] of the measures of the intercepted arcs.

3. Given ⊙Z with tangents $\overrightarrow{XW}$ and $\overrightarrow{XY}$, what is $m\widehat{WVY}$?
   - Ⓐ 70
   - Ⓑ 140
   - Ⓒ 250
   - Ⓓ 270

4. In ⊙E, what is AC?
   - Ⓐ 2.4
   - Ⓑ 5.2
   - Ⓒ 5.6
   - Ⓓ 6.4

5. Given ⊙K with secants $\overline{NS}$ and $\overline{NR}$, which expression represents PS?
   - Ⓐ $\dfrac{(NQ)(NQ + QR)}{NP} - NP$
   - Ⓑ $\dfrac{(QR)(NQ + QR)}{NP} - NP$
   - Ⓒ $\dfrac{NP + NQ + QR}{NR} - NR$
   - Ⓓ $\dfrac{(NP)(NQ + QR)}{NR} - NR$

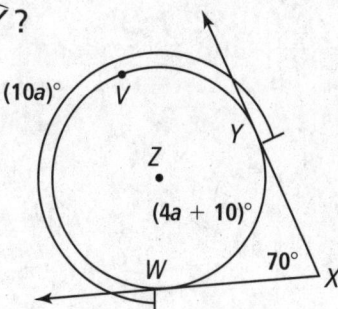

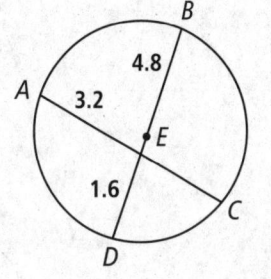

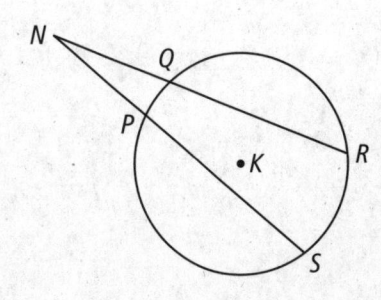

Name _____

10 Topic Assessment Form A

1. What is the length of $\widehat{EF}$? 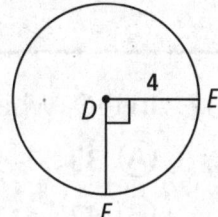
   Ⓐ 8π
   Ⓑ 4π
   Ⓒ 2π
   Ⓓ π

2. If $\widehat{HJR} = \frac{9}{10}\pi$, what is the length of $\widehat{RHJ}$? 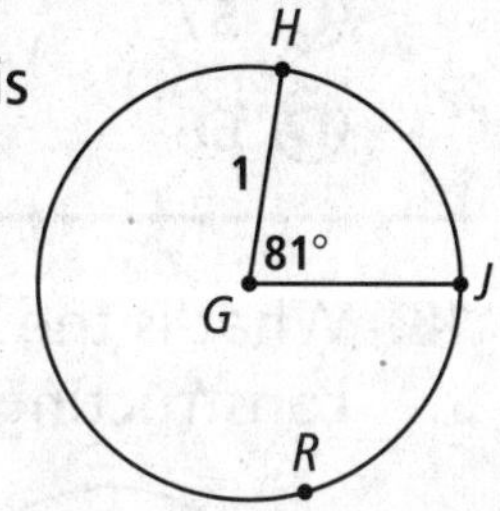
   Ⓐ $\frac{31}{20}\pi$
   Ⓑ $\frac{9}{20}\pi$
   Ⓒ $\frac{11}{20}\pi$
   Ⓓ $\frac{81}{20}\pi$

3. If the area of the shaded part of ⊙K is $\frac{15}{2}\pi$, what is the value of x?

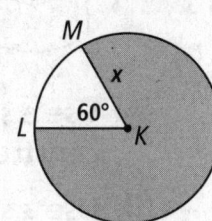

4. $\overleftrightarrow{PQ}$ is tangent to ⊙R at point P and is parallel to $\overleftrightarrow{ST}$. Is each statement true for ⊙R?

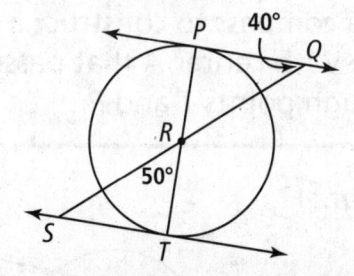

	Yes	No
$\overleftrightarrow{ST}$ is tangent to ⊙R at point T.	☐	☐
$m\angle RST = m\angle SRT$	☐	☐
$m\angle STR = m\angle QPR$	☐	☐

5. $\overline{UV}$ is tangent to ⊙W at point U. What is the value of x? 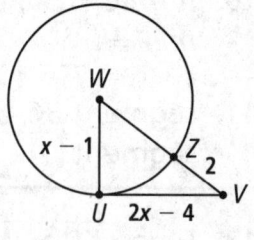
   Ⓐ 3   Ⓒ 5
   Ⓑ 4   Ⓓ 6

6. Select all the steps that are **NOT** part of the construction of a tangent to circle P through point T.
   ☐ A. Draw $\overline{PT}$.
   ☐ B. Construct the ⊥ bisector of $\overline{PT}$ and label the midpoint M.
   ☐ C. Construct a ⊥ to $\overline{TP}$ at P.
   ☐ D. Construct a circle with center M and radius MP.
   ☐ E. Label the intersection of the circles B.
   ☐ F. Construct $\overline{BM}$.
   ☐ G. Construct $\overline{BP}$.

7. Given ⊙A and $\overline{BC} \cong \overline{CD}$, what is $m\widehat{BC}$? 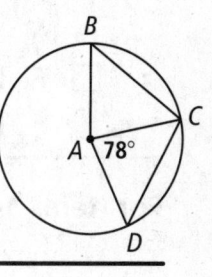
   Ⓐ 39   Ⓒ 156
   Ⓑ 78   Ⓓ 222

8. In ⊙C, $\overline{DE} \cong \overline{FG}$. Select all the true statements. 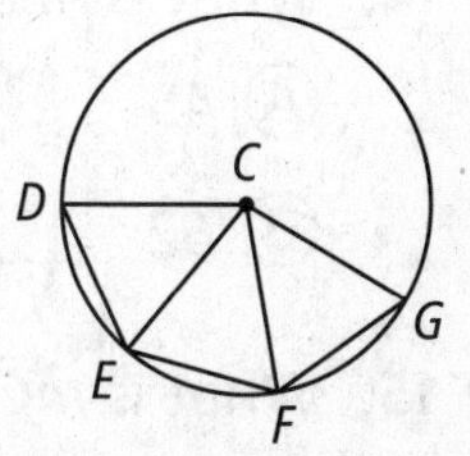
   ☐ A. $\widehat{DE} \cong \widehat{FG}$
   ☐ B. $\overline{EF} \cong \overline{ED}$
   ☐ C. △DCE ≅ △FCE
   ☐ D. △FCE ≅ △FCG
   ☐ E. ∠DCE ≅ ∠GCF

For Items 9–11, use ⊙G with m∠AGC = 90, $\overline{AC} \cong \overline{DF}$, and $\overline{AB} \cong \overline{EF}$.

9. ∠AGB ≅ ∠ ☐

10. If $m\widehat{BC}$ = 50, then $m\widehat{EF}$ = ☐.

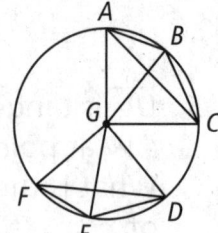

11. segment BC ≅ segment ☐

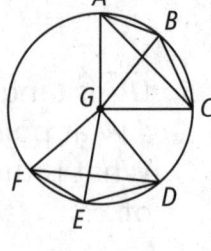

12. Given $\overline{KL} \cong \overline{JM}$, what is JM? 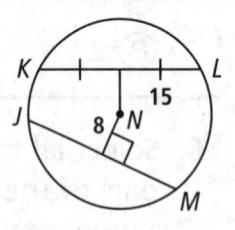
    Ⓐ 8   Ⓒ 17
    Ⓑ 15 Ⓓ 30

13. Which step is NOT part of the construction of a hexagon inscribed in circle P?

    ☐ A. Mark point T on the circle.
    ☐ B. Set the compass to the diameter of the circle.
    ☐ C. Move the compass point to the intersection of the arc and the circle.
    ☐ D. Construct a ⊥ to $\overline{TP}$ at S.
    ☐ E. Draw another arc through the circle.
    ☐ F. Draw chords connecting the points on the circle.

For Items 14 and 15, use ⊙A.

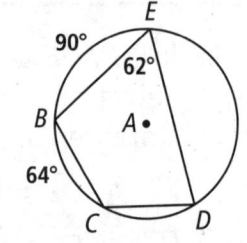

14. What is m∠CDE?
    Ⓐ 45   Ⓒ 64
    Ⓑ 62   Ⓓ 77

15. What is $m\widehat{CD}$?
    Ⓐ 60 Ⓑ 62 Ⓒ 64 Ⓓ 124

16. In order to construct an inscribed equilateral triangle, you must first construct a
    ☐ square.
    ☐ regular hexagon.
    ☐ regular pentagon.

17. In ⊙Q, what is m∠1? 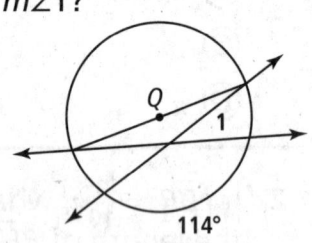
    Ⓐ 33
    Ⓑ 47
    Ⓒ 57
    Ⓓ 66

18. What is the next step in constructing a tangent to ⊙P?

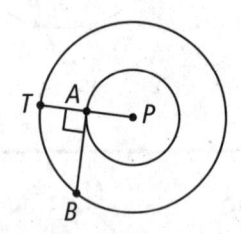

    Ⓐ Use a straightedge to construct $\overline{TB}$.
    Ⓑ Use a straightedge to construct $\overline{BP}$.
    Ⓒ Use a compass to construct a circle with center T and passing through A.
    Ⓓ Use a compass to construct a circle with center A that passes through points T and P.

19. What is m∠1? 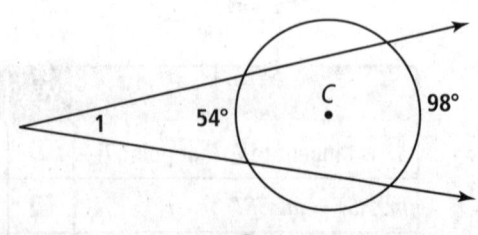
    Ⓐ 22   Ⓒ 46
    Ⓑ 27   Ⓓ 76

10 Topic Assessment Form B

1. What is the length of $\widehat{HJ}$? 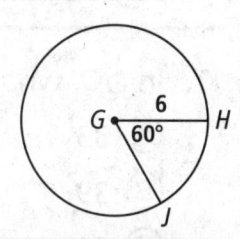
   - Ⓐ $\frac{\pi}{18}$
   - Ⓑ $\frac{\pi}{3}$
   - Ⓒ π
   - Ⓓ 2π

2. If $\widehat{MLP} = \frac{17}{18}\pi$, what is the length of $\widehat{LMP}$? 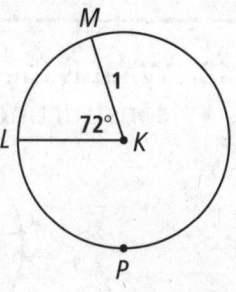
   - Ⓐ $\frac{17}{90}\pi$
   - Ⓑ $\frac{41}{90}\pi$
   - Ⓒ $\frac{72}{90}\pi$
   - Ⓓ $\frac{131}{90}\pi$

3. If the area of the shaded part of ⊙N is $\frac{19}{6}\pi$, what is the value of x?

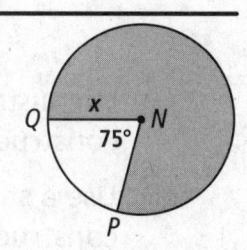

4. $\overleftrightarrow{XY}$ is tangent to ⊙U at point Y. Is each statement true for ⊙U?

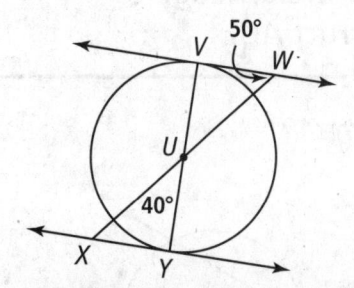

	Yes	No
$m\angle VUW = m\angle UXY$	☐	☐
$m\angle VWU = m\angle YXU$	☐	☐
$\overrightarrow{VW}$ is tangent to ⊙U at point V.	☐	☐

5. $\overline{BC}$ is tangent to ⊙A at point B. What is the value of x? 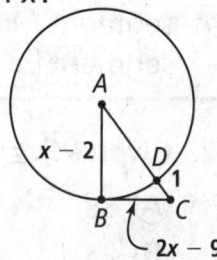
   - Ⓐ 4
   - Ⓑ 5
   - Ⓒ 6
   - Ⓓ 8

6. Select all the steps that are part of the construction of a tangent to circle P through point T.
   - ☐ A. Construct a ⊥ to $\overline{TP}$ at P.
   - ☐ B. Draw $\overline{PT}$.
   - ☐ C. Construct the ⊥ bisector of $\overline{PT}$ and label the midpoint M.
   - ☐ D. Construct $\overline{BM}$.
   - ☐ E. Construct a circle with center M and radius MP.
   - ☐ F. Label the intersection of the circles B.
   - ☐ G. Construct $\overline{BP}$.

7. Given ⊙D and $\overline{EF} \cong \overline{FG}$, what is $m\widehat{EF}$? 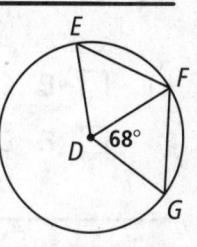
   - Ⓐ 34
   - Ⓑ 38
   - Ⓒ 68
   - Ⓓ 136

8. In ⊙H, $\angle JHK \cong \angle LHM$. Select all the statements that must be true. 
   - ☐ A. $\triangle LHK \cong \triangle JHK$
   - ☐ B. $\overline{ML} \cong \overline{JK}$
   - ☐ C. $\widehat{MLK} \cong \widehat{LKJ}$
   - ☐ D. $\triangle LHM \cong \triangle LHK$
   - ☐ E. $\triangle JHK \cong \triangle LHM$

For Items 9–11, use ⊙P with m∠KPH = 100, $\overline{HK} \cong \overline{LN}$, and $\overline{JK} \cong \overline{LM}$.

9. ∠KPH ≅ ∠ ☐

10. If $m\widehat{LM} = 60$, then $m\widehat{JH} = $ ☐.

11. segment MN ≅ segment ☐

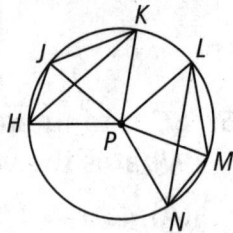

12. Given $\overline{PQ} \cong \overline{SR}$, what is SR?
   - Ⓐ 58
   - Ⓑ 42
   - Ⓒ 41
   - Ⓓ 40

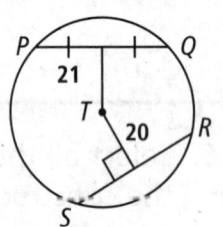

13. Which steps are part of the construction of a hexagon inscribed in circle P?
   - ☐ A. Move the compass point to the intersection of the arc and the circle.
   - ☐ B. Draw another arc through the circle.
   - ☐ C. Mark point T on the circle. and the circle.
   - ☐ D. Set the compass to the diameter of the circle.
   - ☐ E. Construct a ⊥ to $\overline{TP}$ at S.
   - ☐ F. Draw chords connecting the points on the circle.

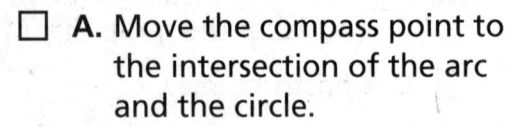

For Items 14 and 15, use ⊙F.

14. What is m∠HJK?
   - Ⓐ 80   Ⓒ 82
   - Ⓑ 81   Ⓓ 84

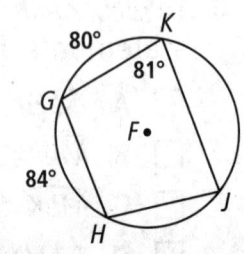

15. What is $m\widehat{HJ}$?
   - Ⓐ 82   Ⓑ 81   Ⓒ 80   Ⓓ 78

16. In order to construct an inscribed square, you must construct
   - ☐ a perpendicular bisector.
   - ☐ an angle bisector.
   - ☐ a line tangent to a circle.

17. In ⊙Q, what is m∠1?
   - Ⓐ 33
   - Ⓑ 39
   - Ⓒ 51
   - Ⓓ 57

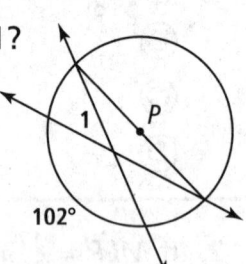

18. What is the next step in constructing a tangent to ⊙P?

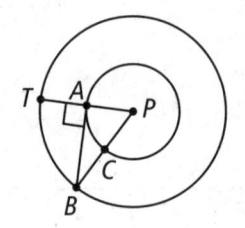

   - Ⓐ Use a straightedge to construct $\overline{TC}$.
   - Ⓑ Use a straightedge to construct $\overline{TB}$.
   - Ⓒ Use a compass to construct a circle through T and B.
   - Ⓓ Use a straightedge to construct $\overline{AC}$.

19. What is m∠1? 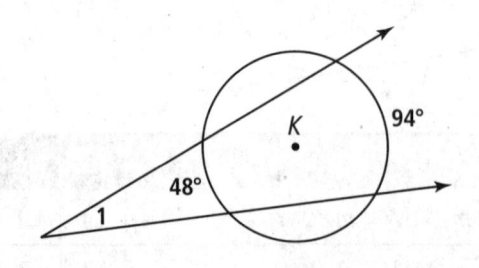
   - Ⓐ 21   Ⓒ 24
   - Ⓑ 23   Ⓓ 47

Name _____

10 Performance Assessment Form A

William is an architect. He is designing a pedestal for a large sculpture that will be placed on a triangular plot of land.

He begins his plans by drawing the plot of land, which he labels △ABC, and then adding a circle with center G tangent to all three borders of the plot, as shown.

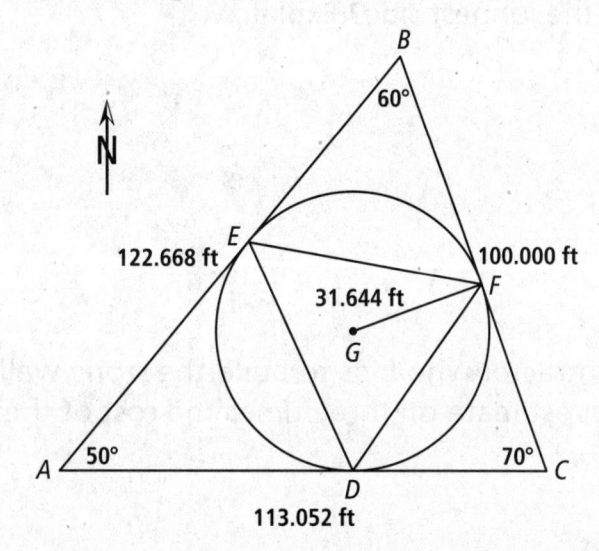

The circle will be a fence. The pedestal will be triangular and bordered by a stone wall, which he labels △DEF, that raises the sculpture above the surrounding land.

1. What type of triangle is the pedestal?

2. Where is the center of the circle located in △ABC? Explain.

3. What is $m\angle BFG$? Explain.

4. The fencing William chooses costs $29.53 per foot, including installation. What will the fencing cost?

5. What percent of the fencing will be used between points D and E? Round to the nearest percent.

William decides to estimate the cost of the stone wall based on three times the cost of the longest side.

6. Which side of △DEF is the longest side? Explain.

7. What is length of the longest side? Explain.

8. William finds a contractor who bids to build the stone wall for $80.72 per foot. If he bases the cost estimate on three times the cost of the longest side, what is the total cost?

9. What are the lengths of the other two sides? Explain.

Name _____

10 Performance Assessment Form B

Kelsey is building a custom bicycle. She has drawn a sketch of the drive train with two circular gears, one with radius 4 cm and the other with radius 10 cm. Kelsey needs to solve a number of problems to complete her design.

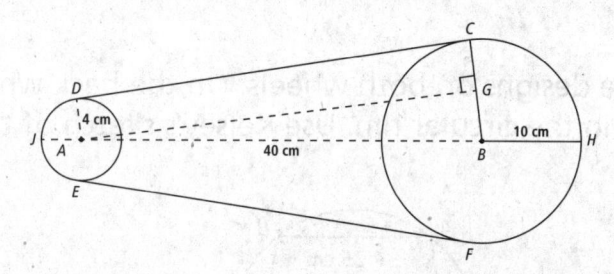

1. Kelsey needs a chain connecting the two circular gears. It will wrap around an arc of each gear and has two straight parts connecting the two gears. What is the length of one of the straight parts, to the nearest tenth of a centimeter? Explain.

2. How long is the part of the chain that goes around the larger gear? Explain.

3. How long is the part of the chain that goes around the smaller gear? Explain.

4. What is the total length of the chain?

5. Kelsey also wants to build a cover to protect the upper area where the chain passes around the larger gear. What is the area of this part of the larger gear? Explain.

Kelsey wants to create designs on both wheels. On the back wheel, she wants a trapezoid inscribed in the circular rim. Use Kelsey's sketch of the design for Items 6 and 7.

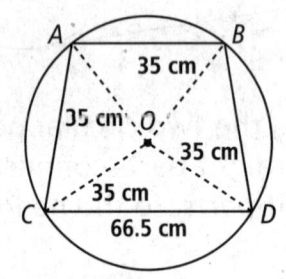

6. Prove that the trapezoid must be isosceles.

7. Kelsey needs to make sure that the longer base of the trapezoid never gets closer than 5 cm from the center of the circular wheel so that it does not get too close to the smaller gear. Will this design meet her needs? Explain.

8. On the front wheel, Kelsey wants two intersecting stripes. She measured some of the lengths of the stripes to their intersection point, as shown in the sketch. How long is the part of the stripes that she has not yet measured? Show your work.

Benchmark Assessment 5

1. Select all the sets of numbers that could be the side lengths of a triangle.
   - ☐ A. 7, 13, 21
   - ☐ B. 6, 6, 2
   - ☐ C. 15, 17, 34
   - ☐ D. 9, 10, 11
   - ☐ E. 4, 8, 12

2. Hector is constructing a regular polygon by following these steps.

   Step 1 Mark Point Q on a circle

   Step 2 Set the compass to the radius of the circle. Place the point on Q and draw an arc through the circle.

   Step 3 Using the same compass setting, place the point on the intersection of the arc and the circle. Draw another arc through the circle. Repeat this step going all the way around the circle.

   Step 4 Draw chords connecting the consecutive points on the circle.

   Hector is constructing a regular
   - ☐ triangle.
   - ☐ quadrilateral.
   - ☐ pentagon.
   - ☐ hexagon.

3. What is the exact value of tan A?

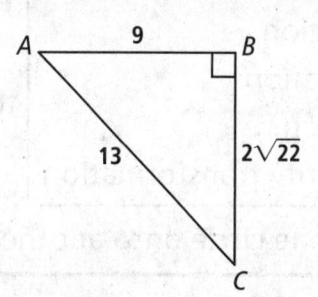

   Ⓐ $\frac{2\sqrt{22}}{13}$

   Ⓑ $\frac{9}{13}$

   Ⓒ $\frac{2\sqrt{22}}{9}$

   Ⓓ $\frac{9}{2\sqrt{22}}$

4. Enrique makes a triangular pen for his pet rabbit with side lengths 15 ft, 11 ft, and 9 ft. What is the approximate area of the pen in ft^2?

   Ⓐ 49

   Ⓑ 57

   Ⓒ 67

   Ⓓ 82

5. If JK = 24, JL = 16, and MT = 5, what is TP?

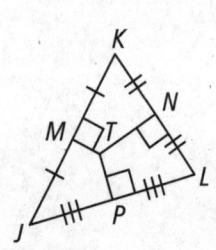

   Ⓐ 10

   Ⓑ 13

   Ⓒ $\sqrt{39}$

   Ⓓ $\sqrt{105}$

6. Complete the statement.

All circles [ ] are / [ ] are not similar because there is always a [ ] reflection / [ ] translation / [ ] rotation / [ ] similarity transformation that will map one circle onto another.

7. Which type of symmetry does the figure have?

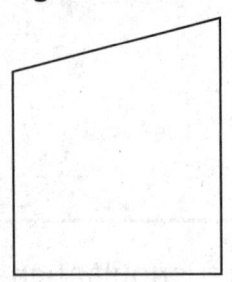

Ⓐ reflection
Ⓑ rotation
Ⓒ translation
Ⓓ no symmetry

8. What is RS? Round to the nearest tenth.

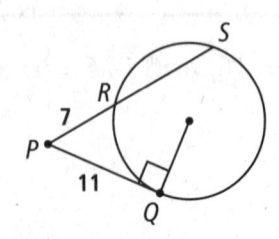

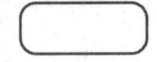

9. A surveying team is measuring the distances between buildings in a city. One surveyor is positioned at Building A and another surveyor is positioned at Building C, which is 530 feet away. One surveyor measures the angle between Building A and Building B to be 39° and the angle between Building A and Building C to be 59°.

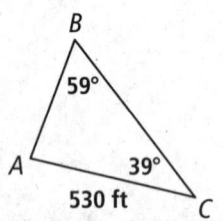

	389 ft	459 ft	612 ft
Distance between Building A and B	☐	☐	☐
Distance between Building B and C	☐	☐	☐

10. Nadeem is constructing a tangent to ⊙Q that passes through A. What should he do next?

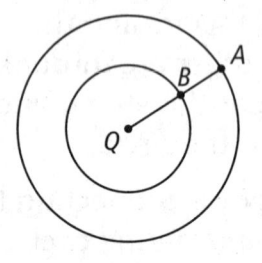

Ⓐ Construct a circle with center B passing through A.

Ⓑ Construct the perpendicular bisector of $\overline{QA}$.

Ⓒ Construct a line perpendicular to $\overline{QA}$ passing through A.

Ⓓ Construct a segment from B to another point on the circle with center Q that contains A.

11. Rays HG and HJ are tangent to ⊙Q. What is $m\widehat{GKJ}$?

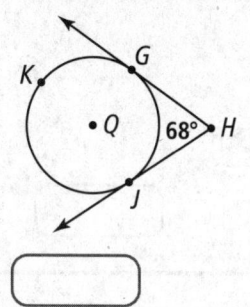

12. Select all the statements that are true.

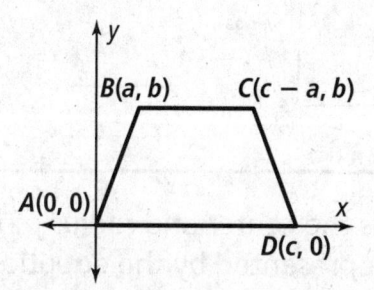

    ☐ A. $AB = CD$
    ☐ B. $AB = BC$
    ☐ C. $AD = BC + 2a$
    ☐ D. $\overline{AB} \parallel \overline{CD}$
    ☐ E. $\overline{AD} \parallel \overline{BC}$

13. Which of the following should NOT be part of the plan for a coordinate proof showing that the perpendicular bisectors of the sides of a triangle are concurrent?

    Ⓐ Write the equation of the line passing through two of the midpoints.

    Ⓑ Use the midpoint formula to find the midpoint of each side.

    Ⓒ Draw and label a triangle on the coordinate plane.

    Ⓓ Find the slope of each side of the triangle.

14. The vertices of △DEF are D(1, 19), E(16, −1), F(−8, −8). What type of triangle is △DEF?

    Ⓐ right
    Ⓑ equilateral
    Ⓒ isosceles
    Ⓓ scalene

15. What is the area of sector MTN?

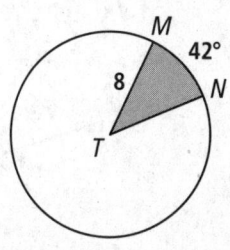

    Ⓐ $\frac{53}{180}\pi$ Ⓒ $\frac{60}{7}\pi$
    Ⓑ $\frac{28}{15}\pi$ Ⓓ $\frac{112}{15}\pi$

16. The vertices of △ABC are A(0, 8), B(12, 3), C(7, −9). What is the area, in square units?

17. What is an equation for the circle?

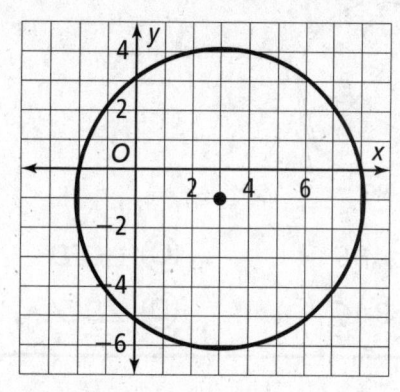

    Ⓐ $(x + 1)^2 + (y − 3)^2 = 25$
    Ⓑ $(x − 1)^2 + (y + 3)^2 = 25$
    Ⓒ $(x + 3)^2 + (y − 1)^2 = 25$
    Ⓓ $(x − 3)^2 + (y + 1)^2 = 25$

18. ∠A and ∠B are complementary. If $\sin A = \frac{4}{7}$, what is $\cos B$?

    Ⓐ $\frac{7}{4}$ Ⓒ $\frac{3}{7}$
    Ⓑ $\frac{4}{7}$ Ⓓ $\frac{\sqrt{44}}{7}$

19. The vertices of GHJK are G(−1, 0), H(1, 6), J(5, 6), and K(5, 2). What is the most precise classification of GHJK?

Ⓐ quadrilateral Ⓒ trapezoid
Ⓑ parallelogram Ⓓ kite

20. What is the ratio of the length of $\widehat{JK}$ to the length of $\widehat{MN}$?

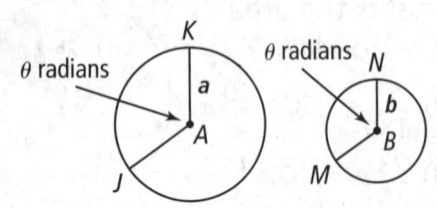

Ⓐ $a - b$ Ⓒ $\dfrac{b}{a}$
Ⓑ $\dfrac{a}{b}$ Ⓓ $\dfrac{a^2}{b^2}$

21. Which angle has the greatest measure?

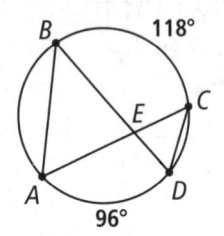

Ⓐ ∠ABE Ⓒ ∠CED
Ⓑ ∠BAC Ⓓ ∠DCA

22. Consider the circle represented by the equation $(x - 2)^2 + y^2 = 13$. Does the point lie on the circle?

	Yes	No
$(0, \sqrt{13})$	☐	☐
$(2, -\sqrt{13})$	☐	☐
$(4, 3)$	☐	☐
$(-2, 1)$	☐	☐

23. Segments AB and CB are tangent to ⊙T. What is the perimeter of ABCT?

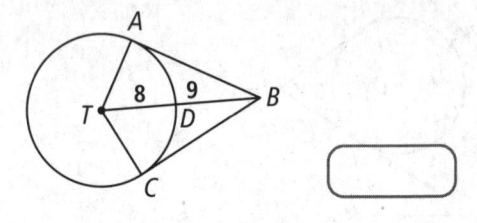

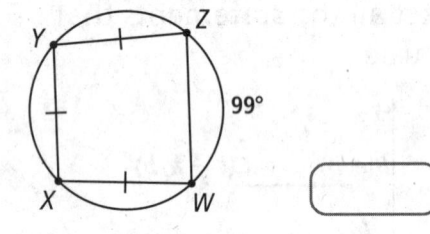

24. What is $m\widehat{XY}$?

25. What is the center and radius of the circle represented by the equation $x^2 + y^2 - 18x + 4y + 81 = 0$?

Ⓐ center: (−9, 2), radius: 4
Ⓑ center: (−9, 2), radius: 16
Ⓒ center: (9, −2), radius: 4
Ⓓ center: (9, −2), radius: 2

26. To begin constructing a square inscribed in a circle with center O with one vertex at point P, first

☐ set the length of the compass to the radius of the circle.
☐ draw a diameter of the circle through P.
☐ draw a radius of the circle through P.

Then

☐ construct a line through P perpendicular to the diameter.
☐ construct the perpendicular bisector of the diameter.

27. Which of the following should NOT be part of the plan for constructing the incenter of a circle? Select all that apply.

   ☐ A. Find the slope of each side of the triangle.
   ☐ B. Draw and label a triangle.
   ☐ C. Bisect each angle of the triangle.
   ☐ D. Use the midpoint formula to find the midpoint of each side.
   ☐ E. Use the distance formula to find the length of each side.

28. A chord is 8 in. long. It is 1 in. from the center of the circle. What is the radius of the circle? Round to the nearest tenth of an inch.

29. Line GH is tangent to ⊙T at N. If $m\angle ANG = 54$, what is $m\widehat{AB}$?

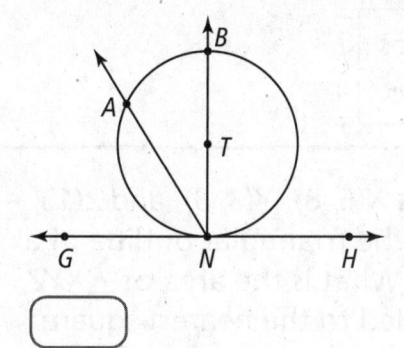

30. Point Q lies on the angle bisector of $\angle BAC$ and is 4 units from $\overline{AB}$. How many units is point Q from $\overline{AC}$?

   Ⓐ 8
   Ⓑ 2
   Ⓒ 1
   Ⓓ 4

31. The area of a rhombus is $\frac{pq}{2}$, where p and q are the length of each diagonal. A rhombus has an area of 600 square units and a perimeter of 100 units. How long is each side, and each of the diagonals?

   Ⓐ side length: 20
      diagonals: 22 and 40
   Ⓑ side length: 25
      diagonals: 26 and 36
   Ⓒ side length: 20
      diagonals: 26 and 48
   Ⓓ side length: 25
      diagonals: 30 and 40

32. What is the value of x? Round your answer to two decimal places if needed.

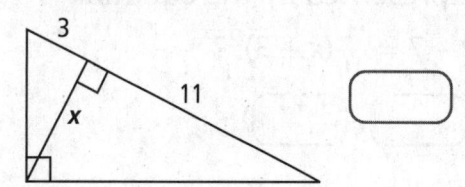

33. The focus of a parabola is (2, 5) and the directrix is $y = 1$. What is the equation of the parabola?

Ⓐ $y - 3 = \frac{1}{16}(x - 2)$

Ⓑ $y - 5 = \frac{1}{4}(x - 2)$

Ⓒ $y - 3 = \frac{1}{8}(x - 2)$

Ⓓ $y - 5 = \frac{1}{16}(x - 2)$

34. What is the equation of the parabola?

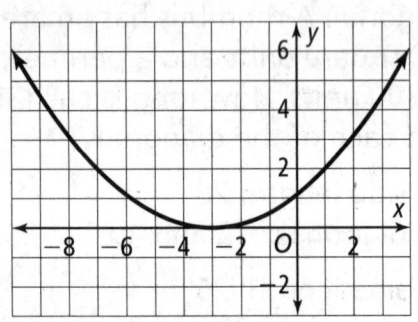

Ⓐ $y = \frac{1}{8}(x + 3)^2$

Ⓑ $y = \frac{1}{8}(x - 3)^2$

Ⓒ $y = \frac{1}{4}(x + 3)^2$

Ⓓ $y = \frac{1}{4}(x - 3)^2$

35. What is the focus of the parabola represented by the equation $y - 7 = \frac{1}{10}(x + 3)^2$?

(⬭ , ⬭)

36. Which point is the center of the circle that contains the vertices of a triangle?

Ⓐ the point of intersection of the altitudes

Ⓑ the point of intersection of the perpendicular bisectors of the sides

Ⓒ the point of intersection of the angle bisectors

Ⓓ the point of intersection of the medians

37. Part A

An arc on a circle of radius 10 has an arc length of $\frac{49\pi}{9}$. What is the degree measure of the corresponding central angle?

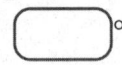

⬭ °

Part B

If the radius is reduced to 2, is an arc length of $\frac{49\pi}{9}$ still possible?

☐ yes
☐ no

38. Points $X(6, 8)$, $Y(3, 3)$, and $Z(13, -3)$ form the triangular outline of a park. What is the area of $\triangle XYZ$, rounded to the nearest square unit?

⬭

Name _____

11 Readiness Assessment

1. A prism is shown. Which polygon can be formed by the intersection of a vertical plane with this prism? 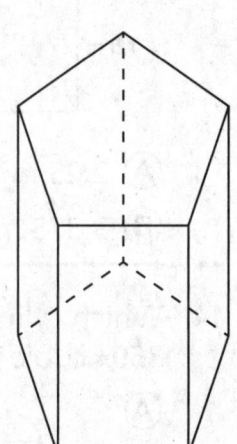
   - Ⓐ triangle
   - Ⓑ rectangle
   - Ⓒ pentagon
   - Ⓓ hexagon

2. What is the area of circle Q?
   - Ⓐ 28π
   - Ⓑ $28\pi^2$
   - Ⓒ 49π
   - Ⓓ $49\pi^2$

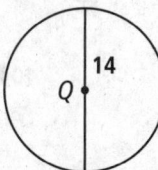

3. What is the area in square units of this trapezoid?

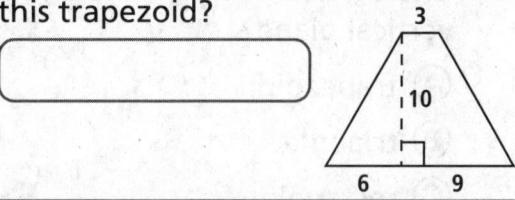

4. What is the volume of a cylinder with radius 5 feet and height 6 feet?
   - Ⓐ 30π ft^3
   - Ⓑ 50π ft^3
   - Ⓒ 150π ft^3
   - Ⓓ 180π ft^3

5. Which expression represents the height of a rectangular prism with length ℓ, width w, and volume V?
   - Ⓐ $\dfrac{V}{\ell w}$
   - Ⓑ $\dfrac{Vw}{\ell}$
   - Ⓒ $\dfrac{\ell w}{V}$
   - Ⓓ $\dfrac{V\ell}{w}$

6. A plane intersects a square pyramid as shown. Which best describes the cross section?
   - Ⓐ square
   - Ⓑ triangle
   - Ⓒ rectangle
   - Ⓓ trapezoid

7. What is the area of the base of this cone?

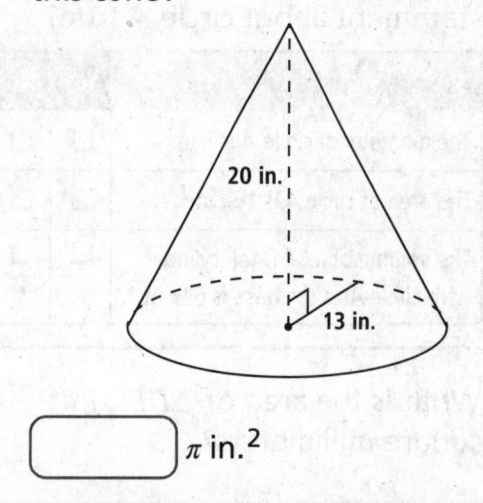

   _____ π in.^{2}

8. The volume of a cube is 216 cm^3. What is the length of each edge of the cube?
   - Ⓐ 6 cm
   - Ⓑ 54 cm
   - Ⓒ 72 cm
   - Ⓓ 108 cm

9. What is the volume of this cylinder, in cubic meters?
   - Ⓐ 81π
   - Ⓑ 99π
   - Ⓒ 108π
   - Ⓓ 891π

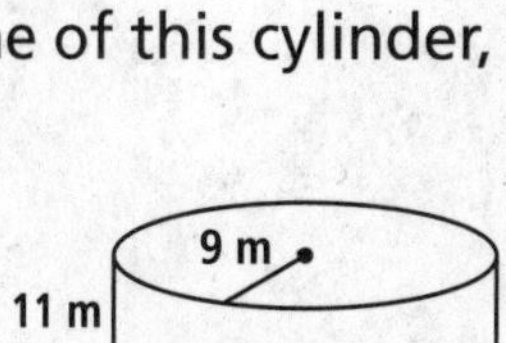

10. Write one of the given expressions for each description below. The variable b is base, h is height, r is radius, w is width, and ℓ is length.

$$\ell w \quad \pi r^2 \quad \ell wh \quad \tfrac{1}{2}bh \quad \pi r^2 h$$

area of a circle ☐

area of a triangle ☐

volume of a cylinder ☐

volume of a rectangular prism ☐

area of a rectangle ☐

11. Circle A has radius 4 inches. Is each statement about circle A true?

	Yes	No
The diameter of circle A is 8 in.	☐	☐
The area of circle A is 16π in.^{2}.	☐	☐
The volume of a 6-in.-tall cylinder with circle A as the base is 64π in.^{3}.	☐	☐

12. What is the area of $\triangle DEF$, in square millimeters?

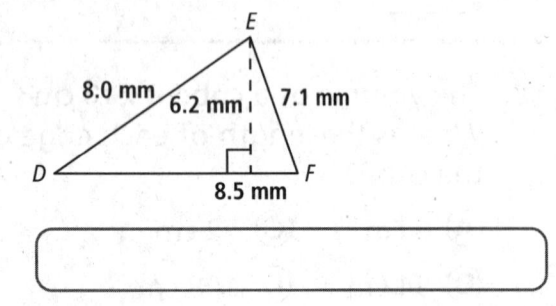

Triangle with E at top, D at bottom left, F at bottom right. DE = 8.0 mm, EF = 7.1 mm, DF = 8.5 mm, height = 6.2 mm.

☐

13. What is the volume of this rectangular prism?

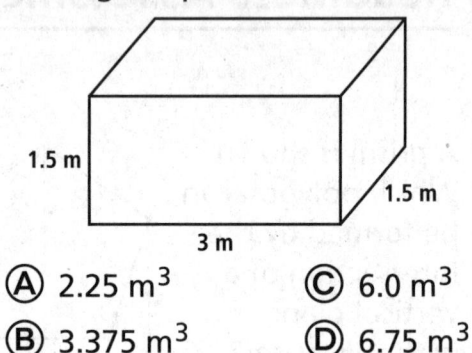

1.5 m × 1.5 m × 3 m

Ⓐ 2.25 m³
Ⓑ 3.375 m³
Ⓒ 6.0 m³
Ⓓ 6.75 m³

14. Which cylinder has a volume of 360π cubic feet?

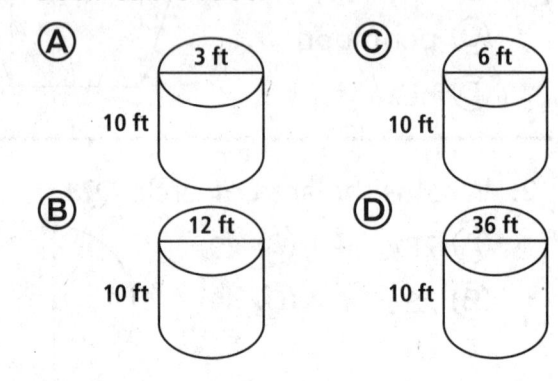

Ⓐ radius 3 ft, height 10 ft
Ⓑ radius 12 ft, height 10 ft
Ⓒ radius 6 ft, height 10 ft
Ⓓ radius 36 ft, height 10 ft

15. Which best describes the intersection of a pyramid and a vertical plane?

Ⓐ trapezoid
Ⓑ triangle
Ⓒ rectangle
Ⓓ cannot be determined

16. What is the area in square units of a circle with a radius of 3.2? Write the answer in terms of π.

☐ π

11-1 Lesson Quiz

Three-Dimensional Figures and Cross Sections

1. Select all the polygons that can be formed by the intersection of a plane and a cylinder either parallel or perpendicular to the base.
   - ☐ A. triangle
   - ☐ B. square
   - ☐ C. rectangle
   - ☐ D. pentagon
   - ☐ E. circle

2. A plane intersects the prism shown parallel to the base. Which best describes the cross section?
   - Ⓐ rectangle
   - Ⓑ pentagon
   - Ⓒ trapezoid
   - Ⓓ parallelogram

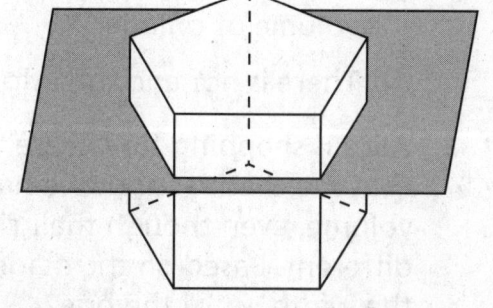

3. A plane intersects the rectangular prism shown through vertices A, C, G, and E. Which best describes the cross section?
   - Ⓐ square
   - Ⓑ triangle
   - Ⓒ rectangle
   - Ⓓ parallelogram

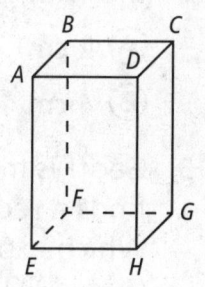

4. Which best describes the intersection of a pyramid and a plane perpendicular to the base of the pyramid through the vertex?
   - Ⓐ square
   - Ⓑ triangle
   - Ⓒ rectangle
   - Ⓓ cannot be determined

5. Match each object to the three-dimensional figure formed by rotating about the axis of rotation shown.

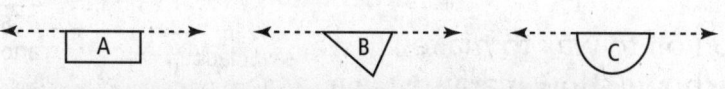

Figure	A	B	C
Cone	☐	☐	☐
Sphere	☐	☐	☐
Cylinder	☐	☐	☐

Name _____

11-2 Lesson Quiz

Volumes of Prisms and Cylinders

1. Which best compares the volumes of cylinder X and cylinder Y?

   Ⓐ The volume of cylinder X is less than the volume of cylinder Y.

   Ⓑ The volume of cylinder X is equivalent to the volume of cylinder Y.

   Ⓒ The volume of cylinder X is greater than the volume of cylinder Y.

   Ⓓ There is not enough information to compare the volumes.

2. Alice is shopping for cheese. She notices that the cheddar and brie have the same volume, even though their shapes are different. Based on the diagrams, what is the width, w, of the brie?

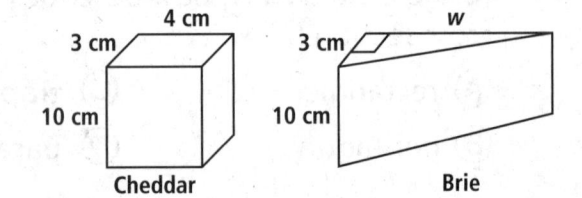

   Ⓐ 2 cm   Ⓒ 8 cm
   Ⓑ 4 cm   Ⓓ 16 cm

3. Geoff is mailing a jar of jam to his grandmother. He finds a rectangular box just tall enough for the jam. Which expression represents the volume of the box that is NOT occupied by the jar?

   Ⓐ $25\pi h$ cm   Ⓒ $(150 - 25\pi)h$ cm
   Ⓑ $125\pi h$ cm   Ⓓ $150h - 25\pi$ cm

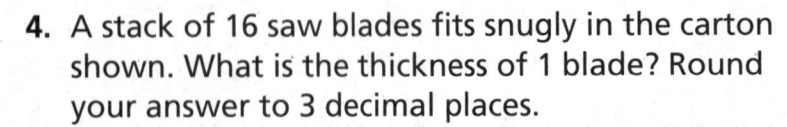

4. A stack of 16 saw blades fits snugly in the carton shown. What is the thickness of 1 blade? Round your answer to 3 decimal places.

   about (_____) in.

5. A candle maker adds lemon oil to wax to make the lemon-scented candle shown. How many ounces of oil will he need for the candle to have 0.0025 ounce of oil per cubic centimeter of wax?

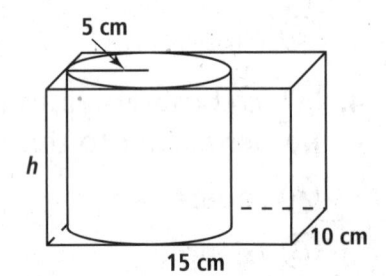

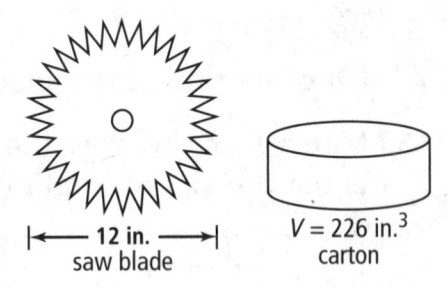

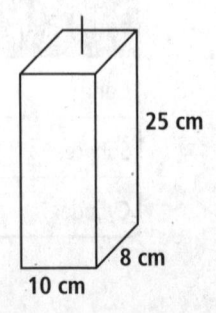

   (_____) ounces

enVision® Geometry • Assessment Sourcebook

Name _____

11-3 Lesson Quiz
Pyramids and Cones

1. Jessica is making a model pyramid out of clay. What volume of clay will she need to make a pyramid with the dimensions shown?
   - Ⓐ 9.072 mm³
   - Ⓒ 27.216 mm³
   - Ⓑ 18.144 mm³
   - Ⓓ 54.432 mm³

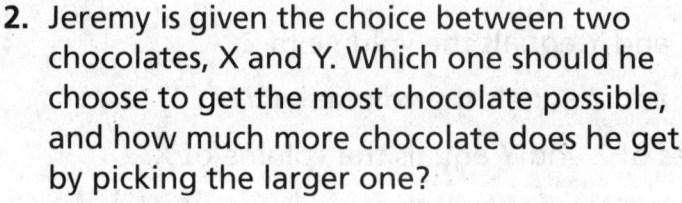

   (Pyramid dimensions: 3.6 mm, 2.4 mm, 6.3 mm)

2. Jeremy is given the choice between two chocolates, X and Y. Which one should he choose to get the most chocolate possible, and how much more chocolate does he get by picking the larger one?

   (X: 5 cm, 6 cm; Y: 10 cm, 7.5 cm, 8 cm)

   - Ⓐ It does not matter. The volumes of X and Y are equivalent.
   - Ⓑ He should choose Y, since he will get twice as much chocolate.
   - Ⓒ He should choose X, since he will get twice as much chocolate.
   - Ⓓ He should choose X, since he will get 10 times as much chocolate.

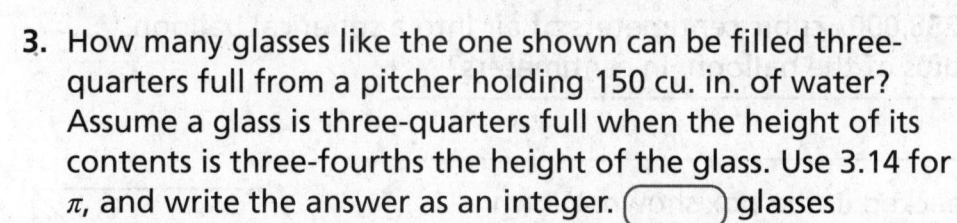

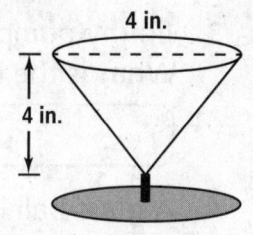

3. How many glasses like the one shown can be filled three-quarters full from a pitcher holding 150 cu. in. of water? Assume a glass is three-quarters full when the height of its contents is three-fourths the height of the glass. Use 3.14 for π, and write the answer as an integer. ⬚ glasses

   (Glass: 4 in. diameter, 4 in. height)

4. A sculptor plans to ship the pyramid shown in one of three boxes. The interior of the pyramid holds 4,500 cm³ of water. The base is an isosceles trapezoid. Into which boxes will the pyramid fit?

Height of box	Yes	No
25 cm	☐	☐
28 cm	☐	☐
32 cm	☐	☐

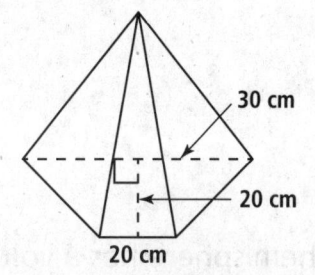

   (Pyramid: 30 cm, 20 cm, 20 cm)

5. Alice is making an octahedron out of origami. The last step requires her to blow into the octahedron to fill it up.

   Which expression represents the volume of air she will need to inflate the octahedron?

   - Ⓐ $\frac{2}{3}a^2b^2$
   - Ⓑ $\frac{2}{3}ab^2$
   - Ⓒ $\frac{2}{3} - a^2b$
   - Ⓓ $\frac{2}{3}a^2b$

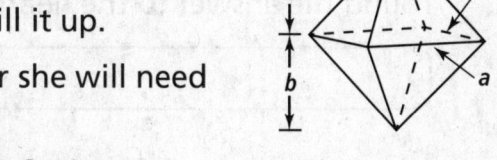

enVision® Geometry • Assessment Sourcebook

Name _____

11-4 Lesson Quiz

Spheres

1. Which best describes the relationship among the volumes of hemisphere X, cylinder Y, and cone Z?

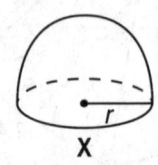

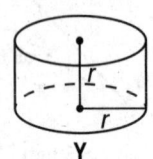

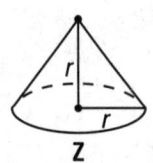

   X   Y   Z

   Ⓐ The sum of the volumes of X and Y equals the volume of Z.

   Ⓑ The sum of the volumes of X and Z equals the volume of Y.

   Ⓒ The difference of the volumes of Z and Y equals the volume of X.

   Ⓓ The difference of the volumes of X and Z equals the volume of Y.

2. A bowling-ball maker starts with an 8.5-inch-diameter resin sphere and drills 3 cylindrical finger holes in it. Each hole is 1 inch in diameter and 3.5 inches deep. Which is the best estimate of the volume of resin in the finished ball?

   Ⓐ 72 in.^{3} Ⓒ 319 in.^{3}

   Ⓑ 313 in.^{3} Ⓓ 330 in.^{3}

3. Jimmy pumps 288,000π cubic centimeters of air into a spherical balloon. What is the radius of the balloon, in centimeters?

4. A glass ball is packed in the box shown. Which expression represents the volume of foam padding needed to fill the space in the box around the sphere?

   Ⓐ $\left(9 - \frac{4}{3}\pi\right)r^3$

   Ⓑ $9r^3 - \frac{5}{3}\pi$

   Ⓒ $\left(27 - \frac{4}{3}\pi\right)r^3$

   Ⓓ $27r^3 - \frac{5}{3}\pi$

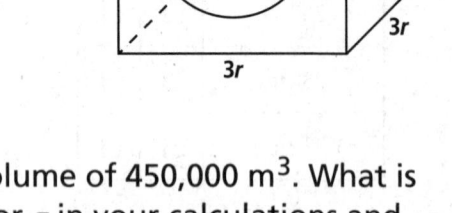

5. A soccer dome shaped like a hemisphere has a volume of 450,000 m^3. What is the area of its floor, in square meters? Use 3.14 for π in your calculations and round the answer to the nearest square meter.

11 Topic Assessment Form A

1. A plane intersects a square pyramid perpendicular to the base. Select all the possible shapes of the cross-section.

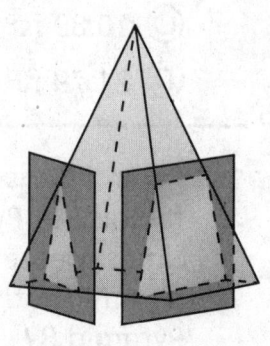

   ☐ A. triangle
   ☐ B. quadrilateral
   ☐ C. parallelogram
   ☐ D. rectangle
   ☐ E. trapezoid

2. Match each object to the three-dimensional figure formed by rotating about the given axis of rotation.

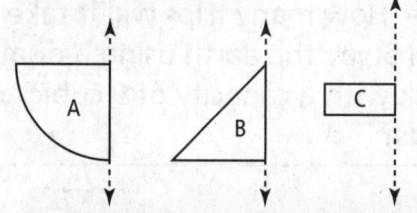

Three-Dimensional Figure	A	B	C
Cone	☐	☐	☐
Cylinder	☐	☐	☐
Hemisphere	☐	☐	☐

3. A plane intersects the prism parallel to the base. Which best describes the cross-section?

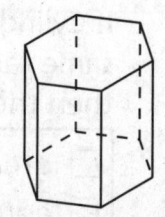

   Ⓐ rectangle
   Ⓑ hexagon
   Ⓒ trapezoid
   Ⓓ triangle

4. Each hemisphere of Isabel's globe has a volume of $60{,}750\pi$ cm^3. What is the radius of the globe, in cm?

5. An orange has a volume of about 113.1 cm^3. What is the area, in cm^2 of the cross-section when the orange is cut in half? Round to the nearest tenth.

6. Assuming that a soap bubble is a perfect sphere, what is the diameter of a bubble containing 1,000 cm^3 of air?

   Ⓐ 6.2 cm
   Ⓑ 7.5 cm
   Ⓒ 12.4 cm
   Ⓓ 15.0 cm

7. Which statement best compares the volumes of the two rectangular prisms?

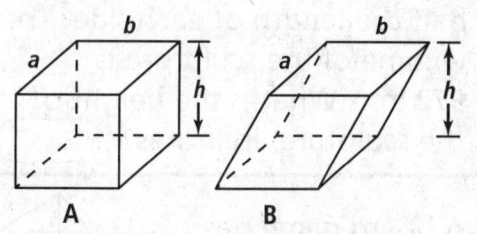

   Ⓐ There is not enough information to compare the volumes of the prisms.
   Ⓑ The volume of prism A is less than the volume of prism B.
   Ⓒ The volume of prism A is the same as the volume of prism B.
   Ⓓ The volume of prism A is greater than the volume of prism B.

8. A steel pipe 100 cm long has an outside diameter of 2 cm and an inside diameter of 1.8 cm. If the density of the steel is 7.8 grams per cm³, what is the mass of the pipe, to the nearest gram?

9. A basketball with diameter 9.5 in. is placed in a cubic box with sides 15 in. long. How many cubic inches of packing foam are needed to fill the rest of the box? Round to the nearest tenth.

10. A stack of one dozen cookies of diameter 2.5 in. exactly fits in a cylindrical container of volume 29.452 in.³. What is the thickness of each cookie?

    Ⓐ 0.25 in.   Ⓒ 1 in.
    Ⓑ 0.5 in.   Ⓓ 2 in.

11. The height of a pyramid-shaped sculpture with a square base is half the length of each side. The volume of the sculpture is 972 in.³. What is the height of the sculpture, in inches?

12. A board game has dice shaped like octahedrons. Each edge of the dice has length 1 cm and $h = \frac{\sqrt{2}}{2}$ cm. What is the volume, in cm³, of each die? Round to the nearest hundredth.

13. A traffic pylon is shown. What is its volume?

    Ⓐ 3.631 ft³
    Ⓑ 7.263 ft³
    Ⓒ 10.89 ft³
    Ⓓ 21.79 ft³

14. Pyramid A is a dilation with scale factor 2 of Pyramid B. How many times greater is the volume of pyramid A than the volume of Pyramid B?

    Ⓐ The volumes are the same.
    Ⓑ 2 times greater
    Ⓒ 4 times greater
    Ⓓ 8 times greater

15. A pile of earth removed from an excavation is a cone measuring 9 feet high and 24 feet across its base. How many trips will it take to haul away the earth using a dump truck with a capacity of 9 cubic yards?

16. Two stacks of coins are shown. Complete the statement.

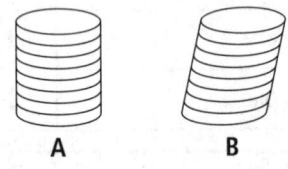

    A   B

    If Cylinder A and Cylinder B have the same radius and the same height, then the volume of Cylinder A is

    ☐ greater than
    ☐ equal to
    ☐ less than

    the volume of Cylinder B.

Name _____

11 Topic Assessment Form B

1. A plane intersects a triangular pyramid perpendicular to the base. Select all the possible shapes of the cross-section. 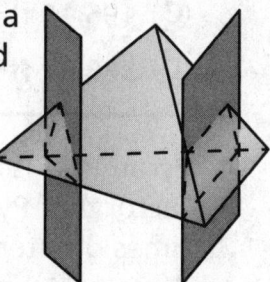
   - ☐ A. triangle
   - ☐ B. quadrilateral
   - ☐ C. parallelogram
   - ☐ D. rectangle
   - ☐ E. trapezoid

2. Match each object to the three-dimensional figure formed by rotating about the given axis of rotation.

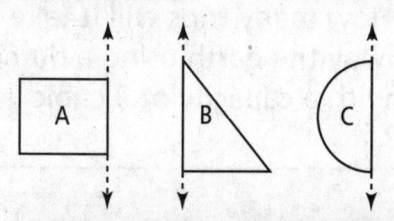

Three-Dimensional Figure	A	B	C
Cone	☐	☐	☐
Cylinder	☐	☐	☐
Sphere	☐	☐	☐

3. A plane intersects the prism parallel to the base. Which best describes the cross-section? 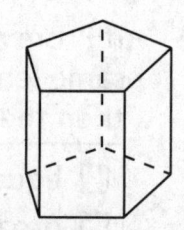
   - Ⓐ rectangle
   - Ⓑ trapezoid
   - Ⓒ pentagon
   - Ⓓ triangle

4. Each hemisphere of a beach ball has a volume of $281{,}250\pi$ cm^3. What is the radius of the ball, in cm?

5. A hemisphere igloo has a volume of about 9,202.8 m^3. What is the area, in m^2 of the floor of the igloo? Round to the nearest tenth.

6. Assuming a soap bubble is a perfect sphere, what is the diameter of a bubble containing 1,200 cm^3 of air?
   - Ⓐ 6.6 cm
   - Ⓑ 8.0 cm
   - Ⓒ 13.2 cm
   - Ⓓ 16.0 cm

7. Which statement best compares the volumes of the two cylinders?

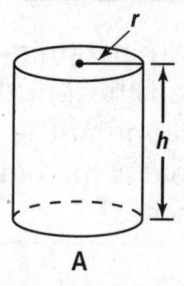

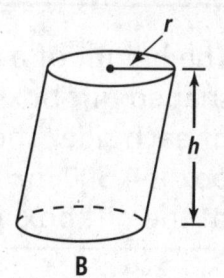

   - Ⓐ The volume of cylinder A is the same as the volume of cylinder B.
   - Ⓑ There is not enough information to compare the volumes of the cylinders.
   - Ⓒ The volume of cylinder A is less than the volume of cylinder B.
   - Ⓓ The volume of cylinder A is greater than the volume of cylinder B.

8. A steel pipe 50 cm long has an outside diameter of 2.2 cm and an inside diameter of 2 cm. If the density of the steel is 7.8 grams per cm³, what is the mass of the pipe, to the nearest gram?

9. A basketball with diameter 9.5 in. is placed in a cubic box with sides 10 in. long. How many cubic inches of packing foam are needed to fill the rest of the box? Round to the nearest tenth.

10. A stack of one dozen cookies of diameter 5 in. exactly fits in a cylindrical container of volume 176.715 in.³. What is the thickness of each cookie?
    Ⓐ 0.25 in.   Ⓒ 0.75 in.
    Ⓑ 0.5 in.   Ⓓ 1 in.

11. The height of a square pyramid-shaped gift box is half the length of each side. The volume of the gift box is 4,500 in.³. What is the height of the gift box, in inches?

12. An ornament is shaped like a regular octahedron, and each edge has length 3 cm and $h = \frac{3\sqrt{2}}{2}$ cm. What is the volume of the ornament, in cm³? Round to the nearest hundredth.

13. A model of a tarp shelter is shown. What is its volume?
    Ⓐ 76.91 ft³
    Ⓑ 98.06 ft³
    Ⓒ 196.11 ft³
    Ⓓ 588.33 ft³

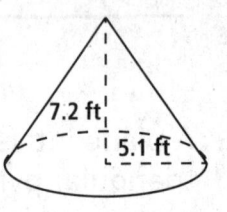

    (7.2 ft, 5.1 ft)

14. Pyramid A is a dilation with scale factor 4 of Pyramid B. How many times greater is the volume of Pyramid A than the volume of Pyramid B?
    Ⓐ 0.25 times greater
    Ⓑ 2 times greater
    Ⓒ 8 times greater
    Ⓓ 64 times greater

15. A pile of earth removed from an excavation is a cone measuring 6 feet high and 30 feet across its base. How many trips will it take to haul away the earth using a dump truck with a capacity of 9 cubic yards?

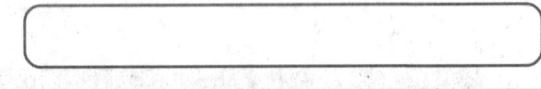

16. Two stacks of newspapers are shown. Complete the statement.

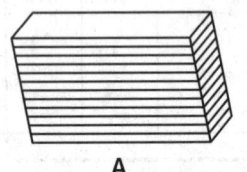

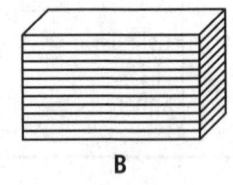

    A   B

    If Prism A and Prism B have the same length, width, and height, then the volume of Prism A is
    ☐ equal to
    ☐ greater than
    ☐ less than
    the volume of Prism B.

Name _____

11 Performance Assessment Form A

Connect-A-Habitat sells habitats for small pets such as gerbils, hamsters, and mice. The habitats are put together from four types of play areas and three types of tubes, shown in the table. To build a set, you select any four play areas and any four tubes and connect them as shown in the diagram. Sets include flexible connectors that allow you to connect any play area to any tube.

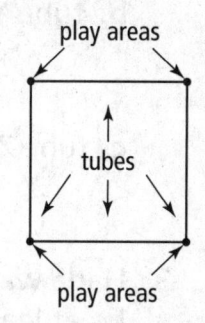

Play Areas			
A	B	C	D
10 in., 9 in., 12 in. (rectangular prism)	circumference = 32 in., 10 in. (cylinder)	13 in. (sphere)	14 in., 14 in., 12 in. (cone)

Tubes		
X	Y	Z
16 in., 2 in. (cylinder)	16 in., 5 in. (triangular prism)	16 in., 2.5 in. (hexagonal prism)

1. What is the volume of each play area? Show your work.

    a. play area A

    b. play area B

    c. play area C

    d. play area D

2. What is the volume of each tube? Show your work.

   a. tube X

   b. tube Y

   c. tube Z

3. Hana wants to buy a set for her hamster. She wants the total volume to be at least 5,000 in.^{3}, and she wants the cross-sectional area of the tubes to be at least 12 in.^{2}. Design a set that meets Hana's requirements. Draw a diagram showing which play areas and tubes are used, and show that Hana's requirements are met.

11 Performance Assessment Form B

Toss It! is a game that is played with balls, cubes, and octahedrons, shown in the table. Each set consists of 12 of each type of piece made from soft plastic with a density of 1.3 g/cm^3. (Density is the ratio of mass to volume.) The game is packaged in an oblique cylinder, shown below, with a mass of 220 g.

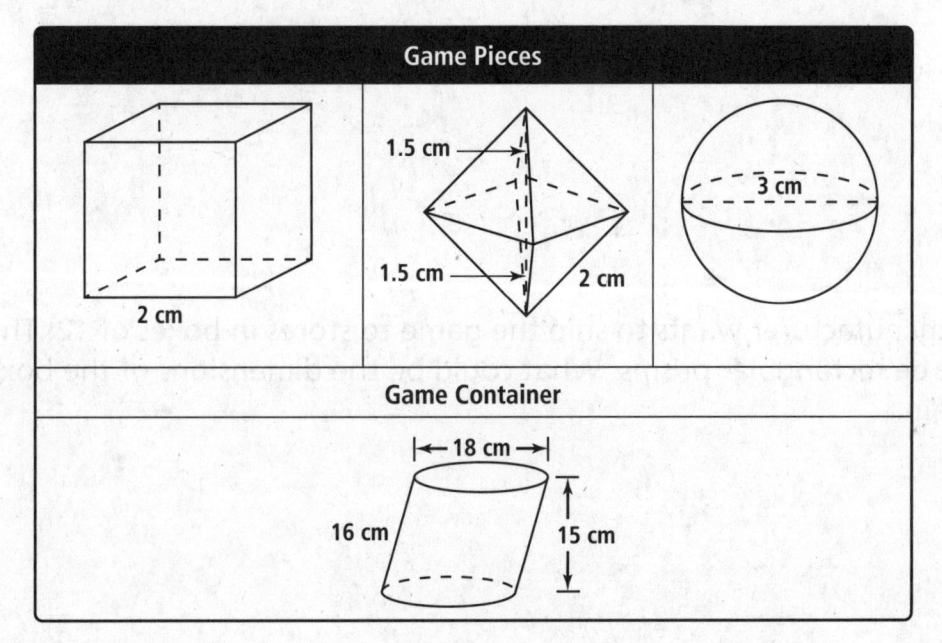

Game Pieces

Cube: 2 cm
Octahedron: 1.5 cm, 1.5 cm, 2 cm
Sphere: 3 cm

Game Container

18 cm, 16 cm, 15 cm

1. What is the mass of each type of game piece? What is the mass of a complete game, including the container? Show your work.

2. The game instructions need to give the number of faces, vertices, and edges for the cubes and octahedrons. What are those values for the game pieces? Show that your answers satisfy Euler's Formula.

3. When the pieces are placed in the game container, what percent of the game container is empty space? Show your work.

4. The manufacturer wants to ship the game to stores in boxes of 12. The boxes must be rectangular prisms. What could be the dimensions of the boxes? Explain.

Name _____

12 Readiness Assessment

1. What is the value of p in the proportion?
   $$\frac{8.7}{1,160} = \frac{p}{100}$$
   Ⓐ 0.0075 Ⓒ 0.029
   Ⓑ 0.75   Ⓓ 0.0029

2. What is the value of the expression
   $100 \cdot (p)^r \cdot \frac{(1-p)^n}{(1-p)^r}$ for $p = 0.7$, $r = 3$, and $n = 5$?

   [ ]

3. What proportion of the surface area is on each face of the shape, to the nearest percent?

	Cube	Tetrahedron (Triangular Pyramid)
Percentage	[ ]%	[ ]%

4. Match the probabilities with the appropriate event.

Event\Probability	0.15	0.5	1	0	0.78
Impossible	☐	☐	☐	☐	☐
Unlikely	☐	☐	☐	☐	☐
Neither likely nor unlikely	☐	☐	☐	☐	☐
Likely	☐	☐	☐	☐	☐
Certain	☐	☐	☐	☐	☐

5. What is the probability that the spinner lands on the letter A?
   Ⓐ $\frac{1}{4}$ Ⓒ $\frac{1}{2}$
   Ⓑ $\frac{1}{3}$ Ⓓ $\frac{2}{3}$

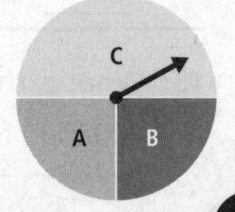

6. A quarter is tossed four times. If heads is worth $0.25 and tails is worth nothing, what is the probability that you end up with exactly $0.50?
   Ⓐ $\frac{7}{16}$ Ⓒ $\frac{11}{16}$
   Ⓑ $\frac{1}{2}$ Ⓓ $\frac{3}{8}$

7. A restaurant owner wants to survey customers. Which method produces a random representative sample?
   Ⓐ Survey the first 20 people that come in after opening.
   Ⓑ Survey every 20th person that comes in after opening.
   Ⓒ Survey 20 customers who leave large tips.
   Ⓓ Survey 20 people on the sidewalk in front of the restaurant.

8. A fair coin is tossed n times. For which value of n is the experimental probability of tossing tails most likely to equal the theoretical probability?
   Ⓐ 5   Ⓒ 33
   Ⓑ 25   Ⓓ 42

9. The number of miles Sheena ran each day since she started her training program are shown.
   $\{3, 4, 6, 2x, 7, 10, 8, 2x - 1, 6, 7\}$
   What is the value of x if she ran an average of $2x$ miles each day during this period?
   $x =$ [ ]

10. Two standard number cubes are rolled, one red and one blue. How many different sums are possible?

    ☐

11. In 20 free throw attempts, Raul made 8. Based on this data, what is a reasonable estimate of the probability that Raul will make his next free throw?

    Ⓐ 8%   Ⓒ 20%
    Ⓑ 30% Ⓓ 40%

12. A bag has 2 red, 3 blue, and 5 green marbles. A marble is randomly drawn from the bag. Select all the correct probabilities.

    ☐ A. $P(\text{red}) = \frac{1}{4}$
    ☐ B. $P(\text{blue or green}) = \frac{3}{7}$
    ☐ C. $P(\text{green}) = \frac{1}{2}$
    ☐ D. $P(\text{not red}) = \frac{4}{5}$
    ☐ E. $P(\text{not green}) = P(\text{green})$

13. Solve $p(1 - p) = 0.24$ for p. Enter the answers in ascending order.

    $p = $ ☐ or $p = $ ☐

14. The data set {80, 85, 85, 80, 85} gives James' scores on 5 math tests. What is his mean score?

    ☐

15. Select all the game moves that are best represented by a negative integer in a game of chance.

    ☐ A. Moving ahead 2 spaces
    ☐ B. Moving back 2 spaces
    ☐ C. A loss of 2 points
    ☐ D. A gain of 2 points
    ☐ E. A drop of 2 points

16. A circular target has a radius of 9 inches. At the center is a red circle with a diameter of 9 inches. Select all the true statements.

    ☐ A. The ratio of the area of the red circle to the remaining target area is 1:3.
    ☐ B. The circumference of the target is double the circumference of the red circle.
    ☐ C. The area of the target not covered by the red circle is $\pi \cdot 9^2$ square inches.
    ☐ D. Doubling both the radius of the target and the diameter of the red circle doubles the ratio of their circumferences.
    ☐ E. Doubling both the radius of the target and the diameter of the red circle doubles the ratio of their areas.

17. A sample of 200 students were surveyed about whether or not they walk to school.

    Part A

    Complete the frequency table.

	Walk	Don't Walk	Total
Grade 10	☐	40	100
Grade 11	70	☐	☐
Total	☐	70	200

    Part B

    Of all the students surveyed, what percent walk to school?

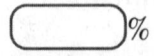

    ☐ %

18. What is the value of the expression $200p^2q^3$ for $p = \frac{2}{5}$ and $q = \frac{3}{5}$?

    ☐

12-1 Lesson Quiz
Probability Events

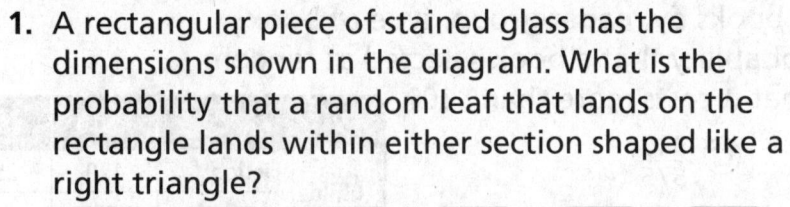

1. A rectangular piece of stained glass has the dimensions shown in the diagram. What is the probability that a random leaf that lands on the rectangle lands within either section shaped like a right triangle?

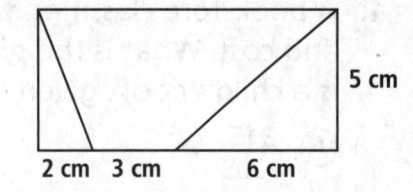

   (2) (3) (4) (5) (6) (8)
   (9) (10) (11) (12) (14) (16)

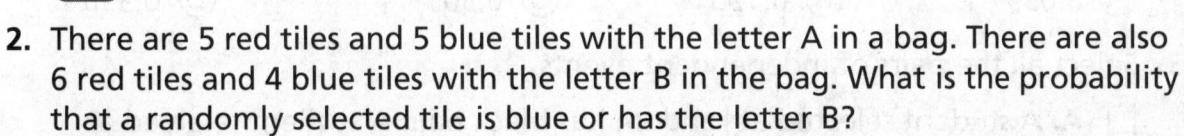

   $\dfrac{4}{11}$

2. There are 5 red tiles and 5 blue tiles with the letter A in a bag. There are also 6 red tiles and 4 blue tiles with the letter B in the bag. What is the probability that a randomly selected tile is blue or has the letter B?

   Ⓐ $\dfrac{9}{20}$ Ⓑ $\dfrac{1}{2}$ **Ⓒ $\dfrac{3}{4}$**   Ⓓ $\dfrac{19}{20}$

3. Select from the following pairs of events all the pairs that are independent.
   - ☐ A. Draw a 2 of clubs from a standard deck of 52 cards, keep it, then draw a 2 of diamonds.
   - ☑ B. Draw a 3 of spades from a standard deck of 52 cards, replace it, then draw a 5 of hearts.
   - ☐ C. Roll a number cube. Then roll again if the first roll is a 6.
   - ☑ D. Roll a 2 on a number cube and spin a 3 on a spinner.
   - ☐ E. Events A and B, where $P(A) = 0.4$, $P(B) = 0.2$, and $P(A \text{ and } B) = 0.8$.
   - ☑ F. Events A and B, where $P(A) = 0.1$, $P(B) = 0.5$, and $P(A \text{ and } B) = 0.05$.

4. On a track and field team, 8% of the members run only long-distance, 32% compete only in field events, and 12% are sprinters only. Find the probability that a randomly chosen team member runs only long-distance or competes only in field events. Write the probability as a decimal.

   0.4

5. The probability that Yuri will make a free throw is 0.3. The probability that he will make two consecutive free throws is 0.09. The probability that he will make the first and not the second in two free throws is 0.21. The probability that he will make neither of the two free throws is 0.49.

Name _____

12-2 Lesson Quiz

Conditional Probability

1. A bookstore classifies its books by reader group, type of book, and cost. What is the probability that a book selected at random is a child's book, given that it costs more than $10?

   Ⓐ $\frac{315}{1005}$ Ⓒ $\frac{315}{575}$

   Ⓑ $\frac{470}{1005}$ Ⓓ $\frac{470}{575}$

		<$10	>$10
Child	Fiction	120	255
	Nonfiction	35	60
Adult	Fiction	200	110
	Nonfiction	75	150

2. Half of a class took Form A of a test and half took Form B. Of the students who took Form B, 39% passed. What is the probability that a randomly chosen student took Form B and did not pass?

   Ⓐ 0.055   Ⓑ 0.195   Ⓒ 0.305   Ⓓ 0.390

3. Select all the pairs of independent events.

   ☐ A. A student selected at random has black hair. A student selected at random drives to school.

   ☐ B. Events A and B where $P(A|B) = \frac{8}{9}$, $P(A) = \frac{3}{4}$, and $P(B) = \frac{2}{3}$.

   ☐ C. A student selected at random is in middle school. A student selected at random is in high school.

   ☐ D. Events A and B where $P(B|A) = 0.9$, $P(A \text{ and } B) = 0.45$, and $P(A) = 0.5$

   ☐ E. Events A and B where $P(B) = 0.15$, $P(A) = 0.25$, and $P(A|B) = 0.15$

4. Three-fourths of a research team worked in a lab while one-fourth of the team worked near a pond. Of the researchers who worked near the pond, 14% collected insects. What is the probability that a randomly chosen researcher worked near the pond and collected insects?

   ☐ %

5. A bag contains 4 blue and 6 green marbles. Two marbles are selected at random from the bag.

   Find each probability. Round to two decimal places if needed.

	With replacement	Without replacement
P(blue second | green first)	%	%
P(green second | blue first)	%	%

enVision® Geometry • Assessment Sourcebook

Name _____

12-3 Lesson Quiz

Permutations and Combinations

1. A chef randomly chooses 5 apples from a case of 24 apples. In how many ways can the chef make the selection?

   Ⓐ 11,628   Ⓑ 42,504   Ⓒ 5,100,480   Ⓓ 1,395,360

2. A game at the fair involves balls numbered 1 to 18. You can win a prize if you correctly choose the 5 numbers that are randomly drawn. What are your approximate chances of winning?

   Ⓐ 0.0001   Ⓑ 0.056   Ⓒ 0.078   Ⓓ 0.278

3. Identify each situation as a permutation or a combination. Then find the number of possible arrangements.

   6 books are placed from left to right on a bookshelf.

   This is a ☐ permutation.   There are ( ) possible arrangements.
             ☐ combination.

   4 goldfish are selected from a tank containing 8 goldfish.

   This is a ☐ permutation.   There are ( ) possible arrangements.
             ☐ combination.

   3 class representatives are chosen from 25 students.

   This is a ☐ permutation.   There are ( ) possible arrangements.
             ☐ combination.

4. A bag contains 7 marbles; one each of red, orange, yellow, green, blue, violet and white. A child randomly pulls 4 marbles from the bag. What is the probability that the marbles chosen are green, blue, red, and yellow? Round your answer to the nearest hundredth?

   ( )

5. Serena has a playlist of 10 songs. She plays 2 songs. What is the approximate probability in each case?

	45%	2.2%	1.1%	90%
She hears her 2 favorite songs.	☐	☐	☐	☐
She hears her favorite song first and her next-favorite song second.	☐	☐	☐	☐

Name _____

12-4 Lesson Quiz

Probability Distributions

1. The probability that a machine part is defective is 0.1. Find the probability that no more than 2 out of 12 parts tested are defective.

   Ⓐ 0.23   Ⓒ 0.89

   Ⓑ 0.66   Ⓓ 0.61

2. The probability that a newborn baby at a certain hospital is male is 50%. Find the probability that 7 or 8 out of 10 babies born in the hospital on any day are male. Round to the nearest hundreth.

   ☐

3. Select all the statements that are conditions for a binomial experiment.

   ☐ A. There is a fixed number of trials.
   ☐ B. Each trial has two possible outcomes.
   ☐ C. The trials are dependent.
   ☐ D. The trials are independent.
   ☐ E. The probability is constant throughout the trials.
   ☐ F. The probability may vary throughout the trials.

4. A tile is chosen at random from a bag containing the following tiles: 7 blue, 3 green, and 6 yellow. You select with replacement two tiles at random from the bag. Define the theoretical probability distribution for selecting a number of yellow marbles on the sample space {0, 1, 2}.

   Write each probability rounded to the nearest hundredth.

   $P(0) =$ ☐

   $P(1) =$ ☐

   $P(2) =$ ☐

5. In an experiment with 50 trials, the number 5 occurred 17 times, the number 6 occurred 8 times, the number 7 occurred 13 times and the number 8 occurred 12 times.

   Let p be defined on the set {5, 6, 7, 8}. Find each of the following. Write each probability rounded to the nearest hundredth.

P(5)	P(6)	P(7)	P(8)	P(6 or less)

enVision® Geometry • Assessment Sourcebook

Name _____

12-5 Lesson Quiz

Expected Value

1. What is the expected value when rolling a fair die in each of the following cases?

   A 6-sided die with the numbers 2 twice, 4 twice, and 6 twice on its six faces. ( )

   An 8-sided die with the numbers 1 twice, 5 twice, 7 three times, and 8 once on its eight faces. ( )

2. The chance of rain is forecast to be 20% each day over the next 7 days. How many rainy days should be expected?

   Ⓐ 0.7
   Ⓑ 1.4
   Ⓒ 2
   Ⓓ 2.7

3. A bag has 8 red tiles and 2 green tiles. In a charity carnival game, you pay $5 to randomly pull a tile from the bag. The payout for pulling a red tile is $1 and the payout for pulling a green tile is $10. Find each of the following.

   The expected payoff per game for the charity is $( ).

   In 20 games, the charity can expect to make $( ).

4. A spinner with 20 equal-sized sections has 5 red, 10 blue, 3 green, and 2 yellow sections. Ann pays $10 to spin the spinner. If she spins a yellow, she wins $20; if she spins green, she wins $15; otherwise, she loses.

   She plays the game twice. The expected payoff for her games is $( ).

5. An insurance company offers two accident policies. Policy A has a premium of $2,000 with a deductible of $800. Policy B has a premium of $2,400 with a deductible of $200. The probability of an accident costing more than $800 in a given year is 15%. Assume a person has at most one accident a year and no accidents costing less than $800. Complete each statement.

   The annual expected cost to the owner for Policy A is $( ).

   The annual expected cost to the owner for Policy B is $( ).

   Policy ( ) has the lesser annual expected total cost to the owner.

12-6 Lesson Quiz

Probability and Decision Making

1. Students from 4 towns attend a conference. Each town is assigned a number 1 to 4.

   A number is drawn and replaced 6 times. Is this a fair way to pick 6 members to give each town representation? ☐

   What is the probability that Town 1 will have at least 1 representative after 6 number draws, to the nearest percent? ☐ %

2. In a two-player game, five cards, numbered 1 through 5, are placed in a bag. A card is drawn at random, and the players look at the number. Which of the following scoring rules makes a fair game?

   Ⓐ If it is greater than 2, Player 1 earns 2 points. If not, Player 2 earns 2 points.

   Ⓑ If it is less than 2, Player 1 earns 3 points. If not, Player 2 earns 2 points.

   Ⓒ If it is greater than 3, Player 1 earns 2 points. If not, Player 2 earns 2 points.

   Ⓓ If it is less than 3, Player 1 earns 3 points. If not, Player 2 earns 2 points.

3. Do the rules described result in a fair situation? Select Yes or No for each rule.

	Yes	No
Roll a 1 through 6 number cube. If the result is 1 or 2, Joel walks the dog. If the result is 3 or 4, Kyle walks the dog. If the result is 5 or 6, Mindy walks the dog.	☐	☐
Write the names of 5 participants on identical index cards. Put the names in a hat and draw a name at random.	☐	☐
Assign each of 10 players a number from 0 to 9. Use a random number generator to select the first 4 to play.	☐	☐
One-half of a spinner is green. The other two quarters are yellow and purple. Spin green and pay $1. Spin yellow or purple and win $2.	☐	☐

4. A caterer needs 12 workers for an event, but each worker has a 5% chance of not showing up. The caterer wants at least a 90% probability that enough workers show up, so she hires 13 workers.

   The caterer's strategy ☐ is ☐ is not effective because the probability that enough workers show up is ☐ 0.14 ☐ 0.65 ☐ 0.86 ☐ 0.95 .

5. At a concert hall, seats are reserved for 10 VIPs. For each VIP, the probability that they will attend is 0.8. The probability that 6 VIPs attend is ☐ .

   The probability that 10 VIPs attend is ☐ .

   The probability that more than 6 VIPs attend is ☐ .

Name _____

12 Topic Assessment Form A

1. A card is selected at random from the set of cards below.

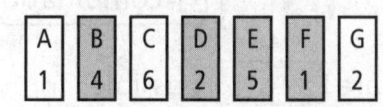

A	B	C	D	E	F	G
1	4	6	2	5	1	2

   (B, D, E, F shaded)

   A sample space for the experiment is {A, B, C, D, E, F, G}. Let W represent the event "the card is white", let S represent "the card is shaded", and let L represent "the number is less than 3".

   Part A

   Select all the correct statements.

   ☐ A. The event W is {A, C, G}.
   ☐ B. The event W or L is {A, D, F, G}.
   ☐ C. The event W and L is {A, G}.
   ☐ D. The event not L is {B, C, E, F}.
   ☐ E. P(W or S) = 1
   ☐ F. P(W and S) = 0

   Part B

   What is P(S or L)?

   Ⓐ 0.23   Ⓒ 0.80
   Ⓑ 0.57   Ⓓ 0.91

2. The local sandwich shop is running a promotion where customers can win $500 worth of free sandwiches. The first 25 customers to buy a $7.99 sandwich are entered into the drawing. What is the expected payoff of the promotion for each customer? $ _____

3. Two-thirds of the juniors at a local high school volunteer in their community. Of the juniors who volunteer, 45% volunteer at least twice a week. What is the probability that a randomly chosen junior volunteers in the community at least twice a week? _____ %

4. If events A and B are independent with P(A) = 0.86 and P(B) = 0.52, what is P(A|B)? _____

5. Seventy-five percent of students are eligible to participate in a school-wide fundraiser. Of the students who participate, 10% earn a prize for their sales. What is the probability that a student who is eligible to participate in the fundraiser will earn a prize for sales? _____ %

6. Collision insurance with a $500 deductible costs $310 per year. With a $1,000 deductible, it costs $255 a year. The table shows the average cost of repairs for two types of accidents and the probability of each type.

	Avg. Cost	Probability
Minor Accident	$683	9%
Major Accident	$4,612	6%

   Which option has the least expected cost for one year?

   $ _____ deductible

   What is that cost? $ _____

7. A sample of juniors and seniors were asked if they plan to attend college.

	Plan to Attend	Do Not Plan to Attend	Totals
Juniors	288	134	422
Seniors	279	107	386
Totals	567	241	808

One surveyed student is chosen at random. Select all the true statements. Percents are rounded.

☐ A. The probability the student is a junior is 52%.

☐ B. The probability the student plans to attend college is 70%.

☐ C. Given the student plans to attend college, the probability the student is a junior is 68%.

☐ D. Given the student is a junior, the probability the student plans to attend college is 68%.

☐ E. Events "is a junior" and "plans to attend" are independent.

☐ F. Events "is a senior" and "plans to attend" are independent.

8. The table shows data for bus arrivals at one stop. By how many minutes can you expect a bus to be late?

Minutes Late	0	1	2	3	4	5
Number of Days	8	7	3	4	2	1

9. **Part A**

In how many ways can 12 gymnasts be awarded first, second, and third place?

This represents a
☐ permutation.
☐ combination.

There are ( ) possible arrangements.

Part B

In how many ways can 3 teachers out of 12 be selected for a committee?

This represents a
☐ permutation.
☐ combination.

There are ( ) possible arrangements.

10. Margo has a bag containing 12 yellow stars and 8 blue stars.

Part A

She randomly selects 6 stars. How many ways can her selection contain 4 yellow stars?

Part B

Margo replaces each star after recording what she draws. What is the probability that she chooses 4 yellow stars and 2 blue stars in 6 draws? Round the answer to three decimal places.

11. There are 3 white marbles and 4 striped marbles in a bag. A marble is selected at random from the bag, and a coin is flipped. Let S represent "the marble is striped", and let H represent "the coin shows heads". Select all the statements that can be used to show that events S and H are independent.

    ☐ A. $P(S) = \frac{4}{7}$
    ☐ B. $P(H) = \frac{1}{2}$
    ☐ C. $P(S \text{ and } H) = \frac{2}{7}$
    ☐ D. $P(S \text{ or } H) = \frac{11}{14}$
    ☐ E. $\frac{4}{7} \times \frac{1}{2} = \frac{2}{7}$
    ☐ F. $\frac{4}{7} \times \frac{1}{2} \neq \frac{2}{7}$

12. Select all of the following equations that are true.

    ☐ A. $P(A) \times P(B|A) = P(B) \times P(A|B)$
    ☐ B. $P(A \text{ and } B) = P(A) \times P(A|B)$
    ☐ C. $P(B \text{ and } A) = P(B) \times P(A|B)$
    ☐ D. $P(A|B) = \frac{P(A \text{ and } B)}{P(A)}$
    ☐ E. $P(B|A) = \frac{P(A|B)}{P(B)}$

13. Ten percent of the students at Memorial High School buy a salad, 18% buy a hot lunch, and 1% buy both. If a student is selected at random, what is the probability that the student buys a salad or a hot lunch?

    Ⓐ 10%
    Ⓑ 19%
    Ⓒ 27%
    Ⓓ 28%

14. A bag has 9 striped marbles, 6 clear marbles, and 5 solid marbles. You draw one marble, report its color, and return it to the bag. You draw another marble and report its color.

    Part A

    Find the probabilities of the following events. Round to the nearest hundredth.

Event	Probability
You have a striped marble in both draws.	
You have a solid marble in the first draw and not a clear marble in the second draw.	
You have a clear marble in the first draw and a striped or solid marble in the second draw.	
You don't have a solid marble in the first draw, and you have a clear marble in the second draw.	

    Part B

    The color of the first marble
    ☐ does
    ☐ does not
    affect the color of the second marble so the events are
    ☐ independent
    ☐ dependent
    .

15. A restaurant gave each customer one free dessert to try, either pie or ice cream. Customers sampled the desserts and then decided if they would recommend the restaurant to a friend.

	Pie	Ice Cream
Would Recommend	36	43
Would Not Recommend	8	13

Part A

What is the probability that a customer who recommended the dessert tried the pie? Round to the nearest whole percent. ( ) %

Part B

Recommending pie is

☐ independent
☐ not independent

from recommending ice cream because the probability of recommending

☐ greater than
pie is ☐ less than
☐ equal to

the probability of recommending ice cream.

16. A town lottery sells 1,000 tickets for $5 a piece. There is a grand prize of $800, two second place prizes of $250, and four third place prizes of $50. The expected value of the game is ( ).

The lottery ☐ is
☐ is not
fair.

17. Chen is going on vacation and packed an orange shirt, a red shirt, a blue shirt, and a yellow shirt. She also packed one pair of pants and one pair of shorts. If she chooses a top and bottom at random, what is the probability that she will wear a red shirt and shorts?

Ⓐ $\frac{1}{3}$

Ⓑ $\frac{1}{6}$

Ⓒ $\frac{1}{8}$

Ⓓ $\frac{1}{12}$

18. Hilaria has a bag of coins, labeled 1 through 20. Her friend draws a coin from the bag at random. What is the probability that the coin shows a number that is even or a multiple of 3?

( ) %

19. Carolina is organizing flowers for her community garden. She purchases a random assortment of flowers from the local nursery, which contains gardenias, pansies, and sunflowers in multiple colors.

	Gardenia	Pansy	Sunflower
Purple	0	12	0
Yellow	16	12	10
White	12	18	0

Carolina will choose one plant at random to plant in her personal garden. What is the probability that she selects a yellow pansy?

( ) %

12 Topic Assessment Form B

1. A card is selected at random from the set of cards below.

Q	R	S	T	U	V	X
7	4	5	7	10	9	4

   A sample space for the experiment is {Q, R, S, T, U, V, X}. Let W represent the event "the card is white", let H represent "the card is shaded", and let M represent "the number is greater than 6".

   Part A
   Select all the correct statements.
   - ☐ A. The event H is {Q, S, U, V, X}.
   - ☐ B. The event H and M is {Q, S, U, V}.
   - ☐ C. The event H or M is {Q, S, T, U, V, X}.
   - ☐ D. The event not M is {R, S, X}.
   - ☐ E. $P(W$ and $H) = 0$
   - ☐ F. $P(W$ or $H) = 0$

   Part B
   What is $P(W$ or $M)$?
   - Ⓐ 1
   - Ⓑ 0.86
   - Ⓒ 0.57
   - Ⓓ 0.29

2. A car dealership is running a promotion where customers can win 10 years of free oil changes, valued at $600. The first 10 customers to buy a $15 carwash will be entered into the drawing. What is the expected payoff of the promotion for each customer?

   $ _____

3. One-third of the sophomores at a local high school participate in school clubs. Of the sophomores who participate, 54% participate in at least 2 clubs. What is the probability that a randomly chosen sophomore participates in at least 2 school clubs? _____ %

4. If events A and B are independent with $P(B) = 0.64$ and $P(A) = 0.58$, what is $P(B|A)$?

   _____

5. Data show 62% of students at a local school buy lunch in the cafeteria. Of the students who buy lunch, 15% buy milk. What is the probability that a student in the school will buy lunch, including milk?

   _____ %

6. Collision insurance with a $250 deductible costs $150 per year. With a $500 deductible, it costs $210 a year. The table shows the average cost of repairs for two types of accidents and the probability of each type.

	Avg. Cost	Probability
Minor Accident	$542	10%
Major Accident	$6,104	4%

   Which option has the least expected cost for one year?
   $ _____ deductible
   What is that cost? $ _____

7. A random sample of voters were asked whether they plan to vote for Doris Brown for mayor.

Plans to vote for Doris Brown

	Yes	No	Totals
Men	246	237	483
Women	288	236	524
Totals	543	464	1,007

One surveyed voter is chosen at random. Select all the true statements. Percents are rounded.

☐ A. The probability the person is a man is 48%.

☐ B. The probability the person plans to vote for Doris Brown is 54%.

☐ C. Given the person plans to vote for Doris Brown, the probability the person is a man is 51%.

☐ D. Given the person is a man, the probability the person plans to vote for Doris Brown is 51%.

☐ E. The events "is a man" and "plans to vote for Doris Brown" are independent.

☐ F. The events "is a woman" and "plans to vote for Doris Brown" are independent.

8. The table shows data for ferry arrivals at a port. By how many minutes can you expect the ferry to be late?

Minutes Late	0	1	2	3	4	5
Number of Days	10	4	6	7	2	1

9. **Part A**

In how many ways can 5 bottles out of a crate containing 10 be randomly selected?

This represents a ☐ permutation.
                  ☐ combination.

There are ( ) possible arrangements.

Part B

In how many ways can 14 science fair participants be awarded first, second, third, and fourth place?

This represents a ☐ permutation.
                  ☐ combination.

There are ( ) possible arrangements.

10. Jonathon has a bag containing 14 red circles and 8 green circles.

Part A

He randomly selects 7 circles. How many ways can his selection contain 3 green circles?

Part B

Jonathon replaces each circle after recording what he draws. What is the probability that he choses 3 green circles and 4 red circles in 7 draws? Round the answer to three decimal places.

11. There are 2 white marbles and 5 striped marbles in a bag. A marble is selected at random from the bag, and a coin is flipped. Let W represent "the marble is white", and let H represent "the coin shows heads". Select all the statements that can be used to show that events W and H are independent.

    ☐ A. $P(W) = \frac{2}{7}$

    ☐ B. $P(H) = \frac{1}{2}$

    ☐ C. $P(W \text{ or } H) = \frac{11}{14}$

    ☐ D. $P(W \text{ and } H) = \frac{1}{7}$

    ☐ E. $\frac{2}{7} + \frac{1}{2} = \frac{11}{14}$

    ☐ F. $\frac{2}{7} \times \frac{1}{2} = \frac{1}{7}$

12. Select all of the following equations that are true.

    ☐ A. $P(A \text{ or } B) = P(A) \div P(B)$

    ☐ B. $P(B \mid A) = \frac{P(B \text{ and } A)}{P(A)}$

    ☐ C. $P(B \text{ and } A) = P(B) \times P(A)$

    ☐ D. $P(A \mid B) = \frac{P(A \text{ or } B)}{P(A)}$

    ☐ E. $P(B) \times P(A \mid B) = P(A) \times P(B \mid A)$

13. Thirty-eight percent of the patrons at a local water park on a specific day use only the Lazy River, 49% use the only the water slides, and 74% use both. If a patron is selected at random, what is the probability the patron uses the Lazy River or the water slides?

    Ⓐ 13%

    Ⓑ 25%

    Ⓒ 35%

    Ⓓ 36%

14. A deck of playing cards has some cards missing. There are 13 hearts, 8 clubs, 12 spades, and 6 diamonds. You draw one card at random, record the suit and return it to the deck. You draw another card and record its suit.

    Part A

    Find the probabilities of the following events. Round to the nearest hundredth.

Event	Probability
You draw a heart in both draws.	
You draw a club for the first draw and not a spade for the second.	
You draw a heart in the first draw and a diamond or club in the second.	
You don't draw a diamond in the first draw, and you draw a spade in the second.	

    Part B

    The suit of the first card

    ☐ does
    ☐ does not

    affect the suit of the second, so the events are

    ☐ independent
    ☐ dependent

15. A bookstore gave customers a free book to read, either fiction or nonfiction. Customers read the book and then decided if they would recommend the bookstore to a friend.

	Non-Fiction	Fiction
Would Recommend	27	61
Would Not Recommend	17	21

Part A

What is the probability that a customer who would not recommend the bookstore read a fiction book? Round to the nearest whole percent. ( )%

Part B

Recommending a non-fiction book is ☐ independent / ☐ not independent from recommending a fiction book because the probability of recommending non-fiction is ☐ greater than / ☐ less than / ☐ equal to the probability of recommending fiction.

16. A school fundraiser is selling 700 tickets for a raffle. Tickets are $3 a piece. There is a grand prize of $500, two second place prizes of $100, and five third place prizes of $25. The expected value of the raffle is ( ).

The raffle ☐ is / ☐ is not fair.

17. Stefano is buying breakfast for his brothers. He buys 2 poppyseed bagels, 3 egg bagels, and 1 plain bagel. He also buys veggie cream cheese and plain cream cheese. If Stefano chooses one bagel and one topping at random, what is the probability that he will eat an egg bagel with plain cream cheese?

Ⓐ $\frac{1}{3}$

Ⓑ $\frac{1}{4}$

Ⓒ $\frac{1}{6}$

Ⓓ $\frac{1}{12}$

18. Micki has a bag of coins, labeled 1 through 30. She draws a coin from the bag at random. What is the probability that the coin shows a number that is odd or a multiple of 5?

( )%

19. Shreya is making sandwiches for her coworkers. She uses three different types of bread and three different types of sandwich fillings.

	White	Wheat	Sourdough
Turkey	10	7	4
Ham	8	4	10
Veggie	5	9	3

Shreya will choose one sandwich at random for herself. What is the probability that she chooses a veggie sandwich on white bread? Round to the nearest percent.

( )%

12 Performance Assessment Form A

A company is trying to reduce the cost of producing one of its tools. It comes up with a much cheaper new method of production. A large box of tools produced by both methods is examined by testers.

	Acceptable	Defective
Old Method	1,640	23
New Method	328	9

1. One tool is selected at random. What is the probability of drawing a defective tool, or one produced by the new method? Explain.

2. Two tools are selected at random, one at a time.

   Part A

   One tool is chosen at random from the box. It is then replaced. A tool is selected again. What is the probability that both selections were acceptable? Are the events dependent or independent events? Explain.

   Part B

   One tool is chosen at random from the box. It is *not* replaced. A tool is selected again. What is the probability that the first one was produced by the old method and the second one by the new method? Are the events dependent or independent events? Explain.

3. Two tools are selected at random from the box, one at a time.

   Part A

   What is the probability that a tool selected at random is defective given that the tool was produced by the new method?

Part B

Is P(defective | new) the same as P(new | defective)? Explain.

Part C

Are the events "select a defective tool" and "select a tool produced by the new method" dependent or independent events? Use conditional probability to support your answer.

4. The company produces 12 different types of tools. Three types will be selected to create a tool set.

Part A

How many ways can the set of 3 tools be selected? Explain.

Part B

Suppose 4 of the 12 types of tools are different types of screwdrivers. If 3 tools are selected at random, what is the probability that they are all screwdrivers? Explain.

Part C

A machine puts one of 12 sticker codes on each tool after it is produced. If the stickers were placed on the 3 tools randomly, what is the probability that each sticker would be on the correct tool? Explain.

12 Performance Assessment Form B

1. Your family is packing for a 4-day trip to another city. The forecast is shown below. Assume that whether it rains on each day is independent of whether it rains on any other day.

	Thu	Fri	Sat	Sun
	high 80°	high 77°	high 79°	high 83°
	low 54°	low 50°	low 52°	low 60°
	rain 30%	rain 40%	rain 20%	rain 60%

Part A

What is the probability it will not rain on either of the first two days to the nearest percent? Explain.

Part B

What is the probability it will rain on both Thursday and Friday to the nearest percent? Does this adding this probability to your answer from Part A total 100%? Explain.

Part C

What is the probability it will not rain on any of the four days to the nearest percent?

Part D

What is the probability it will rain on at least three of the four days to the nearest percent? Explain.

2. For a school project you complete a survey of 50 high school students and 50 adults. Of the 100 people surveyed, 72 said they owned an umbrella, of those, 44 were adults.

Part A

Use the data to make a two way frequency table.

	Student	Adult

Part B

What is the probability that a surveyed person who owns an umbrella is a student? What is the probability that a surveyed person who owns an umbrella is an adult? Round to the nearest percent. Explain.

Part C

Based on the results from Part B, what could you conclude about the relationship between age and umbrella ownership? Explain.

Part D

What is the probability that a person owns an umbrella, given that they are a high school student? Are being a high school student and owning an umbrella independent, based on the survey? Explain.

Name _____

Benchmark Assessment 6

1. Tom thought up two games to play with Lita. Tom has a pair of 6-sided dice, each numbered from 1 to 6. Lita has a pair of 10-sided dice, each numbered from 1 to 10.

   Game A: Roll the dice. If the sum is a prime number, you get 2 points; otherwise, you lose 1 point.

   Game B: Roll the dice. If the product is even, you get 1 point; if it is odd, you lose 2 points.

   Select all that apply.

   ☐ A. Game A is fair.
   ☐ B. Game B is fair.
   ☐ C. Tom expects 0.11 in Game A.
   ☐ D. Lita expects 0.11 in Game A.
   ☐ E. Tom expects 0.25 in Game B.

2. Ms. Gomez is using a computer program to assign each of the 24 students in her class a new seat. Which of the following must be true about the computer program if it is fair?

   ☐ A. The numbers 0 and 25 should be included.
   ☐ B. Each number between 1 and 24 is equally likely to occur.
   ☐ C. The probability of selecting the number 5 is 4.2%.
   ☐ D. The probability of selecting the number 12 is 50%.
   ☐ E. Each number between 1 and 24 must have a different probability of occurring.

3. The following solids have the same height and base area.

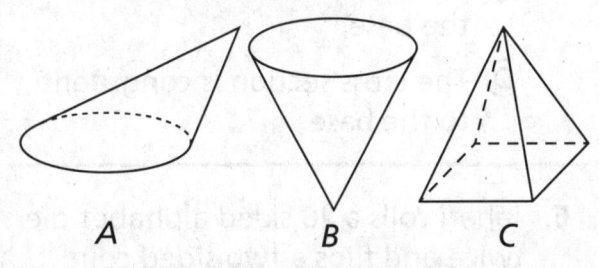

   A B C

   Complete the sentence.

   Cavalieri's principle can be used to show that
   ☐ A and B
   ☐ A, B, and C
   ☐ none of solids

   have the same
   ☐ area.
   ☐ volume.
   ☐ perimeter.

4. To prove the formula for the area of a circle, Madison breaks a circle into congruent sectors. She arranges the sectors into a
   ☐ parallelogram
   ☐ trapezoid
   ☐ triangle
   that has a height equal to the
   ☐ radius
   ☐ diameter
   ☐ circumference
   of the circle and a base length equal to
   ☐ the area
   ☐ half the area
   ☐ the circumference
   ☐ half the circumference
   of the circle.

5. If a pyramid intersects a plane that is parallel to its base, what must be true about the cross section?

   Ⓐ The cross section is a square.

   Ⓑ The cross section is a triangle.

   Ⓒ The cross section is similar to the base.

   Ⓓ The cross section is congruent to the base.

---

6. Jabari rolls a 26 sided alphabet die twice and flips a two sided coin once.

   Part A

   Which of the following represent possible outcomes of this event? Select all that apply.

   ☐ A. {H, Heads, Tails}

   ☐ B. {P, A, Heads}

   ☐ C. {M, M, Tails}

   ☐ D. { L, A, R}

   ☐ E. {Heads, Heads, Heads}

   ☐ F. {D, T, Heads}

   Part B

   Rolling the same letter twice on the alphabet die ☐ is possible / ☐ is not possible so the events are ☐ independent / ☐ dependent.

---

7. What is the value of x? ▢

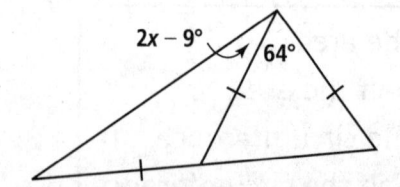

   $2x - 9°$, $64°$

---

8. A plane intersects a square pyramid perpendicular to the base. Which of the following is a possible shape of the cross section?

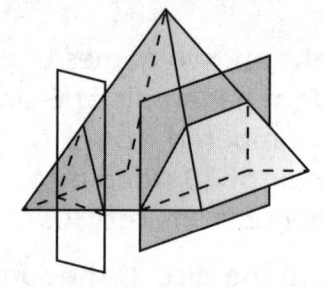

   Ⓐ hexagon

   Ⓑ square

   Ⓒ rectangle

   Ⓓ trapezoid

---

9. Rina is playing a spinner game, where the spinner has 5 equal sections, numbered 1 to 5. On each spin, Rina wins 1 point if the spinner lands on an odd number and loses 1 point if it lands on an even number. What is her expected score after 20 spins?

   ▢

---

10. A set of math flashcards contains 4 addition equations, 2 multiplication equations, and 6 division equations. A card is selected randomly, and a coin is flipped. Let A represent "the flashcard contains an addition equation" and let T represent "the coin shows tails." Select all the statements that can be used to show events A and T are independent.

    ☐ A. $P(A) = \frac{1}{3}$

    ☐ B. $P(T) = \frac{1}{2}$

    ☐ C. $P(A \text{ or } T) = \frac{5}{6}$

    ☐ D. $P(A \text{ and } T) = \frac{1}{5}$

    ☐ E. $\frac{1}{3} + \frac{1}{2} = \frac{5}{6}$

    ☐ F. $\frac{1}{3} + \frac{1}{2} \neq \frac{5}{6}$

11. The cone-shaped game piece is made of a metal with a density of 9.2 g/cm³. What is the mass of the game piece?

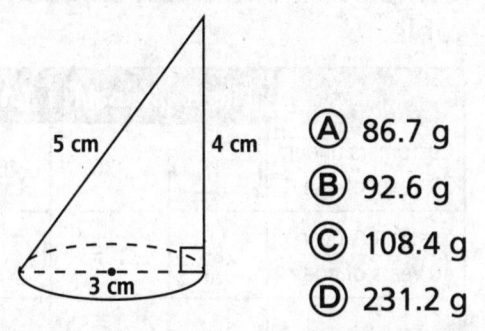

5 cm (slant), 4 cm (height), 3 cm (radius)

Ⓐ 86.7 g
Ⓑ 92.6 g
Ⓒ 108.4 g
Ⓓ 231.2 g

12. Another game piece has the same mass and density as the one shown in Item 11, but it is a right cone with height 5 cm. What is its diameter in cm?

Ⓐ 1.34
Ⓑ 2.68
Ⓒ 3
Ⓓ 6

13. Hiram eats granola, toast, yogurt, or eggs and he drinks coffee, tea, or orange juice. If he picks a food and a drink at random, what is the probability that he will have yogurt and cranberry juice?

Ⓐ $\frac{1}{3}$
Ⓑ $\frac{1}{2}$
Ⓒ $\frac{1}{7}$
Ⓓ $\frac{1}{12}$

14. A cone can be formed by rotating

a(n) ☐ acute
☐ obtuse   triangle about
☐ right

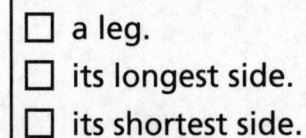

☐ a leg.
☐ its longest side.
☐ its shortest side.
☐ any side.

15. Which is an equation for the circle?

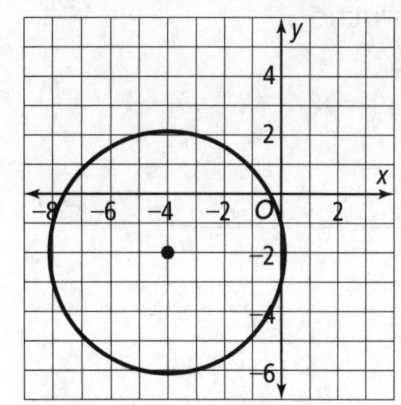

Ⓐ $x^2 + y^2 + 8x + 4y + 4 = 0$
Ⓑ $x^2 + y^2 + 8x + 4y + 15 = 0$
Ⓒ $x^2 + y^2 - 8x - 4y + 3 = 0$
Ⓓ $x^2 - y^2 + 8x - 4y - 5 = 0$

16. A 10 by 8 inch rectangular dartboard contains two overlapping circles. The circles have an overlap of 3 in².

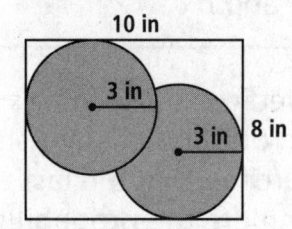

The probability that the dart lands inside one or both circles is ☐ %

17. Elias surveyed his neighbors to find out how many books they had read in the last month. Complete the probability distribution table. Round to the nearest whole percent.

Number of Books Read in the Past Month				
Number	0	1	2	3+
Frequency	6	19	14	4
Relative Frequency (%)	☐%	☐%	☐%	☐%

18. What is the final step in this construction?

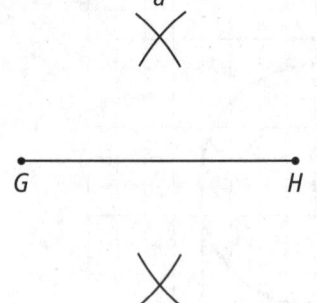

a

G • ———————— • H

b

Ⓐ Use a straightedge to connect points *a* and *b* to *G* and *H*.

Ⓑ Use a compass to make a circle centered at *b* that has *a* as a point on the perimeter.

Ⓒ There is no construction that can be completed with the given diagram.

Ⓓ Use a straightedge to connect points *a* and *b*.

---

19. Benji surveyed customers at his store to find out how many t-shirts they had purchased in the last month. Complete the probability distribution table. Round to the nearest whole percent.

Number of T-Shirts Purchased				
Number	0	1	2	3+
Frequency	5	7	3	1
Relative Frequency (%)	☐%	☐%	☐%	☐%

---

20. A sample of customers at a grocery store were asked if they use plastic or reusable shopping bags.

Complete the two-way frequency table.

	Plastic	Reusable	Totals
Customers under 50 years of age	☐	336	468
Customers over 50 years of age	286	105	☐
Totals	418	☐	859

---

21. A coffee shop classifies its drinks by temperature, size, and cost. Find the probability of each of the following events. Give your answer as a percent rounded to the nearest tenth.

		<$4	≥$4
Iced Drinks	Small	4	6
	Large	2	5
Hot Drinks	Small	7	1
	Large	3	8

Event	Probability
A drink selected at random is a small iced drink, given that it costs $7.50.	☐%
A drink selected at random is a hot drink, given that it costs $2.25.	☐%
A drink selected at random is a large drink, given that it costs $5.75.	☐%
A drink selected at random is a small size that costs less than $4, given that it is a hot drink.	☐%

22. A town conducted a survey to determine how many members of the community would use a new dog park.

Dog Park Survey Results

Town members who plan to use the dog park
- 24% of town members plan to use the dog park
- 10% of town members who plan to use the dog park have more than one dog

Town members who do not plan to use the dog park
- 76% of town members do not plan to use the dog park
- 2% have more than one dog

What is the probability that a surveyed town member plans to use the dog park and has more than one dog?

◯ %

23. A shoe store gave customers a pair of sneakers to test and asked whether they would recommend the sneakers. What is the probability that a customer who recommended their sneakers tested Sneaker B? Round to the nearest whole percent.

	Sneaker A	Sneaker B
Would Recommend	21	35
Would Not Recommend	9	15

P(tested Sneaker B | would recommend their sneakers)
= ◯ %

24. Antony is spinning the spinner for an experiment. Let B represent the event "the spinner lands on a black portion", let W represent the event "the spinner lands on a white portion", let E represent the event "the spinner lands on an even number", and let O represent the event "the spinner lands on an odd number". Select all that apply.

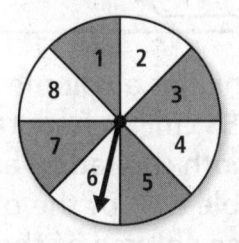

☐ A. The event B is {1, 3, 5, 7}.
☐ B. The event B is equal to the event O.
☐ C. The event W or O is not possible.
☐ D. The event E and B is {1, 2, 3, 4, 5, 6, 7, 8}.
☐ E. P(W and E) = 0.5
☐ F. P(B and E) = 0.5

25. Which is equivalent to sin 51°?

Ⓐ cos 51°   Ⓒ tan 39°
Ⓑ cos 39°   Ⓓ tan 51°

26. The figure shows the shape of a piece Julia is welding together for a sculpture. What is the volume of the figure, in units^3?

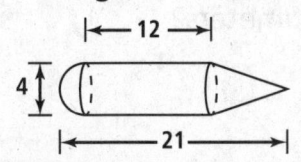

Ⓐ 188.5   Ⓒ 205.3
Ⓑ 196.9   Ⓓ 213.6

27. There are 25 slices of cheese on a cheese board. Of these, 5 of them are cheddar, 8 of them are gouda, and the rest are pepperjack. You select two pieces of cheese from the board at random. What is the probability that both slices of cheese are gouda? Round to the nearest whole percent.

probability = ☐ %

28. A cylindrical tank has a volume of approximately 53 cm³. A new tank is built where both the radius and height are double that of the old tank. What is the volume of the new tank, in cubic centimeters?

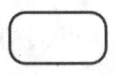

☐

29. In a game, players roll a die. If a 3 is rolled, they get a free turn. To test how many times the number 3 appears, a standard number cube is rolled multiple times and the results are recorded below.

Fill in the blanks to complete the probability distribution.

Number	1	2	3	4	5	6
Frequency	6	10	☐	5	9	8
Probability	0.13	0.22	☐	0.11	0.20	0.18

30. A rectangular prism has a surface area of 84 cm². If the prism is dilated by a factor of 0.5, what is the surface area of its image, in square centimeters?

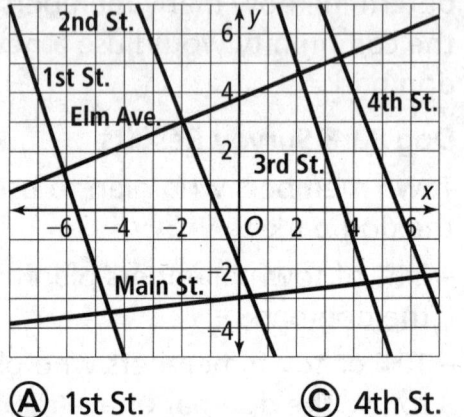

☐

31. Which street is parallel to 2nd St.?

Ⓐ 1st St.
Ⓑ 3rd St.
Ⓒ 4th St.
Ⓓ Elm Ave.

32. A doctor's office is submitting patient data for a study regarding eye color and hair color.

Part A Complete the two-way frequency table.

	Light eyes	Dark eyes	Totals
Light hair	9	17	☐
Dark hair	3	☐	21
Totals	☐	35	47

Part B Determine the following probabilities.

The probability that a patient will have dark eyes is

☐ 0.36.   ☐ 0.49.   ☐ 0.74.

The probability that a patient will have light hair is

☐ 0.55.   ☐ 0.65.   ☐ 0.86.

The probability that a patient will have dark eyes, given that they have light hair is

☐ 0.19.   ☐ 0.36.   ☐ 0.65.